NOVELL'S

Introduction to Networking, 2nd Edition

CHERYL C. CURRID, MARK A. EGGLESTON

Novell Press, San Jose

Novell's Introduction to Networking, 2nd Edition

Published by
Novell Press
2211 North First Street
San Jose, CA 95131

Copyright © 2000 Novell, Inc. All rights reserved. No part of this book, including interior design, cover design, and icons, may be reproduced or transmitted in any form, by any means (electronic, photocopying, recording, or otherwise) without the prior written permission of the publisher.

ISBN: 0-7645-4700-3

Printed in the United States of America

10 9 8 7 6 5 4 3 2 1

2B/RV/QT/QQ/FC

Distributed in the United States by IDG Books Worldwide, Inc.

Distributed by CDG Books Canada Inc. for Canada; by Transworld Publishers Limited in the United Kingdom; by IDG Norge Books for Norway; by IDG Sweden Books for Sweden; by IDG Books Australia Publishing Corporation Pty. Ltd. for Australia and New Zealand; by TransQuest Publishers Pte Ltd. for Singapore, Malaysia, Thailand, Indonesia, and Hong Kong; by Gotop Information Inc. for Taiwan; by ICG Muse, Inc. for Japan; by Intersoft for South Africa; by Eyrolles for France; by International Thomson Publishing for Germany, Austria and Switzerland; by Distribuidora Cuspide for Argentina; by LR International for Brazil; by Galileo Libros for Chile; by Ediciones ZETA S.C.R. Ltda. for Peru; by WS Computer Publishing Corporation, Inc., for the Philippines; by Contemporanea de Ediciones for Venezuela; by Express Computer Distributors for the Caribbean and West Indies; by Micronesia Media Distributor, Inc. for Micronesia; by Chips Computadoras S.A. de C.V. for Mexico; by Editorial Norma de Panama S.A. for Panama; by American Bookshops for Finland.

For general information on IDG Books Worldwide's books in the U.S., please call our Consumer Customer Service department at 800-762-2974. For reseller information, including discounts and premium sales, please call our Reseller Customer Service department at 800-434-3422.

For information on where to purchase IDG Books Worldwide's books outside the U.S., please contact our International Sales department at 317-596-5530 or fax 317-572-4002.

For consumer information on foreign language translations, please contact our Customer Service department at 800-434-3422, fax 317-572-4002, or e-mail rights@idgbooks.com.

For information on licensing foreign or domestic rights, please phone +1-650-653-7098.

For sales inquiries and special prices for bulk quantities, please contact our Order Services department at 800-434-3422 or write to IDG Books Worldwide, 919 E. Hillsdale Blvd., Suite 400, Foster City, CA 94404.

For information on using IDG Books Worldwide's books in the classroom or for ordering examination copies, please contact our Educational Sales department at 800-434-2086 or fax 317-572-4005.

For press review copies, author interviews, or other publicity information, please contact our Public Relations department at 650-653-7000 or fax 650-653-7500.

For authorization to photocopy items for corporate, personal, or educational use, please contact Novell, Inc., Copyright Permission, 1555 North Technology Way, Mail Stop ORM-C-311, Orem, UT 84097-2395 or fax 801-228-7077.

For general information on Novell Press books in the U.S., including information on discounts and premiums, contact IDG Books Worldwide at 800-434-3422 or 650-655-3200. For information on where to purchase Novell Press books outside the U.S., contact IDG Books International at 317-596-5530 or fax 317-572-4002.

Library of Congress Cataloging-in-Publication Data

Currid, Cheryl C.
    Novell's introduction to networking / Cheryl C. Currid, Mark A. Eggleston.-- 2nd ed.
        p.   cm.
    ISBN 0-7645-4700-3 (alk. paper)
    1. Computer networks. I. Eggleston, Mark A., 1974- II. Title.
TK5105.5.C87   2000
004.6--dc21   00-021083
                                                                      CIP

John Kilcullen, *CEO, IDG Books Worldwide, Inc.*
Richard K. Swadley, *Senior Vice President, Technology Publishing*

The IDG Books Worldwide logo is a registered trademark or trademark under exclusive license to IDG Books Worldwide, Inc. from International Data Group, Inc. in the United States and/or other countries.

Marcy Shanti, *Publisher, Novell Press, Novell, Inc.*
Novell Press is a trademark and the Novell Press logo is a registered trademark of Novell, Inc.

Welcome to Novell Press

Novell Press, the world's leading provider of networking books, is the premier source for the most timely and useful information in the networking industry. Novell Press books cover fundamental networking issues as they emerge — from today's Novell and third-party products to the concepts and strategies that will guide the industry's future. The result is a broad spectrum of titles for the benefit of those involved in networking at any level: end user, department administrator, developer, systems manager, or network architect.

Novell Press books are written by experts with the full participation of Novell's technical, managerial, and marketing staff. The books are exhaustively reviewed by Novell's own technicians and are published only on the basis of final released software, never on prereleased versions.

Novell Press at IDG Books Worldwide is an exciting partnership between two companies at the forefront of the knowledge and communications revolution. The Press is implementing an ambitious publishing program to develop new networking titles centered on the current versions of NetWare, GroupWise, BorderManager, ManageWise, and networking integration products.

Novell Press books are translated into several languages and sold throughout the world.

Marcy Shanti
Publisher
Novell Press, Novell, Inc.

Novell Press

Publisher
Marcy Shanti

IDG Books Worldwide

Acquisitions Editor
Jim Sumser

Project Editor
Kurt Stephan

Technical Editor
Ken Neff

Copy Editor
Julie M. Smith

Project Coordinators
Linda Marousek
Marcos Vergara

Quality Control Specialist
Laura Taflinger

Illustrators
Karl Brandt
Shelley Norris

Graphics and Production Specialists
Robert Bilhmayer
Jude Levinson
Michael Lewis
Ramses Ramirez
Victor Pérez-Varela

Proofreading and Indexing
York Production Services

About the Authors

Popular columnist and author **Cheryl Currid** is president of Houston-based Currid & Company, a research and advisory firm specializing in connectivity and information technology. This marks her 13th book.

Mark Eggleston is an industry analyst at Currid & Company with 10 years of information technology experience. He specializes in analysis of the impact of emerging technologies on business.

Preface

Congratulations on choosing *Novell's Introduction to Networking, 2ⁿᵈ Edition*, the ideal first place to turn to for beginning-level, accessible information about network technology.

What You Will Learn In This Book

This book, newly revised, highlights the reasons for networking, the resources available to you, and applications to assist you, as well as introducing you to the interesting possibilities that the Internet and intranets can give you and your business. Besides giving you pointers for creating a network and choosing the best hardware, we also describe appropriate networking software. Finally, we cover the responsibility of managing a network once it is put in place and give you pointers on management tools, security measures, and troubleshooting tactics. The World Wide Web and Internet are threaded throughout the book, as it no doubt is present in everyday business and life. Finally, the appendix gives you recommended sites for accessing more networking information on the web, while the glossary explains unfamiliar terms.

What's New In This Edition

This second edition of *Novell's Introduction to Networking* contains updated information on technologies that have emerged and become popular standards. High-speed Internet working technologies such as DSL and cable modems were only a remote dream when the book first went to print. Fast and gigabit Ethernet technologies, while on the drawing board at that time, now have become the backbone of corporate intranetworking. All these new technologies are covered in detail in this edition.

Also, timely updates have been made to the descriptions of the various network operating systems currently available. In addition, new choices in backup strategies and mediaare presented.

And while the speeds of technologies will outpace any printed word, this book will lay the foundation for a wide knowledge base. With *Novell's Introduction to Networking, 2ⁿᵈ Edition*, you will gain the fundamental skills to pursue a lifelong career in networking. This exciting technology is continuously changing and improving, so you'll never have to worry about knowing everything there is to know—networking will always present you with new knowledge, challenges, and opportunity.

We hope you enjoy reading this book and have great success in implementing your network system.

Acknowledgments

Every book turns into a team effort with a single goal: Put together something to be proud of. This work—its concept and its cast of characters—is no exception.

Thanks must first go to IDG Books' team of professionals. Jim Sumser started the project and helped us dust off the manuscript of the first volume. His work served to focus us for producing a concise new edition. Kurt Stephan took over the reins during the development of the book. His patience and diligence are greatly appreciated. Thank you also to copy editor Julie Smith and technical editor Ken Neff of Novell for their valuable contributions to this edition.

At Currid & Company, our colleagues first rolled their eyes back when they heard that we were going to undertake this project on top of several others that were keeping us working day and night. But, the shock quickly subsided and they supported us with extra research, proof reading, and plenty of freshly ground espresso.

David Diers took a personal interest in some of the research and made sure that our statistics were cross-referenced and valid. Andy Gibbs took over network maintenance at the Currid & Company offices and kept us out of the server room. Darrin Brindle provided great support and navigated us through several surprise events from emergency surgery to the onslaught of Comdex interviews. And, Robyn Wood took over extra duties to clear the path for us. She set up the "friends and family" plan—putting her own children to work. Josh and Chrysa tackled projects that nobody else would touch.

Finally, I want to welcome Mark Eggleston, co-author of this work, to his first (but not last) book-length project. After working with Mark for two years, I'm convinced that he's one of the smartest people I've ever met. Just give him a keyboard, a little bandwidth, and a search engine. He can answer all questions, including the ones I forget to ask.

Cheryl Currid, President
Currid & Company

Contents at a Glance

Contents

Networks: Everywhere

If, as a child, you ever connected cups with a string to make a play telephone, you've already installed your first network. You found that you could send and receive messages, secrets, and jokes with your friends. Chances are that you were both delighted and frustrated with the results.

Initially you were thrilled to receive a message from someone on the other end of the string. While you may have noticed some distortion, messages came through mostly intact. It felt like a technical triumph. If you tried to expand your network, say, with a longer string or more than two cups, you probably began to encounter technical difficulties. Moreover, to get the message through, both you and your friend had to be online (or "onstring") at the same time.

Luckily, with today's advanced technologies, computer networks aren't quite so limited. If you use the right combinations of computer and communications hardware, and good design techniques when planning your connections, you can expand your network to almost anywhere. And because technology lets you store messages, neither you nor your friend has to be at either end of the string at the same time.

Today you can link up with many friends and coworkers by connecting to their computers within a workgroup, office building, or anyplace in the outside world, just like with the cups and string. This chapter begins a journey into the world of networking. It will take you on a tour following two tracks — a philosophical track (why network) and a practical or technical track (how to network).

People build networks so they can share devices, resources, files, messages, and ultimately knowledge. Sharing knowledge makes people smarter and better able to make business decisions. Businesses justify building networks because it saves money when workers share devices, such as printers, fax machines, modems, scanners, and other peripherals. (A peripheral is any device used in conjunction with a computer, whether internally or externally.) But evidence suggests the biggest benefits are in the new ways networks enable people to do business.

The networks of today and tomorrow, however, transcend the physical domain in which they are created. They are more than a compilation of wires, servers, hubs, and nodes (A server is a computer that provides applications or data to a connected computer. Hubs act as the central part of a network, where data arrives from one node and is forwarded to another. A node is a connection point in a network.) Networks are an information utility, transporting information around the globe using impulses of electricity and light.

While the local utility service supplies water and power into homes and offices, networks provide us with a constant supply of information. And comparable to our dependence on water and power for survival, a continuous stream of information can be just as essential for survival.

Networks are becoming seamless, transparent entities that connect anyone with everything — anytime, anyplace.

Yesterday's Networks

Experts disagree on when the first computer networks arrived for business applications. Some like to think that vintage mainframe computers with terminals were the start of network computing. Before the advent of the personal computer a decade ago, computer systems usually consisted of only one real computer (a large central processing unit or CPU), with attached printers and display terminals. Unlike today's networks, the CPU did all the calculating, sorting, storing, and data retrieval, and then sent the requested information down to the terminal as characters that appeared on the screen. The processing seemed to happen quickly, but it had to be managed very carefully.

At the time, computers were very large, very expensive, hard to learn, and difficult to use. Companies created data processing departments to control and set priorities for work the computer would do. Specially trained operators and programmers worked day and night to schedule computing jobs so the system would run efficiently. Every effort was expended to conserve expensive computer power, which was measured in millions of instructions per second (MIPS). The mainframe computer of 1980 cost $250,000 per MIPS.

Slow communication lines compounded the problems of expense and organization. Up to the 1980s, mainframe communication lines usually ran at 4,800 to 9,600 bits per second (bps).

Minicomputers were developed during the 1970s. These computers were less expensive, but also less powerful. They were useful for small departments or groups of people. The architecture of mainframes and minicomputer systems was basically the same, as shown in Figure 1.1. Each was based on the notion that one central computer could manage everything: applications, printers, terminals, and other resources. The terminals displayed the data on the screen, but didn't process anything.

In the beginning, terminals were used more for inputting information than obtaining anything from the CPU. That's what paper reports were for — reams and reams of paper reports. Generally these reports took hours for mainframes to produce (called batch processing), and the addition of a new kind of report required many extra hours to rewrite the programs and include it in the batch.

These "host-terminal" computer systems provided the only way to compute large sets of numbers and business analyses until the very early 1980s, when the personal computer (PC) arrived on the scene. These small computers based on newly invented, inexpensive microprocessor chips changed all the rules of data processing. Because PCs actually had the power to compute independently, people could perform some work without waiting for the mainframe system batch program to run.

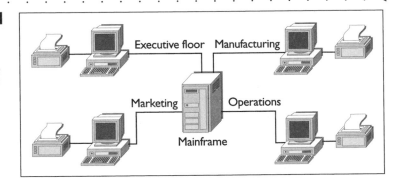

F I G U R E 1.1

For both mainframe and minicomputer systems, all work was performed by the CPU. Attached printers and terminals did not do any processing.

Then came easy-to-use software. Mainframe and minicomputers required difficult-to-learn programming languages. It frequently took months, if not years, to train a specialist to operate and program a computer. Not so with microcomputers. Early computer spreadsheets such as VisiCalc and Lotus 1-2-3 were simple and gave everyday businesspeople the power to do their work independently.

By the mid-1980s businesspeople were ready for a change. All the benefits brought by personal computers seemed wasted because it was so hard to share the results. Also, PC peripherals, such as printers and large fixed disks, were expensive. Most companies refused to buy an expensive, high-quality laser printer for each PC, nor were they willing to spend thousands of dollars for extra disk storage space. While computer work was faster, the arduous process of sharing results made personal computers an inefficient option for businesses.

Still, the enormous cost differences between host-based systems and PCs were too compelling to ignore. Local area networks (LANs) emerged as an experimental technology. A LAN is a high-speed communications system designed to link together computers, peripherals, fixed disks for storage, and communication devices, usually within a small geographic area. LANs were designed originally for connecting the computers within a workgroup, department, or a single floor. But people quickly learned that several LANs could be interconnected within a building or campus of buildings, as well, to extend connectivity.

To put it kindly, early attempts at networking personal computers proved to be challenging. Installing network cards sometimes resulted in a puff of blue smoke with curmudgeons saying, "See, I told you that this technology doesn't work." There were limited diagnostic tools available to determine if initial installations were working well. Sometimes a faulty pin or plug from the wire of a single connection could bring the entire network to its knees.

Also, few well-trained technicians existed. Because the technology was very new, most people learned it on the job. Staffing was difficult.

Early Network Pioneers

Despite the challenges of early network technology, pioneering companies built up networks almost as quickly as the products were brought to market. The benefits of networking people and their computers into more effective teams overshadowed the problems.

Companies like UPS, Coca-Cola Foods, and Manufacturers Hanover Trust Company (now Chemical Bank) were among the first to experience the power of a connected workplace. In each case, users reported great productivity improvements after the installation of LANs.

By putting PCs on the desks of individual workers and connecting the computers through a network, people started working together differently. They shared information differently, coworked more projects, and armed with more analysis, seemed to make decisions faster. While cost savings from sharing resources did occur, the real benefits came from people finding better ways to do their jobs. These early, successful efforts to connect computers made headlines in the mid-1980s.

LANs started to get popular because they could be assembled quickly. For example, The Democratic National Party, in 1988, marked the first use of networks in the political process, which could be hectic to say the least.

Technicians installed ten LANs, hooking up more than three hundred PC workstations, to handle the 1988 convention. The networks ran several types of applications, from counting delegate votes to keeping track of party invitations. The system worked without a hitch.

That same year, the ABC television network (not to be confused with a computer network) tied together 126 PCs in a LAN to cover the Olympic games. The LAN helped coordinate everything from athletes' statistics to travel arrangements. ABC also maintained a video library of twenty thousand tapes for quick retrieval and on-air use.

Network technology went to war in 1991 during Operation Desert Shield and Desert Storm. Such heavy reliance on computer power in military conflicts was previously unheard of, and though it's hard to say that computers won the war, many credit the military's quick access to information as a major influence in the outcome.

Lessons Learned

Networking technology served as a platform from which many different applications grew. Previously, computer systems like minicomputers followed one specific task, such as processing a certain type of data or processing words.

The practice of one computer/one application had interesting results. In some companies, the sheer number of computer terminals made it impossible for anyone to sit at a desk. For example, workers in a Houston-based oil company took pictures of their desks and showed them to their management to make them understand the difficulties of having such a crowded workspace. Some desks contained as many as four terminals — one for access to the company mainframe, one for the department accounting system, one for the database, and one for the personal computer.

With PC-based LANs, a worker access all applications needed on a PC that was connected to the company LAN. It certainly cleaned up desk space.

LAN based networks put vast amounts of data and information within easy reach of people who needed it to make better decisions. As workers learned to share files, spreadsheets, reports, and databases with each other, many were able, for the first time, to get to the information that helped them make smart recommendations or decisions. This, then, was what the early attempts at networking taught the business world: *Connecting people to information and to each other makes them work smarter.*

Today's Networks

The computer networking industry can be measured in dog years. Since the first signs of popularity in the mid-1980s, LAN technology has already progressed through several generations. Most business-oriented networks were originally designed as solutions for people in workgroups. The average network consisted of one server (or master PC) that provided file storage and print services for about ten to twelve personal computers.

Today, there's nothing local about LANs. Servers can host hundreds of users from a single location. Most organizations consider LANs as a part of enterprise computing networks (an internetwork that runs multiple sites and applications). And now with the Internet, the walls of a company don't stop at the enterprise network.

The software that directs the activities of a network is known as the network operating system (NOS). Available from numerous vendors, network operating systems have matured to support a wide variety of configuration needs. Users can share printers, files, and even applications across the network. Most networks today consist of several servers that are optimized to either perform certain tasks or handle the needs of certain users. In that case, the NOS must give an aura of transparency to the users. The user shouldn't know or care exactly what server he or she has accessed. Instead, the user only expects appropriate access to system resources, files, and applications.

LANs by Other Names

Over the short history of network computers, LANs have taken on more than one name and definition. Table 1.1 lists some of the other acronyms that have grown from original LAN technology.

New acronyms often spring up. We, the authors, coined terms for two more emerging types of networks: TANs and FANs. TANs are tiny area networks that connect the computers in very small offices with perhaps two to five PCs. FAN stands for family area network. These networks are emerging as families begin to own more than one PC per household. The FAN may connect shared computers, printers, security system, entertainment devices, and other network-enabled appliances. As of 1999, more than one-half of all the households in the United States owned a PC. And almost half of those households had more than one computer. In fact, many families are already approaching a ratio of one PC per person.

TABLE I.I	ACRONYM	MEANING
Network Acronyms	LAN	Local area network — Refers to a network that services a workgroup or department within an organization.
	WAN	Wide area network — Two or more LANs that are housed in physically different spaces. A WAN can exist when LANs are connected across different towns, states, time zones, or countries.
	CAN	Campus area network — A network of two or more LANs that span several buildings in the same physical location, such as universities, office parks, or large companies with several nearby buildings. CANs are usually connected with wires (copper or fiber-optic) or without wires (through microwave technology or laser repeaters).
	MAN	Metropolitan area network — Two or more LANs connected within a few miles. MANs commonly extend across public roads, highways, or external areas, so they're usually connected wirelessly. Sometimes microwave dishes can be used if there is a line of sight between buildings.

Justifying Business Networks

Businesses have many justifications for using LANs. These include reduced cost, higher worker productivity, and smaller increases in overhead during growth periods. Increased productivity is the most common justification.

With today's acceptance of information technology in the workplace, most companies have abandoned cost-justification requirements for the existence of the network. Managers feel that building a LAN is simply a requirement of doing business. The PC connected to the network is a common, company-issue item, much like a desk, chair, and telephone.

A network reduces cost because it lets people collaborate more efficiently. It lets them share ideas quickly and take action. Overall, software is easier to support on networks and peripherals, such as printers and scanners, and can be shared easily.

From a cost analysis point of view, perhaps the largest gain by networking computers is in freeing up employees' time to accomplish more work. A network can cut down on the time employees spend attending to the copy machine, sharing CD-ROM applications from a single PC, or linking up different word processor applications to churn out consistent reports. Less time spent dealing with tedious processes begets more time to accomplish important work. This means more value for the salary dollar.

Evolution of Network Uses

After deciding that the figurative and literal cost of a network is justifiable, it is time to choose a network configuration. To do this, it is helpful to understand how networks have evolved, so you can see where your company or organization fits in.

It began as a simple way to share files and print services in a workgroup, but network-connected PCs have evolved into nodes on large corporate networks that sometimes connect millions of computers both publicly (Internet) or privately (intranet).

File and Print Services Networks

In the original network plan, file, and print service is where it all began. A single PC stores work through an NOS. The NOS creates the connection to various PCs and peripherals spread out through the office or enterprise (many offices). Different NOSs are available including Novell NetWare 5, Microsoft Windows 2000, Mac OS X Server, and Linux, just to name a few.

Printers, fax machines, voice mail, scanners, and the like can be linked between two PCs or hundreds. The distances vary from a few feet in a small office using a LAN to hundreds of miles using a WAN. The server (the single PC that runs the NOS) is usually expensive at the outset but pays for itself in worker productivity and the increased functionality of existing peripherals.

Sometimes, however, the complexity and expense of dedicated servers is overkill for small businesses. In an effort to provide for the small office/home office (SOHO) market as well as for those with a lower out-of-pocket start-up migration path, peer-to-peer networking was developed as an alternate NOS.

Small-Office Computing

While the rise in file and print service networks was skyrocketing, so were the numbers of small and home-based businesses. This statistic, combined with rapidly falling prices for PCs and their counterparts, created a market for an NOS specifically for SOHOs. Peer-to-peer networking is for those who need to share files and printers and pass e-mail, but do not need the processing power of the server-based network.

Peer-to-peer networking provides SOHOs with the advantages of larger networks without the associated costs of dedicating a PC as a server. The only significant expenditure is for the necessary wiring and NICs. Commonly available peer-to-peer NOSs include Novell Personal NetWare, Microsoft Windows 2000, and AppleShare IP 6.

During the evolution of these different NOSs, the increase in power and decrease in price of PCs and their related hardware gave many companies the opportunity to save costs in both real estate and utility overhead by encouraging people to work at home.

Remote Access

With modem speeds exceeding 56Kbps with the advent of cable, Digital Subscriber Line (DSL), and wireless access, it is no wonder telecommuting is one of the fastest growing segments of business productivity today. Telecommuting means, essentially, that you can work from home yet still be connected to the office network. This is accomplished through specialized software and hardware, which create a simulation of the desktop at work on the desktop at home.

There are three basic methods to maintain office connectivity. The primary method is synchronization. Typically, a server that provides collaboration tools, also known as groupware server, is stationed at the office. It has a dedicated connection to the Internet that allows for dialing in and transferring mail from the home PC. Thus, any e-mail, contacts, or appointments received from coworkers are downloaded to the home PC when the user dials in.

The second method is through remote control. A PC at the office serves as a host to the remote PC (the one at home). Once the two machines are connected over a direct phone line connection or via the Internet, the remote PC can do and see everything that the host PC can.

The third dial-up connection for telecommuting workers is called remote node, which enables a remote PC to use all of the resources on the office LAN as if it were actually at the office. This includes access to file, application, and printer resources.

All three of the methods above may use a direct dial-in to the server, or may connect to an Internet Service Provider (ISP) and use the Internet as a communications medium. For employees accessing the corporate servers from remote cities, using a local ISP and avoiding long distance charges is often most advantageous.

Companies utilize telecommuting to save the rental costs of office space, enjoy higher worker productivity, and decrease commute time. Because employees benefit by spending more time with families and the companies benefit by trimming their overhead and attrition rate, the number of companies connecting their human resources to a corporate network remotely is on the rise and will continue to grow.

In fact, it is estimated that 25 percent of all households in the United States have members who conduct work at home using a PC. Of this figure, 35.7 million users comprise a remote and mobile workforce. And projections show that by 2003, 47.1 million people will work remotely in some fashion.

This increasing use of remote connectivity technology has led in part to the explosive growth of the Internet and World Wide Web.

The Internet

The Internet is the global network that has taken the software, marketing, and business world by storm. Millions of PCs, thousands of networks, all connected by a single communication means that is as simplistic in nature as our telephone numbering system. The Internet can be thought of as an extension of the file and print services and peer-to-peer LANs that permeate the landscape of the business world—with seemingly unlimited information and accessibility, twenty-four hours a day, seven days a week.

Every topic known to humanity can be found on the Internet. It has become the driving force behind the computer industry in the last five years, and barring any breakthrough technology, will continue to be for at least the first decade of the new millenium.

As of January, 1997 there were 57 million people worldwide with Internet access. In June, 1998, the number had nearly doubled to 108 million. And as of July, 1999, there were more than 180 million Internet users worldwide.

The World Wide Web (WWW) is the graphical user interface to the Internet in much the same way that Microsoft Windows is to a PC. Don't be fooled — the Internet is not just a place for the technically savvy computer geek. All major product vendors from Sony to General Motors have sites on the WWW, as well as normally paper-based publications such as Time magazine and The Wall Street Journal. Many companies are even using it to lower their costs in other areas. For example, in 1996, overnight delivery companies created Web pages that enabled customers to track their packages based on their tracking number, thereby significantly reducing the number of calls to their toll-free lines.

Other burgeoning Internet-related technologies include real-time audio conversations with anyone in the world (without long distance charges), video conferences, secure banking, and financial transactions, WBT (Web-based training), video on demand, stock trading, as well as an endless supply of research and demographic data for every category in existence.

What makes the Internet so appealing? Its accessibility. It's not linked to any one type of PC or software product. Any type of PC (Intel, RISC, or Macintosh) running any operating system (UNIX, Windows, System 9, Linux) can access the Internet.

And, as a consequence of the simplistic yet powerful features that make up the Internet, corporations are now developing and refining their own version of the Internet, called intranets.

Intranets

An intranet is a scaled-down version of the Internet. It is used primarily for the employees of a company who are spread out geographically or spend a lot of time traveling. By using the principles of the Internet, such as web browsers and e-mail, corporations can provide access to all aspects of their resources to their users.

Intranets sprung up almost overnight as an important part of corporate computing. Researchers at Boston Research Group estimate that early in 1994, fewer than 11 percent of large business organizations had an intranet. By 1999, 50 percent of U.S. companies with over 500 employees have an Intranet with the remaining claiming to implement one. As the number of large corporations increases, small- to mid-sized firms are also finding the benefits of connecting people through networks.

A key reason for companies to join the intranet generation is the ease of implementation. Intranets have become the cyberspace equivalent of water coolers for getting the news, views, and clues about company activity.

Technically, intranets are secured by private lines rather than run across the same network as the Internet. For example, the sales force headquartered in Houston can access marketing material headquartered in London through real-time interaction across entirely secure lines that are controlled by the corporation itself. Thus, company information such as phone lists that were previously only available on paper and may never be up to date are now obtainable by the click of a mouse and never more than a few seconds old. In addition, scheduling meetings, seminars, vacations, and conferences can be coordinated through a single interface, sometimes called groupware, without ever touching the telephone to call someone or worrying about time zone conflicts, because all the information is truly right at your fingertips.

▶ . . . . ◀

Summary

When all is said and done, the benefits of networking computers far outweigh both the material and opportunity costs. It's not an option for companies — it's a necessity.

Networks based on LAN technology let people connect, communicate, and share knowledge through their computers. When you consider the benefits of optimizing people, the decision to network becomes undeniable.

CHAPTER 2

Networked Resources

Some people like to think of PC networks in the same way as condominium ownership. If you own a condominium apartment, you own the interior walls of your apartment and an undivided interest in the rest of the facility. Generally a management company maintains the hallways outside your door, grounds, and facilities. While you are free to decorate your living room any way you choose, you don't have complete control over the remainder of the building and grounds. You share the pool, exercise room, lobby, and other amenities with other condominium owners.

Similarly, with a PC network users are free to work on any independent application — spreadsheet, word processing, database, e-mail, and so on — as needed. A well-designed network confines most application processing to the local PC with little impact on the rest of the users of the network. To print to a network printer, send e-mail, query a large database, or store files on a network disk, however, users must use a shared resource — a network device. They don't have complete control over how these devices are set up and configured, and usually leave the maintenance and upkeep tasks to a network management organization, such as an information services department.

This chapter, the first of two devoted to how networks work, focuses attention on how networks handle shared devices and resources. It covers the fundamentals in both theory and execution.

Starting with a brief description of how networked devices operate, we lay the groundwork for understanding what and how devices are connected. The Open System Interconnection Model (OSI Model), developed by the International Standards Organization (ISO), sets the standard for services that LANs should provide. Today, most networking devices adhere to the principles, if not the exact letter, of the OSI Model.

Next, we discuss what is required to connect a device to a network, focusing on how devices are recognized by the network. Finally, we turn to examples of shared network devices to give you an idea of the equipment available to you.

Understanding the OSI Model from the Bottom Up

In 1977, the ISO started a process of defining standards for network products. This standardization guide, the OSI Model, enabled network hardware and software vendors to conform to specifics that would enable most of their products to work together.

As illustrated in Figure 2.1, the OSI Model has seven layers that explain logically and sequentially how computers communicate to one another on the network.

FIGURE 2.1

The International Standards Organization's OSI Model for network connectivity and conformity

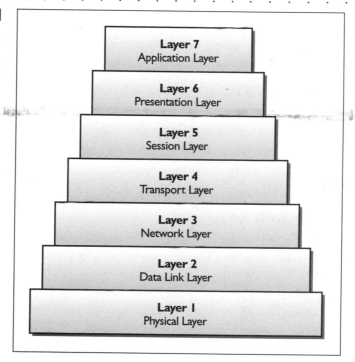

You can think of the model as a seven-layer cake or a staircase like those leading up to a pyramid. You may have also noticed that as you move from layer one to layer seven, the steps get progressively smaller.

In terms of priority, the requirements of each layer must be met from the bottom to the top. For example, it doesn't help to implement a signaling scheme (layer two) or a data link (layer three) unless your cables are connected (layer one). This model provides the building blocks for every network today. Understanding where activity takes place will help you understand why certain network components work.

The Physical Layer

Layer one includes all of the communicating hardware devices on the network. It provides the hardware means by which the bit stream travels. For example, all the specifications for how the Network Interface Cards (NICs) and serial ports for modems communicate are contained in the OSI's Physical layer. Since cabling is required for these devices to communicate, all of the wiring, connectors, and rules concerning how cable should be placed are included here. CAT5, ADSL, and Coaxial cables are members of this layer.

The Data Link Layer

The Data Link layer addresses how the data in each signaling scheme, such as contention or token passing, travels and arrives. It also shows how errors (when signals don't arrive) are dealt with. Ethernet and Token Ring are just a few of the schemes included in this section.

The Network Layer

Sometimes large networks have more than one signaling scheme transmitting across the wires. For example, many large corporate networks have both Ethernet and Token Ring data links. The third layer of the OSI Model, the Network layer, addresses this potential conflict by providing rules on how disparate signals should communicate. In other words, it handles the routing and forwarding of the data. Internet Protocol Version 4 is a component of this layer.

The Transport Layer

For both large and small networks, the Transport layer is paramount. It's at this stage that all of the various network protocols communicate their packets of data to all the different nodes of the network. It determines when all packets have arrived and completes an error-checking process to guarantee an intact data transfer. Transmission Control Protocol (TCP) and User Datagram Protocol (UDP) are examples of protocols comprising this layer.

The Session Layer

Layer five is where the user finally has meaningful interaction with the network. The Session layer is named as such since it is at this point that the user establishes a session with the network by logging in a user name and password. They are then verified by the network operating system's various security measures.

The Presentation Layer

The Presentation layer supports the conversion of data from the form in which it is sent over the network into a representation that the computer understands. For example, external data representation (XDR) use ensures that an Apple computer and a Sun computer can both understand each other despite the fact that, internally, each computer represents data differently.

Included in this layer are compression algorithms, which make files smaller so they take up less network traffic space. An analogy would be the ability to press a button on a Chevy Suburban and shrink it to the size of a Toyota Corolla, but still leaving its six-passenger capacity, color TV, CD changer, full-size spare tire, and leather seats intact.

This layer, which is often referred to as the syntax layer, also includes protocols such as File Transfer Protocol (FTP), HyperText Transfer Protocol (HTTP), and Simple Network Management Protocol (SNMP).

The Application Layer

The top of the OSI Model is the Application layer. The name might make you think of software, but actually this layer deals with print services, database queries, and e-mail. This is where everything starts.

▶ · ◀

Connecting Devices to a Network

To connect any device to a network, the device needs to be physically connected to the network wire, which enables the device to send out an electrical signal alerting other network resources to its existence. Following the bottom layers of the OSI Model, layers one and two must be in place before anything else will work.

To a network at this primitive level, all devices are created equal. Whether it is a PC, a printer, a server, or a connection to the mainframe — the network sees it as a node. The importance of the node isn't determined until later.

The device, such as a PC or printer, may have a Network Interface Card (NIC) physically inside it, or it may be part of another device (such as a printer connected to a PC) that has an NIC. Network interface capabilities come pre-installed in some computers and printers. There's usually a built-in port on the back of the unit, as shown in Figure 2.2. If you need to add networking capabilities to a device that doesn't have an NIC, you must purchase an NIC and install it in the device. The NIC must be designed to work with that device — for example, an NIC for a PC won't work in a printer. Also, not all NICs work in the expansion slots of a PC. Double-check for compatibility with your device before buying one.

As seen in Figure 2.3, an NIC is a piece of hardware that transmits signals, proclaiming its existence across a network. If you imagine the NIC as a homing signal, you've got the right idea. In addition to the signal the NIC sends out, it also has a predetermined address that makes it unique from any other device on the network. The number is actually referred to as a Media Access Control (MAC) address, which is discussed in Chapter 4.

FIGURE 2.2

Some printers and other devices intended to run on networks come with pre-installed ports for your network.

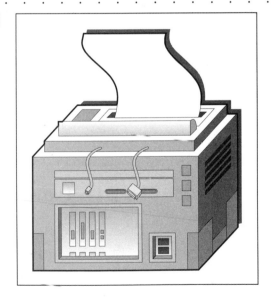

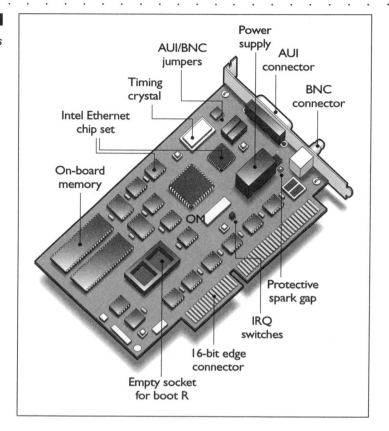

A network interface card fits into such devices as PCs, printers, and modems.

Power supply

AUI/BNC jumpers

AUI connector

Timing crystal

BNC connector

Intel Ethernet chip set

On-board memory

OM

Protective spark gap

IRQ switches

16-bit edge connector

Empty socket for boot R

In addition to the NIC, a device needs a Network Operating System (NOS) to make itself visible to other devices on the network. You could imagine the NOS as a language. Network devices may recognize a newly added device, but won't understand it unless it speaks the same language they do.

The next part of the equation is purely subjective—naming the devices. Each resource that is shared on a network must have a distinct name so that it is identifiable to the NOS. For example, Susie's hard drive in a peer-to-peer network could be called "susies_driveC," just as the 4th floor LaserJet printer could be called "4th_floor_laserjet." This may seem redundant, but giving shared resources names detailing their physical location makes for quick work if problems arise.

▶ · ◀

Examples of Shared Resources and Devices

The advantages of sharing resources across the network include, but are not limited to, decreased cost of ownership for software applications (one complete package is purchased, and additional users may simply buy software licenses), lower maintenance fees on peripherals (several people can share one printer rather than everyone having their own), and most important, the ability to create data that everyone can use on the network (such as a spreadsheet for the budget), rather than having multiple copies.

File Sharing

This is the holy grail of networking. Having the ability to distribute a document, like the budget spreadsheet mentioned earlier, to a central location on the network, where all the appropriate people can access it and use the information without changing the original, is what data sharing is all about. Related to file sharing is application sharing, which is what software applications consist of: many, many files working in concert to perform a certain function, like word-processing. Since the crux of network software applications are covered in the following chapter, it is sufficient to say that sharing applications across the network is not only cheaper due to their one-time fee, but also because it costs less for someone to support and manage than having multiple copies of different software applications on each person's PC.

Drive Sharing (Fixed, Optical, and Removable Disks)

Your next question should be how these files and applications are shared. Aside from the NIC and NOS discussed earlier, files are shared on different types of drives. The most common are hard drives that can hold many gigabytes of information.

Other shared drives may read DVD-ROMs that can contain between 2.6 and 17.0 gigabytes (GB), and CD-ROMs that carry around 650 megabytes (650 million bytes) of data. These drives are shared through networked PCs, servers, and CD-ROM and DVD-ROM towers, which are the devices that actually contain the NICs.

Optical drives include DVD-RAM, CD-R, and CD-RW. These drives may be used on a network to create backups of the data and applications installed on hard drives. Once again, the drives are more efficient when shared between many PCs rather than having one on each PC individually.

The tape drive is especially useful for backing up large amounts of data due to its high capacity and ease of removal for off-site storage. Capacities for this type of storage device may range from 1GB to 50GB.

Drives which contain removable media also must not be forgotten. They allow for quick and easy backup, synchronization, and off-site storage of data. The capacity of these discs may range from 250MB to 2.5GB.

Voice Mail on the LAN

Rather than rely on third-party service providers for voice mail, with a network you can have, control, and monitor all aspects of it yourself. This opens many doors for information tracking. For example, with your own voice mail server, numbers dialed out can be recorded for auditing procedures, your phone answering system can be automated to page users when voice mail is left, and long distance charges can be tracked through the use of codes for each user.

Voice and data transmissions over standard IP networks are quickly converging. Voice over IP (VoIP) is enabling devices such as software controlled PBX switches to route calls to networked PCs or even route voice mail directly into a user's email box. This dynamic field is called computer-telephony integration.

Network Scanners

Network scanners also aid in improving communication by disseminating information more efficiently — transferring paper-based documents to electronic ones. These network scanners enable you to share electronic versions of snail mail (postal mail), incoming faxes, magazine articles, and the like. Through software, individual electronic copies of the information can be sent via e-mail to all pertinent users or stored in a single location on the network shared drive. Either way, paper, and therefore money, is saved.

Document management has resulted from computer imaging technology and has promised to create the "paperless office." Whether or not that tremendous goal will ever be realized, the less-papered office is no doubt a realistic and cost-effective goal.

Shared Modems

A great help in worker productivity is the network pool of modems. From a user's workstation, through various proprietary software, anyone on the network can use pagers, access online services for research, and configure a PC for dialing in from home. Having a pool of modems, rather than a modem on every PC, cuts down on costs. Only a few modems have to be purchased and everyone uses the same communications software. Some have the ability to redirect open serial ports on workstations to communicate the link across standard network wires, and others simply serve as terminal-based links to a modem to the outside world. By pooling the modems, administrators can implement a security firewall that can limit the type and size of data that is transmitted outside of the corporate intranet.

Shared Fax

Sharing a fax machine through a network may seem redundant, considering most offices share a single, centrally located fax machine anyway. However, the amount of time wasted printing documents from the computer, carrying them to the fax machine, and then waiting for the connection to be made and processed is significant.

A LAN-based fax machine enables everyone on the network to send faxes from their workstations. That means no printing is required, tons of money is saved on paper, and worker productivity moves up a notch.

No, we're not referring to a fax/modem on every PC. You can install a fax server, which operates much like a network printer. It accepts and processes each item in the order received, with the additional capability of sending a confirmation message back to the user. You can also redial on busy signals, and you can even have more than one phone line attached to the fax server.

Network Printing

Of course, sometimes the printed word just can't be beat. Next to sharing files across the LAN, sharing printers has got to be one of the most advantageous benefits of networking. Since printers can cost anywhere from hundreds to thousands of dollars, placing one on the network for everyone in the office to use is definitely cost efficient. Plus, there are so many different kinds of printers now, that it is possible to have one of each and still allow all the users to access them.

For example, there are printers that are specifically designed to produce color, while others output dozens of duplexed pages per minute in black and white purity. Some even create the complex engineering diagrams typically produced by computer-aided design software.

There are many companies that produce network-capable printers, such as Hewlett-Packard, Lexmark, Xerox, and Epson. Although more costly, the printers that come with the NIC already installed are the simplest to configure on the network because they typically use integrated Web-based software to allow for complete and remote configurability.

▶ · ◀

Summary

With all of the potential ways to share information on a network, the increases in communication and decreases in cost seem almost boundless. Each new generation of technology presents tools and options for sharing or individualizing resources, so your configuration decisions are likely to change over time.

CHAPTER 3

Networked Applications

Picture this: A fax comes through the centrally located fax machine in a department — a document relevant to the entire company. The department administrative assistant scans it into a network scanner and forwards it to everyone across the network through electronic mail. Or, after scanning it, she places it into a shared directory on the network and notifies everyone of its existence through a single voice mail message, which is then replicated for all the relevant personnel. Because of the importance of the information received, she also tags the voice mail message to page each of the recipients so that they are instantly aware of the need to check their voice mail.

Once the message has been received and viewed, managers decide that a meeting should be called. Instead of calling the participants of the meeting, however, the administrative assistant uses an electronic scheduling program with links to e-mail to reserve the conference room, overhead projector, and coffee bar. Since all the participants' electronic schedules are available on the system, the administrative assistant can easily find a time that is clear for everyone tomorrow afternoon. She sends a meeting request, marks each schedule accordingly, and awaits their confirmation. To help everyone prepare for the meeting, she pastes electronic copies of the documents to be discussed to the appointment e-mail so that it can be edited and approved online. She also creates a quick presentation with the documents and files it on the network, so the managers can pull it up on their networked laptop computers and review it during the meeting. She includes the scanned images of the original documents so that the people in the meeting can review it online using the PC and LCD projector in the conference room.

Did you notice that the only piece of paper mentioned in this scenario was the original? While we'd hesitate to say that a networked office is a paperless office, it may well be a "less paper" office. When information travels over the network there is less need to use paper, and the process of "print out, make copies, and file in cabinet" turns into a matter of "read on-screen, e-mail to others, and file on disk."

Today's networking technology enables almost any office to operate as we just described. People, products, and processes are all linked together to make business more efficient. That is the goal of networking.

Almost any computing application can be networked, whether it needs to be or not. Some applications, however, cannot exist without networks. These are the applications we discuss first. If networking promotes sharing, and a big part of sharing involves messages, then e-mail should top the list of important network applications.

In a network user's view, e-mail becomes part of the fabric of networking. No other application brings functionality quite as fast or quite as far-reaching. Beyond e-mail, applications such as scheduling, discussion groups, collaborative tools, and office automation round out the ability for people to use networks for sharing.

Electronic Mail

For many people, e-mail turns into one of the most important (and most popular) applications available on a computer. E-mail provides people with a way to communicate, escaping the constraints of time, space, and location. Its business benefits can be so far-reaching that Intel's former president, Andy Grove, once quipped that e-mail is a "killer application" because once you've got it, you can't live without it. Lots of e-mail advocates agree.

Network users can communicate information via e-mail when they need to and receive answers when it is convenient. E-mail puts an end to time-robbing phone tag and paper-chasing memos that circulate around until, forgotten, they find a final resting place in an already too-full file drawer. (Even though electronic in-boxes can get pretty full, most e-mail systems allow filters to be created to sort mail automatically, so your messages are better organized than they'd be as a stack of memos on your desk.)

How E-mail Works

In most mail systems (electronic or manual), there is a post office to store and forward the mail, a mailbox for each person, and a vehicle to deliver mail. In good electronic mail systems, there are extra conveniences, such as the ability to attach another file (a spreadsheet, document, or other information) to your message, the option of requiring a return receipt notice; and the ability to store your mail in folders, which can be shared with individuals or groups. With a specially equipped multimedia PC, you can even add voice annotations to your e-mail.

Establishing E-mail Roles

Because the computers do most of the work, with e-mail you won't need a fleet of trucks to move the mail, a team of sorters to sort it, a mail carrier to deliver it, or clerks to file it after it's read.

To establish a successful e-mail system, you do need to define roles for an e-mail administrator and a group of mail users.

The mail administrator sets up the system and periodically performs maintenance chores. For networks of less than fifty people, this is not a difficult or time-consuming task, but for networks with hundreds of users, it can easily turn into a full time job.

Most e-mail administration tasks include the following duties:

▶ Creating the post office

▶ Assigning post office passwords

▶ Adding/changing/deleting mailboxes and users

▶ Monitoring disk space in the post office

▶ Backing up post office data files

▶ Maintaining the e-mail system files

▶ Troubleshooting problems

Also, there are the tasks of training and providing everyday end-user support to consider. Sometimes these duties also rest with the e-mail administrator, while in other organizations, training and support might come from another area within the company.

People must use an e-mail system in order to get any benefit from it. This is a key point. Some individuals and groups may have to make adjustments in their organizational culture to get the full benefits of e-mail. E-mail users will have to check into the e-mail system frequently, reply promptly to their mail, delete unnecessary messages, and adjust their personal habits to accommodate e-mail's advantages.

Best Practices for E-mail Implementation

Since each e-mail package has its own idiosyncratic methods of installation, this section focuses on best practices in general terms for successful e-mail implementation.

The first consideration is disk space. As messages are sent and forwarded between users, disk space is quickly absorbed. Some users will not use more than 100K of disk space for their mailboxes, while others will use much more. Given an average work environment, 10MB per user is a safe number to start with if your network users are unfamiliar with e-mail. If your e-mail users are experienced, or if they expect eventually to link into other e-mail systems, you should allocate 50MB per user from the very beginning. These disk space guidelines are for the post office data only, and do not figure in the amount you'll need for the various e-mail server software and other related applications.

E-mail packages distinguish users by their mailbox name, which must be unique for every user. Before you add the first user, you should establish conventions for making user names and mailbox names unique. Many mail administrators fall into the trap of using everyone's first or last name as their e-mail address. We suggest you don't.

Some first and last names are so common that duplicates will likely occur. Two standards in email addressing have emerged as the most popular. Both include the first name, followed by the last name. The only difference is in the separator used between the names. One uses a period and the other uses an underscore. In addition to identifying post office users when it comes to administration, their Internet e-mail addresses will be easier for them to remember. Many e-mail packages support network names as well, and so make things easier for the administrator and users alike because there is only one name to remember.

While we're on the subject of naming conventions, the post office name should also be considered especially as it relates to Internet mail. Remember, simple is always better. Regardless of the e-mail package used, when naming and setting up the e-mail post office, try to keep it limited to the name of the company. Complex Internet e-mail addresses only spell confusion for users, too much space taken up on business cards, and hassles for the network/e-mail administrator.

E-mail Etiquette

Regular users of e-mail develop their own set of customs. Many e-mail messages take on a much less formal tone than traditional business correspondence. The main purpose is to get a thought across, so messages are often very short. They often lack the salutations and even signatures of formal business letters.

E-mail and the Paperless Trail

If you consider that today's networked office is one with less paper flowing, then e-mail is a critical application. A good e-mail system can provide a paperless trail for documentation of any kind.

Consider this example: Marketing gets three new employees in one week. As the designated human resources representative, your duty is to get these people acclimated to the company through mandatory training, parking, W-2 forms, etc. With e-mail, not only can you create a traceable dialog with each of the respective departments, but you don't have to rely on "telephone tag." With e-mail, you send it and it's there. It's also traceable, meaning that if for any reason a discrepancy arises and it appears that a ball has been dropped somewhere along the process, you have an electronic paper trail detailing and covering every single exchange that has taken place with all the various individuals involved. Best of all, this paper trail is not misfiled in some rickety old filing cabinet that never has been organized to begin with. It is safely stored in an electronic folder residing in your e-mail basket, which is backed up every night.

Group Scheduling Electronically

Like e-mail, a computer-assisted appointment book can become an indispensable tool for today's network member. Manual appointment systems take too much time, are inefficient, and frequently cause people to resort to keeping multiple calendars. How many times have you seen a busy executive with a leather-bound calendar on his desk and a secretary with an almost identical copy? Everything is fine until the phone starts ringing and the schedule starts changing. Before you know it, the calendars get out of sync and nobody is sure what to do, where to go, or when to do it. The problem becomes worse with more people. Getting together for team meetings or bringing in new team members can be a major ordeal to coordinate.

Do electronic scheduling programs really make things easier? After all, there have been scheduling programs available on computers for a number of years. It hasn't seemed to help that much.

The problem with "first generation" computer calendar programs was that they were oriented to the personal users on unconnected computers. This simply doesn't add much to an office environment where people work together. The solution starts with software that is designed for people to share and coordinate information over a network.

What You Can Do with Electronic Schedules

Electronic schedules of any variety serve certain primary functions, all centered around managing and maintaining your projects and day-to-day work. The functions include appointments which maintain your calendar and a planner that schedules meetings, group events, and tasks.

Electronic schedulers typically go where you do. You can work with them on your desktop computer or export files to a laptop computer or personal digital assistant (PDA). This is a great convenience for busy professionals who work both in and out of the office.

Network scheduling programs typically interact closely with their proprietary e-mail system, so users can share schedules and access copies of each other's schedule information. A good scheduling application will let you look into the availability of several people at one time. This is called a busy search, and can save a lot of time.

By granting different levels of access to different members of your organization you can get a good handle on your security issues. For example, you can allow some people to make your appointments for you; permit others to just view your appointments; allow still others to just see whether you are free/busy at certain times, but not your activities; and prevent others from seeing anything at all.

You can also use the program to schedule use of common resources, such as conference rooms, audio-visual equipment, or even other computers.

How Electronic Scheduling Works with E-mail

Typically, electronic schedules and e-mail work hand in hand. For example, in Novell GroupWise, both functions come in the same package. Usually they share the post office directory list of names and the same users' passwords. When an appointment is made through a scheduler, typically an e-mail is sent through the network to the other attendees asking their response to the invitation.

Recall the scenario mentioned at the beginning of the chapter, with the administrative assistant organizing a meeting? How do you think the participants were all brought together? If each person on a network is using a group electronic scheduling package, then individual schedules are viewable by all. One look at all ten directors' schedules and a time can be found and a meeting set in minutes, rather than the hours normally given to playing phone tag. Don't forget about the problems typically associated with reserving a conference room, audio-visual equipment, or even PCs for presentations. All of these items can be placed into network scheduling software too. Some applications do a good job of putting all information on a single screen or printed page.

Collaboration Tools: Beyond E-mail

Fundamentally, there's a big difference between e-mail and collaboration tools. E-mail is basically one-to-one messaging. Joe sends Sue an e-mail. Sue sends Joe a reply. Easy enough.

Of course e-mail can be expanded to share the message with many people. Let's say Joe sends Sue an e-mail and copies the marketing team. Sue sends Joe a reply and copies the marketing team. Basically, the conversation is still between Joe and Sue, but this time they send their messages in public. Carol and Carl can also provide their comments, and take the message to a completely different topic, but that's where e-mail tends to get confusing. If Carol and Carl, Sam and Sandy all want to add their two cents worth, they should take their discussion to a collaboration tool.

In the previous example, the collaboration tool best suited for this type of application would be a discussion group. A discussion group resembles an electronic bulletin board or a meeting without a moderator. Everyone can participate, all at the same time or individually as new thoughts surface.

Products like IBM's Lotus Notes or Attachmate's OpenMind started as this type of group-oriented product. The leading collaboration tools today include Lotus Domino/Notes, Novell GroupWise, and Microsoft Exchange.

Collaboration tools belong to one of two categories: real-time and asynchronous. Real-time collaboration would include discussing a project over the telephone, during a videoconference, or in a physical meeting. Asynchronous collaboration includes discussion groups, centralized file maintenance and updating, group scheduling, or task sharing. Asynchronous collaboration has now become the more popular method of collaboration. It breaks the constraints of time, availability, and location.

The e-mail systems of today have conveniently stretched to accommodate the needs of groups by performing like bulletin boards. Imagine a set of electronic bulletin boards viewable on the computer screen at work. Each bulletin board is designated for a certain type of information. Company phone lists, medical plans, retirement plans, and upcoming social events can all be distributed and viewed on today's e-mail system. For example, specifically, how up-to-date is your company's employee phone and pager list? If it was centrally located within the e-mail bulletin board system, it could easily be updated daily.

The prior examples only address the internal workings of a company. There is an entire world out there, just waiting to be contacted, communicated with, or sold something. Anyone who has Internet-enabled electronic mail can communicate with anyone else who has the same technology.

Best of all, e-mail is a whole lot cheaper than the cost of a stamp, envelope, paper and the labor to put it together. The average postal letter in the United States costs $1.50 to $2.50 to create (including the cost of labor). An e-mail, by contrast, might cost as little as 50¢. It's more personal, too, because there is an etiquette involved in writing business e-mail.

Flip on the computer, pick the e-mail address of an acquaintance, and away you go. Want to add your comments to a group discussion? Just tap out your thoughts and push the send key. E-mail and collaboration tools make networking what it always should have been — easy.

Office Automation

While it is true that many applications don't require networks, all should be networkable, because the end product of most work must be shared with someone — the boss, colleagues, subordinates, customers, suppliers, and so on.

Electronic documents are the way to go. In addition to electronically creating documents once done by hand, today's office automation software all work in conjunction with each other. In other words, numbers crunched in spreadsheets can be applied to charts and graphs in presentation software, as well as databases and word-processing documents. Furthermore, data from any of the applications can be imbedded into any of the other applications in the suite. The standardization of applications and formats across an office suite encourage this type of easy document sharing.

The newest function of office software is for the creation of pages on the World Wide Web. Instead of sharing documents across the LAN or through e-mail, as mentioned earlier, they will be placed on controlled corporate intranet sites, which is covered in Chapter 4. Office automation suites, as they're called, typically include at least a word processor, spreadsheet, database, and graphics software used for presentations.

Word Processing

Modern day word-processing programs have not only replaced the typewriter, but the specially trained typist, too. With standard features such as spell checking, revision editing, tables, columns, and automatic outline and table of contents creation it is no wonder that word processors are one of the leading software packages purchased every year.

Word-processing software on a network has the added functionality of sharing documents in real time with coworkers for editing and collaborative creation, which saves time and money. For example, using standard templates, electronic highlighting, and notations in the margins, all on-screen, are possible without ever printing out the type-written page. Perhaps best of all, with a multitude of file formats in which to save a word-processing document (everything from Microsoft Word to basic text), your work can easily be shared with other companies or clients by attaching these files to e-mail messages just as you would through the office.

Presentation Software

Another way to enhance productivity is with presentation software. It produces multimedia presentations that can be run from your computer to a projection screen in a conference room. That's right—no more creating or paying for those expensive, frail transparencies. Plus, as an added benefit, most current presentation software enables you to display the presentation on a computer screen in front of a large group of people. The presentation never has to be printed to be used.

Networks expand the ease-of-use for presentations by making the files available on the network servers. They can be shared, edited by others, or sent via e-mail to another person or location.

Spreadsheet Software

A tool that fundamentally changed the world is the spreadsheet. Aside from giving people a quick way to add up numbers, it gave them the ability to perform countless "what-if" analyses in a short time. This leads to people making more informed decisions because they can look at a problem any number of ways.

Also, by compiling the numbers and statistics saved in a spreadsheet, the software can automatically create bar graphs, pie charts, and xy plots. Not to mention the fact that people can now retire their ledgers, calculators or, if any still exist, slide rules. A spreadsheet can do it all when it comes to numbers. Spreadsheet software, just to name a few features, can automatically add, subtract, divide, multiply, and perform statistical analysis and even actuaries.

Networks make spreadsheets more powerful by letting people share files and information. In the case of a spreadsheet with graphs, the individual user or someone else on the team can pull just the pertinent graphs into presentation software. In fact, users can create live links between the data and reports. Say, for example, Fred updates his quarterly estimates in a spreadsheet. When his boss wants to update her presentation, she can create a link to Fred's spreadsheet so that each time she pulls up her presentation she has the most current numbers.

Databases

For some people, data and analysis spreadsheets are too limiting. For instance, say a user needs to be able to query (search) for all the dates that a client has been late for payment, arranged quarter by quarter to view a trend. Database software can do all of that. Maybe your business is market or medical research. There is no easier tool with which to produce standard survey forms. These forms can be e-mailed to clients or put on a web site, and when returned, the data can be entered into the database for statistical analysis, trends, and even financial forecasting.

Database software is among the most powerful software on networks. Properly configured, a database lets people share and update records efficiently. Can you imagine an airline trying to assign seats from the ticket counter, reservations desk, and gate area without a real-time, multiuser, seat selection database? Sure it can be done, but not with nearly the same ease and accuracy as with a network.

Tracking Resources Across the Network

Now back to the needs of a network administrator for a minute. You may be thinking, "If I have to manage a network with so many resources, PCs, and applications, how do I keep track of it all?" Easy. Look into the utilities and the network operating system itself. For example, with a Novell NetWare network operating system, everything on the LAN can be efficiently tracked and maintained. The extensive database even includes a way to track where users sit and their phone numbers, departments, and titles. The database, called Novell Directory Services (NDS), maintains all the information related to the network, including user access, printer specifications, file rights, and which user has supervisory access to manage all the resources. NDS also acts as a security guard by maintaining the strictest of access privileges. Thus, the company budget spreadsheet, while shareable on the network, is only viewable by those users with the correct access rights as determined by the network administrator and enforced by NDS. These enforceable rights include permitting admittance to use the various applications on the network as well. Detailed information about rights can be found in Chapter 12.

Should Every Application Be Networked?

While it isn't necessary for every single application to reside on network servers or shared disks, you should consider every application before dismissing it. When it comes to helping people share information, lowering the cost of licenses (when concurrent-use licenses are available), or simply finding the easiest way to centrally update and maintain software — networks look pretty attractive.

Networking applications usually help keep installation, support, and maintenance hassles to a minimum. Keep in mind, however, that individual products do vary. Some applications are written in such a manner that they constantly call sub-programs, which may cause too much traffic on an already busy network. In other cases, software installations are not network-friendly and force files to a local drive. It is best to read the package or contact the software maker's technical support desk if you are unsure.

Summary

Throughout this chapter, three recurring themes present themselves. First is sharing. Networks help people share their work, information, knowledge, and wisdom. Make sure you design your network strategy to share as much as possible. Second, applications should conform to standards. For the benefits to be realized, office automation standardization must take place. Unless end users are very mature and can support special configurations of their own software applications, it helps to choose one set of office automation tools and install them in the same manner, consistently. Third, before purchasing or upgrading, always remember to document and test, test, test software to verify that it will serve your needs.

CHAPTER 4

The Internet and Intranets

For fifty years, people could only dream of having a universal information source that put the world's knowledge within an arm's reach of their desire. Today, for 150 million people, this dream has come true. The path to endless information — every answer and every question you can possibly think of lies only a few mouse clicks away.

It's the Internet, so access to it is free — well, almost. Access costs actually vary widely based on your existing technology infrastructure. It may cost as little as a few hundred dollars for equipment, plus monthly charges for additional telephone lines and an Internet service provider (ISP). Or you could spend thousands to hundreds of thousands of dollars retrofitting your existing network to accommodate the new traffic.

For most organizations, the Internet isn't optional. It's a necessity. In fact, today's version of a LAN is simply the local place to join the Internet. Your company colleagues will want a two way street.

Once you do connect your company's LAN to the Internet, you and your colleagues can pursue either or both of two paths for traffic: e-business and learning.

The e-business path will lead you to assembling your organization's presence on the Internet. Your company may want to advertise, sell directly to consumers, transact business to business activities, or distribute some of its information over the Internet.

Building an e-business site stakes your place in cyberspace, so to speak. For this, you'll need to assemble quite a few skilled workers, from artistic Web page designers to network engineers familiar with setting up servers, network gear, and communications options. Alternatively you can outsource most, if not all the work by using consultants to build your site and host it on someone else's computer. Cyberspace is a virtual world so nothing is location-dependent. For example, Web page designers don't care whether the host computer is across the hall or across the country. With the right communications in place, it doesn't matter.

The learning path takes you in a slightly different direction. If all your organization wants is to improve its ability to learn, you only need to concentrate on providing information access. Your technical architecture can be different, and you won't require an in-house server or a team of Web page creators. Instead, you'll focus on getting solid, reliable, high-speed access to all of your colleagues all of the time. You should also help your colleagues find the right training and support for their individual information needs. Most professionals are excited to see the extensive — and inexpensive — research resources on the Internet. Most information there is free or low cost. But without a road map, people end up wasting more time than they save by fumbling around using the wrong search engines or asking the wrong questions.

This chapter introduces the Internet and intranets (the homespun, in-house version for your organization's insiders). We start with a little history and define the necessary terms that you need to know about sources and resources. If you've been looking for a guide to the fundamentals of the Internet and World Wide Web, then this chapter should give you a reference for how things work. If you are already familiar with the Internet and intranets, but want to know how to connect to it, then skip to "How to Access the Internet and the Web" towards the end of the chapter.

What Is the Internet?

While its root technology was developed during the cold war back in the 1950s and '60s, the Internet was hardly a household word before the early 1990s. Historically, the Internet was used by the U.S. government, educational institutions, and researchers. By 1994, a series of legislative acts and a few accidents cleared the path to open the Internet to everyone.

Things just fell into place. Standards committees quickly adopted the idea of a naming convention to create a world-wide web (WWW). An army of entrepreneurs with heretical ideas set foot into cyberspace and began to re-invent how products were sold. Suddenly it was a modern day gold rush.

Most readers of this book have already started their journey into the online world and, no doubt, found the Internet to be an indispensable resource. Certainly, it is a bit daunting, but still remarkable.

The word Internet literally means network of networks. In itself, the Internet is comprised of thousands of smaller regional networks scattered throughout the globe. On any given day it connects roughly 150 million users in over 300 countries. This number increases daily.

Science-fiction writer Bruce Sterling describes the Internet as functional anarchy. It works, it functions, but it has no controls. No one owns the Internet, and though it has coordinators and groups to suggest standards, there's no real boss.

Some try to describe the Internet as a group of teenagers hanging out at the mall. Since they're all peers, no one member tells the others what to do. Despite occasional squabbles, they tend to stick together. What makes this mode of existence endure is this: funding. Thanks to their moms and dads, these kids have no worries. They can play, be curious, investigate, invest, or throw away the products of their activity. Creativity soars, as does the tab.

The Internet started much like it was run by a giddy group of mall-crawling teenagers. It is a sociotechnical entity that evolved because no one had to worry about paying for it. For the Internet, the parent was the U.S. government under the perceived threat of the cold war forty years ago. It was the Department of Defense who sponsored the Advanced Research Projects Agency (ARPA) and gave it the charter, the funding, and the challenge to invent an indestructible network. And that's exactly what it did. ARPA built a network designed so well that it now carries millions of times more activity than those wild kids (err... designers) ever imagined it could.

The Internet's architecture has no center, hub, or master. Theoretically, no single outage could take it down. If something broke (or was bombed), the network would fix itself and messages would simply find another route, as shown in Figure 4.1.

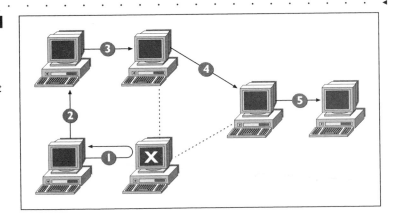

FIGURE 4.1

The Internet was built so that no single point of failure would disrupt all communications. If any host goes down, the traffic is rerouted.

Previously, the Internet existed as a product of the government, universities and selected companies that worked on government projects. The network was built to share resources, never go down, and move information from anywhere to anywhere.

That's where the cosmic-collision theory comes in. In a few short years, the efforts of many teams working under no single master came together.

Among the events that spurred the explosion of Internet access:

▶ Opening the Internet to commercial sites

▶ Development of Wide Area Information Servers (WAIS), making information electronically searchable

▶ Upgrade of the Internet backbone so it supports speeds of 44.7MBps

▶ Establishment of sites for high-profile bodies, such as the U.S. White House

▶ First Internet audio multicast (March 1992) followed by video multicast (November 1992)

▶ Creation of the InterNIC in 1993 to provide specific Internet services; namely, directory and database services, registration services, and information services

▶ Release of Mosaic software in 1993 by the National Center for Supercomputing Applications in Illinois. The Mosaic browser allowed PCs and other desktop computers to access the Web with a graphical point and click interface.

Once commercial sites were granted access to the Internet, the number of Internet hosts increased greatly — by over 400 percent in the first two years.

What Is the Web?

To help differentiate the Internet and the World Wide Web, it helps to think of them as two different parts of the same object. The Internet refers to the physical structure of millions of computers cabled together worldwide. It's the hardware, topology, and technical part. The Web is the content — at least in terms of the snazzy graphics, colorful text, and hyperlinked structure.

The Web received such an early and enthusiastic acceptance, many people believed the Internet and the Web would change the way people work, learn, and live. Within the first five years, just about everyone in the developed world had an e-mail address.

After reviewing many research documents, we decided to provide you with selected summary information to give you a sense of what's happening on the Web, and who is using it. We believe that with time the population of the Web will look more like the general population. In a nutshell, everybody will be there.

GVU Studies

Among the most widely respected survey instruments is the GVU WWW User Survey, a product of researchers at Georgia Tech University. The survey is conducted approximately every six months, attracts from four thousand to twelve thousand participants, and asks basically the same questions each time. Recent surveys have expanded its scope, but we find interesting historical value in comparing the first to the most recent survey. Table 4.1 summarizes some key findings from the surveys.

TABLE 4.1	FACTOR	JANUARY, 1994	OCTOBER, 1998
The Internet and Intranets	Average Age of Respondents	N/A	37.6
	Percentage of Female Respondants	6%	33.6 %
	Percentage of U.S. Respondents	69%	84.7%
	Frequency of Use	36%: >10 hrs./wk. 42%: 0–5 hrs./wk.	99.2%: daily
	Instead of Watching TV	N/A	55.4%: daily
	Average Household Income	N/A	$57,300

Network World 1998 Internet Study

According to the 1998 Network World 500 Internet study, which surveyed 500 companies using Internet/intranet technologies, strong Internet and intranet incorporation was seen. Even allowing for the obvious bias of these corporate respondents, the results are impressive:

▸ 47 percent use the Internet for remote access to their corporate network.

▸ 42 percent responded that all employees have Internet access. Overall, seventy-one percent of all employees have access to the Internet.

▸ 40 percent of the companies are using electronic commerce applications on their Web site. Sixty percent of those that have not implemented electronic commerce on their Web site plan to do so within the next twelve months.

According to Colin Ungaro, Network World's president and CEO, "The Network World 500 study clearly indicates that network IS professionals are discovering new ways to integrate the Internet into their corporate networks today and in the future."

Staggering Internet Statistics

The Internet continues to grow by leaps and bounds. A few more fascinating facts from researchers at Nielsen:

▸ In January 1988, Internet traffic consisted of 85 million packets. In December 1994, Internet traffic had grown to more than 86 billion packets — an increase of 1,000 percent in seven years.

▸ For the first time ever, in 1995, more e-mail messages were delivered in the U.S. than regular postal messages — ten billion more!

▸ 1995 saw an explosion of corporate and commercial sites on the Internet. On December 31, 1994, there where only 29,000 commercial organizations on the Internet in the U.S. By January 5, 1996, the number had grown to over 170,000! Four months later on April 12, the number grew to 276,400.

▶ According to the CommerceNet/Nielson Internet Survey of April 1999, there were 92 million Internet users over the age of 16 in the U.S. and Canada, up from 79 million in July of 1998.

▶ According to information gathered in June 1999 by the OCLC, the Web has approximately 3.6 million sites, with 2.2 million publicly available sites. The number of publicly available sites has tripled since June 1997.

▶ For the first time ever, in October of 1999, the Web received around one billion hits a day, up 49 percent from the year before, according to Media Matrix.

How to Access the Internet and the Web

Accessing information on the Internet and the Web is a very simple process. The most complex part will only occur one time, and that involves hooking up the LAN to the Internet. Once that's done, everyone has access. There's no need to configure separate modems for each desktop computer.

Basic Software

For many users, the only software that's needed is an Internet browser and a few add-in modules for special processing of audio or video information. Products like Netscape Navigator or Microsoft Internet Explorer are easy to set up and provide one access point for all applications.

Once a desktop PC has accessed the Internet, other capabilities, such as transferring files, are accommodated by the browser. No other specialized software is generally required. The search engine software resides on the server, along with most of the file-transfer capabilities. Even some mail capabilities are incorporated into browsers or tightly integrated in links. This architecture is especially helpful to new or infrequent users. They don't need to learn separate tools to accomplish each task.

Putting Your Organization on the Net

If you've been given the project of putting your company on the Internet, don't run for your keyboard to update your secret file, RESUME.DOC. Consider the project as an adventure! Depending on your budget, you can even outsource the adventure to a computer consultant or outside organization that specializes in making good Internet connections.

If you'd rather learn first-hand about putting your organization on the Internet, we can help. Simply open up your word processor software (or project management or spreadsheet software) and lay out your plan. Here's our quick ten-step task list:

1. Choose your access method (dedicated, dial-up, line speed, etc.).

2. Decide on your organization's server and browser software.

3. Locate an ISP.

4. Order your telephone line(s) and schedule installation.

5. Confirm what your needs are regarding connection hardware.

6. Register your domain name.

7. Install the phone lines and hardware.

8. Get connected to the ISP.

9. Install the browser and server software.

10. Educate yourself and enjoy the Internet!

Choose Your Access Method

You need to look carefully at your options to access the Internet. Since the Web is increasingly graphics and multimedia oriented, let us suggest two simple rules of thumb:

▶ Buy as much bandwidth as you can afford.

▶ Use a dedicated line (not dial-up).

Increased bandwidth makes a lot of difference to users. When they experience snappy response time, they tend to use the Internet more productively for more things. They take that extra step to seek another source for information, or feel more comfortable double checking the facts.

You'll more than justify the added costs for faster lines when you consider the cost of people's time awaiting slow graphics screens to repaint. Plus, people will produce higher quality work if they can avoid the anxiety imposed by slow response.

You'll also need to decide if your organization supports two-way traffic. If you plan to host your own Web server as well as give your in-house employees' access, then you should seek advice on capacity planning.

Watch out for surprises! Even if you are a small business, if your organization has many mobile workers or telecommuters, you may find one high speed connection isn't enough. If you are trying to accommodate inbound traffic to your web server, and outbound traffic from your employees to the Web, you could start to slow down your connection quickly. Noticeable speed degradation takes place when only 20 percent of the bandwidth is occupied.

Guides for Web server capacity planning are available on the Internet. For example, Sun Microsystems, among other computer makers, generally keeps current planning worksheets posted on its web site.

If you work in a large organization and are planning for the needs of hundreds or thousands of users, we recommend that you call in some expert help. It never hurts to get a second (or third) opinion.

When it comes to ordering your lines, shop carefully. Because of the many communications technologies available to make the connection, intensive price competition exists among suppliers. Depending on the size and complexity of your infrastructure, you may spend a week to a month searching out your options. For additional details on lines, refer to Chapter 5.

Decide on Your Organization's Server and Browser Software

If your organization doesn't have a standard set for server and/or browser software, you should take some time reviewing the market. There are many packages to choose from, and you should understand the tradeoffs.

For example, using the Netscape browser and server software, you will likely encounter many third-party add-ins or enhancements. Netscape designs an architecture that many other software developers support. If you choose a product such as Microsoft NT Server and Internet Explorer, you will likely have to rely on Microsoft for enhancements. This differentiation continues to evolve.

Locate an Internet Service Provider

The ISP provides you with a tap, or connection to the Internet. This differs from obtaining an access line, or pipe.

Initially, most organizations used different companies; however, that practice isn't always the best. Now that telephone service is deregulated, you'll find both old and new faces when you begin to look for a good ISP. Some telephone companies, such as AT&T, MCI, and Sprint, will sell you both services.

Don't choose your ISP on price or purchasing convenience only. Make sure your ISP has a good reputation, maintains its equipment well, and has a good track record with existing customers. You may even want to visit existing customers to see how they are set up.

Make sure you try to sample their services and call clients for references. Changing ISPs along the way is possible, but a hassle. Since you must first connect to your ISP, then to the Internet, your connection is only as reliable as your ISP. Ask for performance statistics — if the ISP doesn't maintain any, then find someone who does.

Larger sites may wish to host their own access to the Internet; however, it is expensive and complex. You'll need to call in a team of experts to help if you choose to make a direct connection.

Order Your Communications Line(s) and Schedule Installation

Once you've confirmed your needs and selected an ISP, you are ready to order your communications lines and schedule the installation date. Double check your plans and coordinate other activities to take place in a rapid sequence. You can begin to install client software, such as browsers, even before the lines are active.

Confirm Your Needs for Connection Hardware

You need to provide hardware for your connection. At the very least you need a terminal adapter or router to connect your LAN to the new lines. Your ISP will likely help you plan and select your hardware. In some cases the ISP makes this hardware a part of the deal.

Register Your Domain Name

When you first set up your organization on the Internet and the Web, you'll have to register your organization and select a domain name. The process gives your organization an electronic name and address.

To register a new domain name, you need to go through several steps. You must choose a unique top level "domain name." This will be your address in cyberspace.

Creating Your Organization's Domain Name

It's a good idea to have several domain names in mind before you select one. Thinking globally in your selection of domain names and trademarks can keep your business on top.

Keep in mind that there are 191 countries that accept country-code domain registrations and each has different registration requirements. In at least 80 country-code registries, there are no rules about who can register — it's first come, first served.

If you want to protect your brand or company name from infringement or customer confusion worldwide, Network Solutions has a service called idNames (www.idnames.com) that can register a domain name associated with a company's product, brand or name with 80 of these countries at once. You can use a redirect method to send the country-specific domain names to your main site.

If the name is critically important, you should also register as many variations of the name as possible. Otherwise, certain variations could be registered by speculators. If a domain name speculator registers a similar name, you'll either have buy it from the speculator or sue. Legal cases and policies for disputing domain-name registration look at ownership of federal trademarks first. Therefore, it's definitely worth trademarking your domain name so you don't lose it later to the rightful trademark owner.

However, many organizations find it useful to register a unique domain name anyway, so that their employee's e-mail addresses and the organization's electronic address are similar to the company name. Domain names have become a status symbol to some organizations.

You should research the domain name you'd like to register. Network Solutions, a domain name provider, lets you search for existing names and tells you if the name is in use or not. The site is on the web at: `http://www.networksolutions.com/cgi-bin/whois/whois`. The whois service provides a way of finding e-mail addresses, postal addresses, and telephone numbers of those who have registered names with the InterNIC.

If the name you want is in use, your whois query will return a list including information about the organization who holds the name, the name servers, and the contacts responsible for administering it. If it is not in use, the answer you receive will be: "No match for 'yourname.com'."

If you are looking for a special domain name that happens to be owned by someone else, you can negotiate to buy the name. Or, you can search for a list of domain names for sale on a listing service like:

`http://www.domains4sale.com`

Web Naming Conventions

As of the writing of this book, work is underway to expand the domain name conventions. The basic rules of creating a domain name, however, will stay intact.

A domain name can be up to 26 characters long, including the four characters used to identify the top level domain, such as .net, .com, .org. There are seven top level domains, as listed below.

Three of the seven are open, requiring no restrictions on the persons or entities that may register names in them. These three are *.com*, *.net* and *.org*. The other four are restricted, in the sense that only certain entities may register names in them.

The following is a description of these designations:

- ▸ Open domain names:

  - .com is for commercial, for-profit organizations.

  - .org is for miscellaneous, usually non-profit organizations.

  - .net is for network infrastructure machines and organizations.

▸ Restricted domain names:

- .int is restricted to use by international organizations.

- .edu is for four-year, degree-granting colleges and universities.

- .gov can be used only by U.S. federal government agencies

- .mil is reserved for the US military

Expanded Domain Names

In 1997, the Internet Ad Hoc Committee (IAHC) proposed seven new top-level domains. Negotiations with other groups have taken several years and the top-level domains are still not approved for use. When approved, Internet users will have seven new generic affiliations. They include:

▸ .ARTS for entities emphasizing cultural and entertainment activities

▸ .FIRM businesses, or firms

▸ .INFO to set up entities providing information services

▸ .NOM for those who wish individual or personal nomenclature

▸ .REC for entities emphasizing recreation/entertainment activities

▸ .STORE for businesses offering goods to purchase

▸ .WEB for organizations emphasizing activities related to the WWW

What's in a Name?

Most organizations like to use the product name or the company name as the Domain name. If the organization goes by its initials or an acronym, it makes a convenient Domain name. For example, International Business Machines uses ibm.com.

Remember, although your domain name isn't the same as your electronic address, it is used to make up the address. The electronic address or uniform resource locator (URL) is how Web browsers access different places on the Web. For example, International Business Machines (IBM) goes by the electronic address of: `http://www.ibm.com`. Same goes for Hewlett-Packard, which uses `http://www.hp.com`.

Experience says that your domain name is as important as your company name and its physical address. Make it easy for customers and suppliers to remember.

Registering Your Domain Name

You must register domain names and modifications electronically. This is done by filling out an electronic template from a domain name provider, such as Network Solutions. You can get specific information from the provider.

Your application is processed electronically, so the information you send to the domain registration organization is entered into the database exactly as it was submitted on the domain name template. (So, if there is a mistake, you made it.) This also saves time and effort rekeying information. Hard copy registrations of any kind are not accepted.

Avoiding the Name Game

If you use an outside ISP to give you access to the Internet, you do not need your own top level domain name. The ISP can assign you a name under its top level. For example, if your ISP is called newplanet.com then your organization's name could be:

```
www.newplanet.com/your_company_name
```

While it will save you time and energy to avoid the name game, most experts feel that getting your own top level domain adds to the market power of your Web site.

Install the Communications Lines and Hardware

Your activities will increase on installation day. While the telephone or cable company is going to be busy actually installing the lines, you need to coordinate other activities. Depending on how you purchased the service, you may or may not get help from the phone company after your line is installed.

For example, if you decide on an ISDN connection and purchase it through your local telephone company, the service may stop when the installer gets the line working. Historically, the regional Bell operating companies do not install your equipment for you. They only guarantee that the line is working. You may wish to employ a computer consultant for finishing the process where the line installation stops.

You must install the connection hardware and then configure it. This requires a communications device, sometimes called a router. Depending on the device and the service you install, you'll need to configure it with information such as your dial out lines, an IP address, and a method for all the PCs on your local area network to access the Internet.

Get Connected to the ISP

In some cases, such as with cable modems and digital subscriber lines (DSL), your communications company may become your ISP. While this makes it easier on your administration, it doesn't change how you will set up your equipment.

Between your line provider and your ISP, you have plenty of numbers to deal with. At this time you also need to install your router, as mentioned above. Your ISP will provide you with special TCP/IP addresses that identify your server (if you have one), two domain name servers, and dialup telephone numbers.

Install the Browser and Server Software

If you are not hosting your own Web server, then you only need to install browser software on each desktop. Many LAN administrators install the software on a server and either force it to each desktop automatically or make an icon available so that users who want the software can easily install it themselves.

Browser software needs some configuration, but that is usually limited to creating identification information or e-mail addresses.

If you choose to provide content to the Web, you will want to choose a Web authoring tool. While it is possible to create Web pages by using a Notepad-like utility and adding your own hypertext markup language (HTML) tags, we don't recommend it. Check out popular word-processing programs like Corel WordPerfect or Microsoft Word—both can create Web pages. For even more control over your Web page development, use a dedicated tool like Microsoft FrontPage, or Sausage Software's HotDog, which also helps you organize and update your navigation. You will also need to install server software on the computer designated as the Web server. Novell NetWare makes an excellent choice for server software.

Educate Yourself and Enjoy the Internet

Voilá! You did it. Now, just one more task before you sit back and enjoy all the benefits of the Internet. That's end-user training and education. While we discuss general training programs in a later chapter, we want you to make sure that you put "education" up front on your task list.

Without giving end users an effective education program, all your work putting up an Internet connection can go to waste. It's akin to turning over the keys to your brand new car to an untrained (unlicensed) teenager. It's not a matter of "if" they'll have a problem, it's a matter of "when."

Your company should also establish a formal policy of the proper use of the Internet by employees. Because the Internet serves so many diverse interests, and there are no boundaries to content, your company could lose valuable employee time if people surf –the web for non-business activity. The Internet is full of pornography and alternative lifestyle sites which have no business value. Your policy should spell out unacceptable use.

For information on how to restrict access to offensive or unacceptable sites, see our discussion on firewalls in Chapter 6. Also, consider using management tools to monitor excessive use of time on certain sites. While few managers would mind if a person spent 40 seconds to buy or sell stock, most mangers don't want to lose four hours a day while a day-trader tries to get rich by gambling his or her retirement funds.

· ◄

Internet Code of Ethics

Among the things every Internet user should know is how to be a good netizen. Citizens of cyberspace sometimes take their new-found freedom and misuse it. The newly connected should all get the indoctrination and wisdom of those who pioneered the Internet.

In January 1989, the Internet Activities Board (IAB) issued a document titled "Ethics and the Internet." The simple and eloquently stated five key messages establish sensible and responsible behavior. The following are unethical and unacceptable:

Any activity which purposely:

▸ Seeks to gain unauthorized access to the resources of the Internet

- ► Disrupts the intended use of the Internet

- ► Wastes resources (people, capacity, computer) through such actions

- ► Destroys the integrity of computer-based information

- ► Compromises the privacy of users

For the most part, participants on the Internet follow this code of ethics; however, everyone goes through a learning curve when first going out on the Web. Studies show that you'll reduce that curve by a factor of two or three times if you offer end-user training. We strongly recommend it.

Intranets

Intranets are simply a private version of the Internet. This is a closed section that is for the employees and other stakeholders that are close to your company. In some ways, an intranet turns into the company bulletin board or cyber watercooler.

Starting in 1995, people began to take Internet and Web development tools and apply them for local applications. Since many companies already had the infrastructure (LANs and WANs), once they added the TCP/IP protocol for the Web, it was easy to build a private network; hence, the name intranet as the internal version of the Internet. (TCP/IP is discussed in depth in Chapter 6.)

Once the technology is installed and the first applications go up, intranet-based applications begin to grow and multiply almost by themselves. Because Web authoring tools are so easy to use, almost anyone can set up an internal version of a discussion group or post project status reports on a Web-formatted page.

Intranets have proven to be useful from the start. For example, U.S. federal government workers have started pilot programs to share information within and among different government agencies. Some have expanded to include contract bidders who read and respond to government projects. In fact, intranets that appeal to suppliers and customers are sometimes called "extranets" because they bring in so many non-employees.

Overall, intranets solved the "too hard to do" problem caused previously by cumbersome incompatible computer systems that people tried to kludge together. Quick benefits were seen as the technology started breaking down the limitations of physical walls, space, and buildings. Now agencies can share information with each other and with other organizations.

High-profile early adopters started sharing their stories of success. Some examples:

▸ Columbia/HCA Healthcare. In keeping with its goal to find more effective ways of conducting business and servicing customers, Columbia/HCA Healthcare found it could more effectively reach its internal associates with an intranet. Columbia launched its intranet in January 1996, and within months it contained content from more than a quarter of the company. With over 275,000 employees, the company needed a more timely and cost-effective way to handle communications. Paper (and the cost to process it) used up too much money that would otherwise be spent on improving health care. Columbia/HCA's intranet hosts a variety of information sources, including an up-to-date corporate directory, reports, and posts collected from the threaded newsgroups where employees exchange information about process improvements and other topics.

▸ John Deere. This equipment manufacturer installed an intranet so staff members could access an online catalog of equipment and integrate data from multiple sources. The system provides company-wide access to results from remote test sites, furnishes technical documentation to employees, offers a visual front end to all parts of the database, and integrates corporate information with agricultural data on the Web.

▸ Booz Allen & Hamilton. As a leading international management and technology consulting firm with over six thousand staff members in more than eighty offices around the globe, Booz Allen & Hamilton's main asset is knowledge. To facilitate sharing that hard earned asset, the company developed an online information system called Knowledge On-Line (or KOL). The system gives internal staff members around the globe easy and immediate access to the company's current information and best thinking. It lets associates link to company's experts on various topics. More than a dozen applications in four key areas put people within a short reach of valuable information. These include:

- Knowledge Repository. Reviews of more than four thousand knowledge-content documents cross-filed by topic, industry, and locations where the information originates and is applied.

- Expert Skills Directory. Using commercial server software search engines, this system inventories the skills of staff members.

- KOLaborate. A type of bulletin board collaborative tool that allows for both public and private messaging.

- Access to Legacy Systems. The intranet provides a gateway to existing corporate information, such as varied booking systems, human resources, and personnel information.

Another advantage of intranets is that they enable workers to use a browser to access information in a data warehouse. This idea seems to be catching on because it shifts the burden of platform compatibility to the browser vendors and not tool vendors or corporate in-house developers. It also provides a universal client so that the same server application can be easily accessed by both employees and customers. Better yet, it is a low-cost option because Web browsers are only a fraction of the cost of online application programming client tools.

Summary

In this chapter we took a high-level view of the options for building an intranet or Internet presence. Included was a short description of what's available on the Internet and a discussion of how a local version — an intranet — can be conceived. We focused on the practical how-to aspects of putting together an intranet (or access to the Internet). There are many options, and your own investigation will likely lead you to many places. We recommend you steer clear of less traveled roads here. Stick with major products from reliable companies. Once you are connected, enjoy cyberspace!

CHAPTER 5

Designing the Physical Network

Networks—by connecting computers, devices, data, and applications—present endless opportunities for the administrator. In theory, you should be able to connect to, use, view, or update any device or bit of information anywhere on the network. But remember, your own success will vary depending on how well your network was designed and installed.

Good network design will allow your network to grow as large as you need it to. Bad design, especially if followed by slipshod installation, will plague both you and your users forever. Your system may work, but it won't work well, and when the inevitable need for upgrades surface, you'll be faced with hit-or-miss results. Some additions may still be easy but others simply won't work.

We cannot overemphasize the need for comprehensive planning and design. Of course, few people have the budgets to put top-of-the-line components at every twist and turn of the cable, and even if they do, rapidly changing technology can make those components quickly obsolete. Nonetheless, we stress that you familiarize yourself with the consequences your decisions create in selecting network components.

In this chapter we provide detailed descriptions of the various network topologies to consider when planning a network strategy, as well as comprehensive suggestions for selecting actual cable types from today's market. To round out the chapter, we close with a look at dial-up capabilities and other connection options for wide areas.

The Need for Cabling

Everything electric emits electronic signals. These signals can conflict with each other if allowed to coexist on the same plane. In other words, two objects cannot occupy the same space at the same time. A perfect example is when you travel between two cities and get bits and pieces of two different radio stations on the same channel. The problem is only solved when your car moves completely out of range of one station and into the range of the other. Thus, it is important for network cable to have the resiliency to thwart such interference. After all, we don't want radio and TV signals interrupting and possibly corrupting data traveling over our network cable. By the same token, we don't want our data signals leaking from the cables only to be intercepted by those devious enough to capture our valuable information for their own use.

Another very important consideration is installing enough cable in the beginning. There's nothing worse than beginning the installation of additional equipment and discovering you don't have enough spare cable to support it. In the long run, doubling the amount of cable you feel you need at the start is very cost-efficient. Even if you don't foresee your network having much immediate growth, you can count on significant expansion over time. Remember that it is not the cable itself but the labor that is usually the most expensive part of the cable installation. Installing ample cable to begin with will save you money and time.

The type of cable you choose will hinge on your preferences for security, data reliability, and topology.

Cable Topology

As you may have guessed by now, there is a lot of organization that goes into networking computers. For cabling (wiring) purposes, there are three main schemes to organize how the cable connects to the nodes: linear-bus, star-shaped, and ring topology.

Unlike the phone system in your home or business, network wiring must be installed in a certain pattern in order to quickly diagnose malfunctioning cables and to compensate for the signaling pattern of certain network communication.

Linear-Bus Topology

In a linear-bus arrangement, as seen in Figure 5.1, a single cable called the bus or trunk, is installed—usually along a cable path in the ceiling or wall—and terminated at each node on the network. Linear-bus topology may also be referred to as "daisy chain." A good analogy for how this topology works is to think of electrical extension cords. Whether stringing lights for the holidays or linking those orange extension cords when edging the yard, you are using a linear-bus topology. The plug-in points are the terminators.

The bus is a single, branching cable that serves each node.

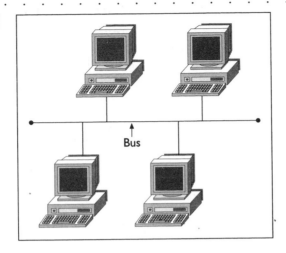

T-connectors, shown in Figure 5.2, are T-shaped metal tubes that serve as connection points for each network node. They work in conjunction with the terminators, which are placed at the beginning and end of the cable (the first and the last PC).

This T-connector resembles a T-joint used by plumbers to join three separate lengths of pipe at one location.

As you might imagine, linear-bus topology is low-cost and simple to design. Assuming you can keep track of the primary cable, it is easy to set up additional PCs by simply tapping into and expanding the trunk cable (like adding more holiday lights to the rooftop). Since each PC is attached directly to the cable, there is no need to purchase additional hardware such as hubs or wire centers. Another advantage is that you will use less cable than with star-shaped topology, discussed next, because the length of cable only has to connect to the next device on the network.

Unfortunately, any break in the cable can cause the entire network, or a good part of it, to fail. A failure can be caused by one end or the other losing proper termination, which can be caused by a pinched cable, loose T-connector, or malfunctioning terminator. As with a string of holiday lights, these failures can be difficult to diagnose.

Convenient and inexpensive, a linear-bus topology is appropriate for very small workgroups of between three and ten members.

Star-Shaped Topology

Utilizing a star-shaped topology, an individual wire is run from each PC to a central location, as shown in Figure 5.3. Here, all the wires are connected to a hub device, which completes the electronic connection. You can think of a hub in a star-shaped topology as a Greyhound bus stop. It provides a central location for all of the signals to meet and then branch out to their individual destinations. Hubs will be covered in more detail in Chapter 7.

Star-shaped wiring uses more cable than linear-bus wiring, but has several important benefits. Since each PC's cable is unique to that machine, if there is a cable fault, only the PC attached to the broken cable is likely to be affected. For example, if you start with a star-shaped network cabled with common unshielded twisted pair (UTP) wiring for Ethernet (covered later in this chapter), and then later decide to replace the Ethernet with Token Ring (covered in Chapter 6), you won't have to rewire your offices.

Star-shaped topology is easier to manage and administer than linear-bus. Once it is set up, it can be easily documented. Most hubs that connect star-shaped networks contain some form of status lights that assist you with locating and diagnosing faults.

The disadvantage of a star-shaped configuration is cost. More cable is needed, as well as a hub to connect all the wires together. However, if greater control over cable network faults is what you're looking for, it may be well worth it to consider this type of network topology.

Even though Ethernet is a bus technology, the most common installation method uses a star-shaped topology over unshielded twisted pair.

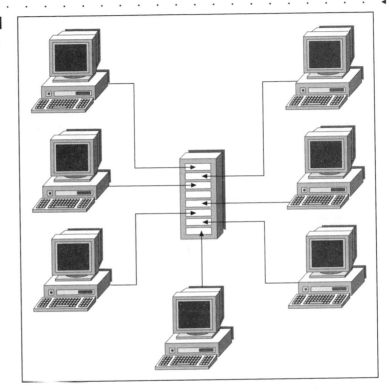

Token Ring Topology

Ring topology networks, where the cable is laid in a circle, are nearly extinct. Although you may hear the word ring used as a synonym for networking, it is mostly used to refer to a media standard such as Token Ring, as seen in Figure 5.4. While token ring networks do actually use a ring topology in the signaling scheme (each signal has to pass by each node sequentially in the ring), they are typically configured with a specialized star-shaped topology.

FIGURE 5.4

A Token Ring topology lays the cable in a circle.

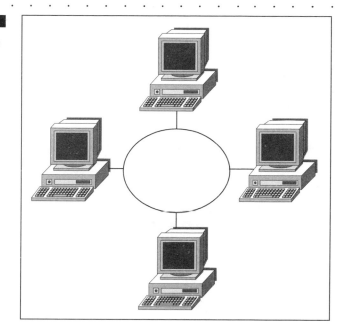

Cable Types

Once you've decided on the topology, you're ready to select the wiring to be used. There are several types of wiring that network electrical impulses will travel over. Each type has physical differences, length requirements, preferred topologies and signaling mechanisms, and a range of pricing structures. The following section will provide both the technical information referred to above as well as descriptions of the most commonly used in peer-to-peer and client-server networks.

Coaxial Cable

Coaxial cable infrastructure accounts for five percent of the computer networks in the United States. Illustrated in Figure 5.5, data is communicated across the network on a single strand of copper wire that is protected from electronic eavesdropping and interference by either more copper wire or foil similar in appearance to that used in your kitchen, surrounding the original strand in a weaved pattern. The topology of choice for coaxial cable is a linear-bus, and is consequently used mostly for peer-to-peer networks.

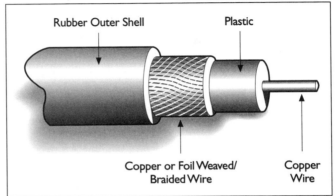

FIGURE 5.5

Thinnet coaxial cable resembles the cable used for your TV.

Rubber Outer Shell   Plastic

Copper or Foil Weaved/ Braided Wire   Copper Wire

There are two types of coaxial cable: thinnet, which looks like the kind used for cable TV, and thicknet, as shown in Figure 5.6. Their main differences include size, price, ease of installation, resiliency to electromagnetic interference, and effective signaling distances.

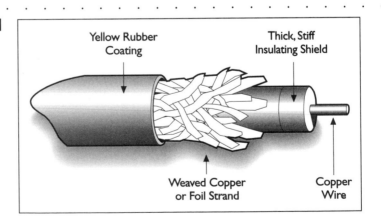

FIGURE 5.6

Thicknet is sometimes referred to as "frozen garden hose" because it's often yellow and rigid.

Yellow Rubber Coating   Thick, Stiff Insulating Shield

Weaved Copper or Foil Strand   Copper Wire

Thicknet Coaxial Cable

Thicknet is commonly referred to as frozen yellow garden hose because of its color and stiff texture; nonetheless, it has the same basic physical make up as thinnet, only with a much thicker protective shielding. Thicknet's inherent installation limitations — it is difficult to put in walls, around corners, and so on — have made it the least popular choice in recent years. Its primary use today is as backbone wiring between buildings, floors of buildings, or areas with high levels of electromagnetic radiation, such as factories and warehouses. Thicknet's ability to carry a signal approximately 541 yards without a repeater (Chapter 7) makes it especially appealing for use in the factory or warehouse setting. It typically connects to the desktop through an attachment unit interface (AUI) connector, which looks similar to a serial port. From the desktop, the AUI cable hooks into the thicknet with what are called vampire connectors, and these can be very touchy if not attached within a few inches of the designated marks along the cable. It is for these reasons thinnet is the more popular of the two.

Thinnet Coaxial Cable

From the outside, thinnet (also called cheapernet because it's less expensive than thicknet) looks exactly like the cable used for cable TV. But don't let appearances deceive you, they're completely different. The correct type of thinnet cable is labeled RG-58 for Ethernet and RG-62 for ARCnet, both of which are described later in this chapter.

Another similarity thinnet has with cable TV coaxial is the connecting ends. The ends of the cable have what are called BNC connectors, shown in Figure 5.7. Affixing these connectors to the cable requires no more than a wire stripper and a pair of pliers. Another difference between cable TV wiring and that used for networking is that cable TV wiring can't be connected to network devices.

FIGURE 5.7

A close-up view of a BNC
coaxial connector

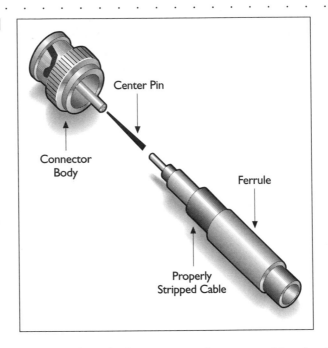

Think of T-connectors as though they are pipe fittings used in plumbing. Data flowing into one connection point continues and flows out of the other two connection points in equal amounts. These connectors aren't valves, but rather three-way converging points, as seen in Figure 5.8, and must occur at every signaling base. In other words, on the back of every network interface card there must be a T-connector in order to branch the connection. Otherwise the signal passing inside the wire will continue on without an opportunity for the node to transmit its data.

Thinnet can support data streams up to 200 yards without a repeater. Granted, this is considerably shorter than the 541 yards of thicknet, but with its more pliable exterior, thinnet is easier to install. Naturally, the type of T-connector is also important. There are many inexpensive imitations available, so make sure they match military specification UG274.

.F I G U R E 5.8

Thinnet coaxial cable must
terminate into T-connectors
at the node.

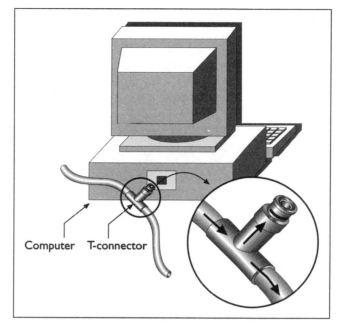

Computer   T-connector

Shielded Twisted Pair

Next to coaxial, shielded twisted pair (STP) is the most electromagnetically resistant copper-based cable used in LANs. Like coaxial, the main data conducting wires are protected with woven copper or metallic foil, as shown in Figure 5.9. In addition to that, the wires are twisted around each other, thus providing the most protection from interfering signals (coming or going) and giving it its name. One pair of wires is used for receiving data while the other pair is used for sending data. STP can be used in both peer-to-peer or client-server networks. However, because of its higher cost of purchase and installation, it is generally only used in large client-server based networks with star-shaped topology and a Token Ring signaling scheme.

As part of the increased shielding properties, STP requires specialized connectors to the various nodes (PCs, printers, and so forth). Rather than the cable being attached to a single connector that then attaches to the NIC (as on coaxial cable), STP cable requires a D-shell connector to the NIC and an IBM data connector to the medium attachment unit (MAU) whose end then goes into the wall towards the hub, as seen in Figure 5.10.

FIGURE 5.9

STP is protected by copper or aluminum shielding as well as the twisting of the main copper wires.

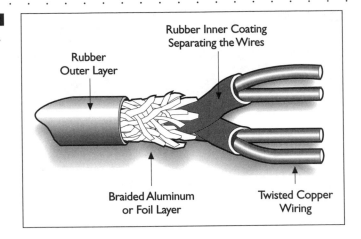

Rubber Inner Coating
Separating the Wires

Rubber
Outer Layer

Braided Aluminum
or Foil Layer

Twisted Copper
Wiring

FIGURE 5.10

The difference between the D-shell connector and the IBM data connector

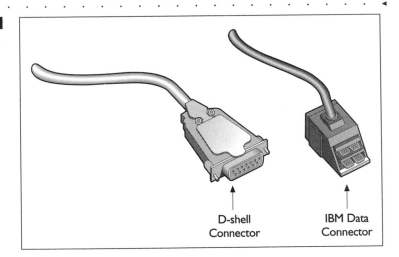

D-shell
Connector

IBM Data
Connector

To prevent data loss from cable deterioration or human error (cutting the cable), as well as crashing the entire network, STP is installed independently between each workstation, server, and wiring hub. In other words, rather than having one long, extended coaxial cable, STP is split between each connection point. As illustrated in Figure 5.11, the extra cable betwesen the nodes and its relative thickness means it quickly fills up the wiring conduits in the walls. All in all, both the purchase and the installation of STP is more expensive than coaxial.

FIGURE 5.11

Because of its thicker, less pliable outer surface, STP can be more difficult to install than coaxial.

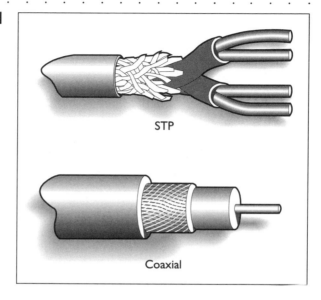

STP

Coaxial

Unshielded Twisted Pair

For low cost, an abundance of qualified installation experts, and an installed base (number of users) of 90 percent within the United States, unshielded twisted pair (UTP) is a great choice for cable. However, UTP is not without complexities. For example, unlike a coaxial cable that runs directly from PC to server, UTP must have an intermediary in the form of a hub, shown in Figure 5.12. This can be expensive depending on how many connections it supports. Furthermore, the installers' "rule of thumb" suggests limiting UTP to 330 feet between the network node and a hub, almost half the usable distance of Ethernet coaxial (550 feet).

UTP looks deceptively like regular telephone line, although UTP cable is slightly thicker. Also, UTP uses RJ-45 connectors whereas telephone wires require RJ-11 connectors, shown in Figure 5.13. Telephone-grade twisted-pair cable is composed of two wires twisted together at six turns per inch to provide electrical interference shielding and consistent impedance (electrical resistance). Because existing buildings usually contain plenty of this wire, it is often used as an inexpensive, easy way to link computers.

F I G U R E   5.12

An eight-port hub is connected to four nodes.

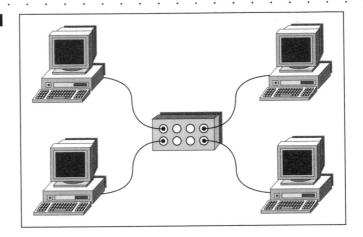

F I G U R E   5.13

Without comparing the number of wires inside the cable, the easiest way to tell the difference between network (top) and UTP phone cable (bottom) is the number of connectors.

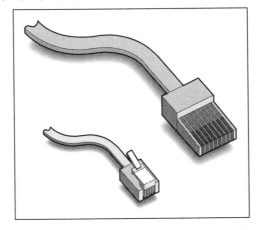

However, using telephone wire for your network, especially when it is already in place, can lead to several major problems. First, unshielded twisted-pair cable is sensitive to electromagnetic interference. In addition, low-quality twisted-pair cables have a varying number of twists per inch, which can distort the expected electrical resistance. Though this cable is usually quite adequate for most telephone communications, network data transmission demands much smaller tolerances.

Also it is important to note that telephone wire is not always run in straight lines. Cable that appears to run a relatively short distance between two offices might actually run through half the building to get from one to the other. A misjudgment could cause you to exceed the maximum cable length specifications.

The technical terms for the differences between UTP types are the category levels. Category 3 is typical phone line and Categories 3 to 5 are network-grade. The differences are in both the speed and amount of data they can conceivably carry. Category 3 has been tested at 16 megahertz (MHz) for attenuation (which describes the rate at which the signal becomes weaker the further it travels) with data capabilities up to 16 megabits per second (Mbps). Category 4 has been tested at 20MHz but has a low installed base, because most people usually move from Category 3 straight to Category 5 when upgrading. Category 5 cable is capable of bandwidth speeds up to 100MHz and can handle up to 100Mbps, which is important when we discuss Fast Ethernet later in this chapter.

While not as shielded as coaxial or STP, all UTP wiring is doubly protected from encroachment by insulation over the copper wires as well as twisting every pair of the wires together, shown in Figure 5.14. The plastic sheath provides absolutely no electromagnetic shielding, although the twists in the wire provide more protection than if it were untwisted.

FIGURE 5.14

UTP is primarily protected by a thin plastic sheath and by the twisting of the conductive copper wires.

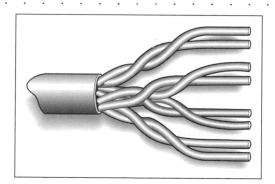

In short, unshielded twisted-pair cable is inexpensive, easy to install, and provides a variety of uses. But be careful: The money that you save may be offset by additional costs later if the network doesn't function properly. To better determine if UTP is worth using, hire an experienced wiring or cable installation contractor to test the signal quality and actual cable lengths of the wiring in your building. This will add to the cost of your network, but it is the best way to avoid cable-quality problems later on.

Fiber-Optic Cable

Fiber-optic cable, the most expensive, uses pulses of laser light to transmit data over glass cables, as shown in Figure 5.15. It is not subject to electrical noise and can handle exceedingly high data rates. While the price of fiber-optic cable has decreased over the years, it still requires skill and expertise to ensure proper connections. The ends of the fiber must be polished with precision to correctly transmit data.

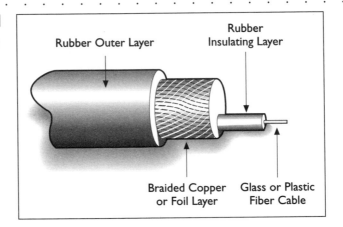

F I G U R E   5.15

Fiber-optic cable can handle extremely high data rates.

The core of fiber optic cable is made from silica glass or plastic. The latter is often called plastic optical fiber (POF), and is less expensive and easier to terminate, although it does have bandwidth and distance limitations.

There are two types of transmission methods that use fiber-optic cable — multimode and single mode. Multimode transmitters are typically used with larger cables such as 62.5/125 fiber. This number indicates a cable with a core diameter of 62.5 microns, and a cladding (layer surrounding the core) of 125 microns. Multimode is used for shorter distances, and requires a less powerful laser light. In fact, most multimode transmitters actually use light-emitting diodes (LED) instead of lasers. Single mode transmitters enable high bandwidth at great distances using a smaller core, typically 8.3/125 fiber, and a powerful laser transmitter. Fiber-optic cable usually carries several warnings relating to the dangerous nature of some laser transmitters. Read and follow warning labels carefully.

Fiber-optic cable has a significant advantage over all metallic cable options. Fiber-optic cable is more reliable because it is not susceptible to packet loss through electromagnetic or radio interference. This feature makes fiber-optic cable appropriate for those who need a high level of security and for electromagnetically noisy environments. Because the light pulses that carry the data are restricted to the cable itself, it is virtually impossible to surreptitiously tap into the medium without getting down into the actual core of the cable. In electromagnetically noisy environments, like those around large cranes and massive mechanical equipment, fiber-optic cable is often used to bypass the interference caused by engines and generators. In hazardous, explosive environments, fiber-optic cabling is suitable since it does not conduct or transmit electricity.

Fiber-optic cable is also very thin and flexible, making it easier to move than the heavier copper cables. Because signal losses while traversing the medium are less than those associated with metallic conductors, fiber-optic cable can support network segments up to 3.5 kilometers (approximately 2.2 miles) apart. Where long runs or links between buildings are required, fiber-optic cable is often the only viable choice.

While it is likely that you or someone on your staff is competent at cable installation for any of the wire-based types, we strongly recommend that you allow only qualified professionals to install fiber-optic cables. Not only does the technology demand close tolerances for tapping and termination, it also requires sophisticated, expensive test equipment to test the quality of the fiber-optic lines installed.

In addition to the preceding examples, there are options available for LANs that are more secure and have higher throughput (the amount of data that passes through). Due to their high costs, however, they're usually reserved for MANs or WANs, where ends are separated by miles rather than feet.

Peer-to-Peer vs. Client-Server

Although it's easy to understand the concept of sharing resources and applications across a network, it's also important to understand several different approaches. Basically, networks conform to one of two methods: peer-to-peer or client-server.

Peer-to-Peer

In some networks, especially very small ones with just a few computers attached, people simply attach each computer to the network wires and set themselves up to share their individual devices. There's no central server to administer sharing. While this approach seems easy and straightforward, it does have limitations. NOSs designed for peer-to-peer networks include Novell Personal NetWare, Microsoft NT Workstation, Windows 98/2000, IBM OS/2, and all of the Apple Macintosh systems.

Sharing Information

As a user on a peer-to-peer network, your experience is similar to having multiple disk drives. Your computer's hard disk is defined as drive C, and you also have access to a directory on Stan's hard disk as drive D, Pam's as drive E, and Jo's as drive F.

CD/DVD-ROM and removable drives are also shared in the workgroup setting. And while most applications will not run directly from CD-ROM titles, files such as clip art can certainly be accessed and taken advantage of by everyone on the peer-to-peer network. Through these means, everyone in the workgroup can easily share data between computers.

Sharing Printers

Printer sharing is a very cost effective and versatile use of printing resources. In a peer-to-peer network, Pam can configure the printer attached to her computer as a sharable device, as illustrated in Figure 5.16. Then if Stan in the office next door wants to use Pam's printer, he ensures the correct print driver is loaded on his computer and sets his default printer destination to Pam's printer. From then on (until he changes it) every time Stan wants to print, his work will go to Pam's printer.

▶ . . . . ◀

FIGURE 5.16

Through a peer-to-peer network, printers connected parallel to workstations can be shared with other workstations.

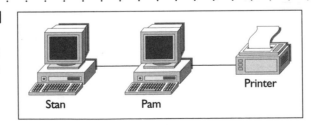

Peer-to-Peer Caveats and Kudos

Peer-to-peer networks differ from traditional file-server or client-server networks in several important ways. Because peer-to-peer networks allow each computer to share its resources, there is no need for an expensive dedicated file server. This allows groups of very small sizes (three to ten people) to justify networking. Peer-to-peer networks are easy to set up. It is a simple matter of installing network adapter cards, connecting cables, and configuring the software. Administration of peer-to-peer networks promises to be simpler than other networks because each user controls access to his or her computer, eliminating the need for a full-time LAN administrator.

Theoretically, peer-to-peer networks can handle hundreds of connected PCs. Realistically, most are quite a bit smaller, containing fewer than five or six computers. If a peer-to-peer network grows larger, it can (and should) be reconfigured to include a dedicated file server. Also, peer-to-peer is deceptively simple. If someone's computer is turned off or crashes while you're trying to print, a peer-to-peer system may not handle it gracefully. Instead it gives users error messages, which users often don't know how to fix.

Application sharing is also more difficult on peer-to-peer networks. Just because Pam has spreadsheet software installed on her computer, and Stan has access to the directory, doesn't necessarily mean he can use her software. Unless Stan installs the software on his own computer, or uses a configuration to use Pam's computer as a server, most software is unlikely to run correctly. Before sharing applications in a peer-to-peer environment, verify that the application software supports this type of usage on each shared computer's operating system.

Even disk, data, and printer sharing has limitations. Let's say Stan's computer holds the data files for the accounting system. Pam won't be able to work on the accounting records if he's gone on vacation and turned off his computer. Likewise for Stan if he tries to print to Pam's printer and she's gone home for the day and turned off her PC. However, even if all the shared devices are turned on and configured properly for sharing, performance is another issue. For instance, if Stan is printing to Pam's printer, she will probably notice a significant degradation in the usual speed of her PC while the print job is being processed. The same principle applies to data sharing. If Pam is accessing large clip-art files from Stan's shared CD-ROM, then he, too, will notice slower response times from whatever application he is using on his computer.

Minimum Requirements for Peer-to-Peer

Each peer-to-peer network operating system will have its own minimum requirements for installation, setup, and hardware requirements (disk space, memory, etc.). Thus, the least you need for the simplest peer-to-peer network is an NIC for each PC you plan to connect, terminated cable and connectors for every workstation, hubs if the topology demands, and of course, the NOS.

As we've watched people try to work with peer-to-peer networks over the years, we've come to the conclusion that they are not suitable for day-to-day office work. With the constantly declining cost of servers, it's more expedient to look at client-server-based approaches.

Client-Server Networking

Client-server networks can be thought of as high-powered peer-to-peer networks. There are still PCs and printers connected and communicating through wires like peer-to-peers, but there are fewer, if any, limitations. Printers don't need a PC attached to be shared with other users, which means they can always be powered on and won't drain a user's productivity by involving the processor of their workstation. Client-server hard disks and CD-ROMs are both larger in size, and faster than those found in peer-to-peer. Consequently, this allows for greater data and application sharing. As illustrated in Figure 5.17, the concepts are the same except that instead of PCs acting as both client and server, there are specific machines that act only as servers, freeing up the client to do the everyday work.

Evolution of Client-Server

So far, client-server has been explained in terms of its differences and similarities to peer-to-peer, but there's more to say than that. Client-server was originally based on a single server with multiple clients. The classic example of client-server is that of Novell NetWare 2.x and higher. All of the shared applications, database engines, and e-mail software ran from the server's hard disks. The server's job was to handle and distribute the various file and print requests regarding the applications (see Figure 5.18). Once the client workstations received the files in its memory, the brunt of the file processing occurred on the workstation.

FIGURE 5.17

Client-server networks include all of the basics of peer-to-peer sharing, but have higher capacities and the ability to expand.

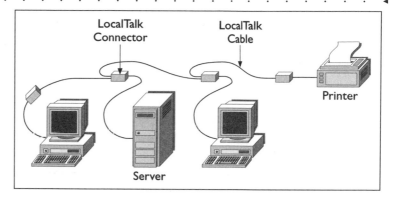

FIGURE 5.18

A client-server network has separate servers designed for file and print services, database engines, and e-mail systems all transferring data independently to clients.

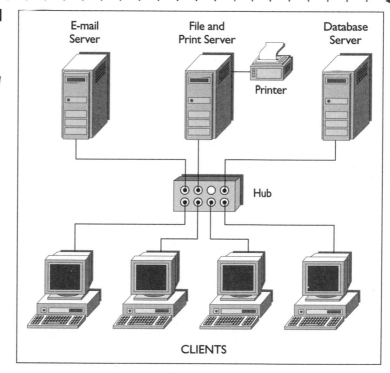

Due to the constant transferring of files between server and workstation, this scenario was not conducive to controlling network traffic, but it was cost effective in that there was only one server. The need for better management of network traffic and larger, more robust databases and applications, led to the next step in client-server.

In order to decrease network traffic, the database transactions needed to occur mainly on the server (much like they did with mainframes), then once complete, be returned to the client PC. For example, a client PC (workstation) at a hospital requests all of the data regarding patients that had late payments for the first two quarters of the last two years. The data for this information is kept in raw form (not organized) on the database server and consequently must be organized into the requested format. Once the information is organized as ordered, the results are sent back to the client PC. Another way to think of this scenario is to imagine the client as the front end and the server as the back end. The front end refers to the client because it is actually what the user sees. The back end refers to the server because it is where all the work is performed. An analogy would be that the front end, or client, is a hand puppet and the back end, or server, is the hand inside the puppet providing life to the client. After all, without the information from the server, the client is worthless.

However, to do this, the back-end servers, as they're called, had to be just as loaded in hardware (if not more so) as the more traditional file and print servers. The result was the need for one dedicated server with high memory, fast disk drives, and a powerful processor per application.

We don't mean to imply that decreasing network traffic was the only justification for the more expensive hardware platform. With the advent of increasingly powerful database engines and applications, the hardware had to match the requirements of the software. These database engines, while still performing within the boundaries of the NOS, can be of different types. Some examples of vendors in this category include Microsoft, Oracle, and Sybase.

On the plus side, back-end servers are not limited to certain platforms or operating systems. A platform is a general term for the type of hardware system on which the PC operates, such as Intel, RISC, Macintosh, and so on. Back-end servers sometimes also need to use operating systems independent of the surrounding NOS to enable its higher processing duties. Some examples include Windows NT and UNIX.

Surprisingly, these differences are actually beneficial for the development of the network. Why? Because the client PC operating system and platform is not tied to that of the server. This creates an environment with infinite means to continually add products and services to the network without jeopardizing the original investment in PCs and network structure (including the NOS). This type of setup is commonly referred to as a multivendor or heterogeneous network. For these reasons, client-server computing can really be thought of as the parents of the Internet and intranets.

Currently, there is no one particular type of back end or client. The Internet and all the many intranets contain thousands of different back ends. Perhaps an example will help.

Remember our discussion in Chapter 3 about e-mail, both LAN and Internet based? This is a perfect instance of how client-server computing can be likened to the Internet, which, so far, is the current end of the client-server evolution.

On the LAN, each client PC has a front end, like Novell Groupwise, that lets the user read and send e-mail messages. On the Groupwise server, requests are taken from other users on the LAN and held until the user's client requests them. Now, think a little larger. Imagine that the company is world-wide and has small LAN-based e-mail client-server setups everywhere. If Nigel is in London and wants to send Nicole in New York an e-mail, he types a message from his client workstation and sends it to the e-mail server in London. If set up on an intranet, the message is forwarded from the London e-mail server through the secure "cloud" shown in Figure 5.19 to the e-mail server in New York. When Nicole's workstation e-mail client requests her new messages, the NY server transfers them. Internet e-mail works exactly the same, with the exception that there is no controlling cloud; e-mail can be sent and received from anyone in the world.

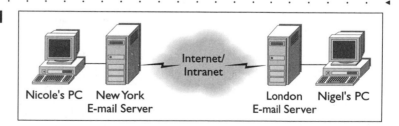

FIGURE 5.19

The native LAN-based, client-server e-mail arrangement can easily be expanded to include both Internet and intranet uses.

Minimum Requirements for Client-Server Networks

Once again, the various NOSs truly dictate the minimum server hardware requirements. Considering the increased complexity and potential for growth, more care and planning is required to implement any client-server network than a peer-to-peer. However, whether installing a single file and print-based server solution or several database servers, you will need various cables, NICs, and a very detailed agenda. Chapter 6 will aid in the creation and understanding of that agenda.

Whether you choose peer-to-peer or some variation of client-server, the important decision will lay in the planning considerations of future growth for your network. Considering all aspects of your network needs, present and future, allows you to lay the groundwork that will enable you to build on top of each succeeding upgraded layer of the network, rather than tear down the past version to start anew every time a new advancement or extended communication link is wanted or needed.

Dial-Up and Dedicated Remote Connections

Generally, any network confined to distances measured in feet comprises a LAN, a few miles between major connections could be considered a MAN, and any network that involves ten or more miles can be thought of as a WAN. For WANs there are several wiring options.

Analog Connections

Simple cable setups use standard analog modems. The modem connected to my PC dials your modem, and through specialized software I can use all of the resources on your PC. This type of connection has many uses in a network, including giving remote users access to it and transferring information between databases or e-mail systems, just to name a few. Modem speeds have peaked at 56Kbps, with 53Kbps being the maximum speed allowed under current FCC regulations. This type of connection is great for establishing quick links and transferring small files between the machines or using remote control to troubleshoot. Analog modems are not good, however, for maintaining static connections, transferring large files (larger than 2MB), or if your office or home only has a single phone line, allowing for simultaneous data and voice connections. Analog modems have these limitations because in addition to transferring data they must also convert it.

While it is true that most phone lines in large metropolitan areas are digital (they transmit an electronic signal in binary code either as on/off pulses or as high/low voltages), they are only digital between the dialing central offices of the phone company. From the central offices to homes and businesses the lines are analog, so that voice can be transferred. Thus, the signal pulses that the computers communicate must be converted from digital to analog (which is the static noise you hear) so they can be converted on the receiving end from analog back to digital. For higher bandwidth, more reliable connections, faster data transfers, and a more simplistic, cleaner dial-up data exchange, one of the digital solutions listed below is a better choice.

Integrated Services Digital Network (ISDN)

ISDN can transmit data up to speeds of 128 kilobits per second (Kbps), maintain static connections, and allow for multiple connections (data and voice). It does this by combining a total of three digital lines.

Two of the lines are for data and transmit at 64Kbps each, for a total of 128Kbps, while the third line has a speed of 16Kbps and is used for telephone communications.

Unfortunately, due to its newness, ISDN is not available everywhere. However, most major U.S. cities offer ISDN services. Call your local phone company for details on availability and pricing.

Digital Subscriber Line (DSL)

Digital subscriber lines use standard copper telephone wiring to bring high bandwidth to homes and offices. DSL comes in a variety of "flavors," differentiated by their speed and transmission types. The generic term, used when referring to multiple DSL technologies, is xDSL.

Similar to ISDN, DSL can carry both voice and data signals over the same cable. Unlike ISDN, DSL maintains a constant data connection, with no need for the end user to dial a telephone number to connect to the Internet. Once an Internet service provider is set up, the user will have instantaneous access to the vast resources available online.

Voice calls, whether inbound or outbound, come through on the line without interfering with the data connection. This allows, for example, users to send a fax and receive a phone call, all while maintaining a constant Internet connection.

Two main types of DSL exist today — splitter-based and splitterless. Splitter-based DSL requires a splitter installed at the physical end location. The splitter allows data to flow simultaneously with other analog communications, such as voice, for instance. Splitterless DSL uses similar technology, but places a splitter at the central office, thereby reducing the installation and hardware costs of individual splitters at each home or office.

Cable Modem

Cable modems provide high speed connectivity over a standard Cable TV (CATV) coaxial cable. The cable terminates at a cable modem in your location, which acts more like an NIC than a modem. Much like DSL, a constant connection is maintained between your PC and your Internet service provider.

Today, Cable TV lines pass by 96 percent of American homes, but so far businesses have much less chance of access. So while this connectivity option will probably be available to part-time home workers, it may not be available for a remote office.

The current dominating standard for cable modem operation is DOCSIS (Data Over Cable Service Interface Specification). DOCSIS standardized the protocols and modulation schemes for carrying bi-directional data over coaxial cable. This standardization encouraged the rapid production and acceptance of cable modems.

Cable modem bandwidth is shared between your location, and everyone else on the same local loop. So while the total bandwith of your local coaxial cable may reach 27Mbps downstream, only a fraction of that speed is available at any time. The more subscribers on your local loop, the slower the data will travel. Upstream rates may range from 128Kbps to 2.5Mbps depending on your subscription type and rate.

Additionally, since the line is shared with others in the area, privacy issues arise. Most cable modems do not address privacy issues, so make sure to research the cable modem that is functional with your cable provider. A firewall, implemented by hardware or software, may be your best bet in thwarting those who seek to compromise your PC or network. Chapter 6 discusses firewalls in more detail.

Next we'll cover the three types of cable modems: external, internal, and set-top box.

With an external cable modem, the coaxial cable is connected to the cable modem, and an Ethernet port (typically RJ45) allows for connection to the PC or LAN. If the cable modem is connected directly to a PC, an NIC will be required. Alternatively, the cable modem can be connected to a hub to share the high-speed connection on the network.

An internal cable modem provides the most direct method of connectivity. The CATV cable connects directly into the cable modem installed into a single PC.

A set-top box connects directly to a television and usually has e-mail, Web browsing, and intelligent television control built in. An interactive set-top box will allow the novice user to easily get on the Web, without even knowing how to use a computer, because it acts as a stand-alone Internet interface.

T1 and T3

If larger pipes of information over long distances are what you need for transferring data, then a T1 or T3 may be what you're looking for. Unlike analog modems or ISDN, T-carriers provide a constant connection, so no dial up is required. T1 is a 1.544Mbps channel that can handle 24 voice or data channels at 64Kbps. The standard T1 frame is 193 bits long, which holds twenty-four 8-bit voice samples and one synchronization bit; 8,000 frames are transmitted per second. T3 is a 44.736Mbps channel that can handle 672 voice or data channels at 64Kbps. T3 requires fiber-optic cable.

Basically, T1 and T3 are direct connections from one end of the country or state to another. Typically this technology is used in the medical community for the remote diagnosing of patients in hard to reach or poverty stricken areas, where families cannot afford to make the trip to a large city. It is also used as a high bandwidth solution for Internet connectivity for large businesses that can afford the exorbitant fees and require the constant connectivity to maintain competitiveness in business.

SMDS

One more option worth considering is Switched Multimegabit Data Service (SMDS). SMDS is a high-speed, switched data communications service offered by the local telephone companies for interconnecting LANs in different geographic locations. It was introduced in 1992 and became generally available nationwide by 1995.

Connection to an SMDS service can be made from a variety of devices, including bridges, routers, and CSU/DSUs (the digital equivalent of a modem), as well as via frame relay and ATM networks. SMDS can employ various networking technologies. Most implementations use rates up to 45Mbps.

Data is framed for transmission using the SMDS Interface Protocol (SIP), which packages data as Level 3 Protocol Data Units (L3_PDU). The L3_PDU contains source and destination addresses and a data field that holds up to 9,188 bytes.

That covers the gamut of cabled options for networks. However, there is still one other option to connect PCs together with a network: wireless.

Wireless Networking

Probably the simplest form of a wireless LAN is the one that is created between a laptop and a desktop (and even a printer) using infrared technology. Basically, there is a red panel on each device that looks and acts exactly like the remote control that goes with your TV set. Some of the low-powered systems behave just like your remote control unit: the infrared ports must be in plain view of each other and within a certain minimum distance in order to transmit and receive data properly. However, high-quality, high-powered systems do not have the same line-of-sight restrictions, and will transmit around objects and over much greater distances.

The next simplest form of wireless LAN technology is that developed by such companies as Proxim, Lucent, and 3Com. These products use radio frequencies to connect PCs. Unless your LAN is on a peer-to-peer network, however, most of your wireless LANs are only one part of your network as a whole, which includes cabled nodes. In other words, some of the PCs will have wired connections to the network while others will be tethered with radio waves. Typical transmission rates over a wireless LAN range from 2–25Mbps.

The wireless standard for LANs is defined by IEEE 802.11. Purchasing a wireless solution that is 802.11-compliant ensures product selection from multiple vendors.

Many vendors, however, also provide products utilizing proprietary protocols. While these products may have higher transmission rates, they are normally not interoperable across vendor lines. Radio frequency LANs are generally much slower than cabled LANs but it is the capability of mobility that makes them attractive. For example, industries with disparate users or structures that don't support standard wiring are prime candidates for wireless networks. In medical institutions all over the United States, doctors and nurses use hand-held wireless devices to record patient data or laptops with wireless adapter cards (PCMCIA cards) to transmit data back and forth to the servers or printers because running cable in patients' rooms is not feasible. Another good example of where wireless technology is used is in the manufacturing industry. With huge warehouses of products, networked computers are a necessity to keep track of inventory, and wireless networked computers allow merchants to transmit data to the network while staying mobile.

Sometimes, though, mobility is not the issue. Earlier we discussed the bandwidths of T1 lines for usage with long distances and large bandwidths. Another option, and probably the ultimate in wireless networking communication is the use of satellites. Satellite communication is primarily used for WANs.

Communication satellites orbit the earth at the equator so that they are motionless relative to earth-based receivers (that way the terrestrial antennas or dishes don't have to constantly restructure themselves to point at different areas of the sky). In comparison to T1 lines, satellite connections are more feasible for several city connections, but only for certain types of data. Because it takes a signal 0.27 seconds to make the trip from the satellite to the receiver, only data transfers like e-mail or overnight database changes are feasible, although someone trying to type in real time using the 0.27 second delay wouldn't really lose much speed on their words per minute. Although the wireless world is a new one for PCs, through continual advantages they are bound to become more prolific.

Summary

This chapter outlines numerous options available in designing the right network for the right job. By now, you've discovered that the term network means much more than simply having two or more computers connected by a wire and transferring files back and forth. Network design can be as unique as the individuals sitting at each node.

CHAPTER 6

Passing Data Across a Network

This chapter builds on the concepts of network design by explaining how data travels across a network. Signaling schemes can be thought of as the roads across which data (information) travels. These roads differ primarily in the amount and speed of traffic they can hold. Typical examples include Ethernet, Token Ring, Asynchronous Transfer Mode (ATM), Fiber Distributed Data Interface (FDDI), and, on the broader bandwidth scale, Fast and Gigabit Ethernet.

Once you build the roads, you can put traffic on them. Electronic impulses called signals are the actual carriers of data. All protocols are carried over signals, though not all protocols are alike. Some can carry more information than others, the same way trucks and cars have different payload capacities. Protocol examples included in this chapter are TCP/IP, SPX/IPX, NetBEUI, NetBIOS, and ODI/IPX.

Network Signaling Schemes

Millions of electrical impulses traverse the nerve fibers in a human body, carrying information to the brain, tissues, and muscles. Basically, signaling and communication across a computer network operate the same way. Electrical signals travel over the wiring from PC to PC, PC to printer, and PC to server, and there are different methods for this communication. These signaling schemes come in two flavors, contention and token passing.

Contention

Networks that use contention schemes, such as Ethernet and AppleTalk, listen to the network cable and wait for the line to go quiet before sending out messages. If two computers happen to send messages at the same time, these messages will inevitably collide and be garbled. When this occurs, collision-sensing electronics take note of the event and the lost messages are resent.

Token Passing

Networks that use token-passing schemes send data in a more orderly way. A token is a specific electronic signal that indicates a node has permission to transmit or receive. A limited number of tokens (usually one) circulate around the network — that is, messages follow a specific order of circulation, and the last recipient in the order passes the message back to the first recipient in the order. Messages to be transmitted are held at the local workstation until a free token arrives that can pick up pending messages and deliver them to their destinations. Once properly delivered, the messages are stripped off the token, freeing it up for other messages. Both attached resources computing (ARCnet) and Token Ring systems use token passing, as does the high-speed FDDI.

Standard Ethernet

The overwhelming favorite of LAN installation is Ethernet, an efficient signaling standard that has been adopted by a majority of the computer market in the United States. Ethernet was invented in the mid-1970s by two Xerox employees, Robert Metcalfe and David Boggs. Its specification is defined by the Institute of Electrical and Electronics Engineers (IEEE) standard as 802.3 (pronounced "eight-oh-two-dot-three").

NOTE

IEEE is a group of electrical and electronics engineers that are at the head of their various industries — medical, manufacturing, computer chip, and so on, who meet several times a year to discuss and provide standards for the hardware everyone uses. This is done so that the myriad components of a single computer or a large network will operate together with the least amount of conflict.

Ethernet is a contention-based protocol standard. Unlike a token passing scheme, all the computers can communicate (send their data) at once. Consequently, messages sometimes collide and disintegrate before reaching their destination. To compensate, Ethernet LANs use a technique called CSMA/CD, which stands for Carrier Sense Multiple Access/Collision Detection. CSMA/CD listens to the wire to determine when it is not being used, then sends the message and listens again to see if the message got through. If a collision occurs, CSMA/CD waits and resends the message, as illustrated in Figure 6.1. As an analogy, consider fax machines. A fax machine will not try to send its data across the line until the other fax machine picks up. If the line is busy, the sending fax machine waits a period of time and then tries to send its data message again.

FIGURE 6.1

*In this example of
CSMA/CD, PCs #1 and #2
listen to the wire before
sending. They're told the line
is busy, because PC #3 is
currently sending data.*

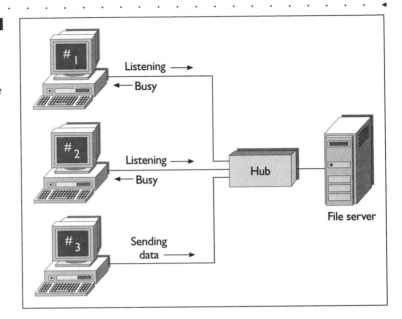

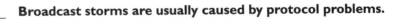

Sometimes, however, Ethernet is not so well behaved. In certain circumstances an Ethernet NIC decides that it doesn't want to wait for an available line to send its data. Instead, the NIC broadcasts information on the network with no regard to other signals, thus causing what is referred to as a broadcast storm.

> **Broadcast storms are usually caused by protocol problems.**
>
> **NOTE**

Our traffic analogy works well here. You can think of CSMA/CD as a four-way traffic light with all of the Ethernet devices respectfully obeying when to stop and start sending information. A broadcast storm occurs when one of the "vehicles" ignores the traffic light and heads into the intersection, wreaking havoc with the orderly flow of traffic.

Depending on their configuration, Ethernet LANs can be very inexpensive. Ethernet works with both linear-bus and star-shaped topologies, giving it flexibility as far as cable schemes are concerned. It can run on thinnet coaxial (also called 10base2 — meaning 10Mbps at 200 meters), thicknet coaxial (also called 10base5 — meaning 10Mbps at 500 meters), twisted-pair (STP or UTP), or fiber-optic cables. Installation prices vary depending on which cable scheme is used.

Perhaps the following will help you make a choice. Ethernet is appropriate for small or large groups of users. Linear-bus-based Ethernet is a good option if cost is a primary concern, and if you have a network of fewer than 20 PCs. Ethernet in a twisted-pair topology, though a little more expensive, is a better choice for larger groups in that it provides fault isolation, better network management capability, and more room for later expansion. It might be a good choice if you are starting from scratch, too, because it provides a great deal of flexibility for both small and large networks.

A standard Ethernet (10BaseT) configuration (a star-shaped configuration based on UTP cable), while it may be slightly more expensive to install, will offer the most flexibility for connecting with other networks.

On the other hand, if installation price is really not an issue and you want more than Ethernet's 10Mbps, then Fast or Gigabit Ethernet is the signaling scheme for you.

Fast Ethernet (100BaseT)

If 10Mbps Ethernet is throttling your network, multiply the bandwidth by ten and use Fast Ethernet's 100Mbps signaling, called 100BaseT. It operates exactly the same as Ethernet's 802.3 standard, except the network interface cards and hubs have to be replaced with 100BaseT models. Fast Ethernet operates over several wiring schemes including Fiber-optic, STP, and UTP (but only at the Category Five level for the TP wiring). Coaxial cable is not an option. Only recently have companies started using Fast Ethernet to upgrade existing networks, as well as build new ones from the ground up. Research data indicates that 18 percent of the U.S. market uses Fast Ethernet right to the desktop. For some, even 100Mbps is not enough where video conferencing, MPEG and JPEG presentations, or x-ray images are concerned. Consequently, the never-say-die computer industry has come up with a new, high-speed technology: Gigabit Ethernet.

Gigabit Ethernet

At 1000Mbps, Gigabit Ethernet is the network speed of the future. It is based on the same IEEE 802.3 format as Ethernet and Fast Ethernet, so upgrading part of a network, such as an enterprise backbone, to Gigabit Ethernet should be straightforward.

Optical cables are the typical connection method to ensure a data rate capacity of 1000Mbps. Hardware, such as switches and hubs, designed to provide 1000Mbps throughput, will specify the type of compatible optical fiber. A specification for running gigabit Ethernet over copper also exists, but is limited to a distance of only 25 meters.

Single mode fiber is often used between buildings, where greater distances are needed. It is more expensive than multimode fiber, which is used mainly within a building.

Increasing the Bandwidth

Standard Ethernet cabling may not be fast enough if you're planning to use high resolution graphic files (MPEG and JPEG), video conferencing, or other multimedia applications across your network. MPEG (Motion Pictures Experts Group) is an ISO/ITU (International Standards Organization/International Telecommunications Union) standard for compressing video. MPEG-1, which is used in CD-ROMs and Video CDs, provides a resolution of 352 × 240 at 30fps with 24-bit color and CD-quality sound. For effective playback, MPEG-encoded material requires either a fast computer (Pentium II, Pentium III, and so on) or a plug-in MPEG board. JPEG (Joint Photographic Experts Group) is an ISO/ITU standard for compressing still images. It has become very popular because it provides compression with ratios of 100:1 and higher. Both MPEG and JPEG are among the most efficient image file types—they're generally smaller than other types containing the same data (say, TIFF).

Video conferencing transfers both voice and images from one PC to another. Because it involves huge amounts of data, video conferencing has to be extremely fast or there will be a delay in the sound and movements of the person you see on the other screen.

Fiber Distributed Data Interface

FDDI is similar to the IEEE 802.5 standard of Token Ring in the way it communicates, with one exception—there are two rings that pass through each network device. FDDI provides an optional dual counter-rotating ring topology. It contains primary and secondary rings with data flowing in opposite directions. If the line breaks, the ends of the primary and secondary rings are bridged together at the closest node to create a single ring again, as shown in Figure 6.2. Not all devices on the network have to include connections to both rings, but what you save in installation could cost you in fault tolerance.

FIGURE 6.2

In dual counter-rotating topology, if the line breaks, the ends of the primary and secondary rings are bridged together at the closest node to create a single ring again.

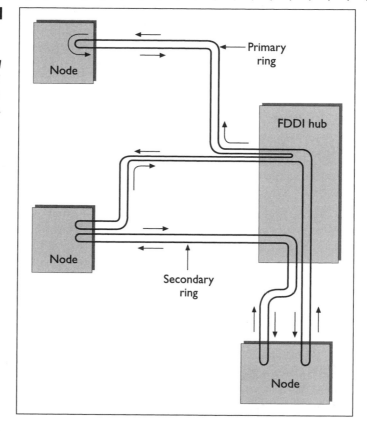

Speaking of the IEEE, FDDI is not one of their standards. FDDI is part of the American National Standards Institute (ANSI) and its abbreviated name is ANSI X3T9.5. FDDI travels at speeds of 100Mbps, which is comparable to Fast Ethernet. Although the fiber portion of the FDDI name implies that the signaling scheme only works over fiber-optic cable, this isn't the case. FDDI also works over both STP and UTP. However, FDDI is typically used as a backbone for large networks or with MANs, so the mileage capability of fiber optics does come into play. An FDDI that runs across fiber optics has a signaling distance up to 2 kilometers without repeaters. It is limited to 100 meters on copper-based UTP and STP.

As you can imagine with the double-fault tolerance, high speed, and preference for fiber, FDDI is expensive to implement all the way to the workstation, though it holds 24 percent of the United States market.

Asynchronous Transfer Mode

In this context, ATM has nothing to do with Automated Teller Machines. That said, what is it?

ATM is a signaling scheme that has the unique ability to simultaneously deliver both video and sound across a network. Real-world applications include the promised cable services with five hundred channels, video conferencing, and remote medical diagnosis (sometimes called telemedicine). It operates over every kind of cable, from coaxial to the twisted-pair twins (STP, UTP), to dial-up connections such as ISDN. ATM has speed and bandwidth greater than the other double-digit signaling schemes, because it has 48-byte cells that travel much smoother and quicker over the network. Some reported speeds are in excess of 155Mbps.

Currently, ATM is neither widely accepted nor implemented. According to data from 1996, ATM is only being used on the backbone side of networks, of which it only holds five percent of the U.S. market. It is still hotly contested as a signaling scheme up-and-comer that may or may not be able to compete with 100Mbps standards, such as Fast Ethernet.

Table 6.1 provides an at-a-glance breakdown of the differences between the types of networks available.

TABLE 6.1	NETWORK TYPE	SIGNALING RATE	CABLE USED
Network Types and Their Characteristics	Ethernet	10Mbps	Coaxial (thin and thick), STP, UTP, Fiber optic
	Token Ring	4 or 16Mbps	STP, UTP
	ARCnet	2.5–20Mbps	Coaxial, STP, UTP, Fiber optic
	FDDI	100Mbps	Fiber optic
	Fast Ethernet	100Mbps	Fiber optic, UTP (Cat 5)
	ATM	1.5, 25, 51, 100, 155, 622Mbps and 2Gbps +	Fiber optic
	Gigabit Ethernet	1000Mbps (1 Gbps)	UTP, Fiber optic

Token Ring

Token Ring networks were popularized in the mid-1980s when International Business Machines (IBM) began to support the Token Ring Protocol standard. A number of IBM computers, including minicomputers and mainframes, have direct connections to Token Ring. Most businesses using Token Ring today do so because they are old IBM mainframe shops from the 1970s. According to our research, Token Ring accounts for 21 percent of computer networks in the United States

Today, the IEEE 802.5 specification defines the workings of Token Ring. There are two speeds available, 4Mbps and 16Mbps. Although Token Ring is commonly associated with IBM, there are a number of third party vendors.

Token Ring uses what is known as a token passing scheme. Rather than PCs broadcasting signals at will, like in Ethernet, Token Ring signaling is more structured. A single token (electrical impulse) will pass by each device on the network. A PC's network card gives its information to the token as it passes, and then no other PC can give data to this "busy" token until it receives the information it needs. This is another way Token Ring differs from Ethernet — there can be no information collision, because only one PC can send data at a time.

Token Ring's physical topology is a cross-breed of both ring- and star-shaped topologies, as shown in Figure 6.3. In other words, data flows from workstation to workstation in sequence (as in a ring network), but continually passes through a central point (as in a star network). The central wiring hub, called a Multistation Access Unit (MAU), uses a twisted wire cable. The central hub makes it easier to troubleshoot failures than a bus topology. This is a completely different type of hub than the one used in a 10BaseT twisted-pair Ethernet network.

 If a PC takes the token and doesn't give it back, the whole ring can crash.

NOTE

Unlike Ethernets, where one PC not communicating doesn't affect the whole network (with the exception of broadcast storms), if one PC on a Token Ring network doesn't cooperate by transferring the token on to the next station, beaconing occurs, thus creating a continuous signaling of error on the LAN.

FIGURE 6.3

Token Ring topology has elements of both ring- and star-shaped topologies.

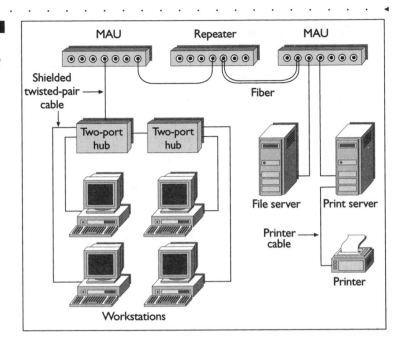

Token Ring networks can run on unshielded twisted-pair (UTP), shielded twisted-pair (STP), or fiber-optic cables. They are available in two versions, supporting transmission speeds of 4Mbps or 16Mbps. Although an individual network must run at either one speed or another, networks operating at different speeds can be bridged or routed together.

Token Ring networks are reliable, even under heavy loads, and fairly easy to install. When compared to the total costs of Ethernet networks, however, Token Ring networks are more expensive. Fewer vendors offer Token Ring equipment than Ethernet.

So, after all of that, is Token Ring right for your network? Token Ring is appropriate for large and small networks. Also, it is especially useful when you are connecting your network to IBM host computers, such as AS-400 minicomputer models or mainframes, because IBM supports the Token Ring Protocol standard more than any other.

If you are starting your network from scratch, and have mostly IBM mini-computers or mainframe equipment to connect to, Token Ring will provide a great deal of flexibility and support.

ARCnet and Macintosh

Last and perhaps least in usage, statistically speaking, are ARCnet and Macintosh. Although the future isn't bright for these two products in terms of networks, they still have a loyal following.

Attached Resources Computing (ARCnet)

ARCnet topology has been widely available since the 1970s, but according to current research, doesn't hold a significant percentage of the U.S. network market. ARCnet passes information around the network using a token passing scheme, meaning each computer has an individual turn to relay information. If this sounds similar to Token Ring, that's because it is, sort of. In Token Ring networks, a token passes around the ring topology until a PC needs it to transmit information. The token is then busy until the information requested is given back to the original requester, during which time no other PC can transmit. In ARCnet, a token is administered by a single PC designed as the controller and identified by the lowest assigned number (more on this further on). The controller passes the token through the network to each PC sequentially, based on its assigned number. Those PCs not needing to send stay quiet; those with information to pass on do so.

ARCnet can run on coaxial, UTP, or fiber-optic cable. If coaxial is used, however, it must be the RG-62 specification. ARCnet requires a topology that is a combination of star and bus, so hubs are mandatory. One of the best features of ARCnet is its traveling distance between hubs. Between active hubs, which function as signal-boosting repeaters, there is a maximum length of 2,000 feet. This is more than double that of other signaling strategies. Unfortunately, the maximum distance of the network from one end to the other is only 20,000 feet. This pigeonholes ARCnet into the small-network end of the industry.

ARCnet network interface cards use no manufactured, pre-assigned network number addresses like those of Token Ring and Ethernet. An ARCnet NIC must be manually configured to give it an assigned number from 1 to 255 where, again, the PC with the lowest number serves as the controller. Thus, it is a good idea to place your most powerful PC in the number-one spot for quicker token processing.

Speaking of speed, the original 1970s version of ARCnet traveled at only 2.5Mbps which, when compared to the 4 or 16 of Token Ring or 10 of Ethernet (not to mention the 100Mbps mentioned earlier) is pale by comparison. However, Datapoint, a manufacturer of ARCnet products, has developed technology that raises the signaling speed all the way up to 20Mbps—even within the existing 2.5Mbps scenarios. (You just have to have new hubs and NICs.) So, if your LAN has no serious growth plans, ARCnet can serve your needs for quite some time.

Macintosh

The good news about Macintosh computers is that they're networkable right out of the box. "Macs" (for short) use two protocols to connect across the network, AppleTalk (older computers) and EtherTalk (newer computers), both of which are contention-based signaling schemes.

AppleTalk can be used over STP or standard telephone wiring. The telephone wire version is actually called PhoneNet. PhoneNet's adapters and wiring are less expensive than LocalTalk's (another variety of AppleTalk).

Either way, both systems allow the sharing of files, e-mail, and printers. Of course the major drawback is AppleTalk's speed—230,400bps—even slower than original ARCnet. Granted, this is still faster than modern modem speeds, which top out at 56,000bps, but it's still rather slow for true networking.

As a result, there is an Ethernet version for Macs called EtherTalk. EtherTalk has all of the usual speeds and features of 10Mbps Ethernet or 100Mbps Fast Ethernet. On the newer Macs, an EtherTalk adapter is included as standard hardware.

An additional benefit of EtherTalk for Macs is the capability to attach to NetWare servers. Granted, PCs still can't read most Mac files, but at least printers and the few file formats that are compatible with both PCs and Macs can be shared.

Protocols: The Electronic Signals of Network Life

For data to travel across the network, regardless of the speed (2, 4, 10, 16, 100, or 1000 Mbps), the methodology used (Ethernet, Token Ring, ARCnet, and so on), or the cable (UTP, STP, coaxial, or fiber-optics), there still has to be a carrier for the information. Think of it this way: Signaling speeds can be seen as speed limits

(4–1000Mbps) on various highways (UTP to coaxial). Regardless, there must be a transport for the data. Protocols serve as those transports. Some can carry large amounts of data, like a school bus, and some carry only smaller amounts, like a compact car.

To carry the analogy further, a protocol is not just the vehicle, it's all the different parts that make up the vehicle. Some portions transmit the data (the wheels), others ensure the data is sent correctly (the steering components), and still other parts of a protocol ensure that data arrives in one piece (the safety belts).

Some protocols carry information more efficiently than others, which is important to keep in mind when choosing a protocol.

The carriers of information include TCP/IP, SPX/IPX, NetBIOS, and NetBEUI. The following section defines the acronyms, explains their individual purposes, and gives their brief evolutionary history.

TCP/IP

Thanks to the Internet and intranets, the most popular networking protocol in the world is TCP/IP. TCP/IP also has something else that the other protocols don't have — a proprietary owner.

TCP/IP stands for Transmission Control Protocol/Internet Protocol. It was developed in the 1960s by the United States Department of Defense as a method for linking computers all across the world to maintain connectivity in the case of another World War. A technical definition of TCP/IP is: an industry standard suite of networking protocols, enabling dissimilar nodes in a heterogeneous environment to communicate with one another. In English, this means that TCP/IP can communicate to any PC using any desktop or network operating system anywhere in the world as long as it supports the TCP/IP suite. The military intended TCP/IP to be a routable, flexible, robust, and fault-tolerant protocol — and it is just that. Consequently, TCP/IP is the bread and butter protocol for the Internet and corporate intranets.

TCP/IP can be thought of as a special set of numbers similar to the numbers used with telephones. The same way each household and business has unique phone numbers, so must PCs using TCP/IP. However, there are two ways to do this. Either TCP/IP is configured on each PC or one PC distributes the TCP/IP numbers through what is called a DHCP or BootP server (Bootstrap Protocol), depending on your NOS.

Configuring TCP/IP

The most time-consuming task in large networks is installing TCP/IP communication software on each PC in the network and assigning each device its very own Internet address.

Internet addresses used with TCP/IP can be just a number or a number represented by a name. The number is split up into four octets with periods, such as "127.248.119.149." An octet is an eight-bit storage unit. In the international community, the term "octet" is often used instead of "byte." Alternatively, this number can be associated with a specific name, like a company (www.ibm.com) or a government institution (www.govt.nasa.gov). So, if you've been surfing the Internet, all of those Internet addresses you see are also represented by unique numbers.

The third octet is known as the subnet. With the typical Class C Internet address you get 253 possible numbers with each subnet. Subnets are used by businesses, for example, to separate addresses according to floors of buildings to keep the numbering schemes organized. This way, when there is a problem, it is more easily identifiable. Businesses can have more than one subnet, it just depends on how large their institution is and how much money they want to pay.

Dynamic Host Configuration Protocol

In this instance, a PC on the network is given the information for all of the available TCP/IP (also called "IP" for short) addresses. Whenever a person in the organization attempts to access an Internet related service (like the World Wide Web), the Dynamic Host Configuration Protocol (DHCP) server assigns an IP address upon bootup for that PC to use temporarily. This method of IP addressing is referred to as dynamic IP addressing because it is an active assignment. Online service providers, such as CompuServe and America Online, operate in the exact same manner. Every time you dial into these services, an IP address is assigned for your usage while accessing the Internet.

Using DHCP is simple because there is less potential for duplicating IP addresses. (Imagine two PCs have the same address and one of them happens to be the network server or another important resource. The resulting busy signal could bring the network to a screeching halt.) Also, DHCP can be cheaper in the long run because not as many addresses are needed.

If money is no object and a large network support staff is available, static IP addressing can be used. In this instance each PC has its own unique IP address that, when installed, must be configured so that it doesn't interfere or conflict with any other PC or device. Although static addressing is simpler than dynamic addressing, problems such as duplicate IP numbers are much more difficult to diagnose. To compensate, make the NIC number, rather than an individual's name or department, the primary associative information link in your record of IP numbers. Names and departments can be used as secondary links in your database. People and PCs are hard to keep track of in corporate America, but the NIC card number never changes. Recording the information in this manner will allow for easier tracking if duplicate addressing does occur.

NOTE

Static addressing is still the norm today, although as the pool of available IP addresses gets smaller, dynamic IP addressing schemes are becoming increasingly popular.

SPX/IPX

SPX/IPX is an acronym for Sequenced Packet Exchange/Internetwork Packet Exchange. Unlike TCP/IP, SPX/IPX is a proprietary protocol, owned and developed by Novell, but also used by other network operating system companies, such as Microsoft.

IPX is a protocol that sends data packets to requested destinations (workstations, servers, and so on). IPX addresses and routes outgoing data packets across a network. It reads the assigned addresses of returning data and directs the data to the proper area within the workstation's or network server's operating system.

SPX verifies and acknowledges successful packet delivery to any network destination by requesting a verification from the destinations that the data was received. The SPX verification must include a value that matches the value calculated from the data before transmission. By comparing these values, SPX ensures not only that the data packet made it to the destination, but that it arrived intact.

SPX can track data transmissions consisting of a series of separate packets. If an acknowledgment request brings no response within a specified time, SPX retransmits it. After a reasonable number of retransmissions fail to return a positive acknowledgment, SPX assumes the connection has failed and warns the operator of the failure.

Because IPX was first developed by Novell, the makers of NICs had to supply their own compliant IPX driver. The results were an IPX driver for each kind of

NIC and a lot of hassle for network administrators to keep track of which went with which. For this reason, Novell developed the ODI/IPX specification protocol.

ODI stands for Open Datalink Interface, a network driver interface from Novell. It is a specification for NIC manufacturers to write a device driver for their NIC that can be used by any network protocol (for instance, SPX/IPX, TCP/IP, AppleTalk, and so on).

NetBIOS

NetBIOS stands for Network Basic Input/Output System. NetBIOS started out as a protocol that could communicate directly with network hardware without any other network software involved. Basically, it enables the use of naming conventions, rather than the typical numbering schemes, such as TCP/IP and IPX.

Unfortunately, NetBIOS does not contain a routing layer and is therefore unable to provide internetworking capability. Other protocols, such as IPX and IP, must be used for internetworking, though NetBIOS is often used to establish the connection.

NetBEUI

The acronym stands for NetBIOS Extended User Interface. Originally developed in 1985 by IBM, NetBEUI is a networking protocol that is an extension of the NetBIOS protocol. Consequently, it has the same shortcomings as NetBIOS. NetBEUI, too, does not travel across other LANs, because it can't be routed (routers are covered in Chapter 7), and is therefore recommended for linking fewer than two hundred PCs on the same segment or where bridging or switching is used to connect segments.

Firewalls

Firewalls are a necessity in today's networking environment if any of the computers on the LAN maintain a connection with the Internet. Luckily, they are easy to install, and may already be inside existing products on your network.

A firewall filters packets — both inbound and outbound — and decides whether or not to let the information pass. In this way, it prevents unauthorized access to internal resources from an external source. It may also be setup to disallow certain types of information being retrieved from the Internet. If a company does not want to tie up bandwidth from employees viewing streaming media files, for example, the firewall can block those types of packets from being retrieved.

Other features that firewalls can provide are reporting and auditing capabilities. Configurable reports can easily be generated on Internet bandwidth use to any single PC, total bandwidth use, or detailed statistics on Websites that the users are accessing. When activity that is specified as suspicious occurs, a recipient can be notified by email, with a detailed log of the incident attached.

Firewalls can be set up through hardware or software means, and are usually located between the top level hub/switch of the LAN, and the router through which packets flow to and from the Internet. The location should provide a single point at which all data flows into and out of the organization. In this way, it can be the sole source of data security management in the organization.

· ◄

Summary

As this chapter illustrates, the dynamics involved in passing data across a network are complicated and they change daily with the evolution of networking. Nonetheless, understanding the most common choices available should help you decide which method best suits your networking needs.

CHAPTER 7

Choosing Network Gear

Don't let the word gear in the chapter title scare you. You're not preparing for a trip through the Amazon or suiting up to climb Mount Everest. We simply replaced the overused term hardware with gear in order to bring a little change to our review of the component parts that make up an average LAN.

It seems not a day goes by that a maker of computer networking hardware (gear) doesn't introduce a new and improved device for LANs. Why? Because there are so many physical components that make up a network. This chapter takes you on a tour of the most common of those components. Depending on the topology and protocol chosen, you will need some of the following items among the gear making up your LAN.

Hubs

In Chapter 5 we introduced you to several network configuration models, or topologies. In our description of these various topologies, we briefly mentioned the hub device as a central location where all the cables come together.

Hubs in general are not unique to any one topology. They're used in Ethernet and Token Ring configurations, to name a few. Often they serve as a central connection point when adding workstations to a network or to strengthen transmission signals when longer cable segments are added between workstations and servers.

Dumb Hubs

First generation hubs, sometimes referred to as basic or dumb hubs were created to provide a basic LAN connection point for workgroups requiring access to shared resources. They're referred to as dumb because these earlier hubs lacked any control or management capability. They simply tied all of the cables together by way of a box with ports to plug cables into. In other words, a dumb hub accepts transmission signals via connected cables, then passes the signals on to other workstations connected to that hub.

Although they're being used less and less today, dumb hubs do provide an inexpensive and effective central connection point for the cables that make up a network. Because of their relative simplicity compared to today's smart hubs, dumb hubs are suitable for less complex environments. Sometimes referred to as workgroup hubs, dumb hubs are used to either split a transmission signal or provide a connecting point for additional workstations added to the single LAN segment. The dumb hub cannot boost a transmission signal and must be cabled directly to a workstation or smart hub for support.

Smart Hubs

Recognizing the limits of dumb hubs, manufacturers developed the second generation or smart hub. Smart hubs usually play the role of a signal amplifier in a typical network topology (much like a repeater, which is explained later in this chapter). These hubs provide limited management capability through software that enables the network administrator to program the way the hub operates. Smart hubs are more versatile distribution points and provide integrated support over several types of cables. You may have heard smart hubs referred to as concentrators because they can take the LAN's capability and concentrate it into one device. Also, smart hubs sometimes take the shape of a card that fits into a slot on the server's motherboard to work jointly with network software and direct communications within the network. These are called internal or card hubs, and they do have limitations that external hubs do not. These include limited on-board random access memory, a limited number of ports per card, a confinement to the capabilities of the buses they're plugged into, and they can slow down server speed. If you ever consider using card hubs, make sure you find out their limitations before you buy and install them.

Intelligent Hubs

This is the level where hubs become significantly more task specific and advanced. Intelligent hubs are sophisticated smart hubs that support multiple LANs and topologies, provide extensive management capabilities, and can house other module types, such as routers and bridges. Intelligent hubs walk a fine line between the traditional role previously mentioned and the role of a switch, which is discussed at the end of this chapter. This fine line comes from the intelligent hub's very comprehensive network management capability and its ability to perform port switching and provide fault tolerance.

If you're considering a LAN that will eventually evolve into a WAN, then also consider investing in a top-end, intelligent hub. In a large network environment, systems administrators are well served by hubs that offer the latest monitoring and management capability. Intelligent hubs keep tabs on the status of the network and correct problems as they occur. In our network management chapter, we tell you how intelligent hubs use management protocols to provide their sophisticated services.

Today's generation of hubs has come so far from the early first- and second-generation roots, it's hard to say how many branches the hub family tree has. Hubs from basic to intelligent come in several shapes and sizes and fall into numerous categories. In other words, not all hubs are created equal. So make sure you do some further, more extensive research on the type of hubs you need (if you need them at all) once you decide the extent of your LAN design.

As you can see, hubs — dumb, intelligent, or anywhere in between — play an essential role by providing significant flexibility in the design of a new network or by expanding the capability of an existing LAN.

Repeaters

Not to be confused with hubs, bridges, or routers, repeaters are the simplest form of a signal booster. A physical device designed to tie two long network cable segments together, a repeater gives the signal the added kick it needs to travel long distances in various cabling schemes. Whether or not you'll need repeaters as part of your network configuration will depend on how long the segments are. Segments consist of cables and computers combined. As mentioned in our chapter on network design, as long as the total length of the segment doesn't exceed the limit requirements for the particular type of cable used, a repeater isn't necessary, as seen in Figure 7.1.

Repeaters accept information in the form of data packets sent by nodes (PCs) and other devices on the network, and basically rejuvenate (or amplify) the packet signal so it can travel a long distance without data loss. Data loss occurs when a signal gets so weak it becomes vulnerable to interference. This phenomenon, known as attenuation, is the sole reason repeaters exist. Weak signals that have been a little distorted by interference are fixed by the repeater before getting a shot of energy and pumped out the other side.

Repeaters are used when the total length of a segment exceeds the maximum signal length of the type of cable used.

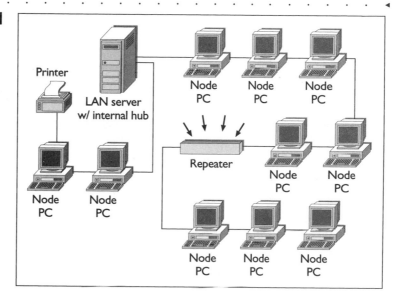

Though this is an important role, this is all repeaters do. They do not distinguish good packets from bad. They do not make computing or switching decisions. Repeaters simply receive data packets, juice them up, then send them on their way. It's as simple as that.

Well, almost. Some repeaters are choosy when it comes to which network signal they will accept on any given LAN. For instance, a repeater designed for an Ethernet network will only accept and pass Ethernet packets. Ethernet repeaters also help control data wrecks. Because Ethernet sends packets after only briefly checking to see if the path is clear, sometimes the checking process doesn't work. Sometimes the network segment is so long, a data packet that is using the cable may not be seen by an Ethernet workstation that's checking it. The workstation, assuming the cable is empty, then sends its packet. The two packets using the same path collide, resulting in a data-wreck. Repeaters designed specifically for Ethernet networks can assist in preventing wrecks by shortening the network. The segments required to accommodate multiple workstations on the network are thus shorter and allow the Ethernet card to see all data packs on the network at any given time.

These days, repeaters used on Token Ring networks are not stand-alone devices, but usually part of the hub device. Since hubs come in different network signaling configurations, there isn't much thought to the process of which complementing repeater to buy.

Repeaters are not choosy when it comes to cable, however. Most repeaters have the ability to link up disparate cable types. They accept data packets from coaxial, UTP, or STP cables on the same LAN and usually come with connectors for all three types.

One last important note about repeaters — no network should have or require more than four repeaters total. Why? Because each time data packets enter a repeater, they are taken apart and reassembled in their original form before they're released. This process, though done quickly, does delay the packet. Now imagine the packet traveling through this process more than four times. Probably not enough to notice, right? Wrong. If the sending workstation does not get a receipt signal back from a packet's destination in a certain amount of time, it will send the same packet again. Therefore, redundant packets could be bouncing all over the network, not only slowing things down, but clogging things up. Save yourself and everyone else some trouble and keep the total number of repeaters on your LAN under five.

Bridges

A step up in sophistication from a repeater, a bridge in its simplest form is a physical device that enables two or more networks to exchange information, regardless of their specific topologies. These box-type devices also play the role of a repeater between different segments on the same LAN or between two or more LANs. For example, a bridge can connect an Ethernet network to a Token Ring network, thus creating one big LAN. Or it can act as a partition used to break a single network into two smaller network segments.

Additionally, a bridge can distinguish good packets from bad. It prevents bad packets from getting any further down the LAN, thereby keeping bad data from cluttering the system. In its capacity as a data traffic regulator, a bridge dividing two segments on the same LAN memorizes all of the addresses for each node on both segments to which it is connected. If the bridge receives a data packet containing an address it does not recognize, the bridge will not allow it to go any further.

Like repeaters, bridges can accept data packets being sent across the network and boost their signal strength to offset the signal-carrying limits of the cable, then send the packets on their way. The advantage a bridge has over a repeater is that it can read the header information of a packet, called the Media Access Control (MAC) address, and determine the packet's intended destination. Then the bridge acts as traffic cop and waves the data on its way.

The MAC address is the unique number assigned to each NIC within each node on the LAN. Since the bridge knows the addresses for all NICs on the segments it is attached to, it can easily ascertain where the packet is going and allow it to cross over. Simply put, a bridge acts like a postal carrier. A bridge delivers packets specifically to the address on the packet. Also like a postal carrier, some packets are intended for all addresses, sort of like those "Dear Resident" letters you get, so the bridge broadcasts the packet to all segments.

Bridges Used Between Segments

A bridge keeps tabs on packets transmitted between nodes on both of the LAN segments to which it's attached. However, bridges don't let any old data pack cross over. For example, there's a bridge installed to separate a LAN into two segments, with one segment designated for Sally and one for Sam. If the bridge receives a data packet from Sam's network going to Sally's, the bridge recognizes it as needing to cross over and allows it to pass. However, if Sam sends a message to someone else on the Sam segment, the bridge recognizes that the signal doesn't need to cross over and thus allows it to continue on the Sam segment.

Bridges Used Between LANs

We've told you how bridges are used to connect segments of the same LAN. Now let's discuss how bridges are used to connect multiple LANs.

Imagine a company housed in one or several buildings, with each floor of each building represented by its own independent LAN network. Now, imagine the need to connect all of those LANs together to create a WAN or CAN. Bridges provide this ability. For example, if Sally's LAN is on the fourth floor of XYZ

Corporation and Sam's LAN is located on the sixth floor, and XYZ wants to connect the two, a bridge can be used to make the connection.

Cascading Bridge Configuration

To perform the function of connecting segments or LANs, bridges are typically used in one of two configurations. The first and least efficient is called cascading. In the cascading theme, a single bridge links one segment to another or one LAN to another in a daisy chain format, as seen in Figure 7.2.

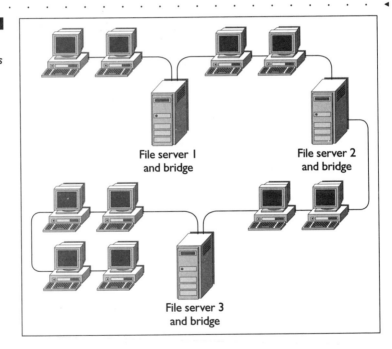

FIGURE 7.2

A network connected to others via cascading bridges

File server 1
and bridge

File server 2
and bridge

File server 3
and bridge

The problem with this arrangement is that for a signal to pass from segment C to segment A, it must traverse through all three segments and both bridges. Remember, a segment can be thought of as a length of network cable with more than two computers on it. For instance, think of the floors in the XYZ building used in our previous example — each floor represents one segment. The cascading configuration is the least popular because it requires data packets to go through several devices before reaching their intended destinations. This in turn provides a lot of opportunity for the data packet to be garbled from line noise or some other interference.

Backbone Bridge Configuration

The more popular and efficient manner of bridging networks is called a backbone. We discuss backbones in more depth in our internetworking chapter. Briefly stated, however, in a backbone configuration, each bridge for each segment is directly linked to the others, as seen in Figure 7.3.

FIGURE 7.3

Networks connected via a backbone

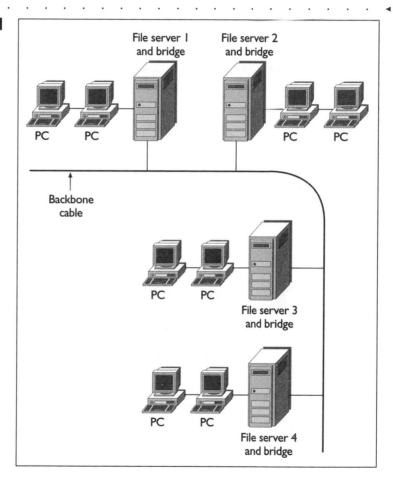

In a backbone configuration the bridges share the responsibility of passing packets around. Each bridge is linked not only to each other but also to each segment — as you can see from the figure. These schemes are also referred to as switching.

With regard to price, the backbone plan is more expensive because of the higher number of bridges required. However, for budgetary justification purposes, the speed and efficiency of the network packets is greatly enhanced.

An added benefit of bridges is the capability to also filter out packets based on preconfigured criteria in addition to the maladaptive ones. For example, if a computer research department is testing a new type of signaling scheme on an active network but doesn't want the new signals to interfere with the mainstay of the network, the bridge can be configured to "segment off" their area. This will allow the test to occur without interfering with the rest of the network.

As is the trend with computers, smarter and more robust bridges exist for even more complicated scenarios. For the purposes of this book, however, let's stick to the basics.

Again, bridges, like the other devices we've discussed, are not all created equal. Some are very basic in design and task, while others are complex and hard to distinguish from routers. This creates a perfect segue to our next device in this stroll through networking gear — routers.

▶ · ◀

Routers

Routers take us to another level of sophistication because they operate on the data transport layer of the OSI model (see Chapter 2). Offering significant capabilities beyond that of a bridge, routers are not beholden to any specific topology or protocol. Unlike bridges, routers don't care what MAC address is attached to a data packet making its way across the network. Routers only pay attention to the destination addresses attached to packets as a set of four decimal numbers separated by periods. This address describes the interface as a node within the network.

Routers come in several shapes, sizes, and capabilities. Some routers are external devices, some are internal, and some are nothing more than sophisticated software on a server.

Some sophisticated routers consist of two distinct devices rolled into one neat box. Designed to work in tandem within the router, these devices can receive, send, and process multiple protocols. A bridge decides when to forward each packet, but it cannot see other bridges or routers. Likewise, bridges are invisible to routers; hubs are invisible to bridges; and routers only know about other routers. Special additions to certain protocols allow routers to know about end nodes, but that is very rarely used. Generally, routers only know about other routers and network segments. Think of a router as a professional makeup artist. It receives data packets masked in one type of protocol, wipes the mask off, puts on a completely different protocol face, gives it the best directions to the stage, and sends it packing (excuse the pun).

How do routers do it? Through the use of routing protocols, which come in the form of sophisticated software designed to make specific decisions regarding the distribution of data packets over a given network. Routing protocols determine what information other routers need to know and keep all the routing decisions current in case the system administrator needs to see the information. Here are just three of the more common routing protocols used today:

▶ *OSPF* stands for *Open Shortest Path First*, one of the most widely used routing protocols for LANs running *Internet Protocol* (IP). OSPF tracks external routing information by using the IP multicasting transmission method. It can talk to all types of other routers, both internal and external, authenticate packets, and avoid routes that may cause transmission problems.

▶ *IGRP* stands for *Interior Gateway Routing Protocol* and offers the capability of managing a wide variety of bandwidths and delays. IGRP gives the user the option of configuring operating characteristics such as internetworking and bandwidth. This protocol manages internal, external, and other system routes.

▶ *RIP* stands for *Routing Information Protocol* and is used in TCP/IP and NetWare to identify all attached networks, as well as the number of router hops required to reach them. The responses are used to update a router's routing table.

Keep in mind, as we mentioned earlier, routers take several forms. Your network may not require an actual physical routing device. You may be able to conduct routing completely through the use of routing software.

Routers at Work

To better illustrate the role both physical routers and software-based routing protocols play, let's look at how multiple protocols are handled by a network. The NetWare operating system provides built-in support for the LAN protocols associated with each type of workstation that NetWare supports. Routing services can be made a part of a NetWare server that provides other services (such as file and print sharing), or they can be dedicated to their routing functions. Both integrated and stand-alone routers function the same way, but performance differences can be considerable. Stand-alone routers almost always offer better routing performance; however, they are more costly to set up and manage.

Internal routers reside within a NetWare server and consist simply of one or more network interface cards (NICs) and protocol NetWare Loadable Modules (NLMs) to provide routing segments (each serviced by a separate NIC in the file server) that are managed by the NetWare operating system. Using internal routing, NetWare can interlink as many LANs as there are distinct NICs in the server. The practical limit, based on cable and common machine constraints, is six to eight distinct network segments. This simple and effective approach to creating an expanded network is illustrated in Figure 7.4.

The principal external routing solution from Novell comes in the Novell Internet Access Server (NIAS), which is bundled with the product. Older versions of NetWare used a stand alone product called the Novell Multi-Protocol Router (MPR), which was a single-user or run-time NetWare operating system, combined with a number of NLMs to support routing for various networking protocols.

The NetWare MPR can be loaded on a full-blown NetWare file services server (which makes it an internal router), or it can be loaded on run-time NetWare (which makes it an external router). If you think of the difference between the two as simply the presence or absence of file services, you'll have an easier time with the concept of the product. When would you choose an external router instead of allowing your server to act as an internal router? There are various practical reasons, some having to do with overcoming physical limitations. A short list of common reasons follows:

- ▶ The file server has no remaining expansion bus slots for additional NICs.

- ▶ The file server is already laden with activity, and performance is crucial.

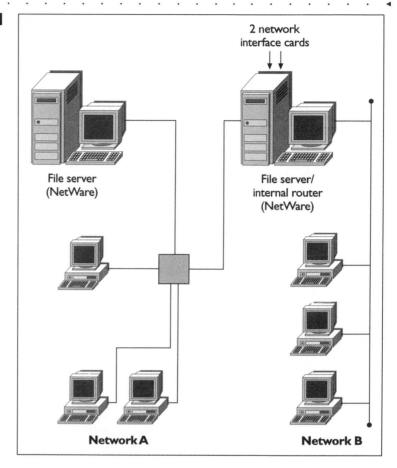

FIGURE 7.4

*Network with server
containing internal router*

- The file server is not conveniently located for interconnection of the dispersed networks.

- The applications in use are critical to the business, and all non-critical functions have to be off-loaded from the file server for fault tolerance. (Fault tolerance is the ability to avoid system failure due to problems with a single component or subsystem, whether hardware or software.)

▸ The routing functions are critical to the business and must be isolated from any possible causes of performance reduction, conflict, disruption, or failure.

▸ One of the links is a heavy-duty, high-traffic network segment that acts as a highway among multiple network segments, known as a backbone. (A backbone typically carries heavy traffic that might take up too much of a multipurpose server's processing capacity. Using a stand-alone router guarantees that the router will do its job properly and that local servers will not be bogged down by routing traffic on and off the backbone.)

▸ A special-purpose link must be integrated. Sometimes cable segments require 32-bit interfaces to be worthwhile; for instance, to get the best use out of a 100Mbps technology like the FDDI.

Figure 7.5 shows a multiprotocol internetwork using an external router. The router in the illustration routes IPX/SPX (NetWare's native protocol), TCP/IP (the native protocol of UNIX systems), and AppleTalk (the native protocol of Apple Macintosh networks). Each of the separate networks can access each of the others by using the routing function of the external router.

Of course, many vendors provide routers that support multiple protocols. These products tend to offer higher performance at a higher cost than a software based solution such as the Novell MPR.

Remote links can be configured when the distance between networks makes it impractical (or impossible) to physically connect them with standard network cables. In this case, telephone lines or public data networks (PDNs) are used to provide an intermediate transmission medium. You can connect networks that are located far apart from one another by configuring a router on each network with modems, as shown in Figure 7.6.

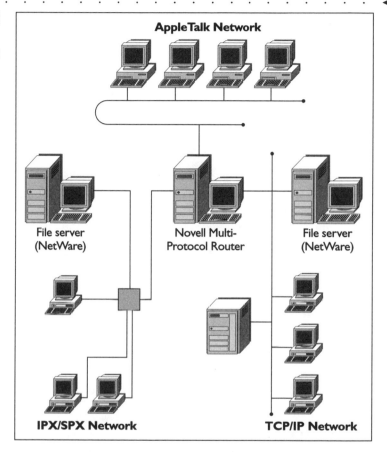

FIGURE 7.5

Multiprotocol internetwork using a Novell Multi-Protocol Router

One last note regarding routers: Consider their role carefully when planning your network. Understand the difference between an external, internal and software router and what types of service you expect them to provide. Also, consider at what level you expect them to perform these services. By understanding the benefits routers can provide when used in conjunction with the right protocol, you avoid a lot of transmission problems and enjoy the performance properly placed routers provide.

FIGURE 7.6

*Use routers for remote
linking to other networks.*

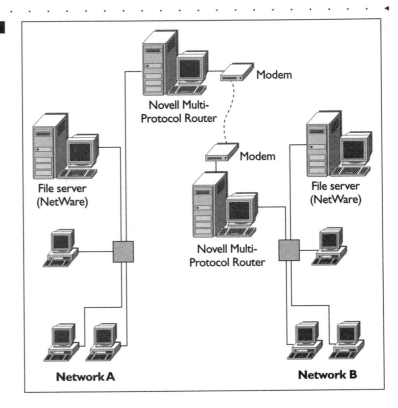

Switches

We close this chapter discussing switches because they have a lot in common with the device we opened this chapter with—hubs. If you recall, we said that today's more sophisticated hubs are difficult to distinguish from switches. (In fact, many of the latest generation hubs are so sophisticated that they are better characterized as switches because they incorporate per-port switching capability.) Switches automate network reconfiguration, and therefore, increase network availability and capability.

The most important difference between switches and hubs is total bandwidth. In an Ethernet hub, data flows into the hub, and then is transmitted to every device in the hub. Since only one stream of data can flow at any one time under

Ethernet, the speed of the hub defines the maximum speed of all devices transmitting to the hub combined. For example, when using an 8-port 100Mbps hub, the total bandwidth of data traveling within the hub is 100Mbps—even when all 8 of the 100Mbps ports are communicating at once. Hubs share the bandwidth, and may cause bottlenecks when not strategically placed within a network.

In a switch, however, each port can operate independently of the others. Inbound packets that are destined to a particular node do not flow to all ports, like in a hub. The packets flow only to the node they are intended for. Here, switched bandwidth is utilized, and allows packets to flow at full throttle through the switch.

Another important feature that some switches provide is disaster recovery. These switches provide LAN managers the ability to build and store alternate configurations in preparation for a potential disaster. If a disaster strikes, the switch can turn on ports connected to specific stations designed to back up the data, or the switch turns off specific ports in order to isolate those segments experiencing problems. This capability provides some security features in that it enables the network administrator to switch off certain ports during certain days of the week or hours of the day, thereby denying access to some users.

Switches also break rules on how many hubs and repeaters may exist between any two nodes on a network. This becomes critical when implementing Fast Ethernet technology, since the number of repeaters between any two nodes is limited to two.

Last but certainly not least, switches provide some degree of fault tolerance. For instance, imagine that in place of the sophisticated switch, Sally uses a typical hub as a central connection point for all of her network cables. If the hub malfunctions or experiences a fault, Sally's entire network could go down. Not a good scenario, is it? A sophisticated switch can sometimes isolate the problem while still allowing the unaffected portion of the network to operate, thereby providing a certain degree of fault tolerance. As per-port costs of switches continue to grow smaller, the value of switches becomes overwhelming. It will ease bandwidth bottlenecks and increase reliability in an organization when strategically placed to meet the needs of its users.

Summary

Remember, there's a lot to learn about the gear involved in setting up a LAN, and you might find it difficult at times to determine the best gear to use on yours. Don't be discouraged. Even the most experienced network administrators must diligently keep up with the faced-paced changes and emerging standards in the networking industry.

CHAPTER 8

Internetworking

Some day philosophers will no doubt look back at the close of the twentieth century and marvel over our sudden rush to get connected. People these days don't just want to connect to devices like printers, or applications like databases, they want to connect to everything and everyone.

Years ago, when Cheryl Currid was designing and building one of the first large scale corporate LANs, a technician came up to her and said, "When are we going to stop hooking up these computers? Every day, we receive new requests for people to hook up." Cheryl looked at him, smiled, and replied, "When we run out of desktops, branch offices, manufacturing plants, homes, hotel rooms, suppliers, customers, and consumers. That's when."

The point: The quest for connectivity doesn't end until everything (and everyone) gets connected. And that quest for connectivity takes us to the topic of this chapter, internetworking.

The notion of networking doesn't stop at the workgroup or department level. Nor is it bound to the physical constraints of a single building, enterprise, or location. Moreover, in business, the desire to connect spans beyond organizational boundaries to the industry and beyond. New business models dictate that companies work efficiently with suppliers and customers. Further, electronic commerce is already here for many industries, and it brings with it special new requirements for connectivity to outside organizations.

Still another opportunity exists. As PCs have become almost as pervasive as the telephone, they may someday replace it. New network switching components and new architectures are beginning to make people question, "Why do I have a separate telephone system for voice and a network system for data. Can't both voice and data run over the same lines?" The answer is yes and no. The capability is possible, the technology is here, it just takes time and motivation to convert.

In this chapter, we turn our focus to the first step beyond the local LAN or workgroup. We lay the groundwork and map out the likely connections that almost any network will ultimately need. Then we discuss the various technologies that you might apply as you extend the physical and logical reach of your network. Even if you are sure that your network will never extend beyond the five people in your workgroup, read this chapter anyway. You never know when you'll want to connect up to external services like the Internet or CompuServe. Likewise, new voice processing technology may turn into a compelling opportunity for you.

The purpose of this chapter is to give you an introduction to internetworking and WAN technology. We don't expect to make you an overnight expert on internetwork design or installation, but we believe it's valuable for everyone to understand the options and choices to expand the network.

What Is Internetworking?

Let's start with a simple three-word definition of the term internetworking: tying together LANs.

The union of networks should operate invisibly or seamlessly, as if they were one. Network users should not know from response time lags that Sue sits in sunny Florida while Sam stays in Syracuse. It shouldn't matter if all the data and devices are on the network. An easy concept, right?

Networks can be tied together by very simple means. Two LANs connected by a cable represents the simplest form of an internetwork. So does a single cable running vertically through the telephone closets of a high rise building. Just as long as it stops at each floor to connect to the local LAN, every network can be easily connected to every other network. As shown in Figure 8.1, internetworking can start out with an extremely uncomplicated design.

Realistically, however, internetworking doesn't start and stop by just tying together a few nearby workgroup LANs. Invariably, your organization's connectivity needs will go far beyond a few local sites. As different technologies are deployed, the simplistic picture of a lone cable connecting LANs disappears, replaced by a complex set of technologies and considerations.

Sometimes people confuse the terms internetworking and WAN. As we described in Chapter 1, a WAN connects LANs that are housed at different physical locations. Most WANs require special long-distance or leased phone lines to make that connection.

By contrast, an internetwork can connect multiple LANs in one single location. For example, several buildings of a campus environment or several floors of a high-rise office building would make up an internetwork. In short, a WAN always involves internetworking but an internetwork doesn't always require a WAN.

We make this distinction to help you think about the technology you'll need when selecting your internetwork. Because you are probably buying your own cable for a local internetwork, you have slightly more control than you would with a WAN. Building a WAN almost always dictates that you work with a long distance carrier, such as AT&T, Sprint, MCI, and so on.

F I G U R E 8.1

Internetworking can be as simple as merely tying together two or more LANs.

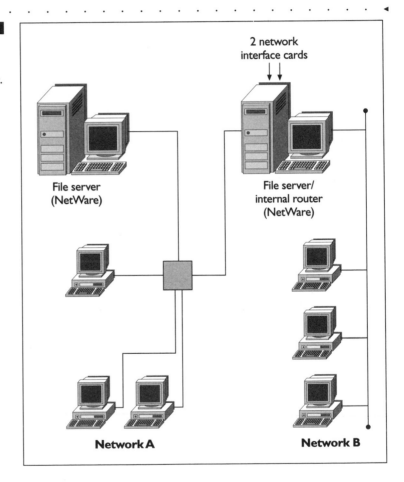

2 network interface cards

File server (NetWare)

File server/ internal router (NetWare)

Network A

Network B

▶ • ◀

Network Connection Devices

On each end of the communications line, you need a device to make the connection to the local LAN. Depending on the type of wire or line you use, you have a choice of devices, from a simple modem all the way up to a complex multiprotocol router.

Bridges often maintain the semblance of a single logical LAN by simply forwarding packets of data from one segment to the next. For example, a two-port bridge splits a logical network into two physical segments. Then it transmits packets across the bridge only if its destination lies on the other side. By forwarding packets only when necessary, it helps to reduce network congestion. This approach works fine for local interconnections or high long-distance bandwidth lines, but isn't as efficient as other means. Newer bridge models combine some of the functions of a router (described next) to manage the packet traffic between networks more efficiently.

Routers select which data packets to route between multiple LAN segments. They make intelligent decisions about the path that packets should take around the backbone and they know where the final destination is located. In so doing, routers are much more efficient. Until the advent of multiprotocol routers, however, routers would only handle one protocol, such as Novell's IPX. Therefore, PCs on a routed internetwork that connected Novell's IPX along with an IBM mainframe running IBM's Systems Network Architecture (SNA) might not see the mainframe. The SNA packets wouldn't have gotten over the router.

Hubs, or concentrators, handle the cabling requirements of linking up internetworks, connecting the ring or bus topology of each LAN to the network backbone. Traditional Ethernet LANs run at 10Mbps over a common bus-type design, even when they are physically attached to a hub, repeater, or concentrator. Every station is capable of receiving all transmissions from all stations, or sending to all stations, although not simultaneously. They can either talk or listen. See Chapter 7 for more information about these devices.

Switches also handle the cabling requirements of linking up networks and internetworks, but they're much faster than hubs and concentrators.

Consider the reality of what bandwidth is really available on your network. Most LANs run at either 10Mbps or 100Mbps. If you have 30 nodes on a segment or ring, that bandwidth is shared among all 30 nodes. Each node only gets 1/30 of 10Mbps, or to be more technically accurate, 1/30 of 25 percent of 10Mbps, which is the maximum traffic for an Ethernet segment. That computes to 83Kbps per node, which is faster than a modem but slower than an ISDN line.

Now you know why switches challenge hubs. Great speed advances come with switched rather than shared media. Replace the hub with a switch, and each node gets a full 10Mbps. Replace the 10Mbps cards with 100Mbps cards, and replace the 10Mbps switches with 100Mbps switches, and each node gets a full 100Mbps. Giving full bandwidth to each user on a LAN ought to speed up those difficult sessions where packets are flowing but not fast.

Switches do more than simply direct packets to one side or the other of a network. They identify the target and send traffic directly to its destination without waiting.

Also, just to tweak up speeds a little higher, there are two types of switching architectures: cut-through and store-and-forward. The cut-through approach reads the destination address of a packet and immediately sends it on its way, without waiting for the entire packet to arrive at the switching device. The store-and-forward technique buffers incoming packets in memory until it runs a cyclic redundancy check (CRC) looking for errors. This approach adds a little time to the process, but avoids problems associated with bad packets going out unchecked and collisions that can slow down the overall performance of the network segment.

Which mode is best? According to Harvard University networking expert Scott Bradner, if you have a noisy network, you might think twice before enabling a cut-through mode; the decrease in network slowdowns might be outweighed by the increase in LAN traffic because of corrupted packets.

Communications Lines

To make the connection, there must be something between the devices, namely a communication line. In a local environment, the communication line might be as simple as a single cable. Generally speaking, internetwork designers use high quality cable that can support the fast traffic, and lots of it.

As described in Chapter 6, most cable choices are made from coaxial, twisted-pair, or fiber-optic cabling. Your specific decision may rest on what's already available in your building or what can be most easily installed.

Wireless Links for Internetworking

Before we talk about the various types of phone lines and transmission options, we must also consider connecting without wires. Depending on your physical environment, you may find the most cost effective connection is the one you make through thin air.

Two primary wireless technologies are available for internetworking: microwave and spread spectrum. Either can make a cost effective option, especially when the only other choice might be to lay your network cable and conduit by digging up a parking lot. Day-to-day operating costs of wireless technologies are low too. Because no one owns the air, you don't pay fees for air time, as long as you control both sending and receiving units. Of course, that also means if your wireless link goes down, you can't call the telephone company. You'll have no one but yourself to fix it.

A microwave signal can travel several hundreds of miles, as long as the transmitters have line of sight with each other. They must be pointed directly at each other without obstructions from other buildings or trees. Speeds of 2Mbps to 34Mbps are available from this technology.

Regulatory issues may affect your ability to use microwave systems. Licenses from national authorities are always required, and some transmission schemes may be restricted altogether. Construction activity may also affect your ability to use microwave technology. If someone decides to build a high rise and disrupts your transmission, you may have to find an alternative technology, or rent roof space on the newly constructed obstruction.

Spread spectrum is a wireless radio technology originally developed by the military for secure and interference-immune communications. Spread spectrum has been available to commercial users since 1985. There are actually two types of spread spectrum in use today, both developed for the military: frequency hopping and code division multiple access (CDMA). Frequency hopping is an analog technique, whereas CDMA is digital.

Frequency hopping is based on the fact that transmissions are hard to intercept. Using short transmissions on many frequencies spreads the message out, making it hard to intercept the whole message. CDMA is far more useful, but much more complex.

Spread spectrum technology also promises some help to interconnect certain nearby LANs. For example, the Proxim RangeLAN2 family of high-speed, wireless data bridges connects LANs in buildings up to three miles apart. This technology is faster than long distance phone lines, but slower than LAN speeds. Most spread spectrum LANs operate at about 2Mbps or less, compared to a standard Ethernet, which is 10Mbps. However, Proxim's 1.6Mbps radio data rate delivers a throughput that rivals most leased line connections, such as 56/64Kbps, Frame Relay, and T1.

RangeLAN2 supports a transparent bridge architecture that works with any protocol or network operating system that supports Ethernet, including Novell NetWare, TCP/IP, Microsoft Windows NT, AppleTalk, and others.

Telephone and Leased Lines

When data traffic must travel beyond the immediate building or campus, you have two options for connections. You may choose from dial-up or leased lines to make the connection from one LAN to another. The speed of the connection will vary too, depending on what type of line you order.

If the concept of internetworking is new to you and your organization, we suggest that you first take a look at the types of applications likely to be used. If workers merely run PC applications and electronic mail from the network, you probably won't need high-speed lines. If, however, there's a chance that you'll be installing distributed databases, groupware, or desktop video conferencing, beware of their hefty bandwidth requirements.

Today, with the right equipment and lines, you have options for almost any type of demand. From dial-up networking with regular modems at speeds of 28.8Kbps to super sonic ATM speeds of over 600Mpbs, you can buy bandwidth. Table 8.1 lists some popular connection technologies and their maximum speed ratings. Table 8.2 shows the same considerations for LANs.

TABLE 8.1

*Popular Connection
Technologies and Maximum
Speed Ratings*

WIDE AREA TECHNOLOGY	SPEED	COMMENTS
POTS	56Kbps	Nearing theoretical limitations as we currently know them.
ISDN	128 Kbps or two 64Kbps	Can be divided into two lines. One line can be analog, for use as a normal phone line. Not widely available, and being replaced by lower cost/higher speed xDSL technologies.
T1	1.544 Mbps	Can be split into numerous channels or divided up into sixty-four 256Kbps lines (called fractional T1).
xDSL	Up to 8Mbps receive 640Kbps send	Quickly gaining consumer popularity due to low costs and high speed.
Cable Modem	From 3 to 30 Mbps	High speed, low cost connectivity option for residential markets. Bandwidth shared, however, among users in the area.
STS-1 SONET	51.84Mbps	Not used.
ATM	25Mbps, 155Mbps, 622Mbps	Popular, but still not widely implemented.

TABLE 8.2

*Popular LAN Connection
Technologies and Maximum
Speed Ratings*

LOCAL AREA TECHNOLOGY	SPEED	COMMENTS
ARCnet	2Mbps and 20Mbps	An all but extinct technology.
Token Ring	4Mbps and 16Mbps	Once the preferred companion to mostly IBM shops; more expensive and less popular than Ethernet.
Ethernet	10Mbps,100Mbps, 1000Mbps (Gigabit)	The most popular choice.
FDDI	100Mbps	Token passing.

These options vary dramatically in cost. Generally speaking, you get extra speed, reliability, and convenience for extra dollars. Don't let that stop you from comparison pricing. Each year, new technology developments tend to change the rules. Your day-to-day operating expenses could quickly change depending on new types of technology introduced.

Watch out about trusting theoretical limitations. Often you'll find today's technical limitations become tomorrow's history. It wasn't too many years ago that no one thought you could transmit data faster than 9.6Kbps over unconditioned phone lines. Today, that figure looks foolish when compared to the low-cost 56Kbps, xDSL, and cable modems available today.

Another consideration is dial-up versus continuous connection. Unless your budget is very tight, let us suggest that you dedicate the line to interconnecting your LANs. While it is possible to share some of the phone line technologies with other applications during the day, it isn't recommended.

People will not learn to use the internetworked resources efficiently when the connection isn't persistent. Imagine Sue trying to set up a weekly report to print for Sam in Syracuse. Say that Sue knows how to print the report to a printer near Sam's office. If she prints the report every Thursday without problems, then both she and Sam will be happy, but if the network connection is up and down sporadically, then she's unlikely to trust the system. Chances are Sue doesn't care that you are trying to save a few dollars on phone lines. In fact, she'll spend so much extra time and effort express mailing the report to Sam that it will more than make up for the savings.

Now for the communication options. For connecting LANs together, consider some of the tried and true options. These alternatives include plain old telephone system (POTS), ISDN, xDSL, cable modem, T1, frame relay-based internetworking, and ATM.

Using POTS and dialing out with the PC's modem or a modem server on the LAN, the maximum speed is slow (only 56Kbps or slightly higher with newer modems that use advanced compression). POTS lines can be dial-up or dedicated. POTS requires a modem for each line on the service.

The bad news about POTS is reliability. Regular phone lines were configured for voice traffic and not data. Line noise during data transmissions can slow down or disconnect a communications session. The good news about POTS is cost. It requires only one extra business telephone line per location.

The latest technology to provide high speed access to the home is xDSL. It provides a constant connection to the Internet at speeds of up to 8Mbps downstream and 2Mbps upstream. It utilizes standard copper twisted-pair cable, and maintains a constant connection.

Unlike xDSL, cable modems share bandwidth with other users in your neighborhood. While cable modems may tout speeds of 3 to 30Mbps, it truly depends on the number of subscribers in your area, as well as the level of use. As in a hub, the speed of a cable modem connection is shared between all the users on the network. xDSL, however, is similar to a switch, in that the connection is not dependent on the amount of bandwidth utilized by others on the network.

ISDN lines are available from most telecommunications providers that serve a local area. Maximum speed is 128Kbps if you use the full capability of these lines. Many, however, split the lines into two 64Kbps channels, one for data and one for voice. With certain types of software overhead, the true throughput speed may actually turn into 56Kbps. This is still a lot faster than POTS, but not as fast as the advertised rate.

ISDN lines can be dial-up or dedicated. To complete the connection, ISDN requires a terminal adapter device to connect the LAN to the ISDN lines much the same way as a router works. Alternatively, the device can be directly connected to an individual PC to service that unit only. These devices are not modems but are starting to look and act much like regular modems. Some makers even call them ISDN modems.

T1 lines are specially purchased or leased lines that let data travel up to 1.544Mpbs. These, like ISDN, can be split up into channels to accommodate other simultaneous traffic, such as voice or slower data traffic. To complete a T1 connection requires a special device. Like ISDN, it is available to multiple users on the LAN, but you also need a router.

Frame relay-based internetworks are strong, fast, and somewhat unsophisticated. Coming from an older technology, called X.25, frame relay is similar, travels over faster lines, and is unencumbered with X.25's error control. Frame relay can be implemented up to T1 speed, which is 24 times faster than X.25. Some phone carriers push it even faster, up to T3 rates, which makes it 672 times faster than X.25.

ATM is an even faster communications technology, with speeds ranging from 25Mbps to 655Mbps. These lines, like other high performance lines, can be divided up to accommodate other types of voice and data traffic. An ATM adapter is required to complete the connection to the line.

Of these choices, you have many options for line speed, as shown in Figure 8.2. It's almost as if you are choosing different sized plumbing pipes for your home.

FIGURE 8.2

Different communications technologies provide you with virtual pipes for data to pass through. It's helpful to imagine them as plumbing pipes of different widths and capacities.

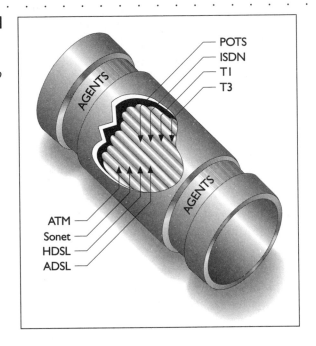

POTS
ISDN
TI
T3

AGENTS

AGENTS

ATM
Sonet
HDSL
ADSL

Connecting LANs to Host Environments

While internetworking LANs is a popular activity, it frequently isn't the only one network managers must face. Organizations that have mainframe computers or minicomputers want those attached to the network, too.

Many minicomputers attach to the network easily through standard Ethernet connections and the TCP/IP protocol.

Many companies still have large data stores in their mainframes to which end users need to have access. Even as companies migrate to more network-centric client-server computing, data still needs to be shared between mainframes and servers.

Connecting LANs to IBM Hosts

IBM brand computers use a different network protocol, SNA. It requires a little special handling when it comes to making a connection.

Gateway servers are used by some organizations to communicate and translate the data stream into a format understood by SNA. The data is then sent to the mainframe over a token ring, Ethernet, or other line. Then, on the mainframe side, a network processing application runs called Virtual Telecommunications Access Method (VTAM), which is responsible for taking the data stream and passing it to the application on the mainframe.

Depending on the exact product, the gateway PC and software sits between your PC and the mainframe and performs protocol conversion. It enables your PC to emulate a dumb 3270 terminal, so you can run any standard mainframe application. The solution also provides software that runs on the individual's PC to provide a shell for the terminal screens that are returned.

On Novell LANs, you can install NetWare for SAA to give you a simple but powerful connection. Using standard IPX/SPX and TCP/IP protocol stacks, the desktop PC and server communicate without the need for SNA and NDIS drivers at each workstation. The network administrator is freed from the time-consuming chore of installing and configuring each PC with special LAN support and NDIS drivers.

NetWare for SAA can support several thousand concurrent sessions with any logical unit (LU) type, such as display, printer, file transfer, and applications. It is sold by the number of host sessions, in packages of 16, 64, 128, 254, 508, or 1,016. You can increase the number of sessions by combining packages.

For the AS/400, the number of independent sessions available can be a little difficult to determine. It varies depending on different AS/400 models, disk space, the type and number of processors, the data link types, data link speed, the specific software applications running, total system usage by users, system memory, and system jobs/applications at any given time.

Summary

As we said at the opening of this chapter, the quest for connectivity is insatiable. That's one of the few indisputable facts of running a network. Your own network design should always keep growth and extra connectivity in mind, even if no one asks for it today.

Even if your company is no longer growing, and the number of computers in the office remains stable, don't count out connectivity. It seems that someone always wants that link that you haven't planned.

As we watch business trends and their effects on technology needs, we see continued changes ahead. So, if you are planning your company's network, remember the advice given to that inquisitive LAN technician so many years ago: We'll stop growing networks "when we run out of desktops, branch offices, manufacturing plants, homes, hotel rooms, suppliers, customers, and consumers. That's when."

CHAPTER 9

Choosing a Network Operating System

So far we've talked a lot about the choices you make when planning a LAN. Among the most basic of all the choices is deciding on the type of network operating system (NOS) as the central platform upon which to start. This chapter focuses on the choices between the major systems.

What's a Network Operating System?

Simply put, the NOS allows people to share "stuff." This definition identifies "stuff" as information, files, applications, and devices, such as printers.

The NOS acts as a switching station to keep track of the location. It also serves to provide the first line of security so that people can read or write only to the areas where they have permission.

In the early days of networks, the NOS simply provided a way to share files and devices. In today's more complex network environment, the NOS takes on more tasks. The NOS stores data about who, when, and how data is stored on the network. It may serve up applications or large parts of applications. It also frequently connects people from widely diverse locations.

The right NOS for your organization depends on how you plan to use your LAN.

As we mentioned in Chapter 1, networks are thought of as peer to peer or client-server. In a peer-to-peer network, there is no need for a server. The NOS allows you to search any shared location on anybody's computer. This is fine for a small environment but not a large one.

For example, certain operating systems like Personal NetWare or the Windows operating system provide file and device sharing. This might be fine for a small workgroup of one or two people, but it would become an administrative nightmare trying to serve the needs of 15 or more people. Imagine trying to use a file from Joe's computer or print to his printer if he had logged out and left the office early for the weekend.

Not All NOSs Are Created Equal

Software developers must carefully weigh how new features are added to the NOS. Since the NOS becomes a primary foundation for how people use computers, its functions and its robustness are important. If you are starting a network from scratch, it's critically important that you study your options.

We suggest that you read our description to start, pick two or three platforms you want to know more about, then surf the Internet or visit a good bookstore and pick up detailed guides for each of your choices.

The more popular NOSs include: Novell NetWare, Microsoft Windows 2000 (server edition), Banyan Vines, IBM's OS/2, and Linux, which comes from a variety of software publishers, such as Caldera or Red Hat.

Before buying a system, you should create a list of key factors. Then study the operating system to see how it handles your needs. A sample list includes:

- Do I need a full NOS or will a peer-to-peer operating system work for my small group?

- How will I support security?

- How will I manage directory synchronization?

- Will I serve applications as well as files?

- Will I administer the network or outsource it?

- What types of client operating systems will I need to support?

Learn as much as you can about the different NOS platforms and what options they offer before you buy. It's time well spent.

Novell NetWare

Positioned as the leading network operating system used today, Novell NetWare has become the NOS of choice for both large and small organizations, not only in the United States, but also around the world.

NetWare runs its own OS, and is compatible with any number of workstations running dissimilar systems. Therefore, NetWare servers can support a variety of clients including DOS, UNIX, and OS/2 workstations or Macintosh clients.

To keep track of network assets and users Novell NetWare uses a directory service called Novell Directory Services (NDS). In addition, NDS enables you to organize network resources, gain easy access to those resources, and centralize the administration of your network.

Imagine a network with thousands of objects, hundreds of servers, and dozens of network administrators in various departments. With Novell NDS, all of these objects and servers exist in one network database. NDS provides consistency and logical organization so large networks can streamline the work of all network administrators. Without this capability, the network is very confusing and cumbersome. Prudent planning, including the use of a directory service, is critical in arranging your entire organization's network into a unified structure.

When planning to use NDS, consider the following issues:

▶ What organizational structure of the directory tree makes the most sense for your network resources?

▶ How are you going to name objects?

▶ How do you want the directory database to be partitioned, and where do you want to store replicas of those partitions?

▶ How should time be kept and synchronized among the servers on the network?

We tackle each of these issues one by one in the following sections.

Planning Your Organization's Directory Tree

To begin planning your directory tree, look first at your organization's structure, functions, and needs. NDS is designed to reflect a hierarchical structure. Generally, this means that your directory tree will be patterned according to the structure of your organization, whether or not that structure is formal.

For example, if your organization is formally divided into departments, you may decide to structure your directory tree by departments as well. On the other hand, if people in several departments work together on long-term projects and need access to common resources, it may make more sense to divide your tree by project teams instead of departments. Also consider the location. If users exist at more than one site, you will want to reflect that in the tree.

When planning your directory tree, also consider who will be running the network. With NetWare, you can centralize network administration so that a single person or small group of people controls the entire directory database, or you can distribute administration so that many network administrators throughout the enterprise control their own portions of the directory database.

If network administration will be distributed among several people, it is crucial that those people be involved in planning the network. They must also be kept informed of all decisions and rules made about creating and naming objects, assigning security, and so on. Otherwise, there is no way to ensure the consistency that makes NDS so powerful. Designing by committee always has its downfalls, but in this case, designing in a vacuum could be even worse. Making massive, fundamental changes to a directory tree once it has been established can be difficult.

Designing the directory tree so that every network administrator is happy could become a political issue, but in most cases, a smooth outcome is in everyone's best interest. Therefore, try to concentrate on simplifying the hierarchy as much as possible. Then publish a description of all rules and guidelines for naming objects and defining information about those objects. Published guidelines make it much easier for network administrators to create new users with correct e-mail names, consistent addresses and phone numbers, and so on.

At some point in the directory-tree planning stage, someone may suggest that different portions of the organization could have separate directory trees. Resist this temptation. There are several problems with having multiple trees. The point of NDS is to unify the organization's network resources. Having separate trees defeats this. Finally, though it is possible to merge two trees after they've been created, it is much easier to set up a single tree in the beginning.

If the reason people want two or more trees is because different people or groups want to "own" their own portions of the network, it is easy to set up a single tree so that administration is distributed to different people. A single person does not have to have control of the entire directory. You can set it up so that several people each have ultimate control over their own portion of the tree.

NDS is designed in large part around the international communications specification X.500. This specification is an attempt to standardize worldwide telecommunications. Before the X.500 specification was even complete, Novell attempted to comply with as much of the specification as possible, while at the same time simplifying some of the characteristics that are not even directly related to computer networking.

The following sections explain more about planning your directory tree.

The Hierarchy of Objects

In its most basic form, your organization can probably be broken down into a beautifully simple pattern. This simple pattern is what NDS uses to organize objects in the directory tree.

There is a top-level, all-encompassing entity to which everything else belongs. This entity may be a company, an organization, an association, a government agency, a school district, or the like. In NDS, this level is called an organization object. Your directory tree must have at least one organization object.

Within the top-level entity, there may be subgroups, each of which has its particular responsibilities. These subgroups may be divisions, departments, subsidiaries, workgroup units, schools, offices, project teams, and so on. In NDS, these subgroups are called organizational unit objects. Organizational unit objects can contain other organizational unit objects as well. For example, the sales department of a company may contain sales teams called Inside Sales, Outside Sales, and Sales Support. If your organization is very small, you may not need any organizational unit objects. If your company is very large, you will probably have many levels of organizational unit objects.

Finally, within any organizational unit, you find all the individual resources of which it is comprised: people, computers, printers, and similar single entities. Each of these entities has its own object in NDS. There are server objects, user objects, printer objects, print queue objects, computer objects, and so on.

These three elements — organization objects, organizational unit objects, and single-entity objects — are what you will use to set up the hierarchy of your network.

There is a fourth level of objects that you can use if you wish, but it is less useful. The country object is an optional object that is even higher than the organization object. If your organization spans countries, you can use the country object to designate in which country each is located. However, it is better to divide a multinational organization into organizational units than into countries. We recommend against using the country object because it will make it more difficult for users to navigate the directory tree. This is explained more fully in the section on naming objects, later in this chapter. Country objects are not necessary for complying with X.500 directory services guidelines, so there really are few reasons to use the country object.

The last type of object you need to know about is the root object. The root object is the very first object in the directory tree, and it cannot be deleted or modified. All other objects, including organizations, are contained within the root object.

Container Objects Versus Leaf Objects

All of the different types of objects fall into two categories: container objects and leaf objects. Container objects can contain other objects. Country, organization, and organizational unit objects are all container objects.

Single-entity objects are leaf objects, because they cannot contain any other objects, just as a leaf on a tree cannot contain other leaves or branches. For further reading on this subject, refer to Novell's Guide to NetWare 5 Networks.

Considering Object Security in the Directory Tree

Another aspect of objects you may need to consider when planning your directory tree is object security, known as trustee rights. Just as there are NetWare trustee rights that control what users can do with directories and files, NetWare 4 and higher include an additional set of trustee rights that affect objects and their properties. These object rights and property rights control how objects can work with one another. For example, a user object might have rights to read the telephone-number property of another user object. The same user might also have the rights necessary to change the postal address property of another user object.

Like trustee rights in the file system, trustee rights for objects and properties can be inherited. If you have certain rights to a container object, you can inherit those rights and exercise them in the objects within that container. However, each object has an inherited rights filter (IRF) that can block some or all of the rights a user inherits on that object. If an IRF is applied at the container level, then inherited rights are blocked for the container object and the entire subtree below.

This concept of inherited object rights is one that may help you plan your directory tree. Grouping users with similar security needs within the same container object may simplify some network administration tasks.

Putting Yourself in the Right Context

Finding your way around the directory tree requires that you understand how objects are named and what their context is in the tree. The following sections explain these concepts.

What Is an Object's Complete Name?

Each object in the directory tree has a name, such as Fred, Anne, Queue2, or Sales_Server. Each object also has a complete name. An object's complete name in NDS is actually more of an address that indicates the object's position in the tree. An object's complete name includes the name of each container object that precedes it, all the way to the root object.

For example, to find Mary at her home, you have to know the country she lives in, the state or province, her city, her street, and finally her house number. In essence, you could say that this address actually defines Mary's complete name. "Mary Whitmore, 1200 Pennsylvania Avenue, Washington, DC, 20044-7566, USA" is a more complete definition than simply "Mary." Without all that information about Mary, you might never reach her.

Similarly, to find Mary on the network, you need to know the organization object and any organizational unit objects that contain her. If Mary is located in an organizational unit object called Sales, which is in an organizational unit called LabProducts, which is in an organization called HighTech, Mary's complete name is Mary.Sales.LabProducts.HighTech. Periods are used to separate the object names. Depending on the tasks you wish to perform, you may need to specify an object's complete name when you work with it in the directory tree.

Using Name Types

Another element of an object's name, called a name type, can complicate the picture slightly. In some cases, you may need to specify not only the complete name but also the type of object each portion of the complete name indicates. For example, Sales is an organizational unit object. To show what type of object Sales is, you use the abbreviation OU, and you would enter OU=Sales.

Each container object has its own abbreviation to indicate its name type:

C   Country
O   Organization
OU   Organizational Unit

Leaf objects all have the same name type: CN (for Common Name). Therefore, regardless of whether the leaf object is a NetWare server object, a user object, a printer object, an alias object, or any other object, its name type is CN.

Therefore, if you have to indicate Mary's complete name with name types, you must use the following syntax:

```
CN=Mary.OU=Sales.OU=Lab_Products.O=HighTech
```

This is obviously a cumbersome method of indicating an object's complete name, and it is another good reason for avoiding the use of the country object. If you use the country object, you will always have to use name types in object names. This is because with the country object, there are four possible object types, and it is more difficult for the system to know which object type you are indicating.

The Name Context

Fortunately, it is not always necessary to use an object's complete name if you are in the same name context as the object you are referring to. An object's name context is its position in the directory tree. If two objects are located in the same container object, they have the same context.

For example, suppose you are trying to tell someone else where Mary lives. If you are both already standing in the city where Mary lives, you can skip the country, state, and city in your explanation. All you need to specify is her street and house number, because all three of you are in the same context — the same city.

Similarly, in the directory tree, Mary's context is Sales.Lab_Products.HighTech. If a printer called FastPrinter is also in the organizational unit object Sales, Mary probably would not have to indicate the printer's complete name when she wants to access it, because the printer is in the same context as she is. Instead, Mary could just select the printer's partial name: FastPrinter. When Mary selects FastPrinter, NetWare will look in Mary's context (meaning within the organizational unit object Sales) for the printer.

Now suppose Mary wants to use a wide-carriage dot-matrix printer that is located in another organizational unit called Accounting. The printer's complete name is WIDE_DOTM.Accounting.Lab_Products.HighTech. Mary could enter the printer's complete name, or she could enter only the part of the printer's name that is different from Mary's own context. Mary and the WIDE-DOTM printer are both located in the Lab_products.HighTech context, so Mary would have to enter only the partial name WIDE_DOTM.Accounting in order for the system to find the printer.

Hints for Planning Contexts and Names

Because names and contexts can become confusing for users, you may want to consider the following hints:

▸ Seriously consider limiting the levels of container objects you have in your tree. Because it is difficult for users to remember long, complete names with multiple layers of organization units, try to avoid having more than two or three levels of organizational units, and keep the names as brief as possible. For instance, using the name Lab instead of Lab_Products would eliminate some typing on Mary's part.

▸ You can have up to one thousand objects in a container object.

▸ If users frequently need to access an object that is not in their context, use alias objects to simplify your user's work. For example, you could create an alias object for Accounting's WIDE_DOTM printer and put the alias object in Mary's context. Then Mary could find the printer in her own context, and she wouldn't have to remember the longer "real" name of the printer.

▸ Avoid using spaces in names when naming objects. You can use them, but they will appear as underscores in some utilities. In other utilities, you may have to enclose the name in quotations marks to avoid having the utilities treat the two-word name as two separate commands or objects.

Windows NT or Windows 2000 Server Edition

Microsoft Windows NT or the more recently released Windows 2000 Server Edition offers a comparable alternative to NetWare, with some distinct differences. Windows NT offers the advantage of keeping your entire network operating on Microsoft. This operating system is an easy to use interface that offers good network security features and is easy to install.

Windows is a good choice for anyone who is looking for a networking environment that easily interacts with other NOSs, like Novell NetWare. The newest release offers cross-synchronization or two-way synchronization capabilities so that network administrators can update information throughout the network regardless of the network platform.

Windows does not handle directory services the same way as NetWare's NDS. Windows uses Active Directory Service (ADS). NDS works best where users rights map to business hierarchy. Hence, a supervisor can see more information than each of the individual employees while employees cannot automatically see each other's information. Rights to files or directories are inherited along a tree. This dynamic inheritance is useful in high-security applications where all users from a group can be locked out by changing the security in the hierarchy.

ADS uses a different form for inheritance that is static. ADS users rights and rules are determined when he or she logs on. The user gets a token based on all groups he or she belongs to and permissions are governed by the token. Unlike NDS, rights in ADS are not inherited in a hierarchy. Developed as one member of an entire family of products, the server edition is part of Microsoft's BackOffice suite. BackOffice also includes a database program, two electronic mail programs, Internet and mainframe access software, and a system management program for managing large networks.

Banyan Systems VINES

Banyan offered a robust NOS called VINES, which was discontinued in late 1999. This network system supported UNIX, DOS, Windows, OS/2 and Macintosh users as clients. VINES, much like NetWare and Windows, provided basic file and printer services.

Similar to Novell NDS and Microsoft ADS, VINES had its own directory name service. StreetTalk allowed every resource on a Banyan VINES network to be addressed by name with the addresses stored in a distributed database. This made objects easy to access and manage. Although StreetTalk didn't offer as complex an architecture as NDS, it was a pioneer in creating a very robust database. For example, in a StreetTalk environment, if Sam has a Hewlett-Packard network printer in his office and Sally has the exact same kind of printer in her office two floors up, and both are running off the same network server, StreetTalk's attribute indicator will show whose office each printer is located in. In other words, StreetTalk takes out the confusion of selecting the right object for the right job.

Macintosh

Though many attempts have been made by Macintosh to gain a competitive edge in the computer networking market, to date they've been, by and large, unsuccessful. That's not to say that they're out of the race.

With the latest estimates putting Mac users at somewhere between ten and fifteen million, Macintosh still commands a large and loyal customer base, both end-user and industry alike. In business and industry, however, users are primarily in specific departmental areas.

Mac's network operating system, AppleTalk, is used by some very large corporate customers, and Macintosh perfected the icon-based graphical user interface concept.

AppleTalk networks are fairly simple to set up and offer many of the same advantages as other, more common operating systems, including the ability to accommodate IBM PC-compatible computers. As an added advantage, all Macintosh computers come configured with a ready-to-use AppleTalk networking port installed.

However, Macintosh has been slow to catch up to the increasing demands of growing LANs and WANs. AppleTalk networks are slow compared to high-speed network systems like Ethernet. Apple does, however, include a high-speed Ethernet solution, EtherTalk, which is compatible with other Ethernet networks.

Linux

Deriving from UNIX, Linux, an operating system available in the public domain, is getting some support as a NOS. Linux is a very fast and efficient operating system but current versions lack scalability features. At the time of this writing, there is no Linux multiprocessor support, albeit one is expected to be released soon. OpenLinux also currently lacks a certificate server.

While it is still a maturing operating environment, Linux shouldn't be counted out of selection decisions. For now, however, Linux may be best positioned as an application server rather than a network server.

IBM OS/2

While it has a smaller market share, IBM maintains support for its own network operating system. It's called OS/2 Warp Server. Originally developed through an ill-fated joint effort between IBM and Microsoft, this Operating System/2 (OS/2) was to be the IBM PC-compatible answer to the 640K RAM barrier, providing high-level simultaneous security programs, and allowing dynamic exchange of information between different applications.

In spite of this highly publicized venture between the two biggest players in the computer business at the time, IBM and Microsoft's new breed of operating system had no real future.

While OS/2 was poorly running the few software programs developed for it, Microsoft was vigorously developing the MS-DOS graphical user interface we now know as Windows. By the time Windows 3.0 hit the streets, industry support for OS/2 began to wither in the shadow of the Microsoft Windows craze.

Today, after several major overhauls, OS/2 primarily provides storage protection and preemptive multitasking services for server platforms, and is used as a back end for such applications as distributed databases.

Although OS/2 has sustained only a small niche market, it's important to know that this particular NOS is available. We recommend, however, that if you consider using one of the less popular NOSs like OS/2 or Macintosh, make sure you're using it for what it can offer in flexibility, compatibility, expandability, and most importantly, survivability.

As you can see, your options for networking software are many. Let us assure you, we've just scratched the surface on a few of the most popular available. Please take the information we've given you and seek out more specific information on the NOSs you feel are best suited to meet your networking needs.

Client Operating Systems

Your network clients, from PCs to PDAs will also have their own operating systems. Likely candidates include Windows, Windows CE, Palm OS, BeOS, MacOS, Unix, or Linux. Java based clients or specialized operating systems will add to the mix of what clients connect to the NOS.

For the industry, interoperability is a goal — but not always realized. When you select a NOS, make sure that you can support all your client operating systems. Also, watch out for compatibility with new operating environments as more digital appliances emerge. With cell phones downloading address books and watches serving as appointment calendars, you can expect that someday every device will talk to every other device.

Summary

As you can see, shopping for an OS is a lot like shopping for a new car. Each make of automobile offers slightly different comforts and levels of sophistication. But when you get right down to it, they're still cars. The question is, do you want to ride in a Cadillac or a VW Beetle? Should you buy a utility vehicle or something economical? These questions are similar to the ones you should ask yourself when considering the operating system that's just right for you. Select the one that will provide the types of services and capabilities specifically associated with the type of LAN you build. After all, a carpenter can't haul much lumber in a Miata. In the next chapter, we discuss choosing the right hardware.

CHAPTER 10

Choosing Hardware

Many people begin networking by choosing the hardware. But this chapter appears near the end of this book because hardware choices should be made only after you understand topology, cable, networking gear, and software choices. In the following pages, we consider such hardware as file servers, workstations, and print servers. Hardware must be matched to the task it is expected to perform. Unless we begin with an empty office, we don't always have the luxury of starting from scratch. Most companies accumulate an assortment of PCs and printers of various makes and configurations prior to tying them all together as a LAN.

Sometimes equipment can be upgraded to handle any increase in load the network places on hardware, but often it's more cost effective either to keep only that hardware that fits squarely into the planned architecture or just start completely from scratch. Today, with the price of new equipment lower than ever, costs associated with upgrading existing equipment often exceed the cost of buying all new components. The hardware market is very competitive, and hardware technology has a short life span.

If your network were a person, the server would be the heart; the software the brain; the cables the arteries, veins, and nervous system; and the workstations the hands, feet, and smaller organs. If the heart stops beating, the entire body dies. If the brain stops working, the body continues living but cannot work. If we lose a hand or a foot, the body continues living but is disabled. This analogy will be used throughout the chapter and helps us understand how to budget appropriately for hardware.

Always purchase the highest quality hardware you can afford. When cutting corners on network hardware, use the analogy of the body. The heart (server) needs to be the strongest part of the network. The circulatory system (cables) is next in importance. You don't want them to get clogged. The workstation is the only place that corners can be cut. If a single workstation is down, or not operating, the rest of the company continues. If the server is down, so is the entire company.

When you are considering less expensive workstations, calculate what any lost productivity will cost the organization. What does it cost to have an employee sitting around waiting for repairs or a replacement computer? The price difference between clones and name brands has drawn closer. Name brands usually offer longer warranties, help desks, and even on-site service. Do the math and make the best decision for your organization.

▶ · ◀

Workstations

Workstations are the last link in the network, often referred to as network nodes. Workstations are configured according to the job they are expected to do. A data entry clerk who enters accounting data into the database does not need the power of an engineer using a 3-D modeling program or the chief financial officer running company-wide sales projections in a spreadsheet.

Workstations access the server, run local software programs, handle network traffic and communicate with attached peripherals such as tape drive backups, CD-ROM drives, modems, printers, and scanners. Diskless workstations, PCs without a hard drive and/or floppy drive (more commonly known as network computers), can be utilized if the user does not need local programs or data and can run all the applications needed from the server. They are also advantageous when all management functions, such as software updates, need to be performed centrally. Most workstations today are IBM-compatible microcomputers or PCs. A minority of workstations are Macintosh. Compatibles are not all created equal. Name brands cost a few dollars more than clones, but they typically use better components, have longer warranties, and have better support options.

It's hard to retire working equipment that shows no signs of failing anytime soon, but the increase in productivity can justify the cost for a better workstation. The general rule of thumb in the computer industry is to expect to get four years from equipment. This time can be stretched if the state-of-the-art or the fastest and largest workstation available is purchased.

A workstation is composed of a motherboard, CPU, accessory cards, keyboard, monitor, mouse, and other attached peripherals. The motherboard is the main board on the computer that memory and accessory cards are plugged into. A CPU is the processor and determines the speed of the computer. Processor speed is referred to in megahertz (Mhz) and usually names the model of processor. For example, a Pentium III 800 refers to an Intel Pentium III processor running at 800 Mhz. Accessory cards add functions to the computer, and include modems, sound cards, and other peripheral-controlling cards.

Next, we discuss the components that affect our selection of workstations for the network.

Memory

Random access memory (RAM) is the component of the computer that executes programs and stores data before it is written to the disk. Most PCs come with two to four memory slots on the motherboard. RAM comes in a variety of flavors including the older single in-line memory module (SIMM) and the newer dual in-line memory module (DIMM). SIMMs utilize 32 data bit dynamic RAM (DRAM) chips. DIMMs utilize 64 data bit synchronous dynamic RAM (SDRAM) chips.

When working with SIMMs, select the largest SIMM the motherboard can handle. This leaves room for expansion later as the need arises for additional memory. If the motherboard has four memory slots and all slots are filled with 4MB SIMMs the only way to upgrade memory is to remove some or all of the memory and buy all new memory. If one slot is populated with a single 4MB SIMM, three slots are left for future expansion. SIMMs must be added in pairs on Pentium processors. A Pentium with 64MB RAM will have two 32MB SIMMs installed. DIMMs, however, need not be installed in pairs, and may be added, or upgraded, individually.

Originally SIMMs were 3.5 inches long and had 30 pins. Newer SIMMs are 4.5 inches long and have 72 pins, as illustrated in Figure 10.1. To further complicate matters, SIMMs can use either 9-bit memory (8 bits plus a parity bit) or 8-bit memory without parity. SIMMs also differ in the number of memory chips soldered to the SIMM board that make up the total memory. Some computers can mix SIMM types and others cannot. When upgrading your PC, if you're not sure what chips your PC takes, make sure whatever you buy is returnable, or have a PC technician do the upgrade. Technicians have most varieties on hand and will find the one that works on your system.

DIMMs have 168 pins, and purchasing may becoming confusing due to the different memory speeds on the market today. To keep up with accelerating CPU speeds, companies have come up with new memory technology. DIMMs may be labeled PC100, meaning it runs at 100 Mhz, the same speed as many system buses. As cautioned above, do some inspection into which type of RAM is compatible with your system before you try and upgrade. The motherboard manufacturer's Web site should contain detailed information about compatible memory chips and types.

Memory requirements are dictated by the programs to be run, type of internal OS, and network OS. Software and network vendors will provide minimum and optimum memory requirements for their respective programs. Always purchase the most memory you can afford. A slower machine with more memory will often run a program faster than a faster machine with less memory. It is better to have too much memory than not enough. A good rule of thumb is to check the memory requirement on the software box and double or triple it. Windows and graphical interfaces in particular require a lot. Try to budget for the optimum suggested memory instead of the minimum.

FIGURE 10.1

72-pin SIMM

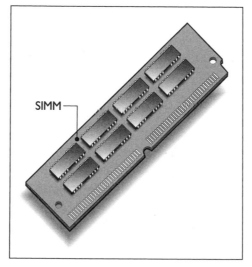

SIMM—

Most users today are multitasking. Multitasking is the running of two or more programs at the same time on a single computer. Mainframes and minicomputers have always multitasked, but the PC was originally designed to do one thing at a time. The advent of Windows made it possible for PCs to multitask.

Two terms that go with multitasking are foreground and background. The foreground program is the one the user is currently working on, and the background program is whatever is running behind the scenes, such as a print spooler or spreadsheet recalculation. Priority is given to the process in the foreground, but if the process in the background is disk or CPU intensive, a slowdown of the foreground program occurs. Users sometimes think that they are multitasking when they have multiple programs open in multiple windows, but really they are just suspending and resuming programs when needed. True multitasking is running multiple processes simultaneously; therefore, the maximum memory possible should be installed to reduce slowdowns and increase productivity.

Processing Speed

Processing speed is the function of the CPU and is measured by the number of instructions that can be performed in a period of time. Intel Pentium chips are the most common CPUs in use today. Each CPU class comes in various speeds measured in megahertz (MHz). To further confuse matters, manufacturers have doubled, tripled, and quadrupled internal clock speeds to increase performance. This does not increase the speed and power incrementally and should only be used as a guide to system performance and power. All components must be matched to provide the best performance.

Processing speed is also a function of the bus, accessory cards, memory, and hard drive interfaces installed in the computer. The processor or CPU can only communicate as fast as the other components in the system. A fast CPU can process data faster than the video, hard drive, or interfaces to other peripherals. We examine these other components in later sections.

The processor plugs into the motherboard, as seen in Figure 10.2. The motherboard affects processor speed because it includes the cache and the bus for the accessory cards. The cache is an additional memory that stores frequently used data and reads and writes the data when the other peripherals are ready for it. The cache acts as a buffer between memory and the CPU. The bigger the cache, the better. The most common sizes are 256K and 512K, but we suggest 512K as a minimum.

Remember that a faster CPU can only pass data to the hard drive, video, and other peripherals as fast as the device can receive them. If all the components are not replaced, performance gains will not be as great as expected. Again, the costs associated with examining the system, finding appropriate upgrade chips and installing them are often greater than the cost of a new workstation.

Bus Performance

The bus is the highway your data travels on. Data travels along this highway between the CPU, monitor, hard drive, and other peripherals. The CPU internal bus, or local bus, operates faster than peripheral buses. The popular bus varieties are *Peripheral Component Interconnect (PCI), Universal Serial Bus (USB), IEEE 1394 High Performance Serial Bus, Industry Standard Architecture (ISA), Extended Industry Standard Architecture (EISA),* and *Video Electronics Standards Association (VESA).* Each handles data in a different manner and at different speeds. A highway with six lanes and a 70 mph speed limit can handle more cars or data faster than a single lane residential road, so select the fastest and widest bus you can afford. The bus is usually the bottleneck in any computer, so it's important to know the difference between the various types.

A CPU on a motherboard

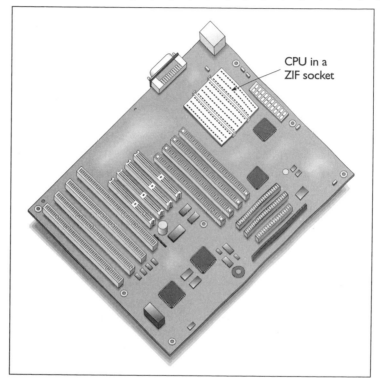

CPU in a
ZIF socket

ISA is the slowest and oldest of the buses. In the past, the vast majority of expansion cards were ISA. Most PCI and VESA computers, however, still have a few ISA expansion slots for backward compatibility. ISA cards are either 8-bit (half cards) or 16-bit (full cards). A half card can fit in any ISA slot, but a full card can only be inserted in a full slot. Half and full slots are readily identified by their respective lengths and the number of pins they accept. ISA cards will fit in all EISA slots.

An EISA bus doubles the ISA 16-bit path to 32-bits, but still uses the same 8MHz clock speed as the ISA card to maintain backward compatibility with it. EISA slots accept all ISA cards. For this reason, VESA and PCI cards are faster than EISA.

Local buses such as the PCI bus and the VESA local bus (also known as VL-Bus and VLB) talk directly to the CPU's internal bus at the same, or nearly the same, speed. They are faster than ISA and EISA because the VLB runs at 40MHz and PCI runs at 33MHz.

Universal Serial Bus, or USB, is a high speed method for connecting peripherals to the CPU. Running at a current maximum speed of 12Mbps, devices are hot-pluggable (can be added or removed to the system while it is powered up, and without rebooting). This standard gained popularity in 1999 as a common interface for everything from scanners to printers to digital cameras.

The IEEE 1394 High Performance Serial Bus, commonly referred to as "FireWire," provides a single socket for connecting up to 63 peripheral devices. Similar to USB, devices on this bus interface are hot-pluggable. Current implementations of 1394 communicate at speeds ranging from 100Mbps to 400Mpbs. The next implementation of 1394 will have speeds ranging from 800Mbps to 3200Mbps. This bus is well suited for bandwidth demanding applications such as video editing and mass storage.

Cards

Thousands of expansion cards are available that will add to a workstation's usefulness. Each card is designed to do either a single job or a number of jobs. Cards exist for video, multimedia, modem, voicemail, fax, hard drive controllers, tape drive controllers, CD-ROM controllers . . . the list is endless. Rather than discuss all available cards, we cover the most popular and most frequently used accessory cards.

Motherboards are manufactured with three to seven expansion slots. Make sure your workstation has enough expansion slots to accept all the cards you want to add. As the previous section on bus speed explains, you want to select cards that use the fastest bus available in the motherboard. Most motherboards come with both PCI and backward-compatible ISA slots. The bus is usually the bottleneck in system performance, so take advantage of the fastest bus available.

Video Cards

Every workstation must have a video card. This card, seen in Figure 10.3, communicates to the monitor and translates computer code to graphics and text on the screen. Video cards have their own memory on board, and the more graphic-intensive a program is, the more memory it needs. Older programs use mostly text screens with very little graphics or pictures.

WYSIWYG (What You See Is What You Get) programs display on the screen exactly what the printer will print. Graphics address the screen by pixels, which are the size of a pin point. It is now possible to display millions of colors in high resolution. The video card controls the speed at which the screen is refreshed or repainted and the speed of the memory on the card buffers, or it stores video information to help speed screen painting.. Simple DOS programs can use 256K or 512K video cards, but any workstation running Windows should have at least 1MB of memory on the video card.

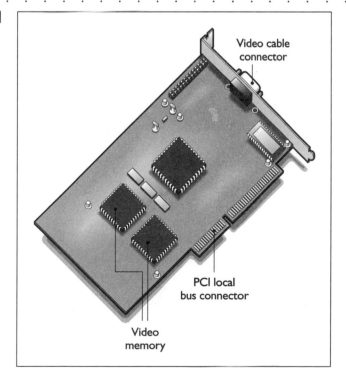

FIGURE 10.3

A standard video card

Video cable connector

PCI local bus connector

Video memory

Multi-I/O Cards

Another card found in all workstations is the Multi-Input/Output (Multi-I/O) card. These cards control the hard drives, floppy drives, and communication ports. Most cards provide two serial ports and one or two parallel ports. Serial ports are used for modems, mice, scanners, and some printers. The parallel ports are used for printers and some special peripherals such as tape drives and external CD-ROM drives.

Hard Disk Controllers

The most common hard drive controllers for workstations are the integrated drive electronics (IDE) and the increasingly popular enhanced IDE (EIDE). The EIDE permits more and larger drives to be installed in the system in addition to faster access and enhanced features over IDE.

The Small Computer System Interface (SCSI) is by far the most popular for servers and larger workstations. SCSI devices transfer data to and from the hard drive at up to 80Mbps, much faster than the IDE and EIDE interfaces. They can also accept from seven to fifteen devices attached to the same controller. Choose the controller that is most cost effective for your application.

CD-ROM Controllers

A CD-ROM controller may be found on nearly all workstations and servers today. Due to the high storage capacity of the CD-ROM, the ease of application installation, and the ability to boot from this drive, it has become a computer standard. Normally, the CD-ROM controller is built into the motherboard.

Modems and Fax Cards

Modem and fax cards, such as the one seen in Figure 10.4, are prevalent on many workstations. Since most faxes originate on the PC, it makes sense to fax directly from the desktop instead of printing the document and standing by the fax machine while it sends. Fax/modems (all-in-one) can be installed internally for convenience or externally if desired. Modems also allow access to e-mail, the Internet, and remote offices or home computers. Fax/modems can also be installed and shared on the network. A communication program routes faxes to a single fax/modem or bank of modems and sends the fax when a port becomes available. This eliminates the need for a modem and phone line for each workstation. Modems are now available that also provide voicemail in addition to fax and data transfer.

▶ • ◀

FIGURE 10.4

A fax/modem card

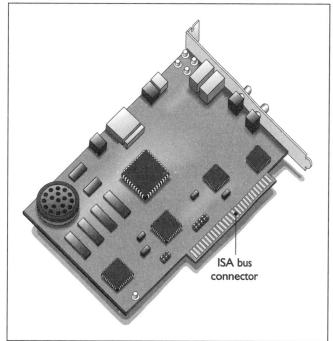

ISA bus
connector

Network Interface Cards

The last card we discuss is the network interface card (NIC), pictured in Figure 10.5. The NIC must be matched to the topology and cables of the network. Cards can be purchased for a single type of network, or combo cards can handle a variety of cable types. Combo cards usually have Thin LAN, Thick LAN, and Ethernet UTP connections. These cards are useful if workstations are moved or a cabling change is imminent. Again, we cannot emphasize enough the importance of purchasing an NIC that uses the fastest bus available on the motherboard. NICs are not the place to save money on a network. Network cards range in price because of their distinct differences. A good, medium-priced card from a reputable company that specializes in networking equipment is your the best choice.

F I G U R E   10.5

A network interface card

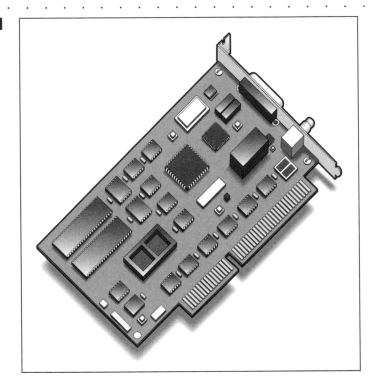

Servers

Everything we discussed about workstations applies to servers. The only difference is the magnitude and scalability of the system. A server is not simply a larger and more powerful workstation, although that was the trend for many years. The server is the heart of your network. It should be the strongest link in your LAN topology. Servers need larger hard drives and more memory to handle all the traffic from users accessing it. You may also want to provide fault tolerance for the hard drives.

Larger networks have multiple servers for applications, databases, engineering, and communications. The term *file server* refers to the most common server that stores applications and files for use across the network. *Database servers* store and retrieve data from a database.

A *print server* handles printing services. A print server can be a microcomputer with printers attached, or it can be a hardware device that handles print spooling or storing output from users and managing when the output is sent to the printer. The *communication server* handles modems and fax/modems and is sometimes called a *modem pool.*

Instead of providing each user with a modem and phone line, a few modems attached to a communications server can service an entire network. Faxes are placed in a queue and sent when the fax modem is free. Users can request a modem for dial out purposes and are notified when one becomes available. Modems can also be configured to accept incoming faxes and permit remote access to the network. A single server fulfills all these functions in a small network, but in larger networks it is advantageous to distribute the communication to a separate server.

Hardware

Desktop, minitower, full tower, rack mount — what size do I need for my network? The answer lies in the projected use and the peripherals to be attached to the server. The main difference is the number of drive bays and number of expansion slots.

The desktop server is only useful in the smallest of networks because of limited drive bays. The smallest acceptable server should have at least five drive bays. It is amazing how quickly the bays become filled with hard drives, CD-ROMs, and a tape drive. Expansion slots are also filled quickly with network cards, SCSI controllers, video cards, and modems. Top-of-the-line servers have external, hot-swappable drive bays, which can be removed and replaced without downing the server (logging off all users, unloading network software, and turning off the server). This is very desirable in mission-critical applications where downtime is unacceptable.

Some rack mount servers are motherboards that install into a large rack that provides power to all the computers. This saves space in large installations where many servers would clutter the computer room. Switches can be installed that share a single keyboard, mouse, and monitor with all the processors. Internal components are easily accessible by opening a door and sliding the component out, instead of opening a case.

Rack mount servers also support symmetric multiprocessing (SMP). A single operating system is loaded in memory and multiple CPUs share the processing. The SMP advantage is scalability — processors can be added when needed to handle additional traffic. SMP computers can also be used on the desktop, but are used most often as servers.

CPU selection in a server should be made carefully. The use of the server determines the level of CPU needed. In true client-server applications, the processing is occurring at the client or workstation. The CPU is managing data storage and retrieval, which is less CPU intensive. A mission critical application or database server needs the fastest CPU available. Servers running accounting programs that process large amounts of data need all the horsepower they can get. Servers used for simple file storage can use a slower CPU. With rapidly growing demands on the server, and CPU prices dropping, it makes little sense to skimp on processing speed.

Another consideration is fault tolerance and diagnostic software. Major manufacturers include diagnostic software that predicts failure, keeps the server running even though a component may fail, and can recover automatically from failures. Predictive software alerts the network manager to potential failures by monitoring system performance and predicting possible problems. Fault-tolerant software can shut down the server in an orderly manner, without losing data, in the event someone accidentally pulls the plug or reboots the computer.

Warranties

The server is the place to buy the best quality you can afford. Servers from the prominent manufacturers come with extended, on-site warranties. Do you want to cease doing business while the server is carried to a service center for repair? Of course not. Let's discuss some warranty terms.

On-site means that the manufacturer comes to your office to repair the unit. Depot or carry-in service means the server must be carried by the customer to a shipping depot that either has a repair shop or ships the unit to a repair shop. Read the warranty before purchasing, not after.

Extended and expanded warranties are offered by most manufacturers. Extended warranties extend the time period equipment is covered. Expanded warranties expand the scope of services. Most on-site warranties provide for service within one business day, meaning a call made on Friday will be answered Monday before 5:00 p.m. This only guarantees the system will be diagnosed. If the technician needs additional parts, the repair takes longer. The maximum coverage available covers equipment twenty-four hours a day, seven days a week, with four hour or less response time.

Wherever possible, try to use the same manufacturer for all components, such as hard drives and memory. Warranty work is simpler and finger pointing is eliminated. For instance, if generic memory or a different brand hard drive is installed in a name brand server, the repair technician cannot replace the memory or the drive. Using all the same brand components greatly simplifies warranty work.

Memory

Server memory should be calculated by a network technician. Factors that affect memory usage are the network OS, number of users, volume size, software to be run, and desired performance. An equation is used, factoring all the variables, to arrive at the optimum memory size. Too little memory on the server can even cause crashes. Use the largest DIMMs to provide room for expansion later. Purchase the best quality memory modules available or memory modules from the server manufacturer. Once again, memory provided by the server manufacturer is tested in the server and makes your life and the technician's life simpler.

Disk Space

You can never be too rich or have enough disk space. Calculate the disk space you think you need and double or triple it. Storage space has steadily dropped in price, so cost shouldn't be a factor. Hard drives are rated for their access rate and spin speed. The faster the spin and the lower the access time, the faster the drive is. SCSI drives are the best choice for servers, as they provide faster throughput and therefore better response time.

Everyone is always complaining about the lack of disk space. However, disk space is usually not the problem. The problem is typically file management. Users are notorious for saving multiple copies of the same document, and should be encouraged to practice good file maintenance. Network managers make copies of entire directories and then forget to purge them. Programs create temporary files and backup files that never go away until someone manually removes them. Files that haven't been used for a certain period of time should be purged. Disk space must be managed by someone in the organization. Technicians have reported freeing as much as 30 percent of a disk from never-used, seldom-used, not-used-for-years, and duplicate files.

Many drive options are on the market that provide fault tolerance and redundancy. These schemes produce a system that almost never goes down. Each scheme has its benefits and drawbacks. We will discuss duplexing, mirroring, and the various levels of *Redundant Arrays of Inexpensive Disks* (RAID).

Duplexing

Duplexing duplicates hard drives, controllers, and power supplies and writes to both drives at the same time. If a drive system goes down, the other takes over with no change in response time.

Mirroring

Mirroring spreads data across two different drives by duplicating the data on one drive and storing it on another (or by repeating data on two different locations on the same drive). If the mirroring writes to two different drives, the system can continue if a drive goes down.

RAID

No, we're not endorsing a bug spray. We're referring to methods of data redundancy and fault tolerance. RAID uses drive arrays, which are two or more disks working together.

RAID 0 is *data stripping*, or spreading data across more than one disk. This speeds transfer rates but does nothing for fault tolerance. If a disk goes down, the data on that disk is lost. If the data is in the middle of a file, the entire file is often lost.

RAID 1 is the same as *disk mirroring*. The disadvantage is that both drives must match. A server with a large, expensive primary drive must have a second, large, expensive drive.

RAID 2 provides fault tolerance by *interleaving data*, or spreading data across several disks. This system can rebuild a failed disk from error correction data spread across the other disks.

RAID 3 is a popular process that transfers data to many disks and stores parity data on a dedicated parity drive. *Parity* is the ninth bit of either a zero or a one depending on the data in the byte. This is checked for accuracy and notifies the user of an error. One byte is written at a time and the controller only permits a single write at a time.

RAID 4 is almost the same as RAID 3, except it permits *multiple writes* at the same time.

RAID 5 is the most popular method. The data and parity information is spread across all the drives in the array with no dedicated parity drive. Performance is boosted by simultaneous reads and writes. Errors that occur on writes can be corrected from the error correcting data.

The bottom line is, if you are willing to pay for redundancy, a system can be designed that, theoretically, can never go down, barring natural disaster. Natural disaster can also be provided for by spreading redundant servers across a WAN in different cities. The days of chronic network crashes are over.

Drive Mapping

Drive mapping is a way of organizing directories on the disk into logical trees and assigning the paths to drive letters. This enables users to find their data quickly and effortlessly. The directory SALES/CORPORATE/SOUTHERN/DATA can be mapped to a drive letter whereby the user simply needs to type F:, or simply double-click on the icon associated with the logical drive, to access that directory. The user is shielded from remembering and typing the long path name, and security can be set according to user, to allow only authorized access to the F drive. This is not a physical drive, as in DOS, where a drive letter denotes a specific piece of hardware such as a floppy, hard drive, or CD-ROM. The mapped drive is a logical drive, and the operating system treats it as if it were a physical drive. Drive mapping is simple when you consider the logical place to put data and files, and who is permitted access to that data.

Print Servers

Print servers control printing to shared network printers by acting as a traffic cop that controls the flow of print jobs. If Sally and Sam both sent a letter to the same printer without the benefit of a print server traffic cop, the document printer might print part of Sam's letter and part of Sally's letter on the same page. The traffic cop permits the output from a program to go to the printer while holding other print requests until that job is completed. When that job is completed, the next print request is sent to the printer. This prevents print output from crashing into each other, confusing the printer and users.

Print servers are workstations or hardware devices specifically designed for the task. A workstation print server can have as many printers attached as there are ports on the PC. Hardware print servers are available with combinations of parallel and serial ports in various numbers. The same distance restrictions apply for network printers as for DOS printers. Parallel printers are suggested to be within 15 feet of the port and serial printers can be up to 50 feet or more away. This distance limitation is important when placing the print server. All printers attached to the print server must be within the suggested distance, unless you use a distance-extending device. Larger networks employ multiple print servers, strategically placed for users' convenience.

Summary

We hope you've gained an understanding of the significance of selecting hardware when planning your network. We suggest that you carefully consider the aspects of LAN computing in the order that we've outlined in this book, because all considerations are uniformly connected.

Network Management Responsibilities and Tools

When is the last time you heard these words: "I'm sorry, I can't help you right now because the server's down. We'll have to wait until the systems people get things back online." A very frustrating experience, isn't it? It's in situations like this when the skills of the network manager are the most crucial. It's also when the LAN architect's principles of design and implementation show their true colors — a well planned success or an embarrassing failure.

In this chapter, we don't spend a lot of time discussing the intricate details of LAN management, but we do familiarize you with many of the general responsibilities and management tools associated with the subject.

Before a LAN can be properly managed, however, a person must be identified to do the managing. This person is usually referred to as the network administrator, network manager, or system engineer. No matter what title this person holds, the job is crucial; duties need to be assigned carefully.

What the Network Administrator Does

If you become the network administrator, you've got your work cut out for you. As a key member of the technology team, you are responsible for installing, maintaining, and troubleshooting the network. You'll need to develop good technical skills as well as good communication skills.

Good communications skills are essential for your success in this role. Stay in touch with the specific goals and objectives your company has established and create a LAN that will function toward meeting them. Keep abreast of departmental changes, for this will allow for more easy and open discussion with the various department managers. Managers, in turn, gain a better understanding of how the LAN uses their data and can then improve on the uses of the data their department generates. Have you ever known a department manager to refuse ideas that will improve the productivity of the staff? Attend departmental meetings, if possible. This gives users a recurring opportunity to express any specific needs or problems they are experiencing. It also gives you the opportunity to provide instant feedback regarding potential or realized solutions. As Network administrator, it is incumbent upon you to think logically, be impeccably organized, and have the skills to develop methodical, recurring task lists.

As Network administrator, dealing effectively and efficiently with people is a skill you constantly work to improve. After all, computers aren't your customers; people are. Constantly look for opportunities to build your one-on-one and group communication skills. Don't just communicate electronically. When possible, spend the time to meet with users as individuals. Let them see a face on the other end of the LAN. Presentations that provide valuable information, group training, and answers to questions are an excellent forum for developing relationships with your customers.

Keep in mind, however, that your responsibilities go well beyond your people skills. You must hone technical skills as well. You will provide technical assistance to your customers in the form of technical reports, online and in-person support, and advice to key decision makers regarding the use of technology within the company. Therefore, as Network administrator you must possess technical expertise that covers a broad range of skills. These skills fall into three major categories, each containing categorical tasks:

- **Maintaining and operating the LAN**
  - Managing files and hardware
  - Organizing directories, files, and hardware
  - Setting up users and access control
  - Allocating disk space
  - Planning for and performing disaster recovery
  - Backing up the network
  - Monitoring performance
  - Providing LAN security
  - Providing risk management for networks
  - Troubleshooting

- **Enhancing the network**
  - Assessing software and hardware products
  - Optimizing LAN performance

- Expanding the network

- Internetworking

▶ **Administering network operations**

- Creating documentation

- Managing support for users

- Developing training for users

- Managing LAN configuration

- Keeping technology current

Add to this the ability to identify and replace failed or malfunctioning equipment and, in some cases, read complex wiring diagrams or technical manuals.

In today's fast moving world of network computing, sometimes even the most seasoned network engineers have difficulty keeping up with the dynamic changes. It is for this reason that the concept of network management was born.

LAN management is not merely a skill, it's also specially designed management tools in the form of hardware and software. Refer to Chapter 7 to review several network management options designed to assist Network administrators in their role.

Equally important as these electronic tools is attitude. The systemic responsibility of managing a LAN is just as important as the know-how. What do we mean by *systemic responsibility*? Perhaps it's best characterized as good habits.

Good Habits to Follow

Just as an automobile engine needs proper care and maintenance to operate smoothly, a LAN requires preventive maintenance and some tender loving care as well. If sound management and maintenance habits are formed during the earliest stages of LAN development and implementation, they're more likely to continue as the network grows.

No, we're not talking about washing and waxing your servers and PCs every Saturday. Preventive maintenance for your network consists of:

► Properly documenting system configurations

► Installing proper power supplies and power backup systems

► Maintaining cables

► Periodic removal of unnecessary data from hard drives

► Establishing data backup and archiving routines

Part of system maintenance does involve cleaning tasks. Dust is an enemy of computer hardware. Although your servers are stable and don't require too much care, make sure the area remains as dust free as possible. Layers of dust, especially on computer parts, can cause overheating.

As the organization's network administrator, you should not have to spend all of your time maintaining the LAN. Establish daily, weekly, monthly, and yearly routines. Daily routine tasks may include the following:

► Adding users

► Cleaning up the file server hard disk drive

► Installing software upgrades

► Making backups

► Restoring damaged or lost files

► Monitoring traffic

► Collecting accounting data

► Generating reports for management

Weekly routine tasks may include:

▶ Monitoring and evaluating network performance

▶ Managing and documenting the network configuration

▶ Exploring and appraising new hardware and software technology

Establishing and continuing good habits like these will pay big dividends when problems do arise, because, as illustrated in the opening sentences of this chapter when the system goes down, productivity usually goes with it. While there is no guarantee a well managed LAN will never go down, remember, it's easier to find a pin in a cushion than to find one in a haystack.

Now that we've discussed starting with good habits, let's talk about bringing skill and attitude together to manage the LAN.

▶ . . . . ◀

What LAN Management Involves

By now you realize all the planning, decision making, and expense involved in developing a well designed networking system. Don't let all of your hard work go to waste by allowing poor management to continue unchallenged. Exert just as much effort into putting solid management practices in place to protect your investment.

Simply put, LAN management is the process of controlling a complex data network to maximize its efficiency and productivity. As we mentioned in Chapter 2, the ISO Network Forum sets standards for computing. Among those standards, network management is divided into five functional areas: *fault management, configuration management, security management, performance management,* and *accounting management.* Let's quickly get a better understanding of each before going on.

Fault Management

First of all, a *fault* is a physical condition that causes a device, component, or element to fail to perform in a required manner; for example, a short circuit, a broken wire, or an intermittent connection. Therefore, *fault management* is the process of locating a fault, isolating it, and then fixing it. Locating, isolating, and fixing a fault are all aided by and almost totally dependent on good fault-tolerant systems.

The first aspect of a disaster plan is not really even a disaster plan. It is the design of the system itself. A network can be designed with manageability in mind, so that many problems (faults) can be avoided entirely, or so that in the event of a problem, recovery will be smooth and easy.

To better illustrate how fault tolerance can be designed into a system, you can look at how network operating systems manage various types of faults.

Hot Fix Redirection

Over time, hard disks develop defects. In the case of NetWare, a technique called *Read after Write Verification* is implemented to ensure the quality of disk writes. It reads back each byte of information after every write. If the data read back does not match the data written to the disk, the process is repeated. If the write fails three times, the area is marked as defective, and the block of data is written to an area of the disk specifically reserved for redirected blocks. This feature is called *Hot Fix Redirection* or *System Fault Tolerance (SFT)* Level I.

Disk Mirroring and Duplexing

With *disk mirroring*, all data written to a hard disk is also written to a second disk. If the server's disks are mirrored, the loss of a hard disk is but a minor nuisance instead of a disaster. With disk duplexing, not only are redundant disks installed, but also redundant disk controllers and cables. Then the system can bear the loss of any component in the disk channel itself. Disk mirroring and disk-channel duplexing are termed SFT Level II.

Disk Mirroring   Mirrored disks are on the same channel. That is, they are attached to the same hard-disk controller. The decision to mirror disks is made during installation or upgrades.

To mirror drives, you need at least two drives, and the second drive must be at least as large as the primary drive. If the secondary drive is larger (in data capacity), most network operating systems will not be able to use the excess hard drive space.

Disk Duplexing   Of course, hard disks are not the only components subject to failure. Disk controllers and cables can also malfunction. *Disk duplexing* is accomplished by installing redundant disks, disk controllers, and cables. All data written to the primary drive is also written to the secondary disk.

One advantage of duplexing over mirroring is that performance is better with duplexed disk controllers. NetWare has the ability to perform split seeks and retrieve information from the disk (and controller) that is closest to the read/write head, thereby improving response time for disk reads.

Configuration Management

The way your network is configured will determine how well it performs. Configuration management put in one word is *documenting*.

This is one of the good habits we talked about earlier. LAN documentation should include the physical layout (floor plans and locations of servers, workstations, printers, cables, bridges, hubs, and so on), the logical structure (login process, scripts, batch files, menus, and so on), and the network infrastructure (a graphical representation of the directory structure of each volume).

You should have a short introduction to the network for new or temporary employees so they can come up to speed as fast as possible, and more importantly, abide by the rules that you set up for system access.

All procedures should be documented. This enables quicker recovery, and it helps technical support personnel give more efficient assistance, whether it's by phone or on-site.

Make a chart of the backup schedule and the location of backup tapes. What is the rotation of tapes that are kept off-site? The list should include names and phone numbers (including pager/mobile phone numbers) of responsible support staff.

Here are the categories we've just discussed in an easy-to-follow bulleted list that you can use as a checklist when documenting your local area network.

- Set up network configuration and operations information.

- Produce network status reports and problem log.

- Create network and user workstation-configuration baseline diagrams and specifications.

- Log configuration change requests.

- Keep daily maintenance documents.

▶ Document modifications or additions of users and groups.

▶ Track installed applications.

▶ Log backups and file server restorations.

▶ Conduct expansion and emergency training.

▶ Create a network expansion plan, including internetworking.

▶ Write test plans for evaluating new products or product upgrades.

▶ Produce network security and risk-management plan.

▶ Formulate disaster recovery plan.

▶ Write user training plans and course materials.

Updating Your Documentation

Document every change to the system, problems, and service calls. If you don't keep the documentation current, there's no point in having it at all. It's difficult to be disciplined, but in the long run it is the only way to run any substantial network effectively.

Document Servers

Make a list of the hardware and software configurations for each file server. Some network operating systems manuals, Novell NetWare 4.x, for instance, come with forms for keeping track of configurations. Copy them (it's legal!) and use them.

Even better, Novell NetWare 5 has an included software utility, CONFIG.NLM, that will create a text file that contains a list of all the modules loaded in the system when the utility is run.

It also helps to print out the configuration files for each server. While you won't necessarily ever have to rekey the information, it helps to have a hard copy available to show what the server does when it starts up.

Document PC Nodes (Clients)

Print out the configuration files for each PC node. Ideally, your clients should be somewhat standardized in configuration.

Network record-keeping and configuration-management documentation is vital to maintaining and operating a successful network. When the network is being installed initially, collect a set of configuration baseline documents that include the things we've discussed: descriptions of the network components, such as cable diagrams, client computers, and file servers; complete lists of all hardware and software, including the version numbers; lists of users and groups; and lists of directories and files. Change requests should be written to document upgrades and modifications to the network hardware, software, and user information.

If some of your nodes use a static IP address, make sure you document this. Besides desktop PCs, your LAN may include a number of other nodes, like shared printers, scanners, or docking stations for notebook computers. Make sure you document the basic files, IP addresses, and other information regarding these devices.

Periodically it helps to review how many people share a device. It often happens that a workgroup starts out with 8 or 9 people sharing a color printer. Six months later, that printer could have 20 people sending jobs to it. This type of growth can cause bottle necks on the system and push printing equipment to the limits. A good set of records helps the network administrator see the growth and change of devices on the network. It's helpful — if not critical — for troubleshooting problems.

All of these suggestions and practices will go along way in assisting the network administrator in providing the best working LAN for it's users.

Security Management

Security management is the process of identifying and authenticating users and controlling or auditing logical access to network resources. Sound security management ensures the network is protected from unauthorized access, accidental or willful interference with normal operations, and destruction. This includes protection of physical facilities and software, and personal security. For more thorough coverage of this subject, refer to Chapter 12. Security becomes even more important when a network is remotely accessible via the Internet or dial-up networking. Please, take this seriously.

Performance Management

Performance management involves tuning the network to increase efficiency and productivity, as well as monitoring performance for overall throughput, percentage of utilization, error rates, and response time; analyzing the data; and optimizing the system to improve identified deficiencies.

Accounting Management

In addition to services that allow for fault, security, and performance management, most network operating systems offer built-in accounting management capabilities that track network usage by keeping a running account of the following:

- ▶ User logins and logoffs

- ▶ Disk space used by specific users and groups of users

- ▶ Network traffic generated (in packets, bytes, or both)

- ▶ Print jobs sent to network printers

- ▶ Number of pages printed

- ▶ Applications used, including when and for how long

- ▶ Changes made to security restrictions

Many of the accounting components work directly with security features and provide many opportunities for managing and auditing all aspects of network usage.

Network Management Strategy

As we've discussed throughout this book, you must have a strategy for managing your LAN. Implementing and operating a LAN without a well planned strategy is like taking a trip in a foreign country without a road map or translation dictionary: You'll eventually find your destination, but you probably won't enjoy the trip.

In your LAN management strategy, consider what you want your management system to provide, both today and in the future. A comprehensive management system should give you the basic features you need now, plus the capability of being easily upgraded as you need it.

Whatever goals you set in developing an effective LAN management system, make sure that the network management software you choose allows you to set up a management console. For instance, Novell has very good network management systems available for every level of complexity, from simple workgroup management packages to extensive LANs and WANs.

Regardless of which LAN management system you choose, most will provide very similar basic features. For example, most management systems implement their capabilities through industry-standard protocols, such as SNMP or CMIP, with the same basic goal in mind—allow the network management console the ability to collect data about the devices it is managing and generate information from that data.

This presents us with a prime opportunity to stop and take a quick look at the key component of effective LAN management—management protocols.

Management Protocols

Management protocols is the language used for communicating with and within a given network. Think of protocol as a set of conventions between communicating processes on the format and content of messages to be exchanged. The simplest protocols define only the hardware configuration. More complex protocols define timings, data formats, error detection and correction techniques, and software structures. The most powerful protocols describe each level of the transfer process as a layer, separate from the rest, so that certain layers, such as the interconnecting hardware, can be changed without affecting the whole. Put very simply, the network management protocol is the method by which your network administrator exchanges information with your network.

Depending on the platform you choose, you may be able to implement several network management protocols in support of your LAN. Here are two common management protocols:

- **Simple Network Management Protocol (SNMP).** This very popular protocol commonly comes with the purchase of hubs. It runs regular diagnostic tests to keep constant status on devices and notes status of each management information base. In case of a problem, SNMP reviews the information base, locates the problem, and allows system administrators to quickly access and correct system problems, remotely if necessary.

- **Common Management Information Protocol (CMIP).** Although it's not used as often as SNMP, CMIP is more complex because it puts system monitoring decisions in the hands of the network administrator. The administrator sets the parameters to be monitored using object-oriented descriptions. This protocol requires much more work and maintenance for administrators, but gives them customized control over all component aspects of the LAN.

The most common methods of monitoring and retrieving information about a LAN at any given time using almost any given network management software are:

- Protocol analysis

- Graphical mapping

- Polling

- Event logging

- Device configuration

Let's take a brief look at each of these common activities associated with most LAN management software.

Protocol Analysis

This particular feature is discussed in more detail in Chapter 12 but is worth mentioning here as well. Because clients or nodes are usually more problematic to secure (due to factors such as telecommuting), it's very important to periodically analyze the protocols traversing the network to ensure proper security and system integrity.

Protocol analyzers offer a tremendous amount of information about network performance, and you can use them to analyze networks from the physical-layer through the upper-layer protocols. Generally speaking, however, most troubleshooting analysis happens at the network layer and below. The errors found there are those that a network administrator can usually handle, such as swapping out a bad network interface card, reloading a LAN driver, or distributing resources or clients to another network or segment.

However, when a problem does occur above the network layer, you can also use analyzers to interpret the communications occurring on the wire. For example, if an application does not load properly from the server, you may wish to use a protocol analyzer to see the downloading process on the wire in order to determine the proper fix.

Graphical Mapping

This is where the graphical user interface really plays a valuable role for network administrators. With this feature as part of the network-management system software, the network administrator can actually generate a visual characterization of the network and its components. This visual map of the network can be color coded and even use blinking lights or sounds to identify system errors. For instance, a network administrator may color code all routers green, hubs red, switches yellow, etc., then set the graphical mapping software to blink that color coded component on the map if it is experiencing a problem. Again, Novell ManageWise provides this type of feature.

Polling

Polling is an important feature of the LAN management system. It should be considered a key component during the strategy and planning phase and definitely be an integral part of any viable network-management system software you consider. It's so important because your network administrator will rely heavily on the network management system to periodically query all devices on the network and determine their status, thus polling them for a response.

Most network management systems allow the network administrator the ability to configure how often the polling takes place. This ability is important because the larger the network, the more devices and traffic. The more devices and traffic a LAN has, the more polling takes place. This will very easily equate to the network management system keeping track of thousands of polling queries and could, in turn, adversely affect network performance. Finding a happy medium between not enough polling and too much is something of a challenge. Too little polling can delay an alert to a system problem and too much can produce a large amount of traffic. We suggest that you follow the recommendations for poll settings provided by the manufacturer of the particular network management software you choose. This usually provides a good starting point.

As a possible alternative to the polling method we've just discussed, there is another specific process known as trap-based polling. With *trap-based polling*, any given device, upon failure or experiencing a problem, sends the network administrator's console a message called a *trap*. The trap message identifies the location of the problem, allowing the network administrator to quickly poll the device in question and determine the nature and extent of the problem.

Event Logging

Event logging is exactly what it's name implies — the logging of events. With this feature, the results of all polling and trap messages can be captured in a file for statistical analysis, future review or comparison, and as a running record of all network administrative activity taking place at any given time.

Device Configuration

Device configuration is a feature that all network management systems should support. Some implement it using industry-standard protocols like SNMP, and some use proprietary agents and protocols. Regardless of the mechanism, a network administrator should have some way of affecting the configuration of large numbers of devices from the management console. This remote access capability proves itself invaluable in situations where the network administrator isn't physically located in close proximity to all LAN servers under his or her responsibility.

► · ◄

Summary

This chapter discusses the technical and administrative functions of a network administrator as well as the functions of LAN management. You need to know both.

The responsibilities for managing a network require both technical and administrative skill, as well as good habits. The success of a network administrator depends on having the ability to work effectively with other network administrators and network users alike. An effective network administrator emphasizes participation in user training, because this better equips end-users to cope with the frequent, easy-to-fix problems associated with network applications. Training one or more assistants ensures continuity of operations and gives the primary network administrator the time to spend on more complicated tasks.

CHAPTER 12

Maintaining Network Security

Security takes many forms. It's not just passwords for logins or combination safes for storing top-secret disks. For your computer network, security includes protecting your company's most important asset: its information. As a network professional, you should be aware of how to protect the network from viruses, improper use or sharing of passwords, incorrect dial-in or Internet based access, improper file access, hardware protection, and rights to the network. Good security can even help prevent a self-inflicted disaster, such as someone inadvertently changing or deleting files.

Often, security is a major concern for large corporations but effective procedures are not implemented. For small organizations security is sometimes overlooked, though it is no less important. Creating and maintaining effective security doesn't have to become a time consuming task. It needs to be thought through and measures put into place.

▶ · ◀

The Nature of Threats

Many are the evil forces waiting to attack your network. Then there are just stupid mistakes. Do you know which is responsible for more crashed networks and lost files? It's usually stupid mistakes. True, we worry more about viruses, hackers, sabotage, and natural disasters, but the user who inadvertently taps the "DEL" key while looking at files in Windows Explorer is often the cause of many problems.

In the past, the mainframe was fairly secure—locked in an air-conditioned clean room, backed up nightly, given dedicated and clean power, and maintained by the hardware vendor. It was programmed by people with pocket protectors, and managed by an MIS director with a staff of hundreds.

The network is different. The server or shared network drive is sometimes under someone's desk, backed up when the mood hits, plugged into the wall, maintained by the person in the office who has had a computer at home the longest, filled with off-the-shelf software (including flying toasters and card games), and managed by the office manager. Larger networks are maintained the way mainframes used to be, because they replaced the mainframe, and the staff and clean room were already in place.

Even the network maintained like a mainframe is more vulnerable than the mainframe was. The mainframe used dumb terminals — terminals without memory, disks, or CPUs. They could only do what the mainframe allowed them to do. Exiting a program meant exiting the user from the operating system. Most mainframe users never touched the operating system functions. If the clean room was locked and the security was correct, the only vulnerability on the mainframe was a modem that permitted vendor support and dial-in access for a privileged few. Break-ins and problems were few and far between.

Today's networks are made up of a bunch of computers (sometimes more powerful than the first mainframes), sitting on employee desks, just inviting someone to do something wrong.

A network has many entry points, and some application software uses files in such a way that the rights must be granted to users so they can read, write, copy, and delete files. This gives access to the operating system, and anyone with those rights can cause problems. Users have access to the Internet and bulletin boards, companies are giving laptops to employees, and users with home computers can dial into the network.

Network resources can be protected with carefully designed security built into the NOS, but how do you protect the workstations and all the hard drives on them? You can protect workstations from viruses, but can you protect them from the user installing bad software, changing configurations, failing to back up, or deleting files? The dangerous user is not the one afraid of breaking something. It's the users that think they know something. Such users are unafraid to tweak configuration files, fiddle with the memory, and poke around to see what they can get into. This type of user is usually just trying to speed up their workstation or add some new software program they use at home. A little power in the wrong hands can be dangerous. With power comes responsibility. Anyone with the power to change things should be trained on the effects those changes could have. We discuss this in greater detail later.

And then there are hackers and deliberate saboteurs. These people enjoy breaking in and doing damage. Serious hackers have found a way around every security measure invented. They have dialers that randomly dial phone numbers until they get a modem. They have password generators that try combinations of passwords, unattended, until they get a hit. Once in, they can transfer large sums of money in and out of accounts at will, destroy good credit ratings or fix bad ones, remove or change records, steal secrets and confidential data, introduce viruses, or just erase the entire system. Disgruntled, terminated employees have been known to make their last act with a company one of revenge and destruction. Easy to use e-mail programs have introduced another peril into the network's existence. Viruses are easily spread by e-mail, where a virus steals names out of e-mail directories to find the next victim.

For example, in 1999, one virus wanted to be the grump that stole Christmas. Virus Prilissa, spread through e-mail, was intended to sit quietly until Christmas day. Then, if opened, the virus would reconfigure your hard drive. A virus alert was publicized by news organizations, such as CNET, to help users become aware of the problem.

With luck you'll never face one of these problems. This chapter alerts you to the possibilities and potential tactics. We recognize that you must weigh the cost of prevention against the cost of the cure. Most of the security measures won't cost anything except the time to learn how to protect yourself.

Identification and Authorization

A big part of security comes from identifying the person and then, his or her authorization. Most often this comes in asking a user for a password at the time he or she logs in to the network. Once the "user" and the "password" are checked as correct, the system assigns the user rights to see, create, modify, or delete information.

Systems have three ways to identify a user. The system must ask for identification by something the users knows, such as a password; or by using something the user carries, such as a key or card key; or by identifying something unique to the user, such as a fingerprint.

Testing for something that the user knows, such as a password, is the most popular, easiest and (unfortunately) the least effective form of security. Passwords are too easily shared or guessed.

Testing for something that the user carries, such as a key, can prevent the sharing or guessing problems. But, carrying cards or keys requires additional hardware to read and authenticate. And, keys can be lost.

Testing for something unique to the user, such as a fingerprint, is the best, and most expensive form of security. Obviously users cannot share (or lose) fingerprints — so identification that performs this test is the most reliable. Let's look briefly at each form of identification.

Passwords

Passwords are the most common form of security. Most people feel safe when they password protect their system. How safe are passwords? Passwords are as safe as we make them. Did you know that many passwords are written on a piece of paper taped to the inside of a top drawer on the user's desk? Have you ever seen a password taped to a monitor? Think about your personal passwords. Are they names of a relative or pet, something to do with your hobby, a favorite word, a curse word, something to do with money, or the ever-popular word "password" for the password? For even better security, suggest that people use a couple of numbers in the password. Naming a password after your dog, "Fido," could be easily guessed — but making the password "Fido1203," after the dog and his birth date would likely foil a lucky guess. A system manager once challenged an intelligent novice to break the security he had set up on the system. The employee got in by guessing a different user's password (a golf term) and moved some vital files to scattered directories, all in under ten minutes. The novice then promised to tell his boss how he did it, if his boss publicly announced what had happened. The system manager had no other choice than to swallow his pride and make the announcement.

Listed below are the top ten rules in using a password system. It might be helpful to share them with the people who use your network.

1. Passwords are a secret.

2. Don't give passwords to anyone.

3. Don't write down passwords.

4. Don't pick common or easily guessed passwords.

5. Don't type passwords while someone is watching.

6. Don't allow users to log in and walk away from the workstation for extended periods of time. Use software that times out the user if there's no keyboard activity.

7. Don't let users place passwords in batch files where they can be read.

8. Encourage end users to quickly change a password if it has been compromised.

9. Require periodic password changes as a safety measure.

10. Reinforce the previous nine steps when training users about passwords.

Let them know that if they forget their password, you can get them another. This is the main reason users write down their password. They're afraid that they'll lose everything if they forget it. Passwords can be beneficial if managed properly or useless if mismanaged or abused.

Some network managers are looking at replacing passwords with a more effective form of determining authenticity, such as identification keys or biometrics.

Identification Keys Hardware or scanning identification offers a better form of identification. Whether you use regular hardlock or smartcard keys, you can more effectively control identification than with simple passwords alone. This used to cost several hundred dollars per desktop, but new technology has brought the prices down and created optimum functions.

For example, companies like RF IDeas, Inc. (www.rfideas.com) use radio frequency solutions for automated security and identification in computer and facility access control applications. Using this type of technology a single ID badge can unlock building doors and allow someone to automatically login to the network.

This technology uses radio frequency that identifies the user as he or she gets within ten feet of the system. It then provides a hands-free login to the network without the user having to remember a password. It also can be programmed to lock the computer when the user walks away.

For less than $100 per station, the cost for this type of security can be well within the reach of many organizations.

Biometrics for Identification

Perhaps the best identification comes when passwords or access keys aren't needed anymore. When systems can identify people based on a unique physical attribute, there will be nothing to share, forget, or lose. Great progress has been made with biometrics identification, which can use anything from your fingerprint, voice, iris scan, or face.

Fingerprint identification has already captured a good share of the market with products that sell as low as $100 per desktop. Companies like Digital Persona (www.digitalpersona.com) with its low cost U.are.U package, provide an easy to use method for people to be correctly identified and logged into a network with a fingerprint. Similarly, keyboard maker, Keytronics (www.keytronic.com) offers fingerprint scanners that are integrated into keyboards.

For other types of biometrics you may consider the following companies listed in Table 12.1.

TABLE 12.1 Biometric Product Vendors	TYPE	COMPANY	PRODUCT
	Face Recognition	Miros (www.miros.com)	TrueFace software recognizes your face and provides a simple-to-use personal ID.
	Face Recognition	Visionics Corp (www.faceit.com)	FaceIt NT recognizes faces for log-on and file-access security for Windows NT networks and PCs.
	Voice Recognition	InteliTrak Technologies Inc. (www.intelitrak.com)	Provides Gatekeeper, which allows a user to logon to a system based on hearing a correct voice logon.

Continued

TABLE 12.1	TYPE	COMPANY	PRODUCT
Biometric Product Vendors (continued)	Voice Recognition	Veritel Corp. (www.veritelcorp.com)	Allows a user to access system or open files by correctly speaking his or her name into the microphone and then answer a question from user profile.
	Iris Scanning	Iris ID	Grants the right to read the values of the property. Compare is a subset of read. If the read right is given, compare operations are also allowed.

Once you identify the individual, the control of the system will then pass to authorization. This involves passing most of the security over to the network security system, which is discussed at the close of this chapter.

Other Security Issues

In addition to the various security techniques discussed previously, you should be aware of other issues that affect your network's security.

Viruses

Viruses get their name from being able to replicate and infect any computer that it comes into contact with. Periodically a virus is so widespread it makes the evening news. Sometimes rumors of a particular virus are themselves a hoax. Where do viruses come from? There are those who claim that the virus-scanning software companies introduce new viruses from time to time to help sell their software, but the truth is that computer hackers are responsible for most viruses. Imagine the feeling of power they get from knowing that something they created is passed all over the world, causes fear in millions of people, and hurts business and establishments. Be forewarned, before you start spending late nights creating your mark on the world. Viruses are illegal, and people developing viruses are being prosecuted whenever possible, with serious consequences.

All of these facts aside, a virus is serious business and should not be taken lightly. A virus can infect a few workstations or completely destroy a network, requiring a complete system regeneration, and causing loss of whatever data was new since the last backup. Does the backup have the virus? If you haven't been affected by a virus yet, you will be sometime.

Viruses take many forms and can enter the network many different ways. A floppy taken from home and copied to the network can contain a virus. Accessing bulletin boards can transfer viruses. A computer technician could be carrying around a virus on one of their utility disks, although there's no excuse for that — they should know better. There have been a few instances of viruses being shipped with very popular commercial software packages.

Recently, viruses have spread through e-mail. Consider the warning:

> VIRUS ALERT
> Within the blink of an eye, you could lose all your spreadsheets, presentations, word processing documents, and personally send 100 of your best friends a virus. And, no, I'm not kidding. If you caught the latest malicious e-mail transmitted virus, you could unwittingly disintegrate the data on your or your colleagues' computers. And you'd do it by simply opening an e-mail attachment.

This attention-getting statement was sent to inform people of the second instance of the worm.explorer.zip virus that was unleashed in late 1999. This was the second strain of a virus that foiled several popular virus checkers and caused certain firms to shut down e-mail systems until files could be checked.

Although there's no airtight method of preventing a virus infection, here's a way to help limit exposure. The three steps we recommend are: backup, protect, and keep informed.

- *Backup:* First, make regular backups (nightly) of your important work. Any spreadsheet, presentation, or word processing document should be backed up automatically on to tape or a separate disk. Make sure the process is automatic, because even if you are normally disciplined, backups are easy to forget.

▶ *Protect yourself and your network.* Pick a virus checker and keep it updated. The two most popular, from McAfee or Symantec (Norton), have automated controls that help you update the system. Although crafty virus strains can foil them for a day or two, these systems are constantly updated to give people the best protection.

▶ *Finally, keep informed.* Keep your eyes on the news. You can set up news filters to search for the word "virus" and e-mail you any new developments. Major portals like CNET (`www.cnet.com`) or Excite (`www.excite.com`) and others let you create such automatic updates. This type of notification makes you among the first to know when there's an outbreak.

Is this meant to scare you? Absolutely! Viruses are mostly preventable. High quality virus scanning software is inexpensive and readily available. It should be installed on every network, workstation, server, and laptop. Updates are available from the software companies to scan for newer varieties as they appear.

Natural Disasters

Natural disasters are often overlooked. Earthquakes, fires, floods, and tornadoes can put you out of business in short order. If you manage a large network that crosses many cities or states, you can install redundant servers around the country. If a server in California is destroyed by earthquake, the redundant server in Chicago can take over without missing a beat. And don't forget those hurricanes on the eastern seaboard or Gulf coast. Small companies do well to have adequate and current backups located in different locations. Two sets of backups in a building that burns down will do little good. Keep one at the office and another in a bank box or the home of an employee; then the odds of both sets being destroyed are slim. Refer to Chapter 13 for more information on creating a network contingency plan in the event of natural disaster.

Dial-in Access

Dial-in access is being added to most networks so employees can work from home or access files and e-mail from the field. Any time a modem is attached to the network, another point of entry has been opened for hackers to gain entry. Passwords can help, but we've already shown that passwords are not foolproof. Be selective in giving access to the system. Make sure the user's rights protect the network. A dial-back modem adds another level of security. The user dials the modem, then enters the name and password. The modem checks a table stored in the modem and dials back the user's phone number. This doesn't work for mobile users who are always using different numbers. There's not much you can do about that. Why do you want to secure the dial-in modems? Because you don't want viruses or hackers hurting your network.

Hardware

An overlooked area of security is availability of hardware. We discussed mainframes and the care with which they are maintained and secured. PCs are ignored because we are accustomed to seeing them on desktops. Servers, routers, hubs, and workstations all benefit from protection.

The server should be attached to an uninterrupted power supply (UPS) that will down the server in an orderly manner in the event that the power is out and the UPS battery supply runs low. Battery backups are needed for mission-critical servers such as airline reservation systems and bank networks.

Is the server console secure and password protected? The console-secure function only permits the console operator to perform certain functions on the server, such as loading software from floppies, changing the date and time, and loading software into memory.

Secure your routers and hubs to protect them from damage, disconnection, and unauthorized access. It doesn't hurt to protect them from lightning either. Routers, hubs, and modems are particularly susceptible to lightning strikes. And beware of laptops, which can be plugged into the network at the hub by disconnecting a cable and plugging in the laptop. The user is then able to run any program on the laptop, with potentially dire results.

Finally, workstations can be protected by requiring passwords to boot the workstation and by removing floppy drives. It is difficult to chain workstations to desks, but they can be protected from theft by commercially produced theft-deterrent devices. Some of these include cables and locks or alarms that are triggered when the device is moved or disconnected from power.

Here again, use common sense when cabling. Use Plenum cables if the building code requires it, and use the best quality cable you can afford. It is important to run the cables in safe areas, such as suspended ceilings, conduits, or channels specially designed to carry cables. Spend a little extra to have the cable terminated in a wall jack instead of run down the wall. Besides being neater, when a workstation is moved, the jumper cable is unplugged from the wall, and there is nothing left hanging out to damage. Cables running across floors are asking for trouble. Refer to Chapter 6 for more information on cables.

Treat your network as if it were a mainframe, as it may very well have been at one time, because it is certainly doing the work of one.

Network Security System

So far, we have discussed the perimeters of network security and the pieces that are outside the network operating system. Now we will examine the security built into the NOS itself. The network security system involves the assigning of various rights to users and administrators. Default settings allow operation of a simple network without an in-depth understanding of all of these features. However, if you are operating a large network, or if you are particular about protecting the data on your network, you will want to take the time to learn all about the security options your network has to offer.

Although rights security is one of the most powerful features of the network, it can be a challenge to learn to use every option effectively. The options include file system rights, object and property rights, trustees and trustee assignments, inheritance, security equivalence, effective rights, and using rights to control access to the directory tree. You can use these security features to define roles in the network to create positions with exactly the authority that you feel is needed to complete assigned tasks.

Another major benefit of network security features is the capability to divide the administration of the network among several individuals, each with authority over only their area of the directory tree. Used correctly, the security system in the NOS can provide you with a highly secure, very structured, and understandable networking environment.

Rights in the File System

Basically, a user is given rights to any file or directory by a trustee assignment that is created by a network administrator. Any user who has rights to a file is a trustee of that file. A trustee assignment contains a list of rights that are granted to a certain user for the file where the trustee assignment is created.

Inheritance allows a trustee assignment that is granted at one point to apply to everything below that point in the file structure. Because of inheritance, network administrators do not have to create trustee assignments for every file that every user needs to use. Inheritance is the main reason that rights can be granted to directories. If a trustee assignment grants a user certain rights, that trustee (user) has those same rights to every file and subdirectory in the directory where the trustee assignment was granted.

A distinction must be made here between a trustee who has explicit rights to a file and a trustee who has implicit rights to a file. Explicit rights are granted to a file when a user has a trustee assignment on that file. Implicit rights are granted when a user does not have a trustee assignment to the file but inherits rights from another trustee assignment. For an example of how inheritance works, see Figure 12.1.

F I G U R E   12.1

The way inheritance works is, when you are granted rights at the top level (or directory), you automatically get the same rights to each folder, sub-directory, and file below it (unless otherwise changed by the system administrator).

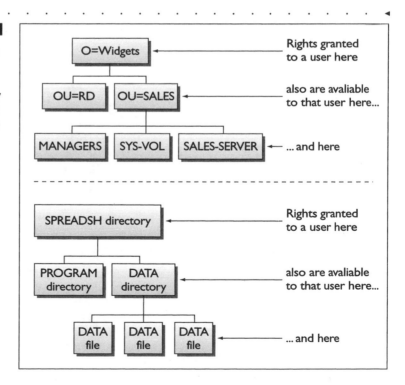

Suppose that you do not want anyone to inherit rights to a certain file. You can block all trustees from inheriting rights to it by creating an inherited rights filter for that file. An inherited rights filter contains a list of rights, just as a trustee assignment does. But these rights are granted solely to the assigned trustee. The file must be kept in the same folder as the inherited rights filter. If a right that the trustee was granted is not listed in the inherited rights filter, that right is blocked and cannot be used by the trustee to whom it was assigned.

Another key mechanism used to simplify the assignment of rights to files and directories is security equivalence. If a network administrator decides that one user should have all of the rights that another user has been granted, the network administrator can make the first user security-equivalent to the second user, and the first user will then have all of the rights that the second user was granted.

The rights that a user can actually use for a file or directory are called that user's effective rights. These are a combination of a user's trustee assignments, inheritance, and security-equivalent rights, as shown in Figure 12.2.

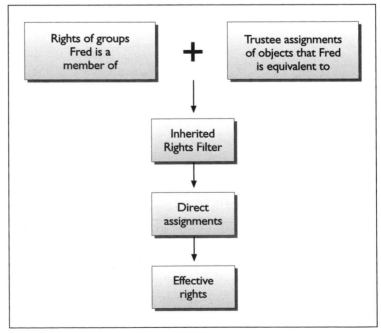

F I G U R E 12.2

How effective rights work

All of the trustee assignments for a file, as well as the inherited rights mask, are stored in the Director Entry Table for the file or directory where they are granted. In order to change a file's or a directory's trustee assignments or inherited rights mask, you must have rights to the file, specifically a right called the access control right. All of the possible rights to files and directories are discussed below.

We have been talking about how users are able to access files by having trustee assignments. Now we need to expand that idea, because any object in the directory tree can be granted a trustee assignment to a file or directory. (An object is an item in a database that represents a real entity on the network, such as a user, group, printer, or server.) For example, a profile object can be a trustee of a directory, or an organizational unit object can be a trustee of a file. This makes it much easier to assign similar rights to a large group of people. We will see how in the next section.

As we talk about granting rights to users and other objects, a question may come to mind about whether there exists a special user account for a network administrator or supervisor who can always make necessary trustee assignments. Some NOSs provide a SUPERVISOR account for that purpose. Also, certain regular user objects in the directory tree can be granted the rights to make changes. There is more about this later in the chapter.

Directory Rights

Table 12.2 lists the rights that a trustee can be granted to work on a directory in the file system. In many situations, you will see only the first character used by itself to indicate the right that has been granted.

Objects: A Simple Review

Objects are entries in a database that hold information about organizational structure or about physical things on the network such as volumes, printers, and users. The objects in the database are organized in a tree structure, which makes some objects higher in the tree than others. We usually imagine the tree as having branches flowing down instead of growing up.

Objects that contain other objects underneath them in this analogy are container objects. These include country, organization, and organizational unit objects. Objects that cannot contain other objects are called leaf objects, and include things like users, printers, and groups (a group has a list of user objects, but it does not contain those user objects). A special case is the volume object, which is both a leaf object in the directory tree and the root directory of a physical volume. You must keep in mind the dual nature of this object so that you can recognize where information that is presented in a volume comes from.

Think of an object as a box. Boxes can have other boxes beneath them in the directory tree's hierarchical structure. The boxes are filled with information about the thing that the box represents. The pieces of information inside the box are the object's properties. One object can contain a great deal of information in its properties. In particular, a user object holds a lot of information about a user and that user's account, such as the user's password restrictions, login restrictions, station restrictions, group memberships, login script, and so on.

TABLE 12.2 Trustee Rights in the File System	RIGHT	DESCRIPTION
	Supervisor	Grants all rights to the directory, its files, and subdirectories. The supervisor right cannot be blocked by an inherited rights mask. Users with this right can grant other users rights to the directory, its files, and subdirectories.
	Read	Grants the right to open files in the directory, read their contents, and run the programs.
	Write	Grants the right to open and change the contents of files in the directory.
	Create	Grants the rights to create new files and subdirectories in the directory. If create is the only right granted to a trustee for the directory, and no other rights are granted below the directory, a drop-box directory is created. In a drop-box directory, you can create a file and write to it. Once the file is closed, however, only a trustee with more rights than create can see or update the file. You can copy files or subdirectories into the directory and assume ownership of them, but other users' rights are revoked.
	Erase	Grants the right to delete the directory, its files, and subdirectories.

TABLE 12.2	RIGHT	DESCRIPTION
Trustee Rights in the File System (continued)	Modify	Grants the right to change the attributes or name of the directory and of its files and subdirectories, but does not grant the right to change their contents. (That requires the write right.)
	File scan	Grants the right to see .the directory and its files with the DIR or NDIR directory command.
	Access control	Grants the right to change the trustee assignments and inherited rights of the directory and of its files and subdirectories.

Security allows us to control access to each object (box) individually, and also to each property (piece of information in the box) individually. We can grant access to the box without granting access to see inside the box, or we can grant access to see and change some information in the box, but not grant access to see other information in the same box.

Such finite control allows creative flexibility and power to the rights system. Unfortunately, it can make things enormously complex if good planning and a sound understanding do not precede your actions.

Object and Property Rights

To illustrate the concept of security using a directory service, the Novell Directory Service (NDS) will be used as an example. Access to the objects and properties of objects in Directory Services is controlled by two sets of rights: object rights and property rights. Instead of a user just having rights to the file system, a user can also have rights to another user, or more specifically, to see or change the information about that user stored in a user object. Object and property rights are different from the file and directory rights that are used in the file system because different information must be protected.

Next we list the object and property rights that are used to access objects and the information that they contain. Then we talk about how file system concepts like trustees and inheritance apply to objects.

Object Rights

Table 12.3 lists the rights that any trustee can be granted in order to work on any object in the NDS directory tree. Except for the supervisor object right, the object rights do not affect what a trustee can do with the object's properties. In many situations, the first character of the right's name is used to indicate the right has been granted.

Property Rights

Table 12.4 lists the rights that any trustee can be granted in order to work on the properties of an object. These rights can be granted to a trustee for all of an object's properties, or for just one of an object's properties. In many situations, you will see only the first character used by itself in the trustee lists (and in some DOS utilities like NETADMIN, RIGHTS, FILER, and so on.) to indicate the right that has been granted.

T A B L E 12.3	RIGHT	DESCRIPTION
Object Rights	Browse	Grants the right to see the object in the directory tree. The name of the object is returned when a search is made and matches the object.
	Create	Grants the right to create a new object below this object in the directory tree. Rights are not defined for the new object. This right is available only on container objects, because noncontainer objects cannot have subordinates.
	Delete	Grants the right to delete the object from the directory tree. Objects that have subordinates cannot be deleted (the subordinates must be deleted first).
	Rename	Grants the right to change the name of the object, in effect changing the naming property. This changes what the object is called in complete names directory.
	Supervisor	Grants all access privileges. A trustee with the supervisor object right also has unrestricted access to all properties. The supervisor object right can be blocked by the inherited rights filter below the object where the supervisor right is granted.

TABLE 12.4	RIGHT	DESCRIPTION
Property Rights	Compare	Grants the right to compare any value to a value of the property. With the compare right, an operation can return true or false, but you cannot see the value of the property. The read right includes the compare right.
	Read	Grants the right to read the values of the property. Compare is a subset of read. If the read right is given, compare operations are also allowed.
	Write	Grants the right to add, change, or remove any values of the property. The write right includes the add or delete self right.
	Add or delete self	Grants a trustee the right to add or remove itself as a value of the property. The trustee cannot affect any other values of the property. This right is only meaningful for properties that contain object names as values, such as group membership lists or mailing lists. The write right includes the add or delete self right.
	Supervisor	Grants all rights to the property. The supervisor property right can be blocked by an object's inherited rights filter.

Rights are granted to objects and their properties in the same way that rights are granted to files and directories—through trustee assignments. As we described for the file system, however, any object can be a trustee of any other object. All of the rights in the tables above are used to grant one object access to another object and its properties.

Inheritance is still an important concept when granting object rights to trustees. If I grant a trustee assignment to a container object, the trustee has the same rights to all leaf objects in that container unless an inherited rights filter blocks some or all of those rights, as illustrated in Figure 12.3. (The figure shows object rights, but it could include property rights as well.) As in the file system, if a trustee has a trustee assignment on the container object, and a trustee assignment on a leaf object within that container, only the trustee assignment to the leaf object is valid; the rights that would have been inherited are not added to the explicit trustee assignment on the leaf object.

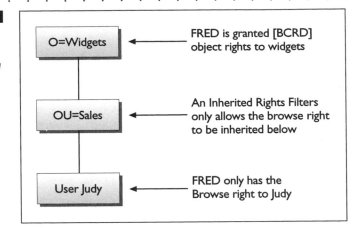

F I G U R E   12.3

A user can have object rights to a container, but those rights can be blocked by an inherited rights filter.

O=Widgets — FRED is granted [BCRD] object rights to widgets

OU=Sales — An Inherited Rights Filters only allows the browse right to be inherited below

User Judy — FRED only has the Browse right to Judy

A trustee assignment to an object can include rights to the properties of that object as well. Such property rights can be assigned in two ways. A trustee may have either the all properties right, which applies to every property of the object, or the specific property right, which applies to individual properties of an object. If a trustee has specific property rights to one or several properties, then only access to those properties is defined, and that access overrides what would have been the default property rights from the all properties right assignment.

Using the all properties and specific property methods together to grant property rights to a trustee is useful when you want to control access to particularly sensitive properties in an object. For example, if you want a user to be able to read all of the properties of a printer object but not change any of them, you grant read all property rights. If you want a user to be able to change all properties of a profile object except the login script property, which the user should only be able to read, then you grant both write all-properties rights and read specific-property rights to the login script property. The all property assignment applies to every property of the profile except login script, which has a specific property assignment.

In Directory Services, it is important to know where trustee assignments to an object and an object's inherited rights filter are stored. All are stored as entries in the object trustees access control list (ACL) property of each object.

To change trustee rights or the inherited rights filter of a file or directory, you must have the access control right to that file or directory. To change rights to an object or its properties, or an object's inherited rights filter, you must have the write property right to the ACL property of that object. If you do, then you manage that object.

Inheritance with Object and Property Rights

Inheritance is even more important when working with objects than it is when working with files and directories. The reason is that objects must have both rights to other objects and rights to the file system in order for work to be done. A user must have rights to its own object, to the profile script that it uses, to printing objects that it uses, and to all areas of the file system that it will access in order to complete assigned tasks. If we did not have inheritance to assist in granting everyone rights to necessary areas, it might be impossible to keep up with the security needs of the users on a large network. Inheritance makes it easy to make assignments to a large number of users with one trustee assignment. Inheritance in the NOS is just like the inheritance that one uses in the file system. If I grant user KIM a trustee assignment to a container object, such as an organization, then KIM has those same rights to every leaf object within that organization, as shown in Figure 12.4. (For simplicity, only object rights are shown in the figure.) If there are any organizational unit container objects in the organization, then KIM's rights continue to flow down into that container. This continues to every object that is underneath the organization where the original trustee assignment was made, unless an inherited rights filter blocks the inheritance of the original trustee assignment at a lower level. If the inherited rights filter is on a container object, then the rights are blocked for everything below that container, not just for that container object.

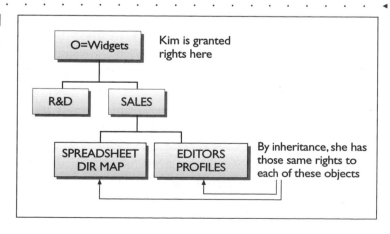

F I G U R E   12.4

Kim inherits object rights to lower objects in the directory tree because she has a trustee assignment above.

Suppose that all or several directory map objects pointing to all of your main application software packages are located under one of three organizational units in your directory tree. User Megan needs to access all of these applications by having rights to each of the directory map objects that contain paths to applications that she uses. You could grant a trustee assignment to Megan for each of the directory map objects that she needs, but that could take hours and would be difficult to update later when changes occurred. Instead, you grant Megan rights to the organizational unit named APPLICATIONS, which holds all of the directory map objects. By inheritance, Megan now has the same rights to each of the directory map objects within the APPLICATIONS organizational unit.

Remember this, however: Only object rights and all properties rights are inherited, or flow down the tree. Because specific property rights might grant rights to a property that does not exist on the object below, only the all properties right is inherited and then applies to all properties of the object below. For example, if you grant a trustee rights to the login script property of an organizational unit, the trustee cannot inherit rights to the login script property of a directory map object in that organizational unit, because directory maps don't have login scripts. The trustee's all properties assignment to the organizational unit would be inherited for the directory map.

In the previous example, we assume that no inherited rights filters on the directory map objects are blocking Megan from inheriting the rights that are granted on the container APPLICATIONS. Objects also use inherited rights filters to control the flow of inheritance, but the inherited rights filter for objects must be more powerful than the one used for a file or directory in order to deal with the increased number of rights used with objects and properties.

We mentioned that only object and all properties rights are inherited. The inherited rights filter, however, can contain entries for each specific property of an object. Why is this so? First of all, the inherited rights filter is not inherited itself, but is a part of each object, so the properties that it must apply to never change. Second, this allows the all properties rights that are inherited from above to be selectively blocked for each property.

For example, suppose that you create an inherited rights filter for a group object named AUDITORS. You don't care if others read the identification information about this object, but you don't want anyone who does not have an explicit trustee assignment to that object to see who is a member of the auditing team. You create an inherited rights filter for the object that includes:

- the browse object right, so that others can see the object,

- the read all-properties right, so that the identification information about this object can be seen but not changed by those with rights above this point,

- and a specific entry in the inherited rights filter for the members property, which includes no rights, so that no one who is not granted rights explicitly to this property can read that membership list. Of course, if a trustee had the supervisor object right, the trustee would also have access to all properties of the object, regardless of which property rights were inherited or blocked.

Figure 12.5 shows the details of this example, including both object and property rights.

An important concept worth repeating about the inherited rights filter for an object is that it can block the supervisor object or property right. This can only be done under certain conditions; namely, that a trustee with the supervisor object right already exists on the object where you want to block the supervisor right from being inherited. The trustee with the supervisor object right at that point is a manager of that branch of the tree. You cannot remove the supervisor object right from that trustee's assignment until the supervisor right is added to the inherited rights filter so it can be inherited again. This prevents cutting off supervisor-level access to a branch of the directory tree.

At least it tries to. If you had a trustee who was the supervisor of a branch of the directory tree, and some other supervisor deleted that user's object (not the trustee assignment, but the user object itself), then the trustee assignment would be invalid and there would be no supervisor of that area of the tree. If that part of the tree included a server and volumes, then supervisor-level access to the file systems on those volumes might also be cut off.

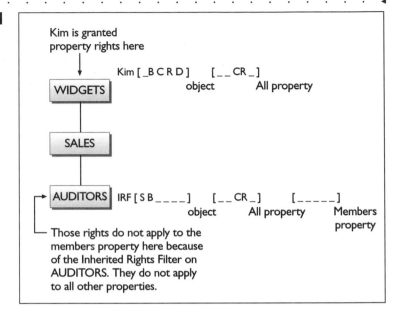

FIGURE 12.5

Kim cannot see the Members property of the AUDITORS group because an inherited rights filter blocks Kim's rights.

Be careful when blocking the supervisor object. You must keep track of which users are branch supervisors and take care not to delete their user objects. NetWare utilities will not stop you from deleting a user, even though the user is the only trustee with supervisor rights to a part of the directory tree.

Let's talk more about access to the file system through the directory tree. Access to the file system is not automatic for any user. Access comes through the NetWare server object representing the NetWare server to which a volume is physically attached. Any user that has supervisor rights to a NetWare server object will automatically have the supervisor directory right to the root directory of every volume attached to that server.

Because the utilities have safeguards to prevent cutting off supervisor-level access to part of the directory tree, every object should always have a supervisor (or several supervisors), including every NetWare server object. This attempts to ensure that every volume has at least one trustee with supervisor-level access at the root directory. A trustee with this access could then grant explicit trustee assignments to the root directory, granting someone rights that did not come through the server object. This might provide a safeguard if you are concerned about cutting off access. Of course, it is also less secure to have more supervisors.

Security Equivalence

The concept of security equivalence that we talked about for the file system is based on the idea that one object can be equivalent in rights to another object. That idea is used even more for rights to other objects in the NDS directory tree. A user object can be security-equivalent to any other object. Each user object has a property that lists all of the objects to which the user is security-equivalent. The user has all of the rights granted to itself, plus all of the rights granted to each of the objects listed in its security equivalence property. Other objects do not have a security equivalence property.

Besides the objects listed in a user's security equivalence property, every object has three other security equivalencies that are not shown anywhere and cannot be changed. These three extra security equivalencies apply to every object, not just to user objects:

▸ Every object is security-equivalent to the [Public] trustee. The [Public] trustee is used mainly to grant rights to users who have not even logged in to Directory Services, such as the \LOGIN directory on a SYS volume. You probably won't use the [Public] trustee much anyway.

▸ Every object is security-equivalent to the [Root] object. This allows you to grant a [Root] trustee assignment to a file, directory, or other object, and every object in the directory tree will have those rights by security equivalence to [Root]. For example, you could make [Root] a trustee of your electronic mail directory so that everyone in the directory tree would have rights to that directory. This odd arrangement prevents you from adding people to a security equivalence list who have more rights than you do, and then using that security equivalence to gain supervisor-level rights to a part of the directory tree or file system.

▸ Every object is security-equivalent to all of the container objects that are part of its complete name. For example, in Figure 12.6, user FRED is security-equivalent to organizational unit SALES, organizational unit WEST, and Organization WIDGETS-INC. This security equivalence is not listed anywhere, but you can always see what an object is security-equivalent to by looking at its complete name. You also cannot change this security equivalence. Every object is always security-equivalent to the containers above it.

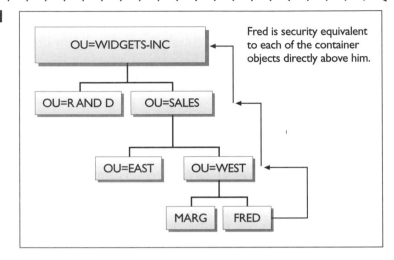

FIGURE 12.6

Fred is security-equivalent to all of the container objects above him in the directory tree.

Fred is security equivalent to each of the container objects directly above him.

The third special security equivalence above provides one of the most powerful security features. You can grant every user in a container rights to a file simply by granting the organizational unit a trustee right to the file. This operates like a group object, but with several advantages. First, the membership of the group is automatic. You don't have to list member users, and when a user is no longer in the organizational unit, you don't have to change any trustee assignments; the user is automatically not security-equivalent to the organizational unit, and all of the rights granted to the organizational unit are not applied to that user.

Group objects should be used in place containers as trustees when the users that are part of the group are a subset of the users in a group, or a combination of a few users from each of several containers. See Figure 12.7.

You must remember three important points about security equivalence to use it effectively:

▶ Security equivalence is not transitive. That is, if KIM is security-equivalent to FRED, and FRED is security-equivalent to MARIA, KIM is not security-equivalent to MARIA through FRED. This also applies to the security equivalence that each object has to every container above it. You cannot make FRED security-equivalent to organizational unit SALES by making him security-equivalent to JUDY, who is in SALES, because the only additional rights that FRED will have are those granted by explicit trustee assignment to JUDY.

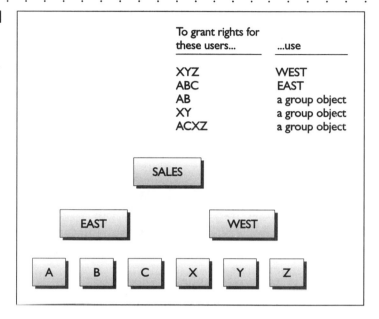

FIGURE 12.7

Group objects should be used when the users that you want in the group are a subset of the users within one container or are not all in the same container.

To grant rights for these users...	...use
XYZ	WEST
ABC	EAST
AB	a group object
XY	a group object
ACXZ	a group object

SALES

EAST   WEST

A   B   C   X   Y   Z

▸ Security equivalence applies to the file system as well as objects. That is, if KIM is granted a trustee assignment to a file, and FRED is security-equivalent to KIM, then FRED can access all the files that KIM has rights to, and not just all the objects that KIM has rights to.

▸ Special rights are needed to make a user security-equivalent to another object. The rights are special because they are different than the rights needed to perform any other action. In order to make BILL security-equivalent to MEGAN, you must list MEGAN in the security equivalence property of BILL. But to do this, you do not need any rights to the security-equivalence property of BILL. Instead, you must manage user MEGAN, which means that you must have at least the write property right to the ACL property of MEGAN. You do not need any rights at all to BILL. This odd arrangement prevents you from adding to a security equivalence list people who have more rights than you do, and then using that security equivalence to gain supervisor-level rights to a part of the directory tree or file system.

What is security equivalence used for? We suggest three areas where it is useful. The first is when rights are granted to a group or organizational role object. Any user listed as a member or occupant of the group or organizational role is automatically listed as security-equivalent to that object, so that any rights granted to the group are also granted to every user in the group.

Second, use security equivalence to temporarily grant one person all access to another person's data while that person is away on vacation or business. Remember, however, that this also grants all rights to the user's home directory and personal data.

Third, use security equivalence to provide backup supervisors for areas of your directory tree. For example, KIM is granted supervisor rights to an area of the tree and manages it from day to day. FRED is made security-equivalent to KIM so that if she is unavailable, FRED has the same rights to complete her tasks. By using security equivalence, FRED always has the same rights as KIM, even though KIM's rights change over time.

[Public] Trustee

A special case of granting rights is the [Public] trustee. [Public] is similar to the GUEST or EVERYONE in some NOSs, but operates a little differently. [Public] is used to grant rights to anyone who does not have other rights granted. Even users who are not logged in to the network have all rights that are granted to [Public]. Nevertheless, [Public] is not a real object of any kind, and no one can log in as [Public]. It simply says "If other rights are not granted to the person requesting access, grant these rights."

[Public] can always be entered as a trustee when creating a new trustee assignment, but should be used sparingly if at all because it grants rights to users who are not even logged in. It can be blocked by an inherited rights filter, like any other trustee assignment. Do not confuse the [Public] trustee, used to grant rights, with the \PUBLIC directory on every SYS volume, which holds utility programs that all users access.

We have talked about many different ways that rights are assigned in Directory Services. Let's regroup by examining how to create effective rights to a file or to an object and its properties.

Look at Figure 12.8 to see an example of how FRED's effective rights to a file are determined by the NOS each time FRED requests access to the file. FRED's effective file rights can come from any of the following:

▶ FRED's trustee assignments to the file, if there are any

▶ Inherited rights from FRED's trustee assignments to parent directories of the file, if nothing exists from the point above

▶ Trustee assignments to objects that FRED is security-equivalent to, such as group objects, or the containers above FRED

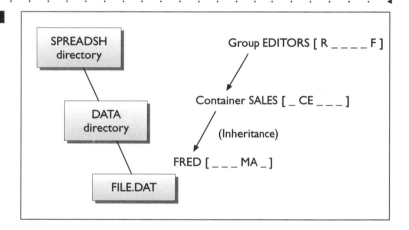

FIGURE 12.8

Group EDITORS and Container SALES are trustee assignments for objects that are security-equivalent to FRED.

If a user has a trustee assignment to a directory on a given level in the directory structure, and also one on a higher level, the current trustee assignment overrides the previous one. Trustee assignments to security-equivalent objects, such as groups, however, are added to individual user trustee assignments.

Rights Granted During Installation

Now that you know how rights work in the NOS, let's look at what rights are assigned during the installation process to get you started.

When you install your first server, a directory tree is created with several objects in place. An organization object, an organizational unit object, a server object, a volume object for each volume attached to the server, and a user object named ADMIN are all created under the [Root] of the directory tree.

During installation, user ADMIN is granted the supervisor object right to the root object of the directory tree. This allows ADMIN, the first user on the network, to perform any action on any object, because the trustee assignment on the [Root] object is inherited for all objects.

Similarly, the [Public] trustee is granted a trustee assignment to the [Root] object with the browse object right. This allows all users on the network to see all objects in the directory tree. You will probably want to remove this assignment if your network is large or your security demands are anything but simplistic. However, this provides a starting point so that everyone can work without the need to first create many trustee assignments. Some time may be needed before all of your users understand the idea of the directory tree and of locating their user object in the tree to log in.

Another important trustee assignment is created when you create a SYS volume object. This trustee assignment allows users to begin using the network and network utilities without first creating many trustee assignments. The container of the SYS volume is granted read and file scan directory rights to the \PUBLIC directory of the SYS volume. By security equivalence, this means that all users in the same container as the SYS volume can access the utilities and information stored in the \PUBLIC directory.

When you create a new user in the directory tree, you are prompted to create a home directory for the new user at the same time by simply specifying a path and directory name.

If you choose to create the home directory while creating the new user, the new user is granted all rights to the newly-created home directory. The new user can then log in to the network and have access to both the \PUBLIC directory for networking utilities and to a home directory on the network for personal work, all without special trustee assignments being made by the network administrator. If your user objects are created in the same container as the SYS volume, and you create a home directory for each user when it is created, you will not have to create any additional trustee assignments for your users to be able to log in and work with the directory. The only catch is that a little additional work will be required to be able to access printing services.

Setting Rights with the NetWare Utilities

The default trustee assignments that are created when you install the network allow users to begin working almost immediately. But how do you make other trustee assignments to serve other needs?

Two administrative utilities are provided with which you can make trustee assignments. One is the text-menu utility NETADMIN. The other is the graphical utility NetWare Administrator, which can be run from OS/2, Windows, or Windows NT/2000.

If you are using the NETADMIN text utility, you can view or change the trustees and inherited rights filters of a selected object by choosing "View or Edit the Trustee Assignments to this Object." You can also view or change the selected object's rights to files and directories on a volume by choosing "View or Edit this Object's Rights to Files and Directories."

The NETADMIN utility does not allow you to work directly with files and directories. You should use the FILER menu utility or the RIGHTS command-line utility to grant rights or change the inherited rights filter of files and directories.

If you prefer to use the graphical Administrator, there are more options available. You can use the Object menu to view or change the trustees and inherited rights filter of a selected object with "Trustees of this Object," or view or change the trustee assignments that the selected object has to other objects with "Rights to Other Objects."

The NetWare Administrator also includes the ability to work directly with files and directories. If you select a file or directory, you can choose "Details" from the Object menu and then view or change the trustees and inherited rights filter of the selected file or directory with the "Trustees of this..." page. If you select an object and then open an object dialog with "Details," you can view or change the selected object's rights to files and directories on a volume with the "Rights to the File System" page.

You need to be careful when working with volumes in the NetWare Administrator, however, because a volume object displays both object properties and information about the root directory of the file system on that volume. Keep your eyes on which rights are listed in the dialog box to keep track of which type of rights you are working on.

Summary

Security is a constantly moving target. As new security measures are implemented or designed, ways around them are also created. Don't assume that you have all the bases covered, and don't assume that what was safe last year is safe this year. Any change in your network means a change in security. Don't ignore security, or you'll be left saying "would've, could've, should've" when (not if) something happens.

Backing Up Your Network

There are two types of network administrators: those who already back up their systems and those who should. Whether it's fire, flood, or failed hard drives, backups can save time, energy, and your job! No matter how hard we try, there are some events that are out of our control, and others that it just isn't reasonable to try to control. For instance, despite years of painstaking research, development, and investment, we still haven't learned to predict earthquakes, deflect hurricanes, prevent fires, or even completely control destructive human behavior such as vandalism, terrorism, and sabotage. Maybe you've never experienced any of those things, but all it takes is one event to make all your hard work go up in smoke. Literally.

Of course, not all data is equal. Some lost data or files won't hurt anything, but others can take a company down. Disaster control experts caution that as many as 50 percent of computer disasters result in companies suffering significant business losses. Some companies become so crippled they cannot re-establish themselves and eventually go out of business. Hopefully you're getting the message: Back up critical data!

Disaster Planning

If the term "big disaster" sounds redundant, stop for a moment and think about what constitutes a disaster. Sure, everyone agrees that an earthquake is a disaster, but suppose you open your departmental budget worksheet file the evening before it is due to be turned in, and your computer casually tells you something like, "Unable to open file: #se)%%x.?x^." You try all those fancy utilities that are supposed to recover corrupted or damaged files, and nothing helps. Your pulse is racing. Your blood pressure is skyrocketing. Go ahead, tell yourself it's not a disaster.

The point is this: Disasters can come in all sizes. So how do you know what to consider when you begin planning? The best answer is to work backwards. Begin by thinking about potential disasters and the magnitude of their consequences. Then consider what options you have for avoiding the consequences (you don't necessarily try to avoid the disaster, although that may well be one of the approaches for minimizing the consequences), and what each approach will cost. Compare the cost of avoiding the consequences with the potential cost of not avoiding the consequences, and factor in the probability of experiencing a particular loss. For instance, it is much more reasonable to prepare for an earthquake if you're on the West Coast of the United States than if you're in the Midwest. That doesn't mean you can't have an earthquake in Chicago, but you may not want to spend the money to cover that risk in Chicago.

So, what are the potential consequences of a disaster? They include loss of physical assets such as computers, loss of revenue due to lost time, and loss or theft of data.

Generally speaking, the kinds of disasters that can reasonably be planned for and recovered from fall into a few basic categories: hardware failure, network failure, and lost data. Lost revenue or lost business is really something that results from one of these other categories, and is the sort of loss that can be indemnified with insurance. To recover lost business means to reestablish a business relationship with former customers. It will require human intervention. However, a rapid recovery from lost hardware, lost communications, or lost data can preserve a business relationship.

Redundancy Strategies

Most people think of backing up as referring to an operations process, usually run nightly, that makes copies of important data and stores it where it can be retrieved if necessary. They don't typically think of backing up hardware. But it's a common and very useful procedure. The simplest form of "catastrophic" hardware failure is probably the loss of a disk drive. This can be catastrophic, especially in a file or database server, not just in terms of lost data, but also in terms of downtime. It can take hours, or even days, to replace a disk drive in a server, format it correctly, restore the appropriate data, mount the drive, and put it back into service. Although the cost of the disk itself, even including service charges for physical replacement of the disk, may be relatively small, the potential loss of revenue, customers, and goodwill as a result of the downtime may be significant. Indeed, if any of the lost data is time-sensitive, the loss may represent a permanently lost business opportunity.

To avoid the potential consequences of such a loss, there are several hardware redundancy strategies from which to choose. These include using alternate servers, keeping hot spares, using mirroring, and the use of hot-swappable drive arrays. Don't worry if it sounds confusing. The basic principle here is redundancy.

Table 13.1 describes five different means of making sure you are protected against hardware failure.

TABLE 13.1	BACKUP TYPE	DESCRIPTION
Redundancy Strategies	Alternate servers	Backing up one server with another, so if one machine goes down, the other can assume the processing responsibilities. An alternate server is not the same as a hot spare (see the following); the alternate is normally a machine that is already in use, but has the excess capacity to handle an increased load under emergency circumstances. Access to disk drives shared with the other server facilitates this approach.
	Hot spares	An inventory of machines preconfigured to be used in place of another machine in the event of a failure.
	Mirroring and duplexing	The process of simultaneously maintaining duplicate copies of data on separate physical disks, so if one disk fails, the operation can continue uninterrupted. This is done primarily with software, but does require multiple disk drives. Duplexing also requires an additional SCSI.
	Hot-swappable	This means that in the event a failed disk is mirrored, the replacement can be installed without bringing down the host computer. Because of the invasive nature of installing a disk, this is normally done in external storage units or a RAID.
	RAID	RAID is an acronym meaning Redundant Array of Inexpensive Disks. It is a standard technology for implementing mirroring across a number of disk drives. RAID technologies also allow performance enhancement by use of other software technologies such as stripping, which are not discussed here.

Hard drives (fixed disks, hard files, disk drives) are the most vulnerable part of any computer for one very easily understood reason: They spin constantly and are read from and written to with movable magnetic heads; therefore, they sustain the kind of wear and tear associated with friction. The rest of the computer is also vulnerable to heat and humidity, as are all electronic devices, but the disk is definitely the most vulnerable. Of course, it also happens to be where the data resides, so it is the most valuable in terms of a potential loss.

Likewise, the principle of redundancy is applied to vulnerable devices other than disk drives. If a primary server fails, an application may be restored to a secondary server in order to make it available, or an alternate server may be able to accept logins from the other's users. A good example of this might be using what is normally a "development" or "test" server to run a mission-critical application if the production server normally assigned to it should fail.

Another approach to implementing this kind of redundancy is to use hot spares, or idle machines preconfigured with all the necessary bells and whistles to fit a particular purpose. This amounts to keeping excess inventory on hand in case of emergency. Depending on the importance of a specific purpose, this may be the best approach to take, but it does have financial consequences. Hot spares may prove particularly useful in highly distributed environments; that is, in environments in which the computing resources are located in a variety of distant geographical areas. By maintaining a centralized stock of hot spares, a machine can be pulled from inventory, the configuration tweaked as necessary, and then shipped to the end location, where it only needs to be installed. This approach also allows for the down machine to be shipped to a maintenance center, rather than requiring on-site maintenance, which is generally more expensive.

Remote installation can be a trickier proposition than it sounds, however. Usually, it is not possible to restore a configuration with 100 percent fidelity to the original at the time of the equipment failure. What usually happens is that the machine is preconfigured as much as possible, shipped to the remote site, installed, and then "polished" until the configuration is right. With a good network design and the proper tools, much of this work can be done remotely once the replacement machine is installed.

When designing the network, it's also a good idea to consider how to build in alternate paths in case a circuit fails. This is actually a kind of hardware redundancy all its own. When a circuit fails, it may be because a router failed somewhere in the network (and if you're using a public network, the router may not be your own), or it may be because someone cut a cable somewhere. In essence, when a circuit fails, the locations at either end of the circuit may be isolated from one another. If that happens, it's wise to have a backup path for communications. When you deal with major telecommunications vendors, and especially if you purchase public data network services, make sure there's more than one way to get from point A to point B.

Even in a private network, it's not a bad idea to build in some redundancy. After all, you never know when a backhoe operator somewhere is going to accidentally sever a cable. There is more than one approach to this situation. One of the more popular (and relatively less expensive) options is dial back up. This means that if a circuit goes down, the router servicing that circuit can use a serial connection to a modem to dial over conventional telephone lines to reestablish connectivity.

While this is a serviceable and fairly inexpensive way to provide circuit redundancy, it has major performance consequences. Most digital circuits are able to communicate at higher speeds than are normally accomplished via modem, even with high-speed modems and data compression technology. Modem data transmission tends to be more error-prone as well, meaning retransmission of data is more likely.

Modems also add a certain amount of overhead to the data transmission, since they must perform the modulation/demodulation process. Finally, many routers are connected to their CSU/DSU units (the digital equivalent of a modem) with v.35 cables, which are able to move data faster than the more common RS-232 serial technology used to communicate with a modem.

But despite these drawbacks and all the various cost implications of redundancy, the idea is to avoid the cost of lost revenue, downtime, and loss of goodwill. In short, it's usually better to tell the customer, "I'm sorry this is taking a little longer, but we've had a system failure and we're doing our best to keep things going" than it is to say, "I'm sorry, our systems are down; can we call you back on that later?"

Mirroring and RAID Technology

A particular approach to redundancy as it relates to the security of data is to use a technique called mirroring, which was first introduced in Chapter 10. This is a technique that does pretty much what the name suggests: Specific areas of a disk or a file system are duplicated, byte by byte, on another physical device (that is, a disk). Yes, this requires more disk space and disk drives, but provides very good protection against the loss of data in the event of a hard disk crash. Anyone who has suffered from a hard disk crash on his or her own workstation knows how difficult the situation can be, and might be willing to spend a little extra money to avoid the experience in the future.

If a mirrored disk fails, the host system simply uses the mirror image until the failed disk can be replaced. In fact, when a volume is being mirrored, the host system actually uses both of them all the time. While the system administrators may find that the disk crash provides a bit of excitement in an otherwise routine day, most of the system's end users will hardly notice any difference. At least, that's how it's supposed to work.

In reality, mirroring is a strategy that requires a good bit of forethought and planning. Some kinds of data are obvious candidates for mirroring, such as system areas. Other areas matter less, such as temporary storage areas or areas reserved for individual users' home directories. Data that is not particularly dynamic in nature, such as executable code that can be reinstalled from the original source, may not be a good candidate for mirroring. On the other hand, if the code is critical to daily business operations and short down times are not acceptable, then it may be advisable to mirror even relatively static code. These are decisions that have to be made on a case-by-case basis, given the demands of the organization and the structure of the systems environment.

Different operating systems may implement mirroring technologies differently, so it is important to consider which file areas are to be mirrored before setting up the systems. Once a file system is implemented on a host system, it can be very difficult and time consuming to change it. Of course, the system must be able to respond to the needs of the organization, and those needs may change, so the system must be able to adapt as well. Careful planning can help to minimize the cost of those changes.

The tendency of data to grow over time is also an important consideration. The system manager who says, "Gee, I really don't need all this disk space" is a rare individual indeed, and the end user who says to the system manager, "Here, please, take some of this storage off my hands" is even rarer. The pack rat syndrome runs rampant among users of networked computer systems, especially when their own local hard disks become crowded with data. The natural inclination is to move data off of the personal workstation to the server, where resources appear infinite. Unfortunately, those resources are neither infinite nor without cost, but the system exists to serve the users — therefore, the tendency is to allow the amount of disk space to grow. This in itself is not a bad thing, but again, it means that the system managers must carefully consider what data and how much data they intend to mirror—before they set up the system.

Mirroring is accomplished by software, provided there are two destination volumes (that is, disks) available, but there is an increasingly popular (and affordable) technology known as RAID that is used in conjunction with mirroring. RAID (introduced in Chapter 10) is an acronym meaning Redundant Array of Inexpensive Disks. Essentially, this is a series of relatively inexpensive disk drives and controllers (the hardware that allows the computer to read from and write to the disks) configured so as to facilitate mirroring. The RAID array may be internal, that is, mounted within the computer cabinet itself, external, housed in its own cabinet, or rack-mounted, meaning it is treated as a separate component, but is mounted in a rack that may contain any number of other components—including the computer, for instance.

RAID technology provides data security through mirroring, and also improved performance and security through the use of multiple controllers. The controllers provide a channel through which the computer communicates with the disks. Think of the controller as a bridge. If only one bridge exists between the processor and the data, then all the traffic going to or from the disks, no matter which disk the data is destined for, must travel across the same bridge. Sound like a formula for a traffic jam? Well, it might be, depending on how much data needs to travel over that bridge. At some point it may be a good idea to build a second bridge. That is basically what multiple controllers provide. Instead of making all the data go over a single channel to the disk drives, multiple controllers allow the computer to use a path that is less congested.

This strategy can be very helpful with respect to mirroring, because when particular volumes are mirrored, the amount of read/write operations associated with that data are increased. That is, if you are keeping a mirror image of all the data on a given volume, then every time you access that volume, you must consider two separate physical locations.

Many RAID arrays also include hot-swappable drives, which aid the recovery from disk failure in a mirrored environment. Hot-swappable means that the disks can be changed without shutting down the computer. This leads to some very dramatic presentations by the vendors hawking the product, as one might imagine, however, there is a real advantage to being able to replace a failed drive.

Finally, it's worth noting that RAID has performance advantages that are not necessarily related to the security of data. There are clear advantages to setting up host file systems so that read/write operations that are normally executed in tandem (such as executing and logging transactions in a database system) can be executed on separate physical structures. This means using different disks and controllers. Stripping (building logical file system structures across multiple physical resources) is another way of enhancing performance in sophisticated environments, and RAID technology can be very useful in implementing stripping as well.

Backup Strategies

Is there anyone left who hasn't lost an important file at one time or another? We've all had nightmares about that file that just blew up for no apparent reason. System managers may have more nightmares of that kind than most people, since they're in charge of files that don't even belong to them.

There's something comforting to the rest of us in thinking, "Oh, it's alright if something happens to that file. I saved it on the server, so it gets backed up every night." That thought isn't so comforting to the system manager. Somehow, the restored file is never exactly the same file you lost, and it's always the system manager's fault, of course. The litany is endless: "Please back up anything you can't afford to lose. Don't assume someone else will take care of it for you, even if we intend to. Accidents can happen to anyone."

We've all heard it. And we've all taken heed and make our own frequent backups . . . in theory. Until you've been burned yourself, you never quite believe that it can happen to you. After you've lost a file, or even a disk, you tend to be more careful, but even then most people, even systems professionals, are not very structured or methodical about it. It tends to be an afterthought, not something that's considered critical.

Well, for the system manager, it is absolutely critical, and it better not be an afterthought. Computers are, after all, machines, and all machines are eventually fallible. When someone is driving a car with over one hundred thousand miles on it, we tend to be impressed. Most of us expect our cars to fail before we get that far. For some reason, we don't ever expect our computers to fail. But they will. Eventually, all machines wear out. And when a computer fails and data is lost, someone is expected to restore the data. That is the reason we do backups. Not for peace of mind, not simply to keep generations of data for historical purposes — although both of those things may enter into it — but because one day we will be called upon to restore data, and we must be prepared to do it. In order to restore data, we have to have a backup.

What is a backup? Essentially, it's just a copy of important data, but that copy may come in a variety of forms. Saving a copy of a file to an alternate disk is the simplest form of a backup. Likewise, there are various utilities to create archives of files, and other backup and restore applications create backup sets (basically a set of files stored — perhaps on multiple disks or tapes — in a single volume). There are various advantages and disadvantages to each approach.

Using Windows to copy a file, for instance, has the advantage of creating a file that can be used as is, in whatever application was used to create it originally. A .ZIP archive file must be unzipped using a utility program. And a backup set usually has to be used with the program that created it (although not necessarily on the same machine). Backup utilities also create a log file in addition to the backup data itself. The purpose of the log file is to provide a record of the backup and restore application of the files that were originally backed up and included in the set.

The log file enables a user, when executing a restore operation, to use the application to select a particular file, a group of files, an entire directory, or even an entire disk drive's contents for restoration. As a result, there is considerable flexibility. In other words, the backup can be used to restore a copy of a single file, or to reconstruct an entire disk, whereas a single file copy can only be used to replace that single file. Most backup and restore applications also include a convenient user interface that makes performing the backup and restore operations easier and more intuitive.

What to Back Up?

It's tempting to make the assumption that anything that's important enough to put on your disk in the first place is important enough to back up, but the truth is, some data really matters and some really doesn't. For instance, if you're a user of any of the versions of Microsoft Windows, you probably make use of a "swap file," which may be permanent or may be temporary. If you use a permanent swap file, then there is a specific file created on your disk for Windows to use. When you exit Windows, the file definition remains (and the file is usually relatively large). This is not a file that needs to be backed up, because it has no purpose after you exit Windows in any case.

Likewise, there may be other files on your hard disk that, in the event of a total loss, would be best restored from an original source medium (disks or CD-ROM, for instance), rather than from a backup set. In fact, in some cases, such as your operating system or your backup and restore application, you may have to reinstall the software in order to be able to use the restore function. So, not all files are necessarily good candidates for backing up.

There are other files and directories that, although it may be wise to have a backup copy, don't change very often. A good example of this is most application software. Your word processing software isn't likely to change very often (although your document files probably are), so it's probably not necessary to back it up every week. One copy of the original is enough. This kind of backup, a one-time-only thing, is referred to as archiving. In fact, most software license agreements prohibit the end user from copying the original disks, except for archival purposes. In other words, even the vendors expect you to make a copy of the original disks, just in case something happens to them.

There are certainly some files that are subject to frequent change. These files, dynamic in nature, are usually the ones that are the most difficult to replace if something happens to them. For example, if a printer driver file used by Windows becomes corrupt, it's usually fairly simple to reinstall the printer. As long as you have the original disks (or an archive copy), Windows will recreate the printer driver and put everything back in order. But if you lose your budget model, the one you've been working on for six weeks, the one that's due to be turned in tomorrow morning, you can bet your last dollar it's going to be next to impossible to recover. This, of course, is more than a matter of inadequate backup planning, it's Murphy's Law in action. But that's why we make backups, right?

Finally, some data files are actually extracts from other sources. Many decision support systems (ad hoc query and reporting systems), for example, are built using databases that actually consist of copies of data maintained in other systems. It's worth asking yourself just how important it is to make a backup of that data. If the extract is fairly complicated in nature — for instance, if the data is organized differently in the decision support system versus how it is kept in the originating system, or if the extract takes a long time to run and impacts performance of the originating system — then it may be a good idea to back it up.

Another reason to backup secondary data sources (data extracted from other original sources) is to preserve the integrity of historical perspective. Many times production systems are oriented toward the current status of the records. Historical data may not be maintained in the production environment. However, historical data can be critical to decision support environments. Marketing analysis, for instance, makes frequent use of historical data to identify trends or pinpoint problem areas.

What about e-mail? The whole issue of whose mail it is remains fairly controversial, although it is now generally understood that e-mail does not possess the same assumption of personal privacy that postal mail has always had. E-mail is, after all, an electronic communication, and the messages end up stored in files on disks. Should that data be backed up? If you think this question is perhaps carrying the debate a little far, think again. Suppose those backed-up e-mail messages constitute evidence of criminal activity—conspiracy, for example. Or perhaps they contain internal communications on the status of sensitive business negotiations or new product developments. Maybe you want to keep copies of those files, maybe not.

There is, of course, a huge difference between losing data and destroying it. Destroying evidence of criminal activity is a crime, and that's obviously unethical. However, that doesn't mean that you have to keep backup copies of sensitive business documents—strategy memos, trade secrets, investment negotiations, and so forth. That's an individual business decision, but then, that's the point of this entire discussion. There are many factors that affect the business decision regarding what data to back up. Table 13.2 gives some guidelines and criteria on strategies for your choice in what to back up.

NOTE

There is another form of backup known as *image backup*. Image backups are fast and easy and work quite well as long as you're willing to restore the entire disk at once. Because you're really just making an image of the physical storage device (that is, the disk) at a point in time, you cannot selectively restore a single file or a group of files. You have to restore the entire disk or nothing at all. That's why they are useful for complex configurations (mostly desktop operating systems). Overall, image backups are not very practical for most circumstances.

How Often Should I Back Up?

It is essential for the organization to plan its backup strategy, and a part of that planning process is deciding what to back up, what kind of backups to do, when to do it (as in what time of day or night), how often, and where to keep them. All of these issues enter into the decision. So far we've discussed what data needs to be backed up. But how often should you do it?

TABLE 13.2 Backup Strategy Decision Criteria	DECISION FACTOR	WHY IS IT IMPORTANT?
	Nature of the files	Do you care if this gets lost? If not, why bother to back it up? Good examples include swap files, temporary space, lab environments that can be easily recreated, and so on.
	Frequency of change	Determine how often you may need to back up this data. Sometimes it may not make sense to back it up at all, as in the case of application executable files, which you may be able to restore from original media just as easily and efficiently as from backups.
	Data sources and use	Secondary data sources do not need to be backed up if it is just as easy to recreate the data by going to the original source and rerunning the jobs that create the files. On the other hand, if some of the data is historical in nature, you may not be able to recreate it from the original sources anymore.
	Security and privacy	Do you have a document shredder in your office? Do you keep electronic files that you might like to put through "the shredder" under some circumstances? Then don't back them up.
	Legal issues	There may be legal or regulatory reasons why an organization is required to keep historical data or to maintain data for a specific period of time before destroying it (tax returns, environmental compliance reports, and so on).

Well, to offer a reasonable answer to that question, it's necessary to consider two others:

▸ How often does your critical data change?

▸ How important is it to capture every nuance of every change in the data?

The first question addresses the dynamic nature of the data; the second, the consequences of losing it.

We've already discussed the importance of backing up data that almost never changes, and we decided that archival is a reasonable approach. But even data that is not suitable for archival doesn't necessarily have to be backed up every time you run a backup. For instance, a file may change daily but only be used at month-end. Is it important to back up that file on a nightly basis, or is it enough to back it up at month-end? Although this example may make it sound as if the decision is a simple one, in reality it involves a detailed understanding of the databases, the way the applications use the databases, and the way the organization uses its applications.

This last issue, the way the organization uses its applications, goes to the heart of the second question we asked a moment ago: How important is it to capture every nuance of every change in the data? Another way of thinking about this question is to consider what might happen if you failed to capture every nuance of every change in the data. What are the consequences?

If the consequences of losing data, even just a particular iteration of some important data, are more than the organization can stand, then obviously it's important to make sure that all the necessary files are covered. The budget model we have mentioned before is a good example of this at the individual level.

If you've ever gone through the budgeting process, you know how many times you may make seemingly minor changes to accounts for different scenarios. And even though the changes seemed minor at the time you made them—after all, you were just experimenting with several possibilities, right?—it invariably turns out that, say, the third variation you did on the staff plan came out with the numbers you need now. But you've already moved past that particular version of the model, and you can't quite remember what your assumptions were. "Now, how did I get the salary and bonuses to work out that way?" you ask yourself. Did you save a copy?

The budget model really relates to how hard it is for you to recreate your work, not how much the organization suffers if you have to stay up late. But the principle is the same: If it's going to hurt to lose it, back it up often. Again, this may sound like a simple decision, but in reality it involves forethought and planning, just as the choices about redundancy involved careful planning.

Backup Media

Once you've got a plan for what files to back up and how often to back them up, you'll probably end up with some kind of a schedule. For instance, you may decide that you'll make a full-system backup (meaning a backup of all the files worth backing up, regardless of whether they've changed since the last time you backed them up) every Sunday morning beginning at 2:00 a.m., and a modified-files backup (a backup of all the files that have changed since the last time you backed them up) every morning, Tuesday through Saturday, beginning at 2:00 a.m.

You may notice a couple of things about this schedule. First, this process is set to begin at 2:00 in the morning, not an hour that many of us wish to be found in the office. There is the occasional hearty soul, but unless your organization runs a late shift, 2:00 a.m. is likely to be a difficult time to find someone to put disks in the drive every couple of minutes.

Second, this schedule runs from Tuesday through Sunday . . . shouldn't that be Monday through Saturday? Well, no—if you begin at 2:00 in the morning—it definitely shouldn't. But the fact is, you may have reasons to make backups every day, even Monday morning (Sunday night, if you prefer). The point is, this is something that needs to be done on a regular basis, and because you cannot usually back up open files, it needs to be done at an hour when most of the files are not in use. Remember, in many production environments, batch processes run from the close of business into the night. If those processes result in updated data files that need to be backed up, the backup can't start until late.

So, backups need to be automated. Let's face it, the graveyard shift is a lonely place. Fortunately, it is possible in most cases to schedule backups for late hours and to run them unattended. That is, they can be run unattended unless the destination medium (tape is the most common) fills up and needs to be changed. At that point, the backup will usually stop and wait for someone to change the tape. And if you started at 2:00 a.m., it's likely that no one will change the tape until people start arriving for work in the morning, at which time they will want to start using their systems and the data files that go with them. That presents a problem, because open files can't usually be backed up. Either the people wait for the backup to finish, or the backup isn't done that night.

It's important to consider the backup target medium. That is, what kind of device you back up to.

Diskettes

Most of us have done back ups to diskettes at some point. Since a diskette can only hold 1.44 megabytes of information — smaller than many office files — this is hardly a plausible solution anymore. Now ask yourself how practical it is to use that medium to back up 5 or 6GB of data stored on various servers. Obviously, it isn't practical at all. Fortunately, other media from removable storage, tape, and redundant disks are available.

Removable Media

Certain types of removable media can be used for network storage. Iomega's Zip or Jaz files provide fast storage for certain types of files. The drives, however, tend to backup only one disk at a time and can be more expensive than other types of media.

Hard Disks

Sometimes the easiest thing to do is to back up data to other online hard disk storage devices. If you need to back up, let's say, 50GB, and you just happen to have an extra 50GB of available disk storage online, it's easily the fastest and simplest target medium to use. With hard disk storage costing well below seven dollars a gigabyte and going on a half-price sale each year, redundant storage is becoming a viable option for certain critical data.

While hard disk backup is convenient and fast, it is not portable. The requirement for off site storage usually requires that you use an alternative method.

Optical

Optical storage devices (CD-R, CD-RW, DVD-RAM) are also used for backing up. These are very reliable, have a relatively high storage capacity per CD or DVD, and last for a very long time. They're also not subject to contamination by magnetic fields. They make a pretty good target medium for archival backups.

Tape

Tape drives continue to be a common form of backup media. Tapes come in all size formats (quarter-inch cartridge or QIC, 8mm DAT, and others), and a wide variety of storage capacities. Since tape storage is a mature technology, so is its refinement when it comes to archiving and storage. As drives and software evolve, compression algorithms have become more and more efficient, resulting in tape formats that hold ever increasing amounts of data. Today it is possible to store gigabytes of data on a single cartridge and get an easy to use catalog of where all the files are.

Another approach is to use more than one type of backup to manage the process. Although this may require the purchase of more than one copy of your preferred backup software and more than one target device, it enables you to run backups of different file areas simultaneously to different target devices. This has the obvious advantage of reducing the time required to complete the backup. It also may be wise to make sure your backup system is behind locked doors in the event of a break-in.

While tape storage remains popular, keep in mind that it's basically an analog process. When you need to restore files saved to tape, the device must fast forward through all other files until it gets to the ones you need. This can be a time consuming process if you are in a hurry when trying to restore files.

Strategy and Implementation

So now you have a backup strategy, a schedule, and the necessary hardware, software, and backup media to perform your backups. Finished? Well, not quite. There's one other issue to consider.

What do you do with your tapes and how many do you need? Although tape backup is less destructive than optical backup, it isn't indestructible. The tapes will eventually wear out. If you've gone to all the trouble to carefully plan your strategy, the last thing you want is to find yourself in the position of needing to restore a file from backup, and discovering the tape is no good. The solution is to develop, in addition to a backup strategy and schedule, a tape rotation strategy.

Consider how many times you can use the tape before it wears out, and how important it is to keep specific versions of your backups. For instance, if you are making a full-system backup once a week and modified-files backups every other night (except Sunday night/Monday morning), and you want to keep each nightly tape for a week before you write over it, you need six tapes. If you're willing to overwrite each tape once a week, that's all you need. If, on the other hand, you want to save each week's full-system backup for a month, then you will typically need an additional three tapes. If you want to do a special month-end backup once a month and save that tape for a year, you will need an additional twelve tapes. This can be simple, or it can be very complicated.

Perhaps the simplest approach is to do a full-system backup every night and keep each day's tape for a month. In that case, you need 31 tapes, and each night you would pull the tape with that day's date on it, insert it in the tape drive, and trust the backup software to kick off the job that night. As long as you can get a full-system backup on one tape and you don't mind having some extra tapes each month, this system will work quite well, and no tape will be used more than twelve times in a year. If that seems like too many uses, you can replace the supply of tapes after six months and no single tape will be used more than six times. However, it does require a lot of tapes, and therefore costs a bit more than a more conservative strategy. (But tape is cheap, so don't be too conservative.)

Finally, you may want to consider periodically sending at least one of your tapes to a safe location away from the office. Why? For the same reason you might send sensitive documents off-site. You spread the risk of loss that way. And to the extent that the off-site storage location is fireproof and maintains tight security, you not only spread the risk, you spread it to a low-risk site as well. For instance, you may want to store your month-end tapes in a safe-deposit box at a bank.

Restoring Data

Thankfully, most of the planning and organization required for the backup strategy is not required for the restore step. On the other hand, the reason it's not as difficult to plan and execute is that you hope you never have to do it at all; and if you do have to do it, there isn't a lot to think about. Usually you aren't asked to restore a file until every other avenue has been exhausted, and by that time, everyone just wants the file back, regardless of what it takes. That makes things simpler, but there are still some things to think about.

For instance, it is important to manage people's expectations, particularly with regard to how long it will take to complete the restoration, and how complete the restoration will be. Generally, when someone asks to have a file restored, they are already frustrated and nervous, so they want it back immediately. They also expect to have everything they need in place as soon as the restoration is done. Occasionally, there is more than one file required to put things back the way they were, which the end user may not realize.

How long should it take to restore a file? That depends primarily on the size of the file and the medium it's on. Bigger files take longer to restore, which isn't usually a problem unless the file begins on one tape and ends on another. Also, the tape medium is sequential, whereas disks are random access devices. To get to a particular place on the tape you have to roll the tape forward to that point. With a disk, the read/write heads can simply move to the correct location. As a result, it may take a few minutes to advance the tape to the point where the file begins. If you have a multiple tape backup set, it may be necessary to load the first tape, read the header to determine which tape contains the affected file(s), load the correct tape, advance to the right location, and begin the restoration.

As for the completeness of the restoration, modified-files backups can make things complicated. If, for instance, a particular file was changed daily for an entire week, then there will be six different copies of the file (based on our previous example of one full-system backup and five modified-files backups). Which version is the correct one? Remember that if the user wants the version with which he or she was working on Wednesday afternoon, then the tape made Thursday morning will have that file. If the user is actually looking for the version he or she saved at 3:30 p.m., but later modified and saved again at 5:15 p.m., the 3:30 version wasn't backed up anywhere.

Occasionally it's not enough to simply restore a particular file. There may be other files associated with the data file that need to be restored also. For example, there may be both a document file and an associated graphic that was imbedded in the document. If the graphic file was not stored in the document (that is, a link to the graphic file was stored, but not the graphic file itself), then it may be necessary to restore the graphic file also. Obviously, it's advantageous to know everything that has to be restored before beginning the process, because it can take a long time to find the right files on the tape.

Finally, it may be wise to perform a verification of the restored file before reporting its restoration to the user. Sometimes the process of restoring a file to disk from tape doesn't succeed for some reason. Most backup and restore software is able to verify that the restored file is identical to what is on the tape. (By the way, this can be done in the other direction when the backup is made, but verifying a backup can add a substantial amount of time to the process.) Whether to verify your backup or not is a question of how much risk you are willing to assume.

Disaster Recovery

Back at the beginning of this chapter we defined a disaster, and we said it could be something as apparently trivial as a lost file, or something as major as an earthquake. Most of this chapter has been devoted to the discussion of backup and restoration because, frankly, if you've had a fire or an earthquake, you probably have a lot of problems to deal with, and recovering your data and systems is only one of them. After all, in a real disaster there may be loss of life, people may have lost their homes — the scale of trouble can easily exceed the kind of issues related to protecting the organization's data.

That is not to suggest that the organization should just cross its fingers and hope for the best. Ultimately, even in a major disaster involving real human tragedy, the resumption of the business that provides people their livelihood is still an important issue. And it is not enough to simply hope it doesn't happen here. You must ask the question, "What do I do if it does happen to me?"

Insurance is very important but it's not enough. Its purpose is to indemnify you against the potential financial losses of a catastrophic event. It doesn't help you get back in business, though. Fortunately, there are some viable strategies for planning the resumption of business.

Most major systems vendors and many management and systems consulting firms provide expertise in the area of creating a business continuation plan or a disaster recovery plan. It is a complicated process, and may well be worth hiring professional advisors to help develop the plan. Even if you don't hire help to create the plan, it's probably worthwhile to consider hiring for other services.

For instance, begin by considering the worst possible scenario. Assume a disaster has resulted in the complete destruction of your place of business. (By complete destruction, understand that we mean your building is simply gone. If this sounds extreme, well, perhaps it is, but it is not excessive — the destruction that Hurricane Andrew brought to South Florida was clearly of that scale.) Where do you begin? Logically, the first thing you need to look for (after checking on your people, of course) is a place to set up shop. Next you need some replacement machines. You have to reroute communications circuits to the new location (if wide-area data communications are an issue, that's one thing, but at the very least you need your voice telephones moved), and you need to reestablish your own operating environment—not just computers and software, but all the various combinations of machines and people that are the real nuts and bolts of any modern business enterprise.

If the disaster was localized to your particular building, then you probably have a chance at finding some space in the same general vicinity where you can begin to restore all your operations. But let's say there's been a hurricane, and the devastation is complete for a radius of fifty miles. Where do you go? How do your people get there?

Even once you've found a place, how fast can you replace the machines? If all you need are PCs, you stand a reasonable chance of finding a good number of the size and type of equipment you need, and can probably have it shipped to your new location quickly. But what if you need some special equipment? Say, a high-performance minicomputer, superserver, or even a mainframe? Those machines usually have a lead time associated with delivery. If you have to wait eight weeks to get your database server, are you going to be able to get back in business at all? Maybe you should just take the insurance settlement and start a new business.

Even if you are able to locate a site, and you miraculously find all the machines you need, do you have sufficient staff to set it all up again? And once you get it all set up, do you have your backup tapes, or were they destroyed with the building?

OK, this is hypothetical and very depressing. But take heart; no matter how bad things look, if you've planned carefully, you've already thought of all this. And if you've signed deals with the right people, you may even have rehearsed for just this sort of situation. Yes, there are vendors who can provide services to address some or even all of these issues. Let's take them one at a time.

Office space—where are you going to find it? Many of the vendors will promise to make space available to you at an alternate site within a specific period of time. It may not be in your general area, especially if the disaster has been widespread, but under the circumstances, will you care? They will also negotiate to provide transportation and housing for your staff at whatever location they have. Of course, the more you want, the more it will cost, but consider the consequences. The vendors we're talking about aren't office space companies, by and large. They are systems vendors and consulting organizations that specialize in disaster recovery planning.

How quickly can you get replacement machines? Remember the hot spares concept? It applies here, too, except you don't necessarily have to buy a spare machine and keep it idle. Most manufacturers will offer some kind of agreement to give you priority access to new machines in case of an emergency, or to temporarily provide you with surplus or reconditioned equipment until you can take delivery of replacement equipment. They even provide the staff to install and configure the equipment at the new location. You will likely have to provide supervision and direction to ensure that things are done according to your standards, but you can get that help on an emergency basis.

As for getting your data back, remember that discussion of off-site storage? If you took care to make sure your data was protected in a fail-safe environment, you should be able to get it all back in relatively short order. In the end, you can negotiate agreements for all the services you need to get your business back up and on-line quickly. But how do you know it will work? You rehearse. Once a year or so you have a rehearsal. You pretend the hurricane just hit and everything's gone. You take a few days and put your vendors and your agreements to the test. If you get your business back in business within tolerable time limits (you have to decide what that is), then you can have confidence that it will be done under real conditions.

Summary

The question isn't whether disaster planning is worth it, but how much is it worth? Like all other business decisions, this one boils down to how much risk you are willing to assume. What's a reasonable risk, and what's not?

Realistically, you can't prevent earthquakes. You can do a lot to prevent fires, but they still happen. In the end, Mother Nature is still bigger than we are. Even the things we do to ourselves aren't completely preventable. As with security, it's not possible to build a completely foolproof disaster prevention system, and if it were, it probably wouldn't be financially responsible to do it. So we try to anticipate the things we can do something to prevent, and we prepare to recover from the things we can't.

The basic lessons are simple. To the extent that you can afford redundancy, practice it. Machines fail; it's just part of the nature of machines. They may last a long time, they may prove to be more reliable than you have a right to expect, but they're still machines and eventually they fail. Rarely do two of the same machines fail at the same time, however, so redundancy is a very effective strategy.

If you can't afford complete redundancy, at least make backups on a regular basis. Make sure to back up the things you really need, and don't waste time on what you don't need. Be careful and methodical. Take care of your tapes and store them in a safe place. If you have to use them, make sure everyone understands the limitations, and make sure you've done everything you can to minimize the impact of those limitations.

And for those things you can't prevent, plan what to do if they happen. Consider what risks you can afford to assume, cover the ones you can't assume, and rehearse so everyone knows what to do when the time comes. Also, remember to keep things in perspective. Real disasters cause real problems for real people. Machines can be replaced, data can be restored, but people are the heart of any organization.

If you plan carefully, implement your plans, test your assumptions, and finally, rehearse, you should be prepared if a disaster comes to pass. Then you can concentrate on the things that really matter, knowing your business will recover.

CHAPTER 14

Training Users

In this chapter we discuss the importance of training everyone in your organization who uses the LAN. You have worked so hard to plan, develop, and install your network — make sure everyone is ready to enjoy it. Just as you wouldn't dare buy an expensive automobile for someone without a driver's license, don't attempt to manage a network or allow users to access your LAN without first preparing yourself and them with the necessary skills.

Network Administrator Training

In keeping with our use of Novell NetWare as an example, Novell provides a host of NetWare-related courses, including those dealing with teaching technical subjects. Attend the training course yourself. Then you can assist novice users by conducting in-house courses yourself, or you can arrange training to be conducted by hardware and software vendors. By explaining how to use the network and teaching the users how to use their applications, you save hours responding to unnecessary phone calls and repeatedly answering hundreds of routine questions. Many users' questions are nontechnical and concern their applications, such as "I can't log in," "the printer isn't working," or "why won't my spreadsheet sort properly?"

Although you need some fundamental training, you can support the organization best with a broad knowledge of the ways the network can improve users' productivity. Of course, you will have to deal with crises from time to time. You may need to have an outside support group help you with the hardware failures, but you should be able to do basic troubleshooting to identify the causes of failures.

If you choose NetWare as your network operating system, you should have the following technical skills as network administrator:

- A good working knowledge of the major NOSs (Novell NetWare, Microsoft Windows NT/2000, and Linux)

- A good working knowledge of the particular NOS software currently used on the LAN you are managing

- An understanding of the NOS's security rights

► An understanding of network hardware and software components

► The ability to create a workable directory structure, construct login scripts, create new users and directories, and provide a working environment for users

► The ability to load applications, perform system backups, and define and control print queues

► The ability to create and maintain a database of network component and workstation configuration information

If you are an aspiring LAN manager, you will need to receive some training to carry out advanced maintenance and operations of your LAN. Some of the subjects with which you need to be familiar include:

Hardware and software basics	Console utilities
Directory structure	Printing
Mapping	Login scripts
Security	Menu creation
Command line and menu utilities	Loading application software
Supervisor utilities	Backup and restore

With the above knowledge and skills, you are well prepared for developing procedures to conduct routine network maintenance and operations tasks.

Training someone to be a comfortable user of applications residing on a LAN isn't complicated and can be conducted in many different ways over a period of time. Let's discuss some of your options, beginning with the basics.

. . . . ◄

User Training

As a thoroughly trained LAN manager, it's important that you participate in the process of developing user training programs. The more knowledge the users have, the less time you will spend supporting them. Beginners should first learn about basic computer operations and networks, followed by training in the applications and procedures they use in their jobs and how the network supports their work. Although self-paced instruction is the least expensive, we have found that classroom instruction is the most effective. Users can return to their desktop PCs and immediately begin to apply what they have learned and then take advanced courses to build on their knowledge. However, always start with the basics.

Covering the Basics

If you ever learned to ride a bicycle as a child, you probably remember the first time you sat on the seat. Perched high, with one foot on a pedal and one firmly on the ground, you looked back to verify that indeed the training wheels had been removed, took a deep breath, then launched yourself on a wing and a prayer. Much to your amazement and exhilaration, you rode. Why? Because you started with the basics.

As a new user riding a PC on a LAN, you probably won't feel anything near the emotions characterized in the above situation, but you should be no less prepared before pedaling yourself onto the local "information bike path."

The basics of network computing can be presented by simply having users take advantage of the tutorials that come with various desktop applications. Another effective basic training method is to require all first-time users to read the user manuals that come as part of the various application software packages loaded on your network nodes.

Formal training can be either conducted in-house or out-sourced, depending on the level of complexity and the resources you have available. We recommend, again, that you start with the basics. The basics include one-day familiarization classes for those members who will typically use Windows 95/98/2000 as a normal part of their job.

It's very easy to set up introductory-level classes designed to familiarize new users with these products, as long as you have the resources available and someone willing to develop the course outline.

Developing a Basic In-House Computer Training Course

A typical course plan will consist of the following general areas:

▶ Course title (to include number of hours or days required)

▶ Course description

- Prerequisites

- List of objectives

- Topical outline

- Class agenda

If you use the above list when developing a computer training strategy for your organization, we feel your courses will be a comprehensive and constructive learning experience. For a better idea of what a typical computer applications course plan looks like, take a look at the sample shown in Figure 14.1.

If you, as the network manager, also end up being the basic computer training course instructor, use this time with your "captive audience" to share your management philosophy and general network rules and procedures. Also, consider issuing user network access and passwords to each trainee upon their completion of the basic computer training course.

Training Environment

Ideally, if you have the facilities, your training classroom should meet some or all of the following criteria in order to provide the best possible environment for effective, hands-on computer-related instruction:

- Convenient location

- Room to accommodate ten to fifteen students (any more becomes too impersonal)

- Good environmental controls (The ideal training class temperature is 68–76 degrees.)

- Comfortable seating and training stations

- One computer training station per student

- Large computer monitor or LCD (to project instructor's own computer screen)

FIGURE 14.1

Sample plan for computer training course

Introduction to Microsoft Office 2000

One Day Course

Course Description
  This class is designed for students who want to learn to use the Microsoft Office Shortcut Bar; start, open, and save Office documents; and use Binders. In addition, students will learn to use the new features of Word 2000, Excel 2000, and PowerPoint 2000.

Prerequisites
  Microsoft Windows 95/98 or Microsoft Word 6.0 for Windows, Excel 5.0 for Windows, and PowerPoint 4.0 for Windows

Objectives
  ▶ Use the Microsoft Office Shortcut Bar
  ▶ Start, open, and save Office documents
  ▶ Use Binders

Topical Outline
  1. Using the Microsoft Office Shortcut Bar
  2. Introduction to Office 2000
  3. Starting the Office Shortcut Bar
  4. The Office toolbar
  5. Changing toolbars
  6. Switching between toolbars
  7. Hiding the Office Shortcut Bar
  8. Moving the Office Shortcut Bar
  9. Fitting the Office Shortcut Bar in the title bar
  10. Customizing the Office Shortcut Bar view options
  11. Creating new toolbars
  12. Adding and removing buttons
  13. Starting a new Office 2000 document
  14. Opening an Office 2000 document
  15. Saving documents in Office 2000
  16. Using the Answer Wizard
  17. Introduction to Binders
  18. Creating a Binder
  19. Adding sections to a Binder
  20. Saving a Binder
  21. Working with sections
  22. Printing a Binder

Class Agenda

7:30 a.m.–8:00 a.m.	Instructor introduction & facilities familiarization
8:00 a.m.–9:00 a.m.	Instruction on topical items 1–5
9:00 a.m.–9:15 a.m.	Break
9:15 a.m.–11:30 a.m.	Instruction on topical items 6–12
11:30 a.m.–1:00 p.m.	Lunch break
1:00 p.m.–2:00 p.m.	Instruction on topical items 13–18
2:00 p.m.–2:15 p.m.	Break
2:15 p.m.–3:15 p.m.	Instruction on topical items 19–23
3:15 p.m.	Formal training ends
3:15 p.m.–4:30 p.m.	Instructor available to provide additional assistance

- ► Proper lighting

- ► Easy access to rest rooms and break rooms

Multimedia Training

Additionally, your corporate intranet can function as a training tool. You can point your users to lists of frequently asked questions (FAQs), offline resources, and even provide multimedia training — with the help of linked HTML pages and built-in multimedia vignettes.

Video and audio can stream across the networks of a corporate intranet to provide just-in-time training on topics ranging from a "How To..." of a particular software package to more complex, work-related problem solving tasks.

These vignettes can be only 30–60 seconds in length and may include screen-captured video demonstrating quick solutions to common computer-related problems, or may have an actor on screen discussing more in-depth topics.

A few innovative companies have even discovered that these training videos were so effective on their intranets, that they posted the vignettes to their Internet site as free training for their customers on their hardware products.

Pursuing Other Options

Not all computer-related training has to take place in front of a computer terminal. Many subjects can be taught in a more traditional classroom or conference room setting. The following subjects could be taught or reviewed without the use of a computer:

- ► Network security features

- ► Desktop (node) security practices

- ► Company network policies and procedures

- ► How a network operates

Network Library

In Chapter 11 we outlined the importance of the extensive documentation that you need to maintain as references for the various aspects of your local area network. These documents don't have to be in paper form; however, until your users become familiar with accessing these read-only files, we suggest they take what we like to call "the temporary form of information" — paper.

We certainly encourage you to use electronic documenting methods wherever and whenever possible, but regardless of the medium you choose for your documentation, make sure it's available to your LAN users and administrators alike.

The following is a basic list of library items you can start with and add to as time goes on:

▶ Binders containing all network documentation (see Chapter 11)

▶ NOS administrator manuals

▶ Miscellaneous software manuals

▶ Miscellaneous hardware and peripherals manuals

▶ LAN troubleshooting guides

▶ This book, of course!

Follow-Up Training

Once you're comfortable that you and everyone else using the network have been adequately trained in the essentials, consider setting up a recurring follow-up training strategy. This strategy will allow for quick skills updates when future revisions to software packages are received from software vendors. Also, having a plan for future training builds upon your goals to not only expand your business, but expand your networking capabilities as well.

As we mentioned earlier, many software and hardware companies offer training opportunities in the form of on-site training, tutorial software, and interactive CD-ROMs, usually available at reasonable rates. There are many independent computer retailers and resellers who offer training classes at their locations. By and large, these training classes have been endorsed by the manufacturers and cater to all skill levels.

Also, look to your local community college for computer skills and software applications training. In many cases, semester-long classes offered by a college or university are credited toward college degrees. These college classes, while more expensive than traditional computer training options, are usually very comprehensive and designed to teach specific disciplines in detail.

Summary

When you train the users of your network, begin with those skills that are essential, build on them, and reinforce them through follow-up sessions. Remember that the more your users know about the LAN and the various applications they use, the more efficient they will be and the less time you will spend answering their questions.

CHAPTER 15

Troubleshooting

Troubleshooting. Just the word invokes fear, trepidation, and pain. Trouble, as in, "Houston, we have a problem." Shooting, as in, "I'm going to shoot someone if this server crashes again!" The file server is down, a file is corrupted or missing, a workstation is dead, Susan's printer won't print, and the list goes on. "It was working yesterday," you hear. "What are we going to do about the spreadsheet I've been working on all week that the boss is expecting today?" "I have to print these invoices today!" You've heard these cries for help before, or you've been the one crying. Don't panic right away. Today's tools and technicians can work wonders.

LAN technology is generally stable. Some LANs run trouble-free for years, while others need only an occasional repair call. NOSs are getting easier to install and maintain, hardware is becoming more standardized and stable, and application software is now more network compatible than ever. But any technology that is comprised of so many pieces — hardware, cable, and software — has potential for problems. And, of course, when problems occur it is always at the least convenient time.

This chapter is devoted to solving common problems quickly. We begin with practical tips for what to do first if something goes wrong. Then we divide up the probable points of failure and describe both what you can check yourself and what you should leave for a qualified repair technician.

. . . .

General Troubleshooting Guidelines

As in life, the first thing to remember when something goes wrong with your network is: don't panic. Sure, it's frustrating when the printer suddenly stops printing, or the drive doesn't read the disk anymore. Maintaining a cool head and using a step-by-step approach to problems will more than pay for itself. Often the user or network administrator can solve the problem if he or she is armed with the right information.

Problems can be intermittent or constant. The intermittent ones are the hardest to diagnose. If the problem is inconsistent and cannot be duplicated, it will be more difficult to diagnose and fix. Does it appear that a single workstation has the problem, a segment of the network, or the entire network? If one workstation is having the problem, look at the drivers, configuration, hardware, cabling, or software installed on the workstation. Try a different login, or a supervisor login from the workstation. Have the user go to another workstation and see if the problem is still there. If the problem persists, a change to their network rights could be the culprit.

Here are a few basic rules for approaching technical problems.

Identify the Problem

The first thing to do is identify the problem. Really identify the problem. "The printer won't work." Is it printing unintelligible characters? Is it printing light on one side of the paper? Is it printing Susan's document but not Tom's? Whether you're the one responsible for fixing the problem or you only have to call a technician to fix it, the first step is to isolate the difficulty. Things are not always as they seem.

A workstation that cannot access the server could be caused by buggy software on the workstation, corrupted or erased drivers, a bad network interface card, loose cabling, a bad port on the hub, a problem with the server, another workstation locking a file you need, or a bad login. The list is endless. The more you can identify, eliminate, and isolate, the better off you will be. Have users try to recreate the problem and write down the steps that lead up to the occurrence.

Is the whole network (that is, every workstation) down, a few workstations attached to one particular hub, or only one workstation? Are all printers down, or just one? Prepare a concise and accurate description of the problem.

Do documents print in Word, but not Excel? Does one user have problems or do all users? Can the problem be recreated? Ask these questions and investigate all variables before going on a wild goose chase. In the long run, you will save time by identifying the problem before you attempt to fix it.

Identify What Has Changed

Many times the cause of the problem is that something has changed, such as new equipment or software being installed. Try to remember the last time everything worked and what changed since then. Did it work last night, but is dead this morning? Someone could have set a desk on a cable, or knocked a cable loose.

Every lead is helpful. Don't think any detail is too trivial. Technicians have been overheard muttering to themselves, "I had a suspicion that was the problem at first, but didn't believe it was so simple." Some software installation programs change the AUTOEXEC.BAT and CONFIG.SYS files. This can create conflicts with memory and TSR programs. Network drivers are TSRs, and any change or addition can affect memory allocation. Table 15.1 (later in the chapter) lists a few common conflicts that may occur on networked workstations.

Discuss the Problem with Someone

Talk over the problem with someone else. Often the act of talking out loud will cause the answer to snap into focus immediately and almost by magic. Maybe this is why many network administrators are found talking to themselves. Talk to a colleague. Call your buddy next door who has a similar configuration. Call the vendor that installed or sold the system. They will have suggestions or may have had the same problem happen to another customer.

The Internet, and online services such as CompuServe and America Online have software forums where questions can be posted. Either software employees or other users will post answers if they have any. Most network software providers furnish an area on their Web sites for just such postings. Remember to state your problem concisely and with as many details as possible. Provide information such as NOS version, cabling, topology, hubs, and software installed on the server and workstation. Also include server information such as brand, processor, memory, installed peripherals, and so on. Be patient when using this medium. Answers are not immediate, but almost always forthcoming with time.

Look for the Obvious First

Many problems can be solved by a quick check of the fittings on cables and plugs. Repair technicians who've responded to "emergency" calls often walk away after just turning on the power switch or plugging in a loose cable. Are all cables connected, free of kinks, not frayed, and plugged into the correct connector? Just because everything was OK a few minutes ago, doesn't mean that it can't be a cable. The cleaning people could have moved or bumped the equipment during the night. You could have dropped something behind the computer and knocked something loose. A chair may have rolled over the cable and damaged it. Rats have even been known to chew through cables. Accessory cards can wiggle loose. The printer could be out of toner or paper. The power cable could be out of the wall outlet. The surge protector could be blown. The workstation can lose its CMOS setup. Reboot the workstation. Recheck everything.

Read (and Reread) the Manual

If there's still a problem after you've checked the obvious, locate the manual for the hardware or software that seems to be failing. Here's where things can get confusing. Sometimes what appears to be a hardware problem turns out to be software, or the other way around.

Generally, however, you can find clues. If, for example, you can't get a document to print from Word, but all your spreadsheets print fine from Excel, chances are something has gone astray with the word-processing software, rather than the printer or the cables. Knowing this, you would look for troubleshooting tips in the Word manual.

Often, just skimming through manuals will provide lots of clues. Look carefully at the installation instructions and ask yourself if everything was followed to the letter. Then look at those parts of the manual devoted to troubleshooting. Many software and hardware vendors anticipate potential conflicts and document them in their manuals.

Is the software a network version or a standalone? If it is a network version, is it tested for your network? Was it installed properly? Even if you don't find your specific problem outlined in the manual, you will have eliminated some possibilities and narrowed your search for the cause of the problem.

Change Only One Thing at a Time

It's all too easy to reinstall software, change out a driver, slap in a new network card, and change the cable in one fell swoop. If, after this, things start working, then fine, you're set. If they don't, you may have inadvertently introduced new complications into the scenario, confusing your search and adding to your problems. If you want to take this approach, replace the workstation with a working PC. If the problem persists, it isn't the workstation.

If you do change several variables at once and things start working, you'll still never know what went wrong in the first place. The symptoms could reoccur, leaving you to go through that whole time-consuming process to fix it again. You may throw out perfectly good equipment. Experienced network troubleshooters gather up all the clues and take one step at a time to find the right solution, beginning with the simplest fix first. Change the cable before changing a network card. Plug the dead workstation cable into another port on the hub if you suspect a single port on the hub is bad. Boot the workstation from a network floppy disk. If your NIC has lights, check the manual to see what they mean. Turn the printer off and on again.

Know Your Own Technical Limitations

Don't try to exceed your own technical limitations. While hardware, software, and network vendors make every effort to simplify the installation and configuration processes, sometimes this technology is best left in the hands of experts. Some changes can be destructive and compound the problem. Always save configuration files before changing them. You can then get back to a starting point by reloading the old files. Simply rename them or copy them to a disk for safe keeping. Saving a good configuration disk is always good policy. If the configuration files are inadvertently changed or erased, they can quickly be restored from disk.

Don't try to change complementary metal-oxide semiconductor (CMOS) settings unless you know exactly what you are doing. CMOS settings are the internal computer configurations that sets things such as hard disk type, number and type of floppy drives, time, date, video type, and other more complicated settings. Changing any one of these settings can cause the computer to not boot or not recognize certain peripherals.

Don't change security and access tables in the network if you don't understand how they affect the users, network, and application software. You may be loading software or drivers that conflict with the network operating system. The individual workstations might include other adapter cards, extra boards with extra serial ports, internal modems, scanner boards, game boards, or other devices that conflict with your network board or an unsupported network card. Sometimes that bargain network card or PC isn't a bargain if you calculate the time spent getting it to communicate with the network.

Give yourself a time budget, say thirty minutes or an hour. If you can't solve the problem by then, don't waste valuable time. Call someone who can take care of it quickly. Call someone before the problem gets bigger.

Visit the Manufacturer's Web Site for News and Updates

Often, you'll find that newer drivers, updates to the printed instruction manual, and FAQs are available directly from the manufacturer's Web site. Information here is usually free, and can be found quickly through a search or by navigating through the links.

Check out the FAQ area of the Web site first. If you're having a specific problem, chances are that other people have run into the same issues. Many times, you'll find the answer to what turns out to be a very common problem or question.

Or, if you find that a device driver is out of date and believe it may be conflicting with another device on the network, download and install the new drivers. Similarly, updated versions of software are often available as a free download.

Call the Manufacturer's Help Line for Support

If you've checked the obvious, not changed more than one thing at a time, read the manual, and still think you can do it within your budgeted time, the next step is to call a help line for support. Be ready to describe the symptoms. Try to paint a complete picture of the problem — it's not very helpful to say, "My printer doesn't work." Instead, tell the support person about the whole problem. It's more helpful to say, "My printer doesn't work in Excel, but it does in PowerPoint." Or, "My printer won't print anything from any software package, and I've already checked the cables, power cord, printer assignment, and print queue."

Often, the manufacturer's help personnel can diagnose and solve your problem in a short time. Support personnel handle hundreds of calls a day similar to yours, and have several solutions to try. They deal with similar problems every day, where you may only face the problem once. Don't be shy about asking for a senior help desk person, if you feel your question is beyond the scope of the first person's experience. If you are working in an organization with in-house technical support, it is also an option to get help there.

Many manufacturers no longer provide free support and use 1-900 numbers or bill you directly for any advice given. This makes it important to identify the problem, be succinct on the phone, and be ready to implement the suggestions immediately to save time and money. Be prepared to stick to your guns if you feel the problem is definitely the responsibility of the company you are calling. Help desks are notorious for trying to pass the blame to someone or something else. Keep an open mind, but if all of your network cards of one brand work fine and a different brand has problems in the same computer, it is probably that brand of network card.

Call in the Cavalry

Some problems just seem to defy detection. No matter how knowledgeable you and your help staff might be, there are times when you have to call in technical experts. At this point, you should contact a local repair facility. Make sure you describe the problem in complete detail so they can dispatch the right kind of expert. A networking guru probably isn't the best person to fix a broken printer. Likewise, a software specialist probably can't tell whether or not the RJ-45 connector on your network cable was improperly made.

Be forewarned, too, that lots of charlatans disguise themselves as LAN consultants. Make sure the technicians are certified for your network. Certifications are available for most network operating systems, and while this doesn't ensure a competent technician, it is a good place to start. The best way to find competent practitioners is through personal referral from a satisfied customer.

Aside from that, interview your candidate by phone or in person about his or her previous networking experience. It helps to find a technician or company with similar priorities and one that will respect your wishes. Does the technician always suggest the most expensive solution or is he or she willing to work within your budget without being insulting? It will help if the firm has previous experience with your operating system and hardware.

Don't hire a technician solely on price. Let's try a third grade math word problem to find out why. If a technician charging $150 per hour solves your problem in an hour, and a technician charging $100 per hour takes two hours, which technician will fix your problem for the least amount of money?

It also helps to stay with a single company, if possible, for your repair. The reasons for this are obvious. The technicians are familiar with your setup and don't have to spend time investigating your installation. The service provider is more likely to do a good job if they can expect repeat business. Credit information and other pertinent information is already on file. The service call can be placed on account instead of collected when the job is complete. It's nice to see a familiar face and know everything will be all right. Once you find a good service provider, treat them right. Don't cry wolf every time any little thing happens. There are real emergencies and there are problems that can wait. Most service companies try to provide service within a specified period of time and charge more for expedited service calls. Expect to pay more if a call is after hours or on weekends. Build trust and rapport with your technician and they'll do their best for you. Treat them badly and you'll get excuses and promises that go unfulfilled.

When the Network Is Slow

This is probably the most common complaint, and also the most difficult to diagnose. There are so many components that make up a network. An individual component can be the bottleneck or it may be a composite problem. In this section we discuss how the server, server memory, cabling, workstations, and topology affect speed.

"A chain is only as strong as its weakest link" and a network is only as fast as its slowest link. Most networks have evolved over the years. You needed to share files, so you turned a workstation into a file server, loaded the NOS, and ran a few cables, and — voilà! — you were networked. Then employees started clamoring for access to the Internet. You ran a few more cables and discovered the NICs that you used for the first workstations weren't available anymore, so you bought different ones. Someone had the bright idea of running the accounting department on the network. "Can't we all fax from the network?" "We need one of those new-fangled laser printers, and let's network it so we can all use it." "Wow, this is a really cool Windows program. Let's install it on the network." "I know our network will run faster with a newer, faster, bigger server." Before you knew it, your network was divided and multiplied until you weren't sure what you had or what you should do — and it had slowed to a crawl. Few of us have the luxury of tossing out all the old equipment and starting over from scratch. You have a big investment and you can't afford to scrap it all. Now is the time to step back and look at what you have. Better yet, call in a disinterested third party to review the state of the network and report on ways to improve speed.

Review of Ethernet and Token Ring

Ethernet is the most popular type of topology today. Ethernet is currently capable of 1000Mbps throughput. A single workstation usually does not, in practice, use all the bandwidth, but it doesn't take advanced math to calculate how many workstations can use the entire bandwidth. When this happens, the bandwidth is divided between the nodes. Token Ring, on the other hand, only allows a single workstation to transmit at a time, with the others waiting their turn. This happens very quickly and each workstation sends small pieces or frames at a time. Each scheme has its proponents and benefits. While not delving into the intricacies of the data passing, it helps to review the fundamentals.

Ethernet

Ethernet is a contention network, which means that each workstation competes to send data across the network. Safeguards are in place that let nodes know when it is OK to send data and resend data if there is a collision. However, Ethernet degrades unpredictably as workstations are added. Only workstations actively transmitting data affect performance. This means that a one hundred-node network with two active logins should give the same performance as a ten-node network with two active logins. Ethernet only transmits when necessary, so this permits large networks of workstations that are not in heavy use. Performance may be adequate when an average number of workstations are active, but can degrade to an unacceptable point when all nodes become very active.

Ethernet can be thicklan (10base5), thinlan (10base2), or most often UTP (10/100/1000baseT). Thicklan and thinlan use coaxial cables. Thinlan is a single cable, which looks like a TV cable, running from the server to all the workstations on the network. A T-connector taps the line for each node, and the last node ends the cable with a terminator. Thinlan has the advantage of being able to connect additional workstations easily and inexpensively. You simply add the workstation to the end of the line or between two existing workstations.

Thicklan is a coaxial cable that is larger in diameter than thinlan, hence the name. The main benefits of thicklan are good shielding and long-distance carriage of signals (up to 500 meters). Adding nodes is the same process as with thinlan, except the cable is pierced with a vampire tap and a fifteen-pin cable connects the tap and the NIC.

UTP looks like the telephone cord you use to attach your phone to the phone jack. Each cable from a workstation is run to a hub or concentrator. A single cable is then attached to the server. This is called star topology because all cables fan out from the hub or center of the network. Hubs can be linked together or chained. This makes multiple smaller hubs operate as a larger hub. One disadvantage of

UTP cable is that to add an additional workstation, you must have a free port on the hub. If no ports are available, a larger hub or additional hub must be purchased. If you have an eight-port hub that is fully populated (all ports connected to a node), to add a ninth node, you will need a ten- or twelve-port hub, or another eight-port to chain to the first. Hubs should be purchased that have a coaxial port to link to another hub or to the server. Hubs with RJ-45 connectors, used with UTP, lose a port or two when linked together.

The top diagram of Figure 15.1 shows a simple 10BaseT network in a star configuration. The server and all workstations are connected to a central hub or concentrator. Any additional workstations are added to available ports on the hub, and additional hubs are added as needed. The bottom diagram in Figure 15.1 shows a thicklan or thinlan network. Additional workstations are added between existing workstations or at either end. The server can be located anywhere along the line.

FIGURE 15.1

Simple diagrams demonstrating 10BaseT or UTP Ethernet cabling in a star configuration (top) and an Ethernet thicklan or thinlan network (bottom)

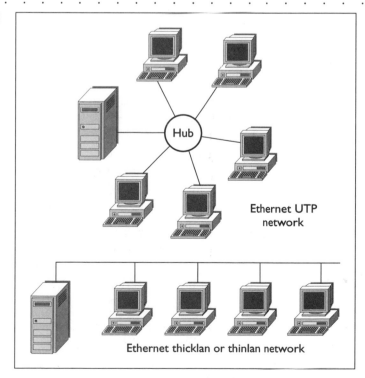

Hub

Ethernet UTP network

Ethernet thicklan or thinlan network

Figure 15.2 shows two ways of chaining multiple hubs together. The top diagram uses hubs with coaxial backbone connections that free all ports for workstations or servers. The bottom diagram demonstrates how hubs without coaxial connections are chained. Ports from each hub connect to other hubs, reducing the available number of ports. For instance, five ports are lost in this diagram.

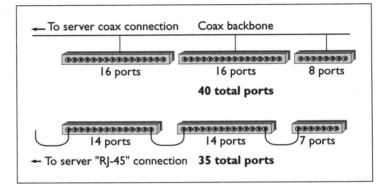

FIGURE 15.2

Simple diagrams demonstrating hub wiring topology with a coaxial backbone (top) and simply chained (bottom)

Token Ring

Token Ring is not a contention network. A single token is transmitted at a time. A token is like a bucket being passed around the network. There is only one bucket. If the bucket is empty, a node can fill it with data. The bucket is passed around the network and each node looks in the bucket to see if the data is for them. If it is, the node empties the bucket and sends it back to the originating bucketto let it know it was received. The originating node then sends the empty bucket around the network again. It circles the network until a node fills it and sends it to another destination. Token Ring networks degrade predictably as nodes are added. Each workstation added to the network drops performance for all other workstations. The ring becomes bigger as nodes are added. The bucket has to go further and more nodes have to look in the bucket to see if the data is for them. This adds time, even if few nodes are active.

Changing Topology to Increase Performance

Learning how data is passed helps you understand what is happening when your network slows down. Is your Ethernet network slow at month's end, or first thing in the morning when everyone is logging on and checking e mail? Is it necessary to change anything in your Ethernet network, or can you live with short periods of slow network access?

In any case, network topology can be changed to increase network performance. The most common way is to segment the network. This increases the throughput dramatically. Remember, the network is able to pass 10/100/1000Mbps of data (Ethernet/Fast Ethernet/Gigabit Ethernet, respectively). Segmenting means adding another network card to the server and moving workstations to the new network card. This adds another physical network to your local network. Each segment, or physical network, is now able to pass 10/100/1000Mbps of data for a total of 20/200/2000Mbps of potential data. There is only a small overhead associated with the server talking to two network cards. This does not affect server performance. If your server is fully utilized (running as fast as it can, all the time) adding the additional card will do nothing, and possibly even slow the network a bit. If the server is under-utilized, this can dramatically improve performance.

Carefully plan which users are attached to which segment. If all the heavy users are still located on one segment, they will still overload that segment. This is similar to a highway. As growth in a city causes a highway to become congested, lanes are added to the highway. Let's say we take a two-lane road and make it a four-lane highway. When completed, the same number of cars are now on twice the number of lanes, thereby reducing traffic congestion in half. If most of the cars still used the old two lanes, congestion would be the same.

Locating servers and the way they are attached can also affect performance. Multiple servers make up many networks. In Figure 15.3 we have engineering, accounting, and communication servers, all connected with coaxial cable. This type of fragmentation occurs when a network grows one server at a time, and performance is not an issue, most often with thinlan coaxial networks.

These servers are all attached to the same LAN, composed of many internal and physical networks. An internal network is created within any file server that has two NICs. Each server in this diagram has two network cards and is therefore an internal network. A physical network is each group of workstations attached to a network card. An internal router in each network must locate the correct destination for each packet and route it appropriately. Internal routers can find the address to deliver the packets anywhere on the physical network. Each hop or pass through a router adds the additional time it takes to pass data. The servers in the middle are always routing packets from both ends of the network. In Figure 15.3, a packet from Workstation 1 must make three hops to get to the communication server.

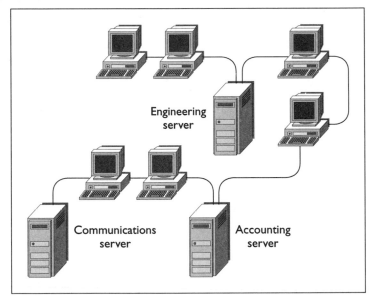

F I G U R E   15.3

Multiple servers in a fragmented network

Hops are similar to bus transfers. Buses don't usually run directly from your front door to your destination. You must ride the bus to another stop, get off and wait for a different bus, transfer to another bus, and so on until you get to your destination. Each transfer or hop adds time while you wait for the next bus. Even if the next bus is waiting, you have to wait for the bus to stop, get off it, and get on the next bus. All this takes time. The fewer the transfers, the less time your trip takes. Let's see how we can reduce the number of hops or bus transfers.

Figure 15.4 shows how connecting all servers to a backbone causes fewer hops and therefore increases performance. Connecting the servers to a backbone eliminates much of the hopping. The servers still have two network cards. The only difference is the order in which they are wired or attached. The middle servers are no longer routing data between the other servers. A request from the engineering server can go directly to the communication server without going through the accounting server. The circuitous route the packet had to travel before is now reduced to two hops, and performance is improved.

Improving Server Utilization

A faster server won't help if the cabling can't carry the additional throughput. A faster server won't help if the current server is not being utilized to its fullest, or is being overwhelmed with errors on the network. Network operating system utilities and third-party programs can measure server utilization. Server utilization is the percentage of time the CPU is processing. If the CPU is sitting around most of the time, waiting for something to do, this is called low utilization. If the CPU is working as fast as it can all the time, this is called high utilization.

Low server utilization and a slow network indicate that software, cabling, bad components, or the workstation NIC is creating errors and resending packets. If the server has high utilization, it still could be any of the aforementioned reasons. A bad workstation NIC, cable, or hub will create additional network traffic as the packets are sent and resent, trying to connect to the server. Server utilization will be up and the workstations that are OK will slow down. If the cabling and other components are optimum, and the server is working as hard as it can, your network would benefit from more memory or a faster CPU. All factors contribute to network speed, and each component must be matched to get the most performance from your network.

▶ · ◀

F I G U R E 15.4

Servers on a backbone

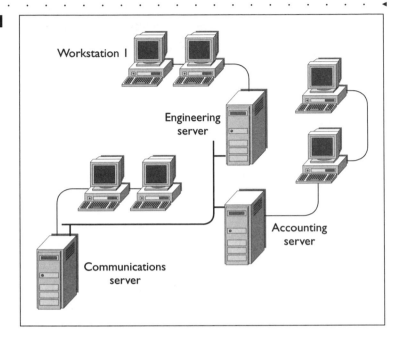

▶ · ◀

Adding Server Memory

The single most cost-effective way to help a slow network that is not hampered by cabling is by adding memory to the network. Networking technicians use formulas to determine the optimum server memory. It's best to let them perform the calculations, because many factors contribute to memory needs. Memory is the fastest storage medium in your server.

Various forms of caching can do much to improve performance. Caching is a way of storing files or information in memory instead of on the hard drive. The CPU can access the information in a cache much faster than on the drive. A hard drive is mechanical, with a spinning platter or multiple platters, and a head that moves to the area on the disk containing the data requested. Memory is electronic with no moving parts. It is just there, almost instantaneously. Servers use various memory schemes to speed access and execution such as:

- ▸ Directory caching

- ▸ Directory hashing

- ▸ File caching

- ▸ Elevator seeking

- ▸ Memory pools

Directory Caching

Networks store information on ownership of files and directories in a directory table. This is similar to the File Allocation Table (FAT) on a hard drive. The directory information includes information such as, information about assigned trustee rights, file names and ownership, directory names and ownership, date and time of last update, and the address of the first block on the network disk, if the entry is a file. The server stores the most recently accessed parts of the directory in memory. The directory table is searched each time a file or directory is used. If the information is in memory, the access is quicker than if it is retrieved from the hard drive.

Directory Hashing

Networks use both the directory table and FAT to store information about files. Both these tables are accessed each time a file is used. Directory hashing is an indexing algorithm that stores the directory table and FAT in memory in a specific order, instead of randomly, as in DOS. The search for information is faster because the server knows where to get the information, instead of searching the entire table until it is found.

File Caching

When parts of files or entire files are stored in server memory, they can be accessed up to ten thousand times faster from memory than from the servers' disks. Files that are not used are replaced by other files that are used. Think of file caching as putting files on your desk while you use them. When you need a number of files from a filing cabinet, you retrieve them and set them on your desk until you're finished with them. You don't find each portion of the file and refile it immediately, since you know you'll have to refer to it again in a few minutes. You keep the files on your desk until you know you are finished with them. This is much faster than going to the filing cabinet each time you need a small piece of information. File caching keeps the files ready for quick access until they are no longer needed.

Elevator Seeking

Files are not stored in contiguous regions of the hard disk — that is, the entire file is not in one position on the physical media. Not all files are the same size. Files written to an empty disk are usually written in one location. As files are erased and written to the disk, empty places for new files are created that are different sizes. New data is then written in pieces to empty portions of the disk, until the file is completely copied to the disk. This creates files that are spread over the disk in many different places, commonly called disk fragmentation. The FAT keeps track of beginning and ending locations of files or portions of files and sends the disk head to those locations until the entire file is retrieved.

Because DOS disks are accessed in order, the action of heads moving over the entire surface of the disk media slows access time. DOS and third-party products provide utilities to defragment disks or reposition data in contiguous areas of the disk. Elevator seeking retrieves data differently. The heads are prioritized to retrieve data as they encounter it, even if out of order. The result is less head movement and quicker access.

Memory Pools

Most schemes for increasing speed are performed in memory, and performance-enhancing functions rely on server memory. When the server is originally brought up, all available memory is allocated to file cache buffers. From this point on, all of the server's memory is reallocated to other memory pools as needed. Because all server memory is originally provided to file cache buffers, the memory needed by other memory pools has to be allocated from this memory.

Because each function is assigned a portion of memory to operate in, most applications determine what memory to use so the administrator doesn't really have options for assigning it. This varies among applications. More memory allows more functions to run. Some functions use memory that is left over or not in use. Other functions need protected memory or a set amount of memory that is devoted to its operation. Each server is tuned by assigning available memory to the various functions.

If a server has insufficient memory, it will swap out processes by writing information temporarily to the server's hard disk. Because it is much slower to write operations to a hard disk for later recall, most network professionals try to add RAM so that operations can be processed more quickly. The performance difference can become very noticeable.

It is impossible to give recommendations for memory assignments because each server is different. A lot depends upon the programs that are run on the server.

Increasing Speed or Access Time

Many factors contribute to the speed of the network. Speed is often confused with access time. Retrieving a file from the network hard disk is usually slower than retrieving the file from the workstation hard disk. A really slow workstation will appear to run faster on the network than a stand-alone. Network equipment must be matched to optimize performance. It does no good to have the fastest server and fastest workstations connected to a slow ARCnet network, or install a 100BaseT network with a 386 server.

It also helps to know whether your application software is client-server based or not. Client-server refers to the way the software handles data and processing. The client is the workstation and the server is the central computer, housing the network software, database, and some application programs. A mainframe does all the processing on a central computer with dumb terminals or video display terminals (VDTs) simply displaying the results. VDTs have little or no memory, and can only run as fast as the mainframe. Distributed applications spread the processing across many smaller computers, reducing the need for a huge central computer.

Non-client applications transfer the entire database to the workstation, so the workstation does all the processing. A 10,000-record, 1,000-byte-per-record database occupies 10MB of space, and this entire file would be transferred to each user requesting a single record in the file. A client-server application will process the query on the server and pass only the requested record to the workstation or client. This places added processing requirements on the server, but transfers are smaller, reducing network traffic.

Other client-server applications have a database server and an application server. The database server stores the database and the application server does all the processing of data for the workstation. This speeds the processing considerably as the tasks are shared by two processors.

No one method is right for all instances, but each application and process should be optimized by programmers to operate in the most efficient manner. This is a programming concern and usually cannot be changed by the user. Understanding the different processes will help when evaluating software. The bottom line is that your network may be screaming, but your software is slowing it down.

Getting out of Bottlenecks

Bottlenecks are numerous. Anything that creates network traffic slows down response time. The more users that are attached to the network, the slower it will be. Response time will be slowed any time the server is running disk-, processor-, and memory-intensive tasks. A single bad, or failing, NIC can create so much network traffic that the entire network slows down. Bad hubs can cause collisions, which slow the network. A kinked cable can cause intermittent problems. Network operating systems provide utilities that display statistics on disk space, volumes, frames received and sent, and system resources and utilization. This data can be used to isolate problems or at least furnish a starting point for your investigation.

The best strategy is to hire an experienced technician to provide recommendations for improving network speed. This is a good idea even if you have a technician on staff. The outside technician draws upon experience with many networks in different environments and configurations. Really pesky problems benefit from diagnostic equipment. A PC with a network adapter and diagnostic software is attached to the network and captures frames passed across the network, displaying the results in reports or on-screen graphs and charts. Information such as the addresses creating requests and the type of request, in code, is captured for reference. This makes it possible to see exactly what type of requests are being processed and who is making them. Armed with this information, the technician can make suggestions for segmenting the network, upgrading or replacing hardware, or making software changes. Don't try this at home, kids, unless you really know what the data means. This is best left to a professional.

When Printers Won't Print

Printer problems can be among the most frustrating of LAN maladies. It seems that printers only fail to work when you need them most. Again, we suggest that you take slow and careful steps to debug printing problems. Use common sense techniques first, then look for more technical issues.

First check the obvious. Is the printer plugged in? Are you out of paper? Are there errors on the printer? Is there a paper jam? Is the toner, or ink cartridge good? Is the printer cable plugged in? After you check the obvious, you can begin to look at the fun stuff, such as printer queues and print servers.

As discussed earlier in the chapter, identify the problem as carefully as you can. Is the network printer working for some users, but not all? If multiple printers are attached to the server, are all the printers down or just one? Is the printer printing from some applications and not from others? Is the printer printing garbage? What changed since the last time the printer worked? Did a software installation change parameters? Did someone change configurations in the network operating system?

A local printer is a printer attached directly to a workstation and only available to that workstation. Local printer problems are usually easy to fix and most users are experienced at troubleshooting them. A network printer is a printer that multiple users have access to. If the printer is working, most other printer problems can be isolated to cabling, print drivers, print servers, print queues, or user rights to the printer.

Printers are attached to the main server, a workstation, or hardware device acting as a print server, router, or workstation. If a workstation printer is to be accessed by other network users, it must be set up as a remote printer.

Use your powers of deduction and eliminate what is working and what isn't. If all printers on a print server are down, suspect the print server hardware, network cables, print queue, or configuration of the print server. Check to make sure all parameters are set correctly in the network software. If a single printer is down, suspect the cable to the printer, printer port, print driver, or configuration of the printer. A remote printer only works if the workstation it is attached to is up and running. If the user on that workstation removes the TSR from memory, the printer will become unavailable.

If a user or group of users can no longer print, check to make sure they're set up as users in the print server configuration. If you are trying unsuccessfully to get a new software package to print, is the software network-compatible? Are the drivers supplied with the software designed for networks? Is the print server overloaded from excessive print requests? Find out what print activities are causing the overload and defer printing of large jobs to evening hours when users are gone. Distribute users to other printers to balance the load. What use is a new printer if everyone is sending all their requests to the old printer?

Printer problems can be isolated if you understand what makes up the print process and the parts of the network that control printing. Be patient and soon you'll be happily printing again.

Troubleshooting Workstation Problems

Here we focus on those more common glitches that can be inspected by nontechnical personnel, including installation and post-installation problems and common solutions. Table 15.1 lists some of these basic problems and solutions at a glance.

TABLE 15.1	PROBLEM	CAUSE / SOLUTION
Workstation Issues	PC doesn't power on (or PC powers on, but nothing comes up on the screen) after the card is installed.	The NIC has a conflict with some other adapter card in the PC. Remove the network NIC and reconfigure any jumpers or dip switches. Consider running a diagnostics program, such as MSD.EXE, which comes with Windows, to determine which IRQs and base I/O ports memory are available. Newer NICs are software configurable and can be configured with utilities instead of physical dip switches and jumpers. Most PCs have IRQ 5,10,11,15 available. IRQ 5 is used for LPT2, so if you have a second parallel printer, use one of the other IRQs.
	The COM2 port doesn't work anymore.	You have set your NIC for IRQ 3. COM ports usually use IRQ 3 and IRQ 4. Reset the NIC for a different IRQ. If the card supports it, try IRQ 10 or IRQ 11.
	The workstation can't log on to the network.	1. Check network cables to make sure your PC is connected to the network. 2. Check the hub to make sure the port is OK. 3. Use a diagnostic utility (usually supplied with your NIC) to make sure your computer can send and receive packets across the network. 4. Check your installation and make sure you correctly specified the NICs and protocols. 5. The network administrator may have a security lock on the port or workstation. 6. Make sure the network drivers are not erased or the batch files and the workstation have not been changed. 7. The network may be down. This can be due to server problems or simply a backup operation that has locked a file until it is backed up.

Summary

We have discussed the guidelines for troubleshooting problems on your network. First, identify the problem, check to see what changed, discuss the problem with someone, and then look for any obvious answer. Read the manual and remember to change only one thing at a time. You don't want to introduce new problems. Recognize the limits of your own technical knowledge and don't be afraid to ask for help, either from the manufacturer's help desk, your company's help desk, or from an outside source.

Recommended Web Sites

What's the biggest library you've ever been in? Was it the Library of Congress, a university library, or perhaps the New York City Public Library? We agree that all of these are very big libraries housing enormous amounts of information. Now, imagine that all of those libraries and thousands more are available to you without leaving your computer terminal. Well, they are — through the Internet. You don't even need a library card. All you really need is Internet access, a Web browser, and the URL of the place you want to go.

Following is our recommended short list of URLs where you can find helpful tips to assist you in gathering more information about network computing and other computing subjects. Each URL will allow you access to the home page for each location. After reaching a home page, where you go from there is purely up to you. We've included the brief descriptions of the company that owns each particular URL to give you an idea of what you'll find at each location.

Network Computing Hardware Companies

Here are some of the major network computing hardware companies whose Web pages you'll find very useful.

Compaq Computer Corporation

www.compaq.com

Compaq Computer Corporation is the world's largest manufacturer of personal computers, and is the second largest computer company. Compaq also offers Internet and enterprise computing solutions, networking products, and commercial PC products.

Hewlett-Packard

www.hp.com

Hewlett-Packard Company designs, manufactures, and services electronic products and systems, with a focus on business, engineering, science, medicine, and education industries.

Dell Computer Corporation

www.dell.com

Dell pioneered the direct business model of computer sales and has grown into one of the largest computer companies in the world.

IBM

www.ibm.com

International Business Machines Corporation is the world's largest computer company. IBM sells an enormous number of mainframes, minicomputers, workstations, and personal computers. To this day, the bulk of the data in most large enterprises still resides in IBM mainframes.

3Com

www.3com.com

3Com manufactures the networking hardware that connects computers to one another across LANs and WANs. These systems, which include adapters, hubs, switches, routers, modems and remote access platforms, enable users to link into computer networks, whether they are in the office, at home, or on the road.

Nortel Networks, Inc.

www.nortelnetworks.com

Nortel Networks, Inc. is a major provider of internetworking products for businesses, workgroups, small offices, and mobile workers. The company offers LAN and ATM switches, hubs, routers, remote and Internet access solutions, and network management applications.

Cisco Systems, Inc.

www.cisco.com

Cisco is one of the largest networking hardware vendors worldwide. It produces hardware and software solutions to provide complete network communications across platforms.

Network Computing Software Companies

Here are some of the major network computing software companies whose Web pages you'll find very useful.

Novell

www.novell.com

As a network software leader, Novell connected PCs to create the LAN market, then interconnected those LANs to build the WAN market. With the advent of global computing, Novell is integrating Internet technologies with business networks to create corporate intranets and business-class Internet services.

Microsoft

www.microsoft.com

Microsoft is probably the world's leading software producer. Although best known for the MS-DOS and Windows operating systems and the Microsoft Office business software suite (and the individual applications that comprise it), it is also the leader in developing network software for small and large networks with Windows 2000 products.

Sun Microsystems

www.sun.com

Sun Microsystems leads the development of Java, a cross-platform computing language that was designed to be utilized in a distributed computing environment, such as the Internet. But Sun is also a major manufacturer of computers ranging from enterprise-scale servers to powerful desktop workstations. Finally, Sun provides a 64-bit operating system, Solaris.

Red Hat

www.redhat.com

Red Hat is a leader in Linux operating system arena. The Red Hat Linux OS has gained incredible popularity, in part due to its ease of use and similarity to the graphical user interface familiar to Windows users.

· ·

Search Engines

If you're looking for a Web site about a specific topic, chances are good that it exists. Although finding its location can be a bit of a challenge, if you start your search at one of the following sites, you're bound to find what you're looking for — and then some. These Web sites provide a single staging point for the most common and efficient search engines in use today. You can choose from predetermined and cataloged search topics or build your own specific criteria. It's easy.

www.infoseek.com

www.hotbot.com

www.yahoo.com

www.northernlight.com

www.google.com

www.ask.com

Glossary

3270 A communications protocol that supports online transaction processing and file transference.

56K service (dedicated or switched) Provided by local telephone companies or long-distance carriers, this service offers customers digital circuits capable of transmitting voice, data, or video at rates of 56Kbps. With switched 56K service, the customer dials up the 56K circuit on demand and pays a per-minute rate based on actual monthly usage.

access charge A charge paid to a local telephone company for the availability and use of exchange facilities for origination and termination of interexchange services.

active hub A networking device that connects the wires of a star shaped network. Used most frequently with ARCnet LANs.

analog/digital Two opposite kinds of communications signals. Analog is a continuously varying electrical signal in the shape of a wave (such as a radio wave), transmitted electronically in a form parallel to the spoken work. Digital is based on a binary code in which the picture or audio information is sent as a series of "on" and "off" signals. This service is more precise and less subject to interference than analog.

analog transmission A continuous wave transmission expressed by bandwidth, or range of frequencies. Some examples using analog channel transmission include: broadcast television, cable television, and AM/FM radio.

application A functional system made up of software, hardware, or a combination of both that performs some useful task. Database managers, spreadsheets, word processors, LAN's, fax machines, and so on, are examples of applications.

application icon A glyph that represents a running application. This icon will appear on your Windows main screen or after you start the application and then minimize (reduce) it.

application switching Moving from one application to another without closing the first application.

architecture A set of rules for building programs, networks, and such as structures.

archive To back up old files and remove them from immediate access. They can be retrieved and used whenever necessary.

ARCnet A network protocol standard that permits computer data, as well as voice or video information, to be carried across a network. It employs a token-passing star topology and is usually connected using coaxial cable.

ASCII character set The American Standard Code for Information Interchange 7-bit character set. It consists of the first 128 (0-127) characters of the ANSI (American National Standards Institute) 8-bit character set and most other 8-bit character sets. The ASCII character set is the most universal character-coding set.

association The relationship between a file type and the application that creates or reads the file.

Asynchronous Transfer Mode (ATM) A high bandwidth, control delay, fixed-size packet switching and transmission system. Because it uses fixed-size packets that are also known as cells, ATM is often referred to as cell relay. ATM will provide the basis for future broadband ISDN standards.

attributes Specific information that is maintained about files. Attributes can show that the file is read-only, hidden, or system, and whether it has been changed since it was last backed up. See also archive attribute, hidden file, read-only file, and system file.

AUTOEXEC.BAT file A file with a set of commands that is automatically run by the operating system whenever the computer is started or restarted. The file generally contains basic commands that help configure the system.

bandwidth The range of frequencies over which signal amplitude remains constant as it is passed through a system. This can also be a measure of the information-carrying capacity of a communications channel or the amount of the electromagnetic spectrum that a given signal occupies; the higher (wider) the bandwidth, the greater the information. This is usually expressed in kilohertz (KHz) or megahertz (MHz).

basic rate interface An ISDN subscriber line consisting of two 64Kbps "B"channels and one 16Kbps "D" channel. This is used for both data and signaling purposes.

baud rate A measurement of speed that is close to 1bps. It is generally applied to modems. For example, a 56K baud modem transfers information at approximately 56,000bps.

Bell system A group of affiliated RBOCs (Regional Bell Operating Companies) in the United States that operates under consistent rules and specifications, many of which are set by AT&T.

binary file A file containing information that is in machine-readable form. The file must have an application capable of reading its format in order for it to make sense of the file .

bisynchronous A data link protocol for synchronizing transmission of binary coded data.

bit A binary digit; the smallest unit of information used by a computer represented by a "1" or "0", or by "on" or "off." A single bit is one digital signaling element; one alphabetic or numeric character is typically represented by 10 bits.

bit error rate (BER) In digital applications, it is the ratio of bits received in error to bits sent. BERs of 10 (one error bit to a billion sent) are typical.

BNC A type of bayonet-lock coaxial cable connector used for video and communications.

bridge A device that passes packets between two similar LAN channels; for example, Ethernet-to-Ethernet. This can also be a device that connects three or more telecommunications channels, such as telephone lines.

broadband Telecommunication capable of transporting multiple data, voice, and video channels over a single medium. Broadband communications have enough bandwidth to stream full motion video, stills, graphics, audio, and text simultaneously.

Broadband Integrated Services Digital Network (B-ISDN) A digital signaling network in which equipment interface data rates operate at speeds of 155–622Mbps.

buffer A place, usually in the computer's memory, used to temporarily store information.

byte A group of bits, usually eight, handled as a unit by a computer operating system.

cable An optical fiber, multiple fibers, or fiber bundle. This may include a cable jacket and strength members, fabricated to meet optical, mechanical, and environmental specifications. See also fiber buffer, fiber bundle.

carrier A provider of transmission capabilities available to the general public, sometimes referred to as a common carrier or a regulated carrier, regulated by the FCC.

A current in a communications channel that can be modulated to carry analog or digital signals.

A telephone company or similar non-private telecommunications service supplier.

The radio frequency wave having at least one characteristic that may be varied by modulation.

Carrier Sense Multiple Access/Collision Detection (CSMA/CD) A technique in which a station on a network determines that no other stations are communicating before it transmits data.

CD-ROM Storage technology that can be used to keep information that can be read by a computer or similar hi-tech device. CD-ROMs use the same technology as audio compact discs and laser discs.

CD-R/CD-RW Storage technology that enables data to be written once (CD-R) or many times (CD-RW) to a compact disc.

channel bank A piece of equipment that typically allows 24 analog circuits to be sampled and converted into digital signals having 64Kbps per channel, which are subsequently merged into a time-divided bit format (such as DS1) at a rate of 1.544Mbps for transmission on a single T1 facility between two points. Channel banks are required at both ends of each link, to combine (at one end) and separate (at the other end) the component signals. Using channel banks, slow-scan TV, data, and phone signals can be sent on the same T1 link.

Channel Service Unit/Data Service Unit (CSU/DSU) On some data networks, these are two separate devices. On most networks that use a codec, this is a box that sits between the codec and the data circuit, used to interface and condition the data coming on and off the network. This box may also contain diagnostic testing functions and indicators, and in the case of switched services, will perform all your dialing functions. A CSU/DSU is required for all SW56 and DDS circuits and is not included with your codec.

client-server network A type of LAN that has at least one computer that is designated as the host computer for some or all of the network's applications.

coax, coaxial cable The copper-wire cable that carries audio and video signals and radio frequency energy, consisting of an outer conductor and an inner conductor that are separated from each other by insulating material. This type of cable can carry a much higher bandwidth than a wire pair.

coder/decoder (codec) Digital encoding/decoding equipment that is necessary to interface analog end-user equipment (such as a television set) to digital transmission facilities. In the case of compressed video, codecs are also used to restore some of the motion that is taken out in the compression process.

COM port A COM port is a serial communication channel on a computer. See also serial port.

common carrier A telecommunications company, such as your local telephone company, that provides communication transmission services.

communications settings Settings that specify how information is transferred from your computer to a serial device, such as a printer or modem. See also serial port.

concentrator A centrally located device for connecting the wires of a star-shaped topology, contention-based network. Concentrators serve as the traffic cop for managing network data. With a concentrator, all network segments are active at the same time. See also hub.

CONFIG.SYS file A text file containing configuration commands used when starting your computer. Commands in the CONFIG.SYS file enable or disable system features, set limits on resources, and extend the operating system's functionality by loading device drivers.

Consultative Committee of the International Telephone and Telegraph Group (CCITT) This committee is working to produce the PX64 standard for compressed video equipment so that the codes of various manufacturers can be used together.

contention-based protocol standard A LAN scheme in which all of the computers can communicate at once. Packets of information can literally collide on the network wire and be destroyed before they are delivered.

continuous audio The audio connection for a switched video network that allows all connected endpoints to speak at the same time, in the same manner as an audio bridge.

CPU The central processing unit of a computer.

customer premises equipment (CPE) Telephone equipment, such as phones and private branch exchanges (PBXs), located on the customers premises.

database Information storage system that can be searched through a number of methods to obtain specific data. "Database" has been associated with computer services, but is now used to refer to general information storage and retrieval systems (e.g., audiotext, teletext, etc.).

data file Any file or document created within an application; for example, a word-processing document, spreadsheet, database file, or chart. See also text file.

data path Secondary network consisting of the "overhead" bits above the 36Mbps video channel.

data port The physical and electrical protocol used by the codec and the DSU or TA to transfer data between each other. A codec comes with either V.35 or X.21 protocol built in. These are actually the number of CCITT international standards which specify pinning, levels, and so on. V.35 is common for networks in North America and X.21 is popular on European-manufactured ISDN terminal adapters.

data rate Analog transmission media is specified in bandwidth (usually in hertz) and signal to noise. Since the principles behind digital transmission are so different, media are specified in different parameters. Rather than how much analog information is passed, a digital user is concerned with how many bits per second can be sent down the channel.

Data Terminal Equipment/Data Computer Equipment (DTE/DCE) To avoid confusion, the data protocols mentioned above designate equipment and ports as either DTA or DCE. In the case of the codec, the CSU/DSU or TA is always the DCE and the codec is always the DTE. Plugging two DTEs together will not establish communication between them, since the DCE provides all the clocks required to run the data.

dedicated file server A master computer that directs the network's operation and applications. It may not be used as a user workstation.

dedicated lines A leased or purchased line that connects two or more data communication sites used exclusively by one vendor or user.

DEMARCATION (Demarc) A line either side of which determines the contractor's and owner's responsibilities. The location(s) where customer-provided equipment is connected to carrier-provided equipment. For example, the splice block where a telephone line enters most homes is a demarc; everything on the line side of the demarc is the responsibility of the telephone company, and everything on the home side (such as the house wiring and the telephones themselves) is the responsibility of the homeowner.

device A component of the system's hardware configuration. Examples include the modem, printer, mouse, sound card, or disk drive.

device driver Software that controls how a computer communicates with a device, such as a printer or mouse. A printer driver, for example, translates information from the computer into information the printer can understand.

Digital Data System The most common point-to-point, dedicated digital telephone service that works well with the codec. The user pays a flat monthly charge to the phone company for a full time link.

Digital Versatile Disc (DVD) An optical disk capable of storing from 4.7 to 17GB of data per side. Similar in form to a CD-ROM, a DVD can hold up to 26 times the amount of data compared to a CD-ROM.

Direct Digital System (DDS) A network whose component parts and signals (representing information of various types) are all transmitted via standardized digital signaling methods. In a DDS network, no analog-to-digital converters are necessary.

disaster recovery The use of alternative network circuits to reestablish communication channels in the event that the primary channels are disconnected or malfunctioning.

document file A file whose extension has been associated with a specific application. For example, an XLS file is frequently associated with the Excel spreadsheet. Opening a file in the Explore or File Manager causes the associated application to start.

downloading A process that involves transferring information from one device to another over a telecommunications channel (telephone, broadcast, and so on). Information received from the originating source can then be stored by the receiver for future use.

DS0/DS3 Designations given to circuits of different bit rates. A DS0 circuit has a bit rate of 56Kbps (actually, the full width is 64Kbps, but the rest is used for overhead associated with the transfer). A single digital telephone circuit uses a DS0. A DS3 has a bit rate capability of 45Mbps, which is equivalent to 28 T1 circuits, or 672 DS0 circuits.

DS1 See T1.

dual 56 Two switched 56K calls made between video conferencing equipment to allow data transfer at 112Kbps. The video conferencing equipment performs a two-channel inverse-multiplexing procedure to assure channel alignment.

duplex On the plain old telephone system (POTS), the audio transmission can be considered half duplex because if both parties speak at the same time, their voices will intercept on the single pair of wires on each end of the call. Most digital systems are duplex, having four wires and allowing simultaneous and independent data (or encoded audio) to pass in each direction. Some systems may be simplex, which pass digits only in one direction.

duplexer A device that combines transmit and receive signals on one antenna

dynamic allocation The ability to add or remove resources to/from a system based on actual need. The alternative to dynamic allocation is to have a fixed amount of resources for a system, which are always dedicated to that system, regardless of whether they are being used.

Dynamic Data Exchange (DDE) A protocol for the exchange of data between applications.

Electronic Bulletin Boards (EBBs) These are systems in which users can read and post short public messages or announcements stored on a central computer. Messages are sent and received by users with microcomputers equipped with modems and communications software. The messages may be screened and posted within categories established by the system operator.

Electronic Industries Association (EIA) A standards organization specializing in the electrical and functional characteristics of interface equipment.

electronic mail (e-mail) A system by which written messages are entered through a keyboard and distributed to individuals or groups subscribing to the service. Messages are generally stored on a computer and forwarded to recipients when they log on to the e-mail server.

encryption/decryption Special coding or scrambling of a communication signal for security purposes.

Ethernet Baseband protocol and technology developed by Xerox and widely supported by many manufacturers; a packet technology that operates at 10Mbps over coaxial cable and allows terminals, concentrators, workstations, and hosts to communicate with each other.

fault management The process of locating a fault, isolating it, and then fixing it.

fax Electronic technology that transmits documents, usually over telephone systems. Facsimile devices are commonly referred to as fax, telecopies, or datafax.

Federal Communications Commission (FCC) The federal agency responsible for regulating all use of the air waves for broadcast and electrical telecommunications purposes.

Fiber Distributed Data Interface (FDDI) A high-speed protocol standard for sending network data over fiber (not copper) cabling.

fiber-optic link Any optical transmission channel designed to connect two end terminals or to be connected in a series with other channels.

fiber optics Method for transmission of information (voice, video, data). Light is modulated and transmitted over highly pure, hair-thin fibers of glass. Bandwidth capacity of fiber-optic cable is much greater than conventional cable or copper wire.

firmware Data and/or program software for the codec stored in a nonvolatile form in a semiconductor memory circuit. For codecs, the firmware is often housed in a plug-in module.

flow control The processes used to regulate the transfer of information from one device to another, usually via modems or communication software. One device sends a signal called a handshake to the other when information can be transferred.

format The way text or data is set up on a page, or the way information is structured in a file. Also, to prepare a floppy disk to hold information. Formatting a disk deletes all information that was previously on it. Be careful not to format the hard disk.

fractional T1 Service offering data rates between 64Kbps (DS0 rate) and 1.536Mbps (DS1 rate), in specified intervals of 64Kbps.

frame relay A form of packet switching using smaller packets and less error checking than traditional forms of packet switching (i.e., X.25); now a new international standard for efficiently handling high-speed data over WANs.

frequency The number of cycles per second of an electromagnetic transmission, usually described in hertz. Generally, high frequency transmissions can carry more information at greater speeds than low frequency transmissions.

full duplex A transmission system, together with its associated equipment, capable of simultaneously transmitting and receiving signals, as opposed to simplex (unidirectional) or half-duplex (one direction at a time) systems.

gateway Used to describe a device that connects two or more dissimilar networks, and makes communication between/among them possible.

gigabits per second (Gbps) A rate at which data may be transferred across a communications line. 1Gbps equals 1 billion bits per second, or approximately 125 million characters per second (assuming 8 bits per character).

gigahertz (GHz) A unit of frequency equal to 1 billion hertz or 1 thousand megahertz per second.

half duplex A circuit that permits communications in both directions, but not simultaneously.

hertz A unit of frequency equal to 1 cycle per second (cps). 1 kilohertz equals 1 thousand cps; 1 megahertz equals 1 million cps; 1 gigahertz equals 1 billion cps.

hub A point or piece of equipment where a branch of a multipoint network is connected. Hubs serve as traffic cops for managing network data. A network may have a number of geographically distributed hubs or bridging points.

hybrid system A system that combines two or more communication technologies.

IEEE Institute of Electrical and Electronics Engineers.

in-band signaling Signaling made up of tones of defined bits that pass within the data transmission stream. Tones sent over digital circuits are encoded into digital PCM bursts and sent as digital data within the data channel.

infrared (IR) The bank of electromagnetic wavelengths between the visible part of the spectrum and microwaves.

Integrated Services Digital Network (ISDN) The worldwide standard for digital telephony. WANs are configured with standardized equipment and digital transmission methods that enable voice, data, and video information to be transferred between user resources simultaneously.

interexchange carrier (IXC) A long-distance supplier.

interface The connection between two devices. Interfaces carry electronic impulses from one place to another. A hardware interface, for example, would connect a host computer to a computer, a modem, or other device.

interrupt A signal that a device sends to the computer when the device is ready to accept or send information. Also used when a device needs the computer's attention.

interrupt request line (IRQ) Hardware line over which devices can send interrupt signals. Usually, each device connected to the computer uses a different IRQ.

inverse multiplexing The creation of a single higher-speed data channel by combining and synchronizing two or more lower-speed data channels.

ISDN multirate A network-based ISDN service that allows users' network access equipment to dial network channels of bandwidth in increments of 64Kbps, up to 1536Kbps. Access to ISDN multirate service is obtained over ISDN PRI lines.

I/O address Input/output locations used by a device such as a modem or printer.

ISO International Standards Organization

IT information technologies

jumper A small set of pins on a computer card that allow for the change of certain settings, such as specifying an IRQ port or address. Jumpers are found on some network interface cards.

kilobits per second (Kbps) A rate at which data may be transferred across a communications line. 1Kbps equals 1 thousand bits per second, or approximately 125 characters per second (assuming 8 bits per character).

kilohertz (KHz) A unit of frequency equal to 1 thousand hertz.

laser Light amplification by stimulated emission of radiation. This highly focused beam of light (or its device) is used in fiber optics and optical video discs.

learning link A computer bulletin board utilized for education-related services.

leased lines A circuit rented for exclusive use twenty-four hours a day, seven days a week from a telephone company. The connection exists between two predetermined points and cannot be switched to other locations.

linear bus topology A network cabling scheme in which all stations are directly connected to one linear cable.

Local Area Network (LAN) A user-owned, user-operated, high-volume data transmission facility connecting a number of communicating devices (computers, terminals, word processors, printers, mass storage units, and so on) within a single building or campus of buildings.

local exchange carrier (LEC) A telephone company that provides local service.

LTP port See parallel port.

management protocols Language used to communicate with and within a given network.

megabits per second (Mbps) A rate at which data may be transferred across a communications line. 1Mbps equals 1 million bits per second, or approximately 125 thousand characters per second (assuming 8 bits per character).

megabyte An amount of information roughly equivalent to 1 million characters. Also denoted as MB.

megahertz (MHz) A unit of frequency equal to 1 million hertz.

memory A temporary storage area for information/applications, such as ROM, RAM, conventional memory, expanded memory, and extended memory.

memory-resident program A program loaded into memory that is available while another application is active. Also known as a terminate-and-stay-resident (TSR) program.

modem (modulator/demodulator) An electronic device used to allow a computer to send and receive data, typically over a phone line.

MS-DOS prompt At the MS-DOS command line, the character or characters that appear at the beginning of the line, indicating the computer is ready to receive input. Also known as the command prompt.

multimode fiber An optical fiber that supports many propagating modes at a given wavelength.

multiplexing The process of combining a number of individual channels into a common frequency band or into a common bit stream for transmission. The converse equipment or process for separating a multiplexed stream into individual channels is called demultiplexer.

multitasking A feature of the computer and its operating system that enables more than one application to run at the same time.

nano Prefix meaning one billionth.

network A group of computers connected by cables or other means and using software to enable them to share printers, disk drives, and information.

network drive A disk drive, available to users on a network, where data files can be stored.

networking The tying together of multiple sites for the reception and possible transmission of information. Networks can be composed of various transmission media, including copper wire, terrestrial microwave, or coaxial.

network interface card (NIC) A printed circuit board installed in a PC that allows network stations to communicate with each other; also called a network adapter card.

network operating system (NOS) The internal set of commands and instructions that directs a network's activities. Novell NetWare, Banyan VINES, Microsoft LAN Managers, and Windows NT/2000 are examples of client-server NOSs.

network printer A printer shared by multiple users over a network.

network topology A network protocol or design that permits computer data, as well as audio and video information, to be carried across a network. The NICs available for network printers use a variety of topologies, including Ethernet and Token Ring.

node A termination point for two or more communication links. The node can serve as the control location for forwarding data among the elements of a network or multiple networks, as well as performing other networking, and in some cases, local processing functions.

null modem A device that interfaces between a local peripheral that normally requires a modem, and the computer near it that expects to drive a modem to interface to that device; an imitation modem in both directions.

Open System Interconnection (OSI) Emerging standard for a layered architecture that allows data to be transferred among systems through networks.

out-of-band signaling Signaling that is separated from the channel carrying the information and sent over an independent out-of-band channel.

packet switching Digital transmissions are broken into data packets that are addressed to their destination and sent by a central switching computer along diverse routes through the network, taking advantage of pauses in voice conversations and interactive data transmissions; the packets are then reassembled at the destination switching center and sent to the end user.

parallel interface An interface between a computer and a printer in which the computer sends multiple bits of information to the printer simultaneously.

parallel printer A printer with a parallel interface connected to a parallel port.

parameter Information added to the command that starts an application, such as a filename or any type of information.

parity A process for error-checking memory chips.

passive hub A small wire connector that can be used to connect certain types of network cables. Usually found on ARCnet LANs.

peripheral device An additional tool that is connected to a computer. Examples include printer, plotter, mouse, and modem.

pigtail A short length of optical fiber permanently fixed to a component, used to couple power between the component and a transmission fiber.

polling LAN managers rely heavily on this network management system to periodically query all devices on the network and determine their status.

port A connection or socket on the computer. Ports are used to connect printers, modems, monitors, or a mouse to your computer. Serial ports (COM) and parallel ports (LPT) are the most commonly used ports.

PostScript A special printing definition language developed by Adobe.

PRI Primary Rate ISDN.

primary rate interface An ISDN subscriber line consisting of twenty-three 64Kbps "B" channels in North America (thirty 64Kbps channels elsewhere) and one 64Kbps "D" channel, used for signaling purposes.

print queue A list of files that have been sent to a printer in the order they are received, including the file currently being printed.

printer driver A program that controls interaction between the printer and computer. This program supplies information such as printing interface, description of fonts, and features of the installed printer.

printer server A network computer that is dedicated to managing requests for a printer.

private branch exchange (PBX) A telephone switch located on a customer's premises that primarily establishes voice grade circuits.

private network A network, usually operated by a single corporate entity, made up of dedicated lines leased from carriers and switching equipment located on the corporate premises.

program file An executable file that starts an application or program. A program file contains a file extension, such as .EXE, .PIF, .COM, or .BAT.

proportional font A font whose characters have varying widths, such as Times New Roman. Courier font is not a proportional font.

protected mode A computer's operating mode that is capable of addressing extended memory directly.

protocol Refers to the communication parameters, such as baud rate and duplex, which are necessary to make a connection between computers.

protocol conversion The process of translating the protocol that is native to an end-user device, such as a terminal, into a different protocol that is native to another device, such as a computer, so they can communicate with each other.

protocol standard A standard method for computers to communicate, such as the Ethernet protocol standard or the Token Ring protocol standard.

public network A network operated by the carriers (IECs and LECs) that includes network-based services and network-based switching.

RAM drive A portion of memory used as a hard disk drive. RAM drives are much faster than hard disks because computers read information faster from memory than from hard disks. Information on a RAM drive is lost when the computer is turned off. This is also known as a virtual drive. See also random access memory.

random access memory (RAM) The most common computer memory, the contents of which can be altered at any time.

read-only An attribute given to a file or directory so that others may view the information in the file or directory but not modify it.

read-only memory (ROM) A type of semiconductor memory device that stores unalterable data or program information.

RJ-11 A standard modular telephone jack.

root directory The top-level or main directory of a disk. The root directory is created when you format the disk, and from this directory you can create files and other directories.

router An interconnection device that can connect individual LANs. Unlike bridges, which logically connect at the OSI's second layer, routers provide logical paths at the OSI's third layer. Like bridges, remote sites can be connected using routers over dedicated or switched lines to create WANs.

RS-232C The industry standard for a 25-pin interface that connects computers with various forms of peripheral equipment.

RS-366 An EIA standard for providing dialing commands to network access equipment. It uses RS-232 electrical specifications but different connector pinouts and signal functions.

serial interface An interface between a computer and a peripheral (like a printer or modem) that allows single bits of information to be transmitted from the computer to the device.

serial port (COM 1) A connection on a computer where you plug in the cable for a serial device.

serial printer A printer that uses a serial interface, which you connect to a serial port.

server A computer that provides disk space, printers, or other services to computers over a network.

smart hub A wire connector for a LAN with built-in management tools. Smart hubs can generally report statistics about the number of packets they receive or turn themselves off if they detect a problem.

soft font A font installed in your computer and sent to the printer before it can be printed. They are also referred to as downloadable fonts.

software-defined network (SDN) A virtually private network in which the network links are assigned to users as needed and are typically invoiced on the basis of bandwidth and time occupancy.

source directory The directory where files are originally located before you move them.

star-shaped topology A network cabling configuration in which one computer is designated as a central hub and all other stations are directly connected to it.

subdirectory A directory within a directory.

switched 56 A service available from local telephone companies that offers a digital channel interface at a 56Kbps rate. It allows the user to place calls between several points and cut costs by only paying for part time service. It is generally used for computer data transmission or compressed video teleconferencing, and is functionally equivalent to a DS0.

switched 64 A dial-up network-based service that provides a data channel operating at a rate of 64Kbps.

switched 384 A dial-up network-based service that provides a data channel operating at a rate of 384Kbps.

switched 1536 A dial-up network-based service that provides a data channel operating at a rate of 1536Kbps.

Switched Multimegabit Data Service (SMDS) A packet-based network service allowing the creation of high-speed data networks (up to 45Mbps).

switching Process of routing communications traffic from a sender to the correct receiver.

SYSTEM.INI file A Windows initialization file that contains settings used to customize Windows for your system's hardware.

T1 Telephone term given to a digital transmission circuit whose bandwidth is equal to twenty-four DS0 voice channels or 1536Kbps (plus 8Kbps bits for overhead).

T3 A carrier of 45Mbps bandwidth. One T3 channel can deliver 28 T1 channels, or 672 voice circuits used for digital video transmission or for major PBX-PBX telephone interconnection.

tail circuit The connection from the central switch location to the individual institution.

tariff A published rate for services provided by a common or specialized carrier, or the means by which regulatory agencies approve such services. The tariff is a part of a contract between customer and carrier.

T-carrier A hierarchy of digital systems designed to carry speech and other signals in digital form, designated T1, T-2, and T-4. The T1 carrier has 24 channels and transmits at 1.544Mbps. The T-2 carrier has 96 channels equivalent with a 6.312Mbps line rate. The T-4 carrier transmits at 274Mbps.

telco Acronym for telephone company.

terminate-and-stay-resident (TSR) program See memory-resident program.

time division multiplex/multiple access (TDM/TDMA) A method for combining multiple data circuits into one circuit (or vice versa) by assigning each circuit a fixed unit of time for its data transmission.

token-passing scheme Each computer on the network has an individual turn to accept and relay information.

topology The physical layout of the cable for a network. Popular topologies are linear bus and star-shaped.

TrueType fonts Fonts that are scalable and sometimes generated as bitmaps or soft fonts, depending on the capabilities of the printer. TrueType fonts can be sized to any height, and print exactly as they appear on the screen.

twisted pair A cable composed of two small insulated conductors twisted together without a common cover. Telephone signals are the most common use of twisted pair technology.

tymnet/telenet Commercial packet-switched networks available in major cities by direct dialing.

Universal Serial Bus (USB) A high-speed serial interface that can connect up to 127 devices, communicating at 12Mbps. A second specification, not yet finalized, but currently know as USB 2.0, will increase the data rate to approximately 480Mbps.

UNIX A computer operating system.

unshielded twisted pair (UTP) Wiring with one or more pairs of twisted insulated copper conductors bound in a single plastic sheath.

V.25 bis An automatic calling and answering command set for use between DTE and DCE, which includes both in-band and out-of-band signaling.

V.35 Commonly used to describe electrical and connector characteristics for a high speed synchronous interface between DTE and DCE. Originally, V.35 described a 48bps group band modem interface with electrical characteristics.

value-added service A communication service utilizing common carrier networks for transmission and providing added data services with separate additional equipment. Such added service features may be store-and-forward message switching, terminal interfacing, and host interfacing.

voice grade channel Used for speech transmission usually with an audio frequency range of 300–3,300 hertz. It is also used for transmission of analog and digital data. Up to 10Kpbs can be transmitted on a voice grade channel.

VT100 An ASCII character data terminal, consisting of screen and keyboard. Manufactured by Digital Equipment Corporation (DEC), the VT100 has become an industry standard data terminal. VT100 emulation software allows a standard PC to act as a VT100 terminal.

wide area network (WAN) A data network typically extending a LAN outside a building or beyond a campus, over IXC or LEC lines to link to other LANs at remote sites. Typically created by using bridges or routers to connect geographically separated LANs.

Wide Area Telecommunications Service (WATS) A bulk rate long-distance telephone service.

WIN.INI file The initialization file for Windows that contains settings for your specific Windows environment. Certain Windows applications modify the WIN.INI file to add extra information that is used when you run those applications.

wireless cable The use of frequencies in the MDS, MMDS, OFS, and ITFS ranges, reserved by the FCC for commercial use, to form a transmission service, typically used for entertainment programming (usually MMDS-multichannel broadcasting to compete with or fill in a niche not served by cable).

X.21 A set of CCITT specifications for an interface between DTE and DCE for synchronous operation on public data networks. It includes connector, electrical, and dialing specifications.

X.25 A set of packet switching standards published by the CCITT.

Index

311

presentation software, 37
preserving historical perspectives, 232
preventing virus infections, 197-198
preventive maintenance, LANs
(local area networks), 176-178
print servers, 167, 172
print services, 9-10
printer sharing, peer-to-peer networks, 78
printers, troubleshooting, 275-276
printing, sharing, 24-25
problems. *See also* troubleshooting
changing one at a time, 259-260
discussing, 258
identifying, 257-258
manuals, reading, 259
manufacturers' help lines, 261-262
repair facilities, local, 262-263
solving, 258-259
technical limitations, knowing, 260
workstations, troubleshooting,
276-277
processing speeds, 160
MHz (megahertz), 157
productivity
enhancing, 36-38
workstations, 157
property rights, 147, 205-212
inheritance, 209-212
protecting
cables, 199-200
hubs, 199
network resources, 191
Plenum cables, 199
routers, 199
workstations, 199
protocols, 102
analyzers, 186
CMIP (Common Management
Information Protocol), 185
DHCP (Dynamic Host Configuration
Protocol), 104-105
FTP (File Transfer Protocol), 19
graphical mapping, 186
HTTP (HyperText Transfer Protocol),
19
IGRP (Interior Gateway Routing
Protocol), 119
MPR (Multi-Protocol Router), 120
NetBEUI, 106
NetBIOS, 106
network management, 184-187
OSPF (Open Shortest Path First), 119
polling, 186-187

RIP (Routing Information Protocol),
119
routing, 119
SNA, 139
SNMP (Simple Network
Management Protocol), 19, 185
SPX/IPX (Sequenced Packet
Exchange/Internetwork Packet
Exchange), 105-106
TCP (Transmission Control
Protocol), 18
TCP/IP (Transmission Control
Protocol/Internet Protocol),
103-105
UDP (User Datagram Protocol), 18
[Public] trustee, 216-217

R

rack mount servers, 167-168
RAID technologies, 170-171, 226-229
RAM (random access memory), 158
Read after Write Verification, 179
reading manuals to troubleshoot
problems, 259
real-time collaboration tools, 35
.REC (domain name), 54
recovering from disasters, 240-242
redundancies
mirroring, 226-229
RAID, 226-229
strategies, network backups, 223-229
registering domain names, 52
remote access, 10-11
remote connections, dedicated, 84-88
repair facilities, local, 262-263
repeaters, 112-114
Token Ring networks, 114
requirements
client-server networks, 84
peer-to-peer networks, 80
research
GVU WWW User Survey, key
findings, 46
Network World 1998 Internet study,
47
Nielsen, Internet statistics, 47-48
resources
networks, protecting, 191
sharing across networks, 22-25
tracking across networks, 38
responsibilities of network
administrators, 174-176

restoring data, 238-240
restricted domain names, 54
RIGHTS utility, 219
rights
directory, 203
effective, 202
file system, 200-212
FILER utility, 219
granted during installation, 217-218
IRF (inherited rights filter), 147,
210-211
NETADMIN utility, 219
objects, 147, 205-212
property, 147, 205-212
[Public] trustee, 216-217
RIGHTS utility, 219
setting with NetWare utilities, 219
trustee, 147, 204-205
RIP (Routing Information Protocol), 119
roles, e-mail, establishing, 20
routers, 131, 118-119, 123-124
external or internal, choosing,
120-122
MPR (Multi-Protocol Router), 120
protecting, 199
routing protocols, 119
Routing Information Protocol (RIP), 119

S

scanners, 23
scanning
identification, 194
documents, 28
schedules
electronic, 33-34
meeting, 28
scheduling
groups by e-mail, 32-34
installations, placing organizations
on Internet, 51
SDRAM (synchronous dynamic RAM),
158
security equivalence, 202, 213-216
security
ACL (access control list), 208
biometrics, identification, 195-196
cables, protecting, 199-200
dial-in access, 198-199
directory rights, 203
directory trees, file system access, 212
dumb terminals, 191

Continued

my2cents.idgbooks.com

Register This Book — And Win!

Visit **http://my2cents.idgbooks.com** to register this book and we'll automatically enter you in our fantastic monthly prize giveaway. It's also your opportunity to give us feedback: let us know what you thought of this book and how you would like to see other topics covered.

Discover IDG Books Online!

The IDG Books Online Web site is your online resource for tackling technology — at home and at the office. Frequently updated, the IDG Books Online Web site features exclusive software, insider information, online books, and live events!

10 Productive & Career-Enhancing Things You Can Do at www.idgbooks.com

- Nab source code for your own programming projects.
- Download software.
- Read Web exclusives: special articles and book excerpts by IDG Books Worldwide authors.
- Take advantage of resources to help you advance your career as a Novell or Microsoft professional.
- Buy IDG Books Worldwide titles or find a convenient bookstore that carries them.
- Register your book and win a prize.
- Chat live online with authors.
- Sign up for regular e-mail updates about our latest books.
- Suggest a book you'd like to read or write.
- Give us your 2¢ about our books and about our Web site.

You say you're not on the Web yet? It's easy to get started with IDG Books' *Discover the Internet,* available at local retailers everywhere.

'POLL, AS IF HE HAD BEEN MY FAVORITE, WAS THE ONLY
PERSON PERMITTED TO TALK TO ME.' Robinson Crusoe

handkerchief from his trousers pocket and with great deliberation wiped his chest and forearms, the base of his throat and his armpits. Once rid of the thin film of sweat which had protected it until that moment, his skin began to glow like fire, red with light. Adam got up and walked quickly to the back of the room, into the shade; from the pile of blankets on the floor he pulled out an old shirt made of cotton, flannelette or calico, shook it and slipped it on. When he bent down, the tear in the middle of the back, between his shoulder-blades, opened in a way it had, to the size of a coin, and revealed, at random, three pointed vertebrae which stuck out beneath the taut skin like fingernails under thin rubber.

Without even buttoning his shirt, Adam took from among the blankets a kind of yellow exercise-book, the sort used in schools, in which the first page was headed, like the beginning of a letter:

My dear Michèle,

then he went back to sit in front of the window, protected now from the rays of the sun by the material that clung to his ribs. He opened the exercise-book on his knees, ruffled briefly through the pages covered with closely-written sentences, produced a ball-point pen from his pocket, and read:

'My dear Michèle,

I would so much like this house to stay empty. I hope the owners won't come back for a long time.

This is how I'd dreamt of living for ages: I put up two deck-chairs facing each other, just under the window; like that, about midday, I lie down and sleep in the sun, turned towards the view, which is beautiful, so they say. Or else I turn away a little towards the light, throwing my head into full relief. At four o'clock I stretch out further, provided the sun is lower or shining in more directly; by that time it's about ¾ down the window. I look at the sun, perfectly round; at the sea, that's to say the horizon, right up against the window-rail, perfectly straight. I spend every minute at the window, and I pretend all this is mine, silently, and no one else's. It's funny. I'm like that the whole time, in the sun, almost naked, and sometimes quite naked, looking carefully at the sky and the sea. I'm glad people think everywhere that I'm dead; at first I didn't know this was a deserted house; that kind of luck doesn't come often.

When I decided to live here I took all I needed, as though I were going fishing, I came back in the night, and then I toppled my motorbike into the sea. Like that I gave the impression I was dead, and I didn't need to go on making everyone believe I was alive and had heaps of things to do, to keep myself alive.

The funny thing is that no one took any notice, even at the beginning; luckily I hadn't too many friends, and I didn't know any girls, because they're always the first to come and tell you to stop playing the fool, to get back to the town and begin all over again as though nothing had happened: that's to say cafés, cinemas, railways, etc.

From time to time I go into town to buy stuff to eat, because I eat a lot, and often. Nobody asks me questions, and I don't have to talk too much; that doesn't worry me, because years ago they got me into the habit of keeping my mouth shut, and I could easily pass for deaf, dumb and blind.'

He paused for a few seconds and wiggled his fingers as though to relax them; then he bent over the exercise-book again, so that the little veins in his temples swelled and the egg-shaped, hirsute lump of his skull was exposed to the savage thrusts of the sun. This time he wrote:
'My dear Michèle,
Thanks to you, Michèle—for you exist, I believe you—I

3

have my only possible contact with the world down the hill. You go to work, you're often in the town, at the different street crossings, among the blinking lights and God knows what. You tell heaps of people you know a chap who lives alone in a deserted house, a complete nut; and they ask you why he isn't shut up in a loony-bin. I assure you I've nothing against it, I've no cervical complex and I think that's as good a way as any other to end one's days—in peace, in a comfortable house, with a formal French garden and people to see that you get your meals. The rest doesn't matter, and there's nothing to prevent one from being full of imagination and writing poems—this kind of thing:

> today, day of the rats,
> last day before the sea.

Fortunately I can make you out amidst a mass of memories, like when we used to play hide-and-seek and I would catch sight of your eye, your hand or you hair between clusters of round leaves, and thinking about it all of a sudden I would discard my faith in appearances and cry shrilly: "Seen you!".'

He thought about Michèle, about all the children she'd be having sooner or later, in any case; irrationally, that didn't matter, he could wait. He would tell those children a whole heap of things, when the time came. He'd tell them, for instance, that the earth was not round, that it was the centre of the universe, and that they were the centre of everything, without exception. Then they would no longer be in danger of losing themselves, and (unless they got polio, of course) they would have 99 chances in a hundred of going about like those children he had seen last time he went to the beach—shouting, yelling, chasing rubber balls.

He would tell them, too, that there was only one thing to

4

be afraid of—that the earth might turn over, so that they would be head downwards with their feet in the air, and that the sun might fall down on the beach, about six o'clock, making the sea boil so that all the little fishes would burst.

Dressed now, he sat in the deck-chair and looked out of the window; to do this he had to raise the cross-bar of the chair to the highest notch. The hill went down to the road in a slope that was half gradual and half steep, jumped four or five yards; and then came the water. Adam couldn't get a complete view; there were lots of pines and other trees and telegraph poles in the way, so he had to imagine parts of it. Sometimes he wasn't sure whether he'd guessed right, so he had to go all the way down. As he walked along he could see the skein of lines and curves unravelling, different things would splinter off and gleam; but the fog gathered again further ahead. One could never be definite about anything in this kind of landscape; one was always more or less a queer unknown quantity, but in an unpleasant way. Call it something like a squint or a slight exophthalmic goitre; the house itself, or the sky, or it might be the curve of the bay, would become obscured from view as Adam walked down. For shrubs and brushwood wove an uninterrupted screen in front of them; at ground-level the air quivered in the heat, and the far horizon seemed to be rising in puffs of light smoke from among the blades of grass.

The sun distorted certain things, too. Beneath its rays the road would liquify in whitish patches; sometimes when a line of cars was going by, the black metal would burst like a bomb for no apparent reason, a spiral of lightning would flash from the bonnet and make the entire hill blaze and bend, shifting the atmosphere by a few millimetres with a thrust of its halo.

That was at the beginning, really at the beginning; for afterwards he began to understand what it meant, monstrous solitude. He opened a yellow exercise-book and wrote at the top of the first page, as though beginning a letter:

'My dear Michèle,'

He used to play music as well, like everyone else; once, in the town, he had stolen a plastic pipe from a toy-stall. He had always wanted a pipe and he'd been delighted to have this one. It was a toy pipe, of course, but good quality, it came from the U.S. So when he felt inclined he would sit in the deck-chair at the open window and play gentle little tunes. Rather afraid of attracting people's attention, because there were days when fellows and girls used to come and lie down in the grass, round the house. He played softly, with infinite gentleness, making almost inaudible sounds, blowing hardly at all, pressing the tip of his tongue against the mouthpiece and pulling in his diaphragm. Now and then he would break off and rattle his fingertips along a row of empty tins, arranged in order of size; that made a soft rustling, rather like bongo drums, which went zigzagging away in the air, rather like the howls of a dog.

And that was the life of Adam Pollo. At night he would light the candles at the back of the room and take up his position at the open window in the faint sea-breeze, standing absolutely erect, full of the energy that the dusty noonday takes from a man.

He would wait a long time, without moving, proud of being almost dehumanized, until the first flights of moths arrived, tumbling, hesitating outside the empty hole of the window, pausing in concentration and then, maddened by the yellow blink of the candles, launching a sudden attack. Then he would lie down on the floor, among the blankets, and stare fixedly at the hustling swarm of insects, more and more of them, thronging the ceiling with a multiplicity of

6

shadows and collapsing into the flames, making a wreath of tiny legs round the corolla of boiling wax, sizzling, scraping the air like files against a granite wall, and smothering, one by one, every glimmer of light.

For someone in Adam's circumstances, and who had been trained to meditation by years at a university and a life devoted to reading, there was nothing to do except think of things like this and avoid madness; hence it was probable that only fear (of the sun, to take one example) could help him to remain within the bounds of moderation and, should the occasion arise, to go back to the beach. With this in mind, Adam had now slightly changed his usual position: leaning forward, he had turned his face towards the back of the room and was looking at the wall. Seeing the light dimly across his left shoulder, he was forcing himself to imagine that the sun was an immense golden spider, its rays covering the sky like tentacles, some twisting, others forming a huge W, clinging to projections in the ground, to every escarpment, at fixed points.

All the other tentacles were undulating slowly, lazily, dividing into branches, separating into countless ramifications, splitting open and immediately closing up again, waving to and fro like seaweed.

To make sure, he had drawn it in charcoal on the wall opposite.

So now he was sitting with his back to the window, and could feel terror creeping over him as the minutes went by and he contemplated the tangle of claws, the savage medley that he could no longer understand. Apart from its special aspect of something dry and charred which was shining and sprinkling, it was a kind of horrible, deadly octopus, with its hundred thousand slimy arms like horses' guts. To give himself courage he talked to the drawing, looking at its exact centre, at the anthracite ball from which the tentacles

7

flowed out like roots calcinated in some past age; he addressed it in rather childish words:
'you're a beauty—beautiful beast, beautiful beast, there, you're a nice sun, you know, a beautiful black sun.'
He knew he was on the right track.

And sure enough, he gradually managed to reconstruct a world of childish terrors; seen through the rectangle of the window, the sky seemed ready to break away and crash down on our heads. The sun, ditto. He looked at the ground and saw it suddenly melting, boiling, or flowing beneath his feet. The trees grew excited and gave off poisonous vapours. The sea began to swell, devoured the narrow grey strip of beach and then rose, rose to attack the hill, to drown him, moving towards him, to numb him, to swallow him up in its dirty waves. He could feel the fossilized monsters coming to birth somewhere, prowling round the villa, the joints of their huge feet cracking. His fear grew, invincible, imagination and frenzy could not be checked; even human beings become hostile, barbarous, their limbs sprouted wool, their heads shrank, and they advanced in serried ranks over the countryside, cannibalistic, cowardly or ferocious. The moths flung themselves on him, biting him with their mandibles, wrapping him in the silky veil of their hairy wings. From the pools there rose an armoured nation of parasites or shrimps, of abrupt, mysterious crustaceans, hungering to tear off shreds of his flesh. The beaches were covered with strange creatures who had come there, accompanied by their young, to await no one knew what; animals prowled along the roads, growling and squealing, curious parti-coloured animals whose shells glistened in the sunshine. Everything was suddenly in motion, with an intense, intestinal, concentrated life, heavy and incongruous as a kind of submarine vegetation. While this was going on he drew back into his corner, ready to

8

spring out and defend himself pending the final assault that would leave him the prey of these creatures. He picked up the yellow exercise-book of a little while back, looked again for a moment at the drawing on the wall, the drawing which had once represented the sun; and he wrote to Michèle:

'My dear Michèle,

I must admit I'm a little frightened, here in the house. I think if you were here, in the light, lying naked on the ground, and I could recognize my own flesh in yours, smooth and warm, I shouldn't need all that. While I'm writing you this, just imagine, there happens to be a narrow space, between the deck-chair and the skirting-board, that would fit you like a glove; it's exactly your length, 5 ft. 4, and I don't think its hip measurement is more than yours, $35\frac{1}{2}$. So far as I'm concerned the earth has turned into a sort of chaos, I'm scared of the deinotheria, the pithecanthropes, the Neanderthal man (a cannibal), not to mention the dinosaurs, the labyrinthosaurs, the pterodactyls, etc. I'm afraid the hill may turn into a volcano.

Or that the polar ice may melt, which would raise the level of the sea and drown me. I'm afraid of the people on the beach, BELOW. The sand is changing into quicksands, the sun into a spider and the children into shrimps.'

Adam closed the exercise-book with a snap, raised himself on his forearms, and looked out of the window. There was nobody coming. He reckoned how much time he would need to go down to the sea, bathe and get back. It was too late in the day; he had rather forgotten how long it was since he'd last been out of the house—two days, or more.

It looked as though he had been living entirely on biscuits —cut-price wafers bought at the Prisunic. Now and then he felt a pain in his stomach, and there was a sour taste round his glottis. He leant out of the window and contemplated

9

element, cooler and thicker than air, and the soles of his feet were sliding, pushing back the layers of sea-water, and finally, after several ice-cold slithers, encountering an unstable, slimy surface covered with rootlets, with microscopic pods of weed that burst under his weight and coloured the liquid, near the bottom, with dark green particles, like a mist of leaves minced up in the process of decomposition.

Fortunately the dog hesitated when it came to concealed hollows, and each time Adam was able to make up the ground he had lost. Feeling that it was being followed, the animal looked round once with a stare that caught Adam on the chin. Then it set off again, towing the man behind it as though on a leash; in a few minutes it had managed to acquire an incredible dignity and now went forward, indefinably steadfast, chest-deep in the sea, exclusively concerned with getting to the right-hand end of the beach and the group of bathing huts that stood there.

They walked like this all the way, one behind the other. As could be surmised from a distance, the bathing huts formed a half-circle, backed up against the concrete jetty with the harbour beyond it. Further down the beach the bathers were lying in a confused mass of brightly-coloured towels and bikinis; they were facing the light and because of the way their bodies were foreshortened when seen from the water's edge, they all seemed to have sloughed their old skins for new, faintly orange-tinted ones on which the sun had dribbled, leaving shiny traces.

The dog halted, began to turn its nose towards Adam, stopped half-way, and jumped ashore. It climbed the ridges of pebbles, skirted past two or three groups of sleepers, and settled itself beside a young woman.

Adam imitated it; but while the dog took up a position on the right, he went to the left. Before sitting down he hastily unfolded the towel he had been carrying round his neck and spread it on the ground; then he squatted there, hugging his knees. For ten or fifteen seconds, a few inches from the woman's stomach, he watched the dog, which was licking its paws; its eyelids were lowered and its nose pointed downwards. Adam looked at his feet and decided to follow the dog's example; oil must have accumulated along the tide line since the last storm, and the soles of his feet were black. He began scraping between his toes with a sliver of driftwood.

Adam quite realized that time was going by in this unexpected way; it was one of the kinds of time you can take to yourself completely, one of the elastic kinds that you need only adjust to the scale of whatever it is you have to do, in order to enjoy it in peace. So Adam told himself in a whisper that he was in control of things; there was no fundamental difference between the two points of the beach that he had occupied in turn. Sitting on the bath-towel, he could let his gaze roam slowly round, carrying it to infinity in concentric circles. Either one was prepared to admit that a pebble, plus a thousand pebbles, plus brambles, plus refuse, plus traces of salt, far from being motionless, lived a life of secretion and moved within a different time-system; or else one must declare that life can only be measured by the evidence of the senses. In that case Adam was undoubtedly the one and only living creature in the world.

'Hadn't you better try this?' the young woman suggested.

Adam smiled his thanks, took the paper handkerchief she held out to him—noticing as he did so that it had left a kind of fluff or snow on the tips of her fingers—and went on wiping away the oil. He thought he ought to say something. He muttered:

'Yes—it is easier like this.'

He tried to meet the young woman's eyes, but it was no use: she was wearing the kind of very dark sun-glasses, with thick lenses and frames, that are a speciality of tourists from New York at Portuguese seaside resorts. He was too shy to ask her to take them off, though he felt what a relief it would be to see her eyes. Sentimentally, he could only see his own reflexion in each plastic-rimmed lens; he looked just like a big, fat monkey, bending over and working at his feet. As though, by swaying the body forward, that position set up the concentration needed to produce the intuition that one was living, yes, living all alone in one's corner, isolated from the death of the world.

The young woman suddenly drew up her legs, a little slanting, with her head and shoulders raised just above the ground, sighed voluptuously and sent her fingers groping along her spine, brushing over the white mark on her tanned skin, as she refastened the strap of her bikini. She paused for a moment in this position, a captive figure, arms crossed behind her back, making hollows below the shoulder-blades, as though indicating to some matador the chink in her armour, the point where the sword can be thrust through to the heart. She was sweating very slightly under her arms and between her breasts. She said:

'I must go now.'

Adam followed up with 'Do you come here often?'

'It depends,' she said. 'And you——?'

'I come every day. Haven't you seen me?'

'No.'

He went on:

'I've seen you before, sitting down here—or around here. I mean at this end of the beach. Why do you sit in the same place every day? I mean, is there anything special about it? For instance, is it really cleaner than anywhere else, or cooler, or hotter, or does it smell nice, or what?'

18

'I don't know,' she said. 'I suppose it's just a habit. Is that what you mean?'

Adam registered this as though it really deserved attention.

'No—no, I don't believe you. Or at least what you say about having habits. It seems to me your dog is the one that has habits. In fact I wouldn't be surprised if he brings you to this part of the beach every time. If you'd watched him you would certainly have noticed how he arrives on the beach, goes in for a bathe, up to the neck in water, with his nose pointing straight ahead, and afterwards sleeps in the sun for a bit, and licks his paws. And then how he trots away, composedly, always stepping on the flat stones so as not to hurt his paws, until he's far enough from the children, so that they won't poke his eye out with their spades and rakes. Isn't that so? And without ever changing his clothes.'

'Listen,' said the young woman, 'you seem to me to be very young.'

Suddenly she had her clothes on, her hair was dry, she lit a Du Maurier cigarette, flashed her sun-glasses darkly two or three times, called her dog, and walked away, up to the road.

C. 'You remember that time in the mountains?' Adam asked. The girl smiled, but her smile was certainly pursuing a different conversation. He had to repeat his question, rather gravely, in a louder, more level tone, in more deliberate words not uninfluenced by a boyish desire to shock.

'Now look, Michèle, surely you remember?'

She shook her head, already beginning to find this tiresome.

'As a matter of fact,' he said, 'every girl has some story like that to tell her mother. When she tells it she says "the time I was raped." You too.'

'Couldn't we talk about something else?' Michèle retorted; but Adam ignored this; he went on telling his story, for other people's benefit, in a cheap parody of uneasy recollections.

'Then you remember, too, that we'd gone off together on the motorbike. First of all I'd taken you to a couple of cafés, because it was in the middle of winter and practically freezing. Couldn't have been more than 1 or 2 degrees above, or perhaps even down to zero. We'd both drunk black coffee, big cups of it. Or rather I'd watched you drinking it; you had a funny way of drinking black coffee, I liked the way you did it, in those days. You used to take the cup in your left hand, like this, put your hand under your chin like a saucer, and stick out your upper lip. You'd dip it daintily into the coffee and before beginning to drink —remember—you'd raise your head slightly, so that one saw the semi-circular shadow the coffee had left round your mouth.'

The waiter brought their order; Michèle extended a hand, chose one of the glasses of beer and swallowed several mouthfuls without pausing for breath. Then she put the glass down, with an abrupt movement of her wrist. The froth round the glass began to evaporate, slowly widening the gaps between the trails of bubbles. Little shafts of effervescence traversed the almost opaque yellow liquid from the surface downwards; to take only one of its aspects, it looked as rich and virile as the sea. Part of it, about a quarter, was now collected in the pit of Michèle's stomach, like a liquid stone, a little petroleum, a suspicion of brilliantine. As for the other three-quarters, waiting in the glass, it might have been an empty goldfish bowl standing at noon on an Empire *guéridon*, its fish having died.

Or even one of those fish-tanks you see in the windows of big restaurants, where solemn gourmets come to have fat carp hauled out for them in a net, each fish leaving a hole in the water between the pilot-light, the oxygen blowpipe and the artificial weeds—departing from behind its emerald-green bulkhead to enter a world of torture, of butter, of parsley in the eyes and tomato in the mouth.

'After the cafés we went off again on the motorbike, along the main road. Then I took that narrow lane that led away into the country, and it got dark and began to drizzle a bit. It's good to remember things so well. Really it is. Does it sound true, anyway? Won't you tell me? Won't you take your turn and tell me a little? Or just say "And then? And what happened next?" Because there's only one way of telling that kind of thing, and that's in the sentimental style—you see what I mean, it gives people confidence and has a certain air of truth about it. I like that.

'D'you know what you said? You said—they were your very words—"It's not worth it." It's not worth it! Not worth what? The extraordinary thing is that I understood, and yet I went ahead all the same. Until we came to a big patch of mud that barred the way. Besides, no—after all, I hadn't understood what you said "It's not worth it". I think I was doing everything without realizing, just anyhow. I propped the bike against a tree and we walked on, through the wet grass; the grass was wet. You said you were cold, or something, and then I said we ought to shelter under a tree till the rain stopped. We found a big umbrella -pine and we stood with our backs to the trunk, one on each side. That was where we got sticky patches on our shoulders. There was a carpet of pine-needles and grass all round, very pretty. That's true. All of a sudden the rain came on harder, and then I sidled round the trunk and put my hand behind your neck and pulled you down on the ground. The raindrops were coming through the leaves, I don't know if you remember, joining together in twos and threes and splashing down on us, as big as your hand. Yes, I tore your clothes, because you were getting frightened and beginning to yell; I slapped you twice, full in the face —not very hard. I remember you had a zip that was absurdly stiff; it kept on sticking; in the end I managed to pull it down by tugging with all my strength. Wait— afterwards you went on struggling, but not too hard. I think you must have been scared stiff, of me or of the consequences. At least I think so. Well, and when all your clothes were off I held you down on the ground with your feet against the trunk of the tree and your head right out in the rain, and I held your wrists in my hands and squeezed

22

your knees between my legs. And in theory I raped you—like that, easily, you see, as wet with rain as though you'd been in a bath; listening all the same—if you'll excuse me—to your cries of rage, the little noises of the storm, and the shots fired by the sportsmen who were beating the underwood on the opposite hillside. I say "in theory". Because in practice it was a flop. But after all, perhaps that doesn't matter much so far as I'm concerned. Once I'd managed to get your clothes off. Anyhow—to make a good story out of it, literary and all that—let's say I saw you getting gradually covered with wet hair, earth, prickles and pine-needles and I saw your mouth wide open, you were breathing hard through it, getting your breath back, and a trickle of muddy water was coming from an imperceptible spring somewhere near the roots of your hair. Honestly, by the time it was all over you looked like a garden. You wriggled free and sat up with your back against the tree. For me, you understand, you'd become just a heap of pinkish earth mixed with grass and raindrops. With some vestiges of a woman here and there; perhaps because you were waiting. All the same we stayed there for quite a while, doing nothing—I couldn't say how long exactly, ten minutes, perhaps twenty—less than an hour in any case. That was absolutely ridiculous, considering it was icy cold, zero degrees above zero in fact. When we—or rather no, we got dressed without looking at each other, you on one side of the trunk and I on the other. And as your clothes were torn I lent you my raincoat. It was still pouring as hard as ever, but we were tired of waiting, so we got on the bike again and went away. I left you outside a café and, without your asking me or anything, I made you a present of my raincoat. You didn't look too good in it, did you? I don't know what you told your father, whether you went to the police or not, but——'

23

'Yes, I did go to the police,' said Michèle. This was pretty incredible.

'You knew what you were about? I mean, you knew what it might lead to?'

'Yes.'

'And then?' said Adam. 'And then?' he repeated.

'Then, nothing . . .'

'What d'you mean, nothing? What did they say?'

Michèle shook her head.

'They didn't say anything. I shan't tell you, so that's that.'

'I didn't see anything in the papers, so far as I know.'

'The papers have other things to talk about—haven't they?'

'Then why did you go to the police?'

'I thought—oh, I don't know; I thought you needed a lesson.'

'And now?'

Michèle swept her hand in a curve, presumably by way of negation.

Adam pretended not to be satisfied with this.

'Now?'

'Now it's over, what the hell does it matter?' she retorted, almost shouting.

It was his turn to be annoyed; he explained:

'You ask me what the hell it matters, do you, when a chap's a deserter into the bargain? You don't realize that a charge like that might land me in the nick? Are you really crazy, or what, Michèle? Can't you see, can't you see that Adam Pollo, a deserter from the army, is at the mercy of the first informer who comes along, and that any day—or rather any hour, any minute—two fellows in uniform may appear on the scene, beat me up, kick me, shove me into a strait-waistcoat, handcuff me—the lot—and not rest content till they've clapped me into the darkest cell in some army barracks, with no food, no heating, no women, no nothing, and even less than that?'

Michèle, after a moment's hesitation, decided to call a halt to the game.

'That'll do, Adam, you're beginning to make me really tired.'

He went on, however.

'Michèle, I can't understand you! Do you really favour the version of life where people always pretend to disbelieve everything? According to you I deserve hanging, or don't I? Answer me!'

'Adam, please, I really have a headache, I——'

'Answer me first.'

'Shut up.'

'Well? Do I deserve hanging?'

'Yes—there—are you satisfied?'

Adam decided to say no more. As for Michèle, she took a mirror out of her handbag and smoothed her eyebrows with a fingertip. Some people going by along the pavement glanced at her furtively. She looked by no means one in a thousand. Defeated by her obstinacy, Adam waited while she combed her hair, powdered her nose and touched up her lipstick; all he had left was to drink his nearly cold coffee.

Then for a few minutes they played a game; it consisted of moving the things on the table by a fraction of an inch; they took turns, attacking and counter-attacking, shifting the beer-mats, the saucer, the cup, the spoon, some scraps of wool, a dead fly, the little square paper the bill was marked on, the white ashtray, a match, their sun-glasses, the butt of a gauloise cigarette, a drop of coffee (spread towards the right), etc.

Adam won in the end, with a big speck of fluff that had

fallen off Michèle's sweater; he pushed it forward by a hair's breadth. Immediately after that they got up together and left the café. The waiter called to them as they went past the bar; Adam was the only one who looked round. He paid with small change, glanced at himself in the big mirror on the wall, and went out.

They walked side by side without a word, staring straight ahead; the street ran gently down towards the sea, and they were watching for any glimpses of the horizon that might appear between the square blocks of the houses. On reaching the promenade they paused and almost turned in opposite directions; finally Adam followed Michèle. A bit further on they sat down, on a bench that had lost its back three months previously in a driving accident: a six-ton lorry had knocked over a scooter which had suddenly appeared from the right, and had then lost control and toppled onto the pavement—damaging the bench and causing two deaths.

'I wrote to you,' Adam said. 'I wrote to you and I raped you. Why didn't you do something as well?'

'What did you expect me to do?' asked Michèle wearily.

'I wrote to you, and I put my address.'

'You surely didn't expect me to answer?'

'Of course I did! For heaven's sake!' He enjoyed shouting. 'Of course I did! Or else you should have fetched the cops.'

'I've no use for the cops.'

'You brought a charge, or didn't you?'

'I can't help that . . .'

'I can't help that . . .' she protested several times.

They walked along the seafront for a considerable distance; the wind was blowing in gusts, now cold, now hot. Nobody went past on their pavement. To one side lay the sea, absolutely smooth, dirty with oil in places, the beacon flashing from the sea-wall, and a few street lamps whose vertical reflections seemed to be moving forward. On the other side was the great mass of dry land, systematically covered by the town, by telegraph-poles and trees, exaggerately curved, as though one were looking at it with one's head upside-down. In Adam's mind, they say, the scene was reversed, as though in a convex mirror. So he felt he was balanced on his toes, perched right above the continents, with the round earth like a globe under his feet, imitating the position of Mary and doing the opposite of Atlas's task. It was like the time when (aged twelve or thirteen) he used to throw his whole weight on his rubber beach-ball, forcing it below the surface of the water so that, dilated by the pressure, it slipped up along his calves in little uncoordinated jerks.

As they walked they exchanged a few more remarks.
'Why can't you help it?'
'Because. Because I don't know.'
'Do you know what? You lack concentration.'
'Is that so?'
'And you're too emphatic.'
'Anything else?'
'Wait. You're not persuasive.'
'Really?'
'Yes, really. Not that you care a damn. Because it makes no difference in the long run. I believe just as much in whatever I do; the great thing is always to talk as if it were to be put in writing; that way one feels one's not free. Not free to talk like oneself. And then one mixes better. One's no longer alone. One exists with the coefficient 2, or 3, or 4, instead of that infernal coefficient 1. You understand?'

'I understand. I've got a headache,' said Michèle.

She waited a little for him to reply; then, sensing that

27

he would say nothing more for a long time, she kissed him, said goodbye, and turned back towards the middle of the town. She strode away, with her man's raincoat tightly belted, her hair flattened by the rain, a black spot of oil on her left ankle; her face was set, almost vicious.

D. It almost seemed as though raising artificial problems had become a habit with him. He had four or five tries before making up his mind; asking questions to right and left, consulting old postcards received at Christmas or on New Year's Eve and calendars dating from last year or last month; even asking the advice of grandparents. Several people invited him to have an apéritif, a little glass of Cinzano at the bar; kind of them, but he had his own idea. He refused their invitations and sat down at the far end of the room, with his back to the wall. He dwelt on the fact that by now he must be the oldest of them all, something like twenty-eight to thirty, or thereabouts. That was certainly the age when, if ever, one should be able to understand everything at a hint and capable of action, especially where resolutions of this kind were concerned.

28 August, heat-wave, height of summer; 7.30 p.m.; he stared straight ahead of him, past the customers moving about in the foreground, and saw it was beginning to get dark outside. He had chosen his bar carefully, as one of those where Michèle often went. He sat waiting, with a glass of orangeade in front of him; he was searching his memory.

Three American sailors, probably drunk, came into the bar, singing American songs. Adam watched them as they

29

walked across to lean on the bar, beside the till. One of them left the others and came past Adam's table. He pushed a coin into the slot of the juke-box, bent down to read the titles on the screen, and then suddenly realized that this was unnecessary because every song in the box must be American. He pressed two buttons at random and stepped back, finding it hard to tear his eyes away from the circle of light on the record. Nevertheless he walked off, found his way to the cloakroom door, and was going out just as he heard the first words of the Red River Rock:

'Heigho Johnny rockin'
Rock-a-goose by the river,
Ho red river rock 'n roll.'

Adam listened to the song right through, beating time with his left hand on the table-top. When the record was over he paid and was leaving the bar as the American sailor came out of the cloakroom and joined his friends.

An hour later Adam ran into them again in a grill-room in the old part of the town. One of them recognized him, heaven knows why, caught him by the arm and muttered into his ear in English. Adam didn't listen; he offered the man a cigarette, lit it for him, and sat down beside him on a stool. He ordered a cheese and salad sandwich and then turned to the American sailor. His mind was empty of thought, he was half-dead. The sailor said his name was John Beaujolais and he came from Portland, Maine. Then he asked 'What's your name?'

'Puget-Théniers,' said Adam, taking a bite of his sandwich and wondering why he had chosen that particular town.

'I used to know a French girl, Mireille her name was,' said the American; he turned to his companions and told them some story, in an undertone; they all burst out laughing. Adam went on eating for a time; he felt a kind of boredom stealing over him, as though he had spent the afternoon among Martians, trying one language after another on them.

'Are you fellows still at war?' he asked Beaujolais, pointing to his uniform with a crust of bread.

'No, not at war,' said Beaujolais, 'but—*le service national*, eh? You too, I guess?'

'No, I'm through with that,' said Adam. He paused to swallow a mouthful of bread and salad and then went on:

'I like American books. I enjoyed reading Wigglesworth, Child, and that poet Robinson Jeffers, who wrote *Tamar*. I enjoyed Stuart Engstrand. You know him?'

'No,' said Beaujolais. 'Me, I'm a jazz musician. Tenor sax. I played with Horace Parlan and Shelly Manne, a couple of years back. Romeo Penque, too. He's a flute-player. I know John Eardley well. He's great. Real great.' He tapped the counter with his finger.

'But I had to quit—yes, quit—so . . .'

'Yes, Stuart Engstrand,' Adam went on. 'He's not well known here, and in America he's looked upon as a guy who rather writes down to the public, isn't he? But personally I think he's good; he writes straightforward stuff. He tells simple stories. Guys who want pretty girls and marry them. And because they're pretty it doesn't go so well. But the fellows are tough, not like over here. So they always win out in the end.'

'French girls are pretty, isn't that so?' said the American. 'I'd like to—marry one.'

'Yes,' said Adam, 'so would I.'

'Listen,' said the American, 'you want to know what Mireille was like? She was like this; like this! In summer she used to wear hats, how d'you call 'em? She had a white dog. He's died since, I believe. I wanted her to go back with

31

me afterwards, to the States. Yes. I said to her, you come; but she said no. I'd have liked her to, no kidding.'

The sailor stared hard at Adam for a moment. Then he said: 'You want a drink?'

'No,' said Adam. He revolved slowly on his stool and leant back with his elbows on the edge of the bar and the middle of his spine pressed against its metal rim. He looked at the three uniformed figures moving about on his right. The peace, thus composed of talk between strangers, tips, parts of evenings joined together without rhyme or reason, could easily be transformed into hostilities, stale bread, scraps of terror by night, and then, all of a sudden, into war, with code language, passwords, blood, trails of black smoke. He could sense wars going on all over the world; in his brain there was a peculiar region that encroached upon the others, a jungle site where nature was truly strange; the vegetation consisted of barbed wire like hard, stiff lianas, with small, spiky knots every six inches instead of leaves.

But the great thing was to know what one would do when the war was over. One might go into business, take up teaching or spend the rest of one's life writing novels about the army. Failing that, one might become a jazz musician, like John Beaujolais of Portland, Maine. Or join up again, pick up one's kitbag and make off into the North African mountains, carrying a big machine-gun—wastelands, pylons, expeditions at 6 in the morning, with a heavy mist clinging to the contours of the ground so that the flights of ducks are half-concealed—just enough for purposes of slaughter. But after that, on leaving the army, would one be able to climb a hill and live all alone in a big, empty house, put two deck-chairs face to face and lie sweating in the sun for days on end, almost naked and sometimes quite naked? To believe that one needn't

32

make money in order to keep alive, but that one does need to defend oneself against all those (and there are plenty of them) who'd like to murder one?

Adam was trying to recapture some link with the past ten years; some phrase, some army habit, the name of some place; anything that would make clear to him how he had spent his time and finally, finally, later on, where he had been before this.

A French soldier came into the restaurant; he wore the uniform of the Alpine regiment and seemed to be looking for somebody; he had the alert, forceful expression customary to those who disregard the petty details of life. Adam felt irresistibly drawn towards him; he could not prevent himself from getting up, walking over to the man and speaking to him without more ado; sweat broke out on his chest as he did so.

'You're a soldier, are you?' he asked.

'Yes. Why?' replied the other.

'What company?'

'Twenty-second *Chasseurs alpins.*'

'Do you know a place called Msila?' Adam demanded.

The other stared at him, surprised.

'No . . . Where is it?'

'In Algeria.'

'I've never been over there,' said the other man. 'Besides . . .'

'Wait a minute!' Adam continued, 'I'm trying to think—I know the map, you see. It's near Bordj-Bou-Arreridj.'

'I daresay,' said the soldier. 'But excuse me, I haven't got time . . . I'm waiting for a girl . . .'

He turned away as if to sit down at a table; Adam followed him, pressing his point:

'Msila, in Bibania. In the foothills of the Hodna mountains. The nearest town is Setif. You must have heard of Setif?'

'But I tell you,' the man interrupted, 'I've never set foot in your damned sector . . .'

'How many months have you been in the army?'

'Three!' he shouted, 'Three, and I——'

'Then it's possible,' said Adam, 'it's possible I've never been there. You understand, I'm trying to remember—anyway, what does it matter? I'm sure to find out one day. You won't have a drink while you wait for your girl?'

'No thanks, I'm not thirsty,' said the soldier. He added 'Good night,' and walked quickly to an unoccupied table. When Adam got back to his stool he found the three American sailors had gone. He lit a cigarette and tried to think things out. But his attention was constantly distracted by a host of small happenings he had scarcely noticed before, but which now swelled to huge proportions and clung to his sensory structure like iron filings to a magnet, accumulating and getting in the way.

A handsome auburn-haired girl came into the restaurant, holding herself very straight but wriggling her hips in a slightly ridiculous manner, and walked across to the French soldier's table. The man reddened, stood up and pulled out a chair for her, smearing the edge of his khaki jacket with ash from a cigarette he had dropped on the table and forgotten; it now rolled jerkily to the opposite corner and fell to the ground by its own impetus, not making the slightest sound when it hit the floor; when Adam, in imitation, pushed a cigarette across the metal top of the bar until it fell off, the noise it made was at least a thousand times louder.

Adam huddled on his stool; shut in by a strange old age, he was quietly resuming his place in the sun, in the deserted house at the top of the hill, taking no interest in the countryside, in the town or the sea, no interest in the aircraft that flew along the horizon, sometimes noisy, sometimes

34

silent, no interest in ocean cruises or in the fine, realistic books people occasionally write after their military service, recording in meticulous detail that on a certain day in a certain month of June they were told to swill out the latrines directly after being made to peel forty pounds of potatoes; no interest in the many who are incapable of dying for love of a diadem spider, for the languors of nature, who cannot be brought to the verge of tears when the silence is rent by a drop of water falling into the waste-pipe of a washbasin. Those who refuse to live in the bosom of the earth, in the warm bosom, the bosom full of scents, rustlings and haloes, of the earth; of our microbial earth.

Step by step he was taking up his withdrawn position at the open window, crouching on the ground between the two empty deck-chairs, and he was becoming aware that he did not understand anything at all. There was nothing in the actual structure of these horrible things to show him definitely whether he had just come out of a mental home or out of the army.

E. Michèle had an awful job finding Adam's house. The bus put her down on the road at the first turn after the beach. She looked round at the houses and gardens and the hills rolling softly into the distance, covered with thicker vegetation; but recognized nothing that could guide her in all this. She walked slowly along the bank that bordered the road, stepping cautiously on the gravel as though intent on bending either sandal in turn to the exact point—an angle of about 30°—where the instep stretched the leather straps absolutely taut, making them squeak, just once, a sharp squeak that kept time with her steps.

From her jacket pocket she took a plan Adam had drawn one day on the underneath of a beer-mat. Both sides of the card bore a printed slogan, something like:

'Drink Slavia, it's different . . . your very good health!' but she did not look at that; she studied the plan, a rough pencil-sketch running across the words of the advertisement. A curved line represented the bay beyond the harbour. Two parallel lines marked the road, the one she was on now. To either side of the road and below the S of Slavia a number of little circles or squares had been hastily scrawled, and Michèle remembered what Adam had said:

'There are some shanties there, up and down the hillside. I won't mark them all, because it would take the whole blessed day—there are so many of them. I'm telling you that so you won't think I've under-estimated the landscape. Look, I'll write it for you—there: shanties.'

Further on there were two more parallel lines, closer together this time; that was the path. To left and right of the path the cardboard was covered with a very light net-work of crisscross lines; a word had been written on top of the cross-hatching, but it was too rubbed to be legible. Some distance up the path, on the left, there was a square which was perfectly clear; it had obviously been drawn with care and was much larger than the others. It was marked in the middle with a kind of St. Andrew's cross. That was where Adam lived—the little, insignificant spot on the earth's surface that one underlines, that one marks in perpetuity somewhere or other, just as one scribbles an indecent drawing on a lavatory door so that, for once at any rate, all the lavatories in the world shall have their centre of gravity.

On reaching the top of the parallel lines of the path, Michèle looked to the left. But the rectangle indicated by the cross could not be seen, owing to the uneven ground, the houses and shrubs. She had to set off at a venture, through a tangle of brambles, at the risk of emerging too high up or too low down, or trespassing on private property. Below her stretched the rounded sea, pricked here and there with white sails. The sun's reflection swung over its surface, flashing like a crystal chandelier, and the waves lay motionless like furrows. The sky was twice its proper size, and in places, particularly in the vicinity of the line of mountains that cut off the horizon beyond the bay, the land was badly put together; its colours clashed and its planes were often heaped one upon another, with a curious dis-regard for the most elementary notions of balance and perspective; one felt that this landscape would seize any opportunity—a red sunset or a purple eclipse, to take only two examples—of being cheaply melodramatic.

Michèle kept coming upon what might be clearings or uneven patches, craters like shell-holes, inhabited by snakes and ant-lions, or great beds of prickly plants. She caught sight of Adam's house some distance away and realized she must have misread the map, for she was well below the marked point.

She began climbing the hill again, her shirt drenched with sweat and the hook at the top of her check swim-suit digging into her back as the bra was stretched by her bowed shoulders. This time the sun was behind, throwing her shadow directly ahead and painting the front of the house a sickly white.

Adam, at the window, had seen her approaching; he drew back for a moment, uncertain, wondering who the intruder could be; at less than fifty yards he recognized Michèle. Thus reassured, he left his observation post and sat down again in the deck-chair. A voice, hoarse with heat or fatigue, hailed him by his first name:

'Adam! Hi, Adam!'

In this arid terrain the cry sounded so unpleasant that for fear it should be repeated he climbed out of the window and stood at the edge of a flower-bed. Without noticing it, he trod on and squashed two red and black ants, one of which was carrying the remains of a dung-beetle. He waited till Michèle was only a few yards away, and then said, with a perfect imitation of naturalness:

'That you, Michèle? Come on up.'

He took her hand and helped her over the last lumps of earth; he watched her when she stopped, out of breath, her face glistening and her damp clothes clinging to her body.

'You gave me a fright,' he said. 'For a moment I wondered who it could be.'

38

'What? Who did you think it might be?' Michèle panted.

'I don't know—one never knows . . .'

He cast a glance of concern at his naked stomach.

'I'm terribly sunburnt there, round my navel,' he said.

'Why—why do you always have to be talking about your navel, your nose, your hands or your ears, or something of that kind?' asked Michèle.

He ignored the remark.

'I ought to get dressed,' he muttered. 'Just feel that—no, not there, my stomach.'

She touched his skin and flapped her hand as though she had burnt herself.

'Go and get dressed, then.'

Adam nodded and went indoors by the route he had taken to come out; Michèle followed him, but in a way he didn't care. After putting on his shirt he lit a cigarette and turned to look at her. He saw she had a parcel in her left hand.

'You've brought me something?' he enquired.

'Yes, some newspapers.'

She undid the parcel and spread out its contents on the floor.

'About a dozen daily papers, a *Match* and a movie magazine.'

'A magazine? Which one? Show me . . .'

She held it out to him, Adam turned over a few pages, sniffed them near the cover, and dropped the magazine on the floor.

'Interesting?'

'I took what I could find.'

'Yes, of course,' he said. 'Anything to eat?'

Michèle shook her head.

'No—but you told me you didn't need anything.'

39

'I know,' said Adam. 'And money? Can you lend me some?'

'Not more than a thousand,' said Michèle. 'Want it now?'

'Yes, if possible.'

Michèle held out a note; he thanked her and thrust it into his trousers pocket. Then he pulled one of the deck-chairs into the shade and sat down.

'Would you like a drink? I've got two and half bottles of beer left.'

She said 'Yes.' Adam fetched the bottles, took a penknife from somewhere near the heap of blankets, and prised the cap off a full bottle. He offered it to Michèle.

'No, give me the half that's left over, it'll be enough for me.'

They drank straight out of the bottles, several good gulps without a pause. Adam was the first to put down his bottle; he wiped his mouth and began to talk, as though continuing some old story:

'Apart from that, what's the news?' he asked. 'I mean, what's the news on the wireless, the TV and so on?'

'The same as in the newspapers, you know, Adam . . .'

He persisted, frowning:

'All right, then, let's put it another way: what news is there that isn't in the papers? I don't know, but for anyone who lives among other people, like you do, it's not the same, is it? There must be things the papers and the radio don't mention, but that everybody knows? Aren't there?'

Michèle reflected.

'But things like that aren't news. Otherwise they'd be in the papers. They're people's opinions, and so forth——'

'Call it what you like—people's opinions, rumours going around—What's the latest? Is there going to be—at least, do they think there's going to be an atomic war, soon?'

40

'Atomic?'

'Yes, atomic.'

She shrugged.

'I haven't the faintest idea—how should I know? No, I don't believe they think that. I don't think they believe there'll be an atomic war. As a matter of fact I don't believe they give a damn.'

'They don't give a damn, eh?'

'I think, perhaps . . .'

Adam sneered.

'Okay, okay,' he said, with a shade of absolutely unjustifiable bitterness, 'so they don't give a damn—Neither do I. The war's over. I didn't finish it, nor did you, but that's beside the point. It's behind us. You're right. Only one day, it's a hopeless business, you see funny cast-iron animals, painted khaki, the camouflage colour, real tanks, appearing from all directions and swooping down on the town. You see little black dots spreading over the whole district. You wake up, pull back the curtains, and there they are, down in the street; they're coming and going, you wonder why, they're very like ants, you might mistake them for ants. They have kind of hose-pipes that they drag after them everywhere; and with a very soft sound, puff! puff!, they spout jets of napalm onto the buildings. Where can I have seen that, I wonder? The tongue of flame that comes out of the pipe—it goes on through the air by itself, in a slight curve, and then it stretches out longer and longer, it goes in at a window, and suddenly, without your really noticing, the house is on fire, it's erupting like a volcano, the walls are collapsing all in one piece, slowed down by the air, which is incandescent, with big curls of sooty smoke, and the fire pouring out in all directions like sea-water. And the guns and the bazookas, the dum-dum bullets, the trench-mortars, the hand-grenades, etc., and the bomb that drops

41

on the harbour when I'm eight years old and I tremble and the air trembles and the whole earth trembles and sways under the black sky? When a big gun goes off, I tell you, it jerks back with a graceful, agile movement, just like a shrimp if you stretch out your hand towards it, with your fingers all swollen and red because the water's cold. Yes, when a big gun goes off it makes a graceful movement like a well-oiled machine, a graceful mechanical twitch. It growls, it springs back like a piston and it makes splendid holes three hundred yards away, holes that aren't too messy and that turn into pools afterwards, when it rains. But one gets used to it—there's nothing one gets used to as easily as war. There's no such thing as war. People die every day, and so what? War is all or nothing. War is total and permanent. I, Adam, I'm still in it, come to that. I don't want to get out of it.'

'Stop it for a second, will you, Adam? In the first place, what war are you talking about?'

She had taken advantage of Adam's speech to finish her bottle of beer quietly; she liked to drink beer unhurriedly, taking big mouthfuls and letting them filter down slowly between her tongue and her uvula—all but counting the thousands of bubbles that fizzed through her mouth, that searched every tiny crevice and spot of decay in her teeth, took possession of her entire palate and went up into the back of her nose. Now she had finished, and as what Adam was saying did not interest her she thought this would be a good way of stopping him.

'Well, what war are you talking about?' she repeated, 'The atomic one? It hasn't happened yet. The 1940 war? You didn't even fight in that one, you must have been twelve or thirteen years old at the time . . .'

So that's it, said Adam to himself; so that's it. The atomic war hasn't happened yet. And of course I didn't fight in the

1940 one, I must have been twelve or thirteen years old at the time. And even if I did fight in it, I'd have been far too young to remember about it now. There had been no wars since then, otherwise they would have been mentioned in the modern history textbooks. And Adam knew, from having read these comparatively recently, that they did not report any war, anywhere, since the one against Hitler.

Perplexed, he fell silent; and suddenly, by pure chance, he realized that the whole universe was redolent of peace. Here, as no doubt elsewhere, there was a wonderful silence. As though they were both coming up from a dive into the sea and breaking surface, both carrying deep inside their ears, against the ear-drum, a ball of warm liquid setting up an imperceptibly rhythmic palpitation, pressing against the brain as a no-man's land of sibillant sounds, warblings, kindly whistles, single notes and the splash of waterfalls, where the worst rages, the most horrible ecstasies, sound like flowing brooks and seaweed.

They spent the rest of the day listening to this peace, to the few sounds that came from outside or the imperceptible displacement of objects inside the house. In any case the silence was not absolute; he had referred to sibillant sounds and whistles; to these must be added other sounds, grating noises, friction between layers of air, specks of dust brushing past one another and falling on flat surfaces; all amplified 1,500 times.

In case of need they huddled together in a corner of the first-floor room and made love mentally, thinking all the time 'We're spiders or slugs.' And much other childishness of the same kind.

Towards evening they arrived at a kind of imperfect state of themselves, as though everything they were doing was off-beat, even their slightest gesture, their faintest breath, and they had become mere halves of people. In this

43

upstairs room, immediately above the one Adam lived in, there was a large billiard-table with a threadbare cloth. They had lain down on this, side by side, gazing up at the ceiling. Adam's face had kept its bored, yet somehow pleased expression; his left hand was lying horizontally across the billiard table with the open palm upturned. Michèle lit a cigarette for the satisfaction of dropping the ash into the pockets of the table; without moving her head, she looked sidelong at Adam's profile; she felt a few seconds' irritation because it had something fastidious about it, an air of satiety; she said she found all this horrible, that she had the impression of waiting for God knows what—the Strasbourg train, or her turn at the hairdresser's.

Adam held his pose perfectly, but one felt that for a fleeting instant he had considered moving his legs or raising his eyebrows. He said something through motionless lips, and Michèle had to get him to repeat it.

'I said,' he repeated, 'that that's what I can't stand about women.' He was still scrutinizing the ceiling; for he had discovered that if one looked straight at the middle of it, owing to the fact that there were no rough patches in the pale green paint that was spread evenly over the plaster, the eye was not arrested by any protuberance. One saw no walls or corners, and there was thus nothing left to indicate that this was a plane surface, theoretically parallel to the horizon, characterized by its pale green colour, smooth to the touch, vaguely sandy, and at all events a man-made affair. Aiming right at the centre, with half-puckered eyelids, one was suddenly faced by a new type of communication which ignored relief, the force of gravity, colour, the sense of touch, distance and time, and drained all genetic desire from you; the effect of which was to atrophy, to mechanize; which was the first stage of anti-existence.

'That's what I dislike—their need to express all their

44

sensations. With no decent restraint. And they're nearly always inaccurate. As though it mattered in the least to other people, anyhow . . .'

He sniggered:

'We're stuffed with sensations, all of us! In my opinion it's more serious to reflect that we all have the same ones. But no—people want to describe them and then go on to analyse them, and then construct arguments on them—which have no more than a documentary value, if that.'

Adam drove his argument home:

'So one gets metaphysics at a café table, or in bed with a woman, or at the sight of a dog that's been run over in the street, because its eyes are popping out and its belly has split open, letting out a tumble of guts and a froth of blood and bile.'

Finally he propped himself up on his elbows, determined to convince Michèle:

'You feel as though you were waiting for something, don't you? Something unpleasant—unpleasant rather than dangerous?—Isn't that right? You feel as though you were waiting for something unpleasant. Well, listen to me. I'll tell you. It's the same with me. I have the same impression of waiting. But you must realize one thing: I personally shouldn't worry about this impression of waiting, except that I'm positive that it's bound to happen—that this unpleasant something-or-other will inevitably happen to me sooner or later. So that now, in point of fact, it's no longer something unpleasant that I'm expecting, it's something *dangerous*. You understand? It's simply a way of keeping one's feet on the ground. If you'd told me what you haven't told me, for instance that you have the impression of waiting for something and that you know, you understand, you *know* that it must be death, then okay. I understand you. Because there always comes a day when

45

one proves to be right in waiting for death. But you understand, don't you, that what matters is not your unpleasant impression, but the fact that not a moment goes by without our consciously or unconsciously waiting for death. That's the point. You know what that means? It means that in a certain system of life, which one puts into application by the mere fact of existing, you're leaving a negative element—which, as it were, perfectly rounds off the human unit. It reminds me of Parmenides. You know, what he says, I think: "How, then, can what *is* be going to be in the future? Or how could it come into being? If it came into being, it is not; nor is it if it is going to be in the future. Thus is *becoming* extinguished and passing away not to be heard of." That's the way to talk. One must have an inkling of it. Otherwise, Michèle, it's not worth being able to think. Talking's no use, you know, Michèle, no use at all.'

It suddenly occurred to him, for no reason, that he had hurt Michèle's feelings, and he was sorry about that, in a way.

'You know, Michèle,' he said, to make up for it, 'you may be right. You may tell me—why not—that the whole involves the whole—in the long run that might perhaps be truest of all to Parmenides . . .'

In his turn he looked sideways, watching the girl's profile with eyes that were nevertheless not so perceptive; it brought him the satisfaction of a connection that suddenly became possible, a real link between the two halves of his speech.

'I mean, in the dialectical system of reasoning—rhetorical seems to me to be a more accurate term from this point of view—yes, in this system of reasoning that isn't concerned with experience, you only have to say to me: "What time is it?" and I interpret your question like this: *What,* interrogative pronoun, belongs to a fallacious conception

46

of the universe, in which everything is listed and classified and where one can pick out of a drawer, as it were, a suitable adjective for every subject. *Time*—an abstract idea, is divisible into minutes and seconds which, added together in infinite number, produce another abstract idea which we call eternity. In other words, time includes both the finite and the infinite, the measurable and the incommensurable; which is a contradiction and therefore a logical absurdity.

Is? Existence—just another word, an abstract anthropomorphism, existence being the sum of the individual's associations of ideas. *It?* Same thing. *It* has no existence. *It* is the general extension of the male concept to an abstract idea, that of time, in addition to which it contributes to an aberrant grammatical form, the impersonal, bringing us back to the business of *Is*. Wait. And the whole sentence relates to a matter of time. There you are. What time is it? If you knew how that little sentence tortures me! Or rather, no. It's I who suffer through it. I'm crushed by the weight of my consciousness. *I'm dying of it*, that's a fact, Michèle. It's killing me. But fortunately one doesn't live logically. Life isn't logical, perhaps it's a kind of disorder of the consciousness. A disease of the cells. Anyhow, it doesn't matter, that's no reason. One has to talk, I agree, one has to live. But Michèle, isn't it just as well to say only what's really useful? It's better to keep the other things to oneself until one forgets them, until one comes to live solely for one's own body, seldom moving one's legs, huddled in a corner, more or less hunch-backed, more or less subject to the crazy impulses of the species.'

Michèle still said nothing; she was not vexed, but her whole being was concentrated on the discomfort built up, over what would soon be a period of hours, by movements one is hardly certain of having made, disconnected words, and all the rare or microacoustical sounds in the house and outside; she was perhaps discovering—who knows?—that we have in our ears a kind of amplifier which needs to be constantly regulated and which we must not turn up beyond a certain point, or we shall never understand anything again.

'What time is it?' Michèle asked, yawning.

'After all I've been saying to you, you still keep it up?' said Adam.

'Yes, what time is it?'

'The time when, *bright in the darkness, wandering around the earth, a light from elsewhere . . .*'

'No, listen, seriously, Adam—I bet it's past five o'clock.' Adam looked at his watch:

'You've lost your bet,' he said, 'it's ten to five.'

Michèle sat up, got off the billiard table and walked across the darkened room. She looked through the chinks in the shutters.

'It's still sunny outside,' she announced—and added, as though suddenly suspecting the fact that the back of her shirt was drenched with sweat:

'It's really hot today.'

'We're right in the summer,' said Adam.

She buttoned up her blouse (in actual fact it was a man's shirt altered to fit), never for a moment taking her eyes off the slit in the shutter and the little bit of landscape to be seen through it; she was black all over, except for a white streak that cut across her face at eyebrow level. It was as though someone had taken control of their bodies, depositing them in a furrow and only letting them see parts of things. She, whose view was restricted by the size of the slit in the shutter, measuring about ¾ inch by 12 inches; he, still lying on the table, only half-aware that she was looking out.

'I'm thirsty,' said Michèle, 'you haven't got a bottle of beer left?'

48

'No, but there's a tap in the garden, on the other side of the house . . . The only one the Water Board hasn't cut off . . .'

'Why do you never have anything to drink in the place? It seems to me you could easily buy a bottle of grenadine or something, now and again.'

'I can't afford it, little girl,' replied Adam. He had still not moved. 'I expect you'd like us to go into town for a drink?' Michèle swung round on her heel. She peered into the depths of the room and the shadows were mirrored in her eyes, as black dots against a background of dazzle.

'No, let's go down to the beach,' she said decidedly.

They agreed to go for a walk on the rocks, along the headland. There was a kind of smugglers' path starting from the beach, and they followed this, side by side, in almost total silence. They passed groups of anglers going home as though from work, with their rods over their shoulders. They went soberly along the path, which followed the line of the shore at a convenient height, not too near the water or too far up the hill. Clumps of aloes had been planted at regular intervals, to rest the eyes and the mind. In the same way, the surface of the sea was decorated with an almost geometrical design of sharp crests, imitating waves. The whole thing looked as carefully done as a piece of cloth in hounds-tooth check or a huge allotment laid out to suit the tastes of beetles or snails.

There were at least a dozen houses on this stretch of the hill; one could see faint traces of their drain-pipes, winding along just below the ground, like roots. A few yards further on the path ran below a concrete pill-box; a steep flight of steps went down a shaft and came up again bringing with it a hot smell of excrement. Adam and Michèle skirted round the building without realizing it was a pill-box. He simply thought it was one of those modern-styled villas, and wondered how the owners could bear to live in the vicinity of such a stench.

When they reached the tip of the headland the sun had quite disappeared. All signs of the track petered out here; they had to leap from rock to rock, almost at sea-level, with only half of the sky overhead, the other half being cut off by the overhang of the hillside. Jumping from a bit too high up, Michèle twisted her ankle, and they both sat down on a flat rock, to rest. They smoked—he had two cigarettes, she one.

About a hundred yards from the shore a big fish was swimming along, its black, cylindrical body half out of the water. Adam said it was a shark, but they couldn't be certain because, in the gathering dusk, they could not make out if it had fins or not.

For half an hour the big fish swam round and round in the bay, widening its circle each time. The spiral it traced was by no means perfect; it was more in the nature of a lunatic figure, the practical illustration of a species of delirium in which the dark creature was losing its way, endlessly and blindly running its nose against superimposed layers of hot and cold currents. Hunger, death or old age was perhaps gnawing its belly, and it was prowling aimlessly, almost a ship in its desires, almost a sandbank in its imperfection, its almost invisible negative eternity.

As Michèle and Adam stood up it appeared for the last time, its menacing torpedo shape gliding between the waves; then it moved out to sea and was obliterated. Michèle said very softly, pressing close to Adam:

'I'm cold . . . I'm cold, I'm very cold . . .'

Adam did not shrink from the touch of the girl's body; indeed, he even took her hand—a soft, slender, warm hand —and repeated, as they walked on:

'You're cold? You're cold?'

To which Michèle replied:
'Yes.'

After that came the holes in the rocks; there were all sizes of them, large and small; they chose an average-sized one, a one-person hole, and sprawled in it at full length. Especially Adam: not a day went by without his achieving the miracle that consisted of whipping up his mythological sense to a frenzy, surrounding himself with stones and rubble; he would have liked to have all the rubbish and refuse in the world and bury himself under it. He surrounded himself on all sides with matter, ashes, pebbles, and gradually turned into a statue. Not like one of those Carrara marbles or mediaeval Christs which always sparkle to some extent with an imitation of life and pain; but like those pieces of cast-iron, a thousand years old or twelve, which are not dug up but are occasionally identified by the dull sound the spade gives back when it encounters them between two crumbling lumps of earth. Like a seed—just like the seed of a tree—he lay concealed in the cracks in the ground and waited in beatitude for the water that would germinate him.

He moved his hand a little towards the right, gently, already knowing what he would touch. In a second's infinite pleasure he felt his knowledge vacillating, a tremendous doubt overwhelming his mind; while a certain logical, memorable experience tried to make him recognize the feel of Michèle's skin (the bare arm lying beside him), his fingers groped blindly to left and right and met only the soil, granulous to the touch, hard and crumbling.

Adam seemed to be alone in this ability to die whenever he wanted, a private, hidden death; the only living creature in the world who was passing insensibly away, his flesh not decaying and putrefying, but freezing into a mineral.

Hard as a diamond, angular, brittle, at the heart of the

crystal, held in position by a geometrical pattern, confined within his resolute purity, with none of the weaknesses characteristic of the shoals of codfish which, in their collective refrigeration, never lose the little drop of moisture that glitters at the junction of their fins, or the glazed eye, two evidences of a painful death.

Michèle got up, dusted her clothes with her hands, and said plaintively:

'Adam—Adam, shall we go?'

She continued:

'Adam, you frighten me when you're like that—not moving, not breathing, you might be a corpse . . .'

'Idiot!' Adam retorted, 'you've disturbed my meditations! That's finished it, I should have to begin all over again.'

'Begin what?'

'Nothing, nothing . . . I can't explain. I'd already got to the vegetable stage . . . To mosses and lichens. I was just coming to the bacteria and the fossils. I can't explain.'

It was over. He knew now that the danger had been averted for the rest of the day. He got to his feet, seized Michèle by the shoulders and the waist, threw her to the ground and undressed her. Then he took her, with his mind far away, concentrated, for instance, on the leaden-hued body of the shark which must be describing wider and wider circles in the world as it sought for the Straits of Gibraltar.

Later on, with a shout of HAOH, he ran off by himself over the rocks and along the path that led back to the beach, through bushes and thorns from one slab of rock to the next, peering into dark hollows, divining the host of obstacles that might have tripped him up, barked his shins or snapped him in two with a sharp crack down there on some flat stone, leaving him still quivering, to be devoured by those disgusting parasites. The night had achieved a sort

52

of black perfection; each object was a fresh disturbance on the map of the district. The earth's surface was striped black and white like a zebra's hide; the concentric circles of the mountains were like fingerprints laid one beside another, sometimes one above another, with no pause for rest. The tips of the cacti had piled arms in anticipation of a mysterious battle.

The liquid mass on the left had ceased its headlong rush and become a sea of ice; all slumber and all steel, it had turned into a metallic carapace.

Adam was now running through a vista of iron, by no means dead, but living in depth, an enigmatic life of enclosed animation which no doubt found expression in currents or bubbles a hundred yards underground; the polished crust of the world was like a knight asleep in his armour, motionless but possessed of potential life so that the icy gleam indicates blood, resolution, arteries or brain. A smokeless fire, an electric fire, was smouldering under the black soil. And the earth's surface was drawing off the whole strength of that fire, to such an extent that the rocks, waters, trees and air seemed to burn still more fiercely, *to be* the flames of petrified nature. The path, widening already, brought Adam to the bottom of a shaft beside the pill-box, steeped him in foul odours and sent him hurtling up the flight of steps. This was the culminating point of the road. The only place along the coast where the view was multiplied thousands of times over the three expanses of sea, land and sky. At the apex of this ascent Adam suddenly realized that running had become unnecessary and he stopped, petrified.

Coming from the vista that lay before him, the chilly wind covered him from head to foot, transformed his paralysis into pain. He stood there, prominent as a lighthouse, contemplating his own intelligence in the universe, certain now that he would be occupying its centre to all eternity, without intermission; nothing could break this embrace, drag him out of the circle, not even death which, on a certain day in a certain year, would photograph his human form between two thin planks, at the centre of his geological Age.

He took a few steps forward, against the breeze.

He was almost hobbling as he walked, as though facing up to a tremendous blaze; coming to a rock below the level of the path, he sat down, with an indifferent glance towards the horizon. His body was completely insignificant, as puny as a nerve against the blood-red background of a kind of dream.

A sailing boat, half hidden from the other side of the sea, was crawling imperceptibly forward. After a quarter of an hour Adam began to feel cold; he shivered and looked in the direction of the pill-box, wishing more and more that Michèle would come along at last, out of breath from running after him and discomfited by having lost the race.

F. The sun went on blazing in the naked sky, and the countryside shrank back into itself, little by little, under the heat; the soil cracked in places, the grass turned a dirty yellow, sand heaped up in holes in the walls, and the trees were weighed down by dust. It seemed as though the summer would never end. Now the fields and terraced hillsides were occupied by cruel hordes of grasshoppers and wasps. The rutted lanes ran through the tumult of their wings, cut like razor-blades through these excrescences of the air, these hot bubbles full of spicy scents, which jostled one another at stubble height. The atmosphere made unremitting efforts.

Men cycled across the fields, emerged on to the main road and mingled with the flood of cars.

In the distance, all round the great amphitheatre of mountains, the houses flashed back the sunlight from their windows, and it was not difficult to assimilate them mentally to the stretches of cultivated land along the roadside. One could defy perspective and make a deliberate mistake about them, likening them to the splinters of mica that lay among the clods of earth. The boiling countryside looked pretty much like a black blanket thrown over red-hot coals; the holes sparkled violently, the material was blown into folds by subterranean gusts, and here and there columns of smoke rose as though from hidden cigarettes.

A sort of cast-iron grating encircled the park. On the south side it bordered the main road, parallel to the sea, and there was a big gate half-way along; on either side of the gate stood a kind of wooden sentry-box, keeping the sun off a pair of women in their fifties who sat knitting or reading thrillers. In front of each of the women, on a board that stuck out from the window of the sentry-box, lay a roll of pink tickets traversed at regular intervals by rows of perforations so that they could be easily torn off. A man in a blue uniform and cap lounged beside a stand of geraniums, taking the tickets bought at the sentry-box and tearing them with the tips of his fingers; little pink crumbs were clinging to the rough cloth of his jacket, at about stomach-level. The man did not so much as cast a bored glance behind him at the area under his charge, where he would have seen a crowd of people walking away, their faces inquisitive yet apathetic, and vanishing behind the barred cages. He didn't speak to the women in the sentry-boxes either, and he barely replied to questions from the visitors; when he did, he spoke absent-mindedly, not looking at the questioners' faces but staring at the roof of a restaurant on the beach—Le Bodo—all decked with flags and streamers. Occasionally, of course, he couldn't avoid saying 'thank you', 'yes', 'go ahead', or something of the kind. And there were a few people who knew nothing, hadn't a clue; as he took their tickets, tore them gently with a double twist of the wrists and dropped the useless scraps into a basket on his left, he would bring out a whole sentence:

'Yes, Madame, I know. But we close at half-past five, Madame.'

'You have plenty of time. At half-past five, yes, Madame.'

56

Adam set out at random past the cages, listening with half an ear to the talk going on around him, and sniffing a bit at the variety of smells emanating from dung and wild beasts; the yellowish smell, laden with urine, had the special faculty of bringing things—particularly animals—into sensuous relief. He stopped in front of a lioness's cage; for a long time he stared through the bars at the supple body, full of vague muscles, reflecting that the lioness might have been a woman, an elastic woman moulded of rubber, and this acrid smell might have come from a mouth accustomed to Virginia tobacco, mixed with a suspicion of lipstick, a smell of peppermint tablets from the teeth, and all the faint, indefinable shadows, downy growths and chapped skin that leave a halo round the lips.

He leant on the railing that kept people away from the cage, and surrendered to an invading torpor dominated by a longing to touch the beast's fur, to thrust his hand into the thick, silky pelt, to fasten his claws like iron nails at the back of the creature's neck and overlay the long, sun-hot body with his own body, now sheathed in a leonine hide and covered with a mane, extraordinarily powerful, extraordinarily typical of the species.

An old woman went past the cage, leading a child, a little girl, by the hand; she went past, and as she walked on, against the light, her shadow blinking across each bar in turn, the lioness raised her head. Two flashes passed in opposite directions; at some point above the sand the black shaft, heavy with human experience, encountered the strange, greenish steely flare from the lioness and it seemed for an instant that the old woman's white, almost naked body was mated with the beast's tawny coat; both of them reeled, then sketched an advancing and receding movement of the loins, as though in this barbarous understanding they were performing an erotic dance-step. But a split second

57

later they drew apart and their gestures were separate again, leaving beside the cage only an immaculate white patch like a pool in the sunshine, a kind of peculiar corpse, a phantom where the wind stirred twigs and leaves. Adam, in his turn, looked at the woman and the child and felt himself gripped by an unfamiliar nostalgia, a quaint need to eat; unlike most of the people who went by he had no wish to speak to the lioness, to tell her she was beautiful, that she was big or that she was like a great cat.

He spent the rest of his afternoon walking all over the zoo, mingling with the tiniest races that lived in its cages, at one with the lizards, mice, beetles or pelicans. He had discovered that the best way to mix with a species is to make oneself desire a female member of it. So he concentrated, round-eyed, stooping, elbows propped on all the railings. His searching gaze penetrated the smallest concavities, the folds of skin or plumage, the scales, the fluffy hairs that sheltered the visibly ignoble slumbers of balls of black hair, masses of flabby cartilage, dusty membranes, red annulations, skin that was cracked and split like a square of earth. He stripped the gardens of their grass, dived head-first into mud, devoured humus voraciously, crawled along burrows at a depth of twelve yards, pawed a new, kindred body born from the putrified corpse of a field-mouse. With his mouth drawn down between his shoulders he pushed forward his eyes, his two big, round eyes, gently, with a thousand precautions, waiting for a kind of electric shock that would contract his skin, activate the ganglions that propelled him, and throw the rings of his body against one another like copper bracelets, with a faint tinkle, when once he had become subterranean, coiled, gelatinous—yes, the one and only real, tenebrous earthworm.

At the panthers' cage, this is what he did: he leant

forward slightly, over the railing, and suddenly waved his hand at the bars. The animal—a dark-furred female—flung herself towards him with a roar; and while the terrified bystanders fell back a step and the beast, mad with fury, tore the ground with her claws, Adam, paralysed with fear, trembling in every limb, heard the voice of the keeper, which set up a delicious vibration somewhere in the back of his head.

'That's a clever thing to do, that is! That's clever! That's a clever thing to do! Clever! Clever, eh?'

Thus divided again from the panther, Adam retreated a little way and muttered, without looking at the keeper:

'I didn't know . . . I'm sorry . . .'

'You didn't know what?' said the man in uniform, trying at the same time to quieten the animal with words such as 'Ho there! Ho there! Ho! Ho! Rama! Rama! Quiet! Quiet! Rama!' 'You didn't know what? You didn't know that there's no sense in teasing wild animals? It's clever, yes, clever, to play tricks like that!'

Adam did not try to make excuses; he muttered again, in embarrassment:

'No . . . I didn't know . . . I wanted . . .'

'Yes, I know,' the man interrupted, 'It's amusing to play tricks on the animals when they're shut up in cages! It's fun; but it wouldn't be such fun if the cage happened to come open, would it, eh? That wouldn't be such fun. And it would be fun if you were the one who was inside, don't you think?'

He turned away in disgust and appealed to a woman bystander:

'Some people just don't seem to have a clue. That there beast hasn't eaten for three days and as if that wasn't enough, there are people who think it's a joke to come and jeer at the creatures in their cages. Yes, I sometimes

59

wish the cage would open a crack and let one of those devilish brutes out. Then you'd see 'em running—oh yes, they'd understand fast enough then, they'd know fast enough.'

Adam moved away without waiting for the end of the sentence. He did not shrug his shoulders, but walked slowly, dragging his feet. He went past the mammals' cages; the last of these, the smallest and lowest, held three gaunt wolves. A kind of wooden kennel had been set up in the middle of the cage, and the wolves were circling round and round this, tirelessly, incessantly, their slanting eyes stubbornly fixed on the bars that rushed past at top speed, level with one's knees.

They circled in opposite directions, two one way and one the other; after a certain number of turns, let's say ten or eleven, for some sudden, queer, unaccountable reason, as though at the snap of someone's fingers, they wheeled about and went on again in the other direction. They were mangy beasts, grey with dust, mauve round the jaws; but they never stopped circling their den and the steely glint of their eyes was reflected all over their bodies—they looked as though they were covered with metal plates, violent, full to vomiting with hatred and ferocity. The circular movement they were making inside the cage became, owing to its regularity, the one really mobile point in the surrounding space. All the rest of the park, with its human beings and its other cages, sank into a kind of motionless ecstasy. One was suddenly frozen, fixed in an unbearable rigidity that spread all round as far as that bell-shaped structure of iron and wood, the wolves' cage; one was like a luminous circle seen through a microscope and containing, stained in bright colours, the basic elements of life, such as chromosomes, globules, trypanozomes, hexagonal molecules, microbes and fragments of bacteria. A structural geometry

60

of the microcosmic universe, photographed through dozens of lenses; you know, that white disc, dazzling as a moon, coloured by chemical products, which is true life, without movement, without duration, so far away in the second infinity that nothing is animal any longer, nothing is apparent; nothing remains but silence, fixity, eternity; for all is slow, slow, slow.

They, the wolves, were in the middle of this desiccated landscape, its only sign of movement; movement that, seen from above, perhaps from an aircraft, would have resembled some strange palpitation or the ant-like stirring that sets up on the surface of the sea, diametrically below the plane. The sea is round, whitish, crested, and hardened like a block of stone, it lies 6,000 feet below; yet if you look carefully there is something independent of the climbing sun, a sort of little knot in the substance, a flaw that glints, advances, has a scrabbling centre. That's it; for if I suddenly turn away from the electric light I see it, that tiny star that looks like a white spider; it struggles, swims, makes no progress, it lives on the black landscape of the world, and it falls, to all eternity, past millions of windows, millions of engravings, millions of chasings, milliards of flutings, lonely as a star, never to die of its perpetual suicides because it is long since dead in itself and buried at the back of a sombre bronze.

When Adam left the wolves' cage he went to another enclosure; an artificial glade in the middle of the park, with several ornamental basins to left and right where a few big pelicans, their wings clipped, could come to drink. The pink flamingoes, the ducks and penguins, were the same kind of life too; the discovery that Adam had made little by little, since a certain day that summer on the beach, then in two or three cafés, then in an empty house, a train, a motor coach, a newspaper, he was now making again, a

61

little more completely each time, as he watched the lions, the wolves and the puffins.

It was so simple that it stared you in the face and made you crazy, or at any rate most unusual. That was it, he'd got it, he grasped it and let it escape at the same moment; he felt sure, and yet he no longer even knew what he was doing, what he was going to do, whether he had escaped from a lunatic asylum or deserted from the army. That was what was happening, what was going to happen to him; by dint of *seeing* the world, the world had gone right out of his eyes; things had been so thoroughly seen, smelt, felt, millions of times, with millions of eyes, noses, ears, tongues, skins, that he had become like a faceted mirror. Now, the facets were innumerable, he had been transformed into memory, and the blind spots where the facets met were so few that his consciousness was virtually spherical. This was the point, verging upon total vision, where one sometimes becomes unable to live, ever to live again. Where sometimes, lying on a sickening bed on a hot summer afternoon, one sometimes empties a whole bottle of Parsidol into a glass of cold water and drinks and drinks and drinks, as though there were never to be another fountain on the face of the earth. People had been waiting centuries for that moment, and he, Adam Pollo, had reached it, had suddenly got there and appropriated all things to himself; he was no doubt the last of his race, and this was true, because the race was approaching its end. After that one need only let oneself expire gently, imperceptibly, let oneself be stifled, invaded ravished, no longer by milliards of worlds but by one single, solitary world; he had effected the junction of all times and all spaces, and now, covered with ocelli, huger than a fly's head, he was waiting, solitary at the tip of his slender body, for the strange accident that would flatten him on the ground and encrust him, once more among the *living*, in the bloody pulp of his own flesh, his shattered bones, his open mouth and blind eyes.

Towards the end of the afternoon, just before the zoo's closing-time, Adam went into the snack-bar, found himself a table in the shade, and ordered a bottle of Coca-Cola. To his left was an olive-tree in which someone had thought fit to set up a kind of wooden platform with a chain; and at the end of the chain there was a lively black and white marmoset, evidently put there to amuse the children and cut down the animals' food bill; children were never satisfied until they had bought a banana or a bag of sweets from a toothless old woman who was there for the purpose, and offered them to the monkey.

Adam leant back in his chair, lit a cigarette, took a sip out of the bottle, and waited. He waited without knowing exactly for what, settling down vaguely between two layers of warm air and watching the monkey. A man and woman went slowly past his table, loitering along with their eyes fixed on the small, furry animal.

'Pretty things, marmosets,' said the man.

'Yes, but bad-tempered,' said the woman. 'I remember my grandmother had one for a time; she was always giving it titbits. But do you suppose it was grateful? Not at all, it would bite her ear till it bled, the nasty brute.'

'That may have been a sign of affection,' said the man.

Adam was suddenly seized by a ridiculous impulse to get things straight. He turned to the couple and explained.

'It's neither pretty nor bad-tempered,' he said, 'it's just a marmoset.'

The man burst out laughing, but the woman looked at him as though he were a complete imbecile and she had always known it. Then she shrugged and walked away.

The sun was quite low by this time; the visitors were beginning to leave, emptying the space round the cages and the café tables of a multitude of legs, shouts, laughter and colours. As dusk came on the animals emerged from their artificial lairs and stretched themselves; barking was heard on all sides, with the whistling of parrots and the growling of the carnivores impatient for their food. There were still a few minutes left before closing time; Adam got up, went across to the old woman and bought a banana and some sweets; while he was paying she said crossly:

'Do you want to feed the monkey?'

He shook his head.

'No I don't—why?'

'Because time's up. It's too late now to feed the animals. It's forbidden after five o'clock, otherwise they'd have no appetite left and they'd get ill.'

Adam shook his head again.

'It's not for the monkey, it's for me.'

'Oh well, if it's for yourself it's not the same thing.'

'Yes, it's for me,' said Adam, and began to peel the banana.

'You understand,' the old woman went on, 'After the time-limit it would upset the creatures.'

Adam nodded; he ate the banana, standing in front of the woman but with his eyes fixed, as though abstractedly, on the marmoset. When he had finished he opened the bag of sweets.

'Will you have one?' he asked; he noticed she was staring inquisitively at him.

'Thank you,' she said, taking one.

They shared the rest of the sweets, leaning on the counter and watching the monkey all the time. Then Adam crumpled the empty bag into a ball and put it in an ashtray. The sun was level with the tree-tops by this time. After that Adam put a great many questions to the old woman, asking how long she had been working in the snack-bar, whether she was married, how old she was, how many children she had, whether she enjoyed life, whether she liked going to the cinema. Leaning closer and closer, he gazed at her with growing affection, just as, a few hours earlier, he had gazed at the lioness, the crocodiles and the duck-billed platypus.

In the long run, however, she grew suspicious. While Adam continued to ply her with questions and badgered her for her Christian name, she seized a damp cloth and began rubbing the zinc top of the counter, with vigorous movements that made the fat of her arms quiver. When Adam tried to take her hand as it went by, she blushed and threatened to call the police. A bell rang somewhere on the far side of the park, to announce closing-time. At this, Adam decided to leave; he said goodbye politely to the old woman; but she, standing with her back to the light, made no reply. He added that he would certainly come to see her again one of these days, before winter.

Then he left the café and made for the gate at the other end of the zoo. Men in blue uniforms were swilling buckets of water over the floors of the cages. A kind of purple shadow filled the hollows of the landscape and savage cries rose to the surface in waves, witnessing to the presence on all sides of stifling heat that smelt of viscera. The sentry-boxes on either side of the entrance were closed. But as far as the road, almost as far as the sea, despite the general withdrawal of men and beasts, there hovered here and there a vague odour of she-monkey, gently insinuating itself into you till you began to doubt your own species.

G. After that I know he went to wait for the dog, every day at the same time, on that kind of breakwater to the right of the beach. He didn't go and sit on the pebbles, among the bathers, although he could have waited more comfortably there; partly because it was hot and partly because he liked to feel he could move more freely in a more open space, where the wind would all the same bring a gust of fresh air from time to time, he used to sit on the edge of the breakwater, with his feet dangling over the side. The entire beach lay before his eyes, the stones, the little heaps of greasy paper, and of course the bathers, always the same people, always in the same places. He used to spend quite a time watching like this: his shoulders propped against a block of concrete brought there by the Germans in 1942, his body sprawling full length in the sun, one hand in his trousers pocket, ready to fish out of the packet one of the two cigarettes he allowed himself per hour. With the other hand he would be scratching his chin, fumbling in his hair, or raking through the stones on the breakwater to find dust and different kinds of sand. He kept an eye on the whole beach, the people coming and going, the imperceptible rolling of the pebbles. But above all he watched for the black dog to emerge from the unknown mass of bathers and trot towards the road, sniff the clumps of grass, and leap and

66

run and throw itself headlong into the little adventure on the pavements.

Then, as though lassoed out of his torpor, he would set off once more to follow the animal, with no suspicion of where he was being led, without hope; yes, with the strange sort of pleasure that makes one continue a movement automatically or imitate everything that moves because, being a sign of life, it justifies all possible suppositions. One always likes to carry on a movement, even when it is trotting briskly on its four paws with their damp, brushing sound, propelling along the tarmac a light fleece of black hairs, two pricked-up ears and a pair of glassy eyes and is called, called once and for all, a dog.

At ten minutes to two, the dog left the beach; he had splashed about in the water for a bit before he set off, and the hair on his chest was still matted into little fluffy locks. He scrambled up the embanked pebbles, panting with the effort, went past Adam at a distance of a few yards and stopped at the roadside. The sun made him blink and threw a white patch on his cold muzzle.

He paused, as though waiting for someone; this gave Adam time to jump off the breakwater and get ready to leave. For a moment Adam was tempted to whistle or snap his fingers or just to call to him as most people do with most dogs— something like 'Come on, dog!' or 'Hi, Fido!' But the words were cut short in his head before he had even begun to utter them.

Adam merely stopped and looked at the animal from behind; seen from this angle he was curiously fore-shortened, standing foursquare on his pawns with arched back and the hair thinning out along his spine; and his neck looked bulgy, thickset and muscular, the kind of neck dogs never have.

He looked at the top of the dog's head, with the furrow

down the middle of the skull and the ears cocked. A train made a noise as it entered a tunnel—a long way off, of course, far up in the mountains. The dog's right ear moved forward a fraction of an inch to catch the rattle of the engine; then twitched smartly back, as a child down on the shore began to yell and went on and on at the full pitch of its lungs—smitten by some grief, a burst ball or a sharp stone.

Adam waited, motionless, for the starting signal; but the dog took him by surprise—darted forward, ran round a car, and went on up the road. He trotted rapidly, keeping close to the bank, rarely glancing to right or left. He stopped twice before reaching the crossing where the main road runs through the village: once beside the back wheel of a parked Oldsmobile; although there was nothing special about that car, he didn't look at it, or sniff it, or lift his leg quietly against the metal hub-cap. The second time was when that elderly woman was coming down to the beach with a boxer bitch on a lead; she glanced in his direction, gave a slight tug at her dog's leash, and then looked at Adam. She felt entitled to remark, as she went by:

'You should keep your dog on the lead, young man.'

Adam and the dog both followed the bitch with their eyes—their bodies turned the way they were walking, but their heads twisted back over their shoulders. They went on like this for a few seconds' silence, with little yellow flecks at the back of their eyes. Then the dog barked and Adam growled wordlessly, deep down in his throat: rrrrrrrrrrrrrrrrroa, rrrrrrrrrrrrrroaa, oaarrrrrrrr, rrrrrrrro.

At the fork in the road Adam hoped the dog would turn right, because a bit further along was the hill where he lived, the path you've heard about and the big house—still empty—that he occupied. But as usual the dog unhesitatingly turned left, making for the town. And as usual Adam followed him, merely regretting, in a particular corner of his memory, that such an imperative reason should draw the quadruped towards the crowds and the houses.

After the road along the sea-front there came a sort of avenue, with plane-trees set at regular intervals along the pavements, casting dense black shadows. The dog made a point of walking through these shady patches, and at such moments, because of his curly coat, he disappeared among the black ringlets and discs of the leaf-shadows.

Once this business of shade and sunshine began, hesitation became more frequent; the dog would veer abruptly from left to right and then back from right to left; he was weaving his way among the pedestrians, whose numbers were increasing all the time because by now they were well into the town: open shops, hot or cool smells coming in waves, colours everywhere, faded canvas umbrellas—all this clamped between walls, together with posters, shreds of posters bearing snatches of print that announced events over and done with three months ago:

> 'Squa   ıd   ATCH
> Bar de Band and James W. Brown
> Fem in
> MARTI
>   ritive'

The dog had slowed down considerably, partly because the crowd was growing thicker and thicker and partly, no doubt, because he must be approaching his goal. So Adam was able to relax and smoke a cigarette. He even took advantage of a moment the dog spent in sniffing at an old patch of urine, to buy a chocolate-filled roll from the stall outside a confectioner's shop; he had eaten nothing since morning, and felt weak. He nibbled at the warm roll while he followed the dog along the main street. Coming to a red light, the animal stopped, and Adam came and stood beside him; he was still holding a small piece of roll in the grease-spotted paper from the shop, and he thought of giving part of it to the dog. But he reflected that if he did that the animal might take a liking to him, which would be risky; afterwards it would be the dog that would follow him, and he didn't know where to go, he didn't want the responsibility of leadership. And besides he was hungry and would rather not give away what little food he had left. So he finished the chocolate roll and looked down at the dark, hairy body panting beside his feet, sniffing, with back legs tense, and waiting obediently for the traffic policeman to wave people across the road.

The town was curiously empty of dogs; except for the boxer bitch they had passed just now on the way up from the beach, led on a leash by the old woman, they had only met people. Yet the streets bore the stigmata of a secret animal life; such as smells, patches of dried urine, excrement, tufts of hair left on the kerb where a sudden, compelling coitus had taken place in the full flood of the sunshine, among the hurrying feet and growling buses.

The signs of canine life thus to be found—by looking carefully, as one went along, at the pattern of the pavement —made a cryptic record of comings and goings through the labyrinth of the town. They all helped to build up a concept of space and time with nothing human about it, and to bring hundreds of dogs home to their usual lairs every evening, safe and sound and sure of being themselves.

He, Adam, was well and truly lost; not being a dog (or not yet, perhaps) he could not steer himself by all these notes inscribed on the ground, these smells, these microscopic details that rose up from the resonant tarmac and automatically enveloped the rachidian bulb via the muzzle, the eyes, the ears or even the mere contact of padding

70

paws or scratching toe nails. And being in any case no
longer human—never again—he passed, unseeing, right
through the town, and nothing meant anything to him any
more.

He did not see 'Studio 13', 'Gordon's Furniture',
'Frigidaire', 'High Class Grocers', 'Standard Oil', 'Café La
Tour', 'Williams Hotel', 'Postcards and Souvenirs',
'Ambre Solaire', 'Galeries Muterse', 'Bar and Tobacconist',
'Place Your Bets', 'National Lottery'.

Who had drawn lines on the pavement? Who had carefully laid sheets of glass over the showcases? Who—yes,
who—had written 'Pyjamas and Matching Striped Sheets'?
or 'Today's Menu'? Who had said one day 'Wireless Sets
and Spare Parts', 'Come In and Look Round', 'Great Sale
of Bikinis', 'Autumn Fashions', 'Wholesale and Retail
Wine-merchants', etc., etc.?

Yet there it all was, put there so that in the summer people
like Adam could find their way about, be reminded that
they were greedy or that they longed to sleep naked in
striped pyjamas with matching striped sheets and striped
pillows, perhaps with striped wallpaper on the bedroom
walls, and striped moths bumping into striped lampshades
during the striped nights streaked with neon lighting and
days striped with railway-lines and cars. So when people
saw Adam, round-shouldered, his hands thrust into the
pockets of his grubby-kneed trousers, following just ONE
dog, not even on a leash, a dog covered with blackish wool,
the least they murmured under their breath was 'there are
some weird types along this coast', even if they didn't go
as far as 'some people would be just as well in a loony-bin'.

A dog is certainly much easier to follow than most
people suppose. In the first place it depends on the angle of
vision, the level of one's eyes; one has to search among the
swarms of legs to find the black patch living, palpitating,

71

running below knee-height. Adam managed this without much difficulty, for two reasons: the first was that his slight stoop gave him a natural tendency to look down at the ground, and thus at the quadrupeds that live there; the other reason was that for a long time he had been training himself to follow something. They say that from the age of twelve or fifteen, when he came out of school, he would spend half an hour at a time following people—often teenage girls—through the crowded streets. He didn't do it with any purpose, but because he enjoyed being led to a lot of different places without bothering about street-names or any serious considerations. It was at this period that it had been revealed to him that the majority of people, with their stiff bearing and self-willed expressions, spend their time doing nothing. At the age of fifteen he was already aware that people are vague and unscrupulous and that, apart from the three or four genetic functions they carry out every day, they go about the town with no inkling of the millions of cabins they could have had built for themselves out in the country, to be ill, or pensive, or nonchalant in.

There was, after all, another dog, just across the street, accompanying a man and woman who were both about forty; this was a very beautiful bitch, slender and silky-haired, poised confidently on long legs; and Adam and the other immediately wanted a closer look at her. She had gone with her owners into a department store, packed with people, which was engorging and disgorging every second through its glass doors a flood of visitors, mostly women, laden with parcels and paper bags. The dog kept its nose to the ground, following some kind of trail, and Adam followed the dog. They entered the shop almost together. As they went through the door a neon sign flashed above their heads, reflecting downwards between people's feet, on the dog's woolly back and on bits of the linoleum-covered floor, in reversed letters, 'Prisunic', 'Prisunic', 'Prisunic'.

At once they were surrounded by people, women or children, or by walls, ceilings and displays of goods. Over-head was a kind of yellow slab from which there hung at intervals, between two strips of lighting, cards bearing inscriptions such as 'Bargain prices', 'Hardware', 'Wines', or 'Household Goods'. People's heads were right up among these cardboard rectangles and sometimes knocked into one, making it twirl round on its string for a long time. The counters were set at right-angles, with gaps for the cus-tomers to pass through. The whole place shone with a multitude of bright colours, jostling you to left and right, calling 'Buy! Buy!', displaying goods for sale, smiles, the click of women's heels on the plastic floor, and then putting records on the record-player at the back of the shop, between the bar and the photomaton booth. The whole thing was covered by the generalized strains of piano and violin music, except now and again when the low, placid voice of a woman, speaking with her mouth close against the microphone, was heard to say: 'Beware of pickpockets, ladies and gentlemen.'

'Section 3 Supervisor is wanted in the Manager's Office . . . Section 3 Supervisor is wanted in the Manager's Office. . . .'

'Hello! Hello! We recommend our snag-proof seamless nylon stockings, all sizes, three different shades—pearl, flesh or bronze—now on sale in the lingerie department on the ground floor. . . .'

The dog found the bitch again in the basement, at the electrical goods counter. He had been obliged to search the entire ground floor, slipping past hundreds of human legs, before he saw her. When he caught sight of her she was beginning to go down the stairs that led to the basement;

Adam hoped for a moment that the dog would not venture to follow her to the bottom. Not that he himself was not eager to get closer to the female—on the contrary; but he would willingly have foregone that pleasure so as to escape from this horrible shop; he was dazed by the noise and the lights and felt somehow caught up in the human swarm; it was rather as though he were moving in reverse, and a hesitant nausea lingered in his throat; he sensed that the canine species was eluding him in this stuffy place, all formica and electricity; he couldn't resist reading the price-tags all round him; a sort of commercial instinct was trying to put things to rights in his consciousness. He did some half-hearted mental arithmetic. An ancestral attachment to all this material that man had taken a million years to conquer was stealthily awakening, defeating his will-power, flooding right through him, translated into diminutive shufflings, tiny movements of the eyelids and the zygomatic muscles, shivers passing down the spine, dilations and contractions of the pupils as they adjusted themselves; the dog's black spine was bobbing up and down, ahead of him, and he was almost beginning to *see* it again, to weigh it in the depths of his brain in a native tremolo of unborn judgments.

The dog did indeed pause at the top of the stairs, intimidated by this dimly-lighted pit that kept swallowing up the crowd. But a little girl tried to pull his tail as she went by and babbled 'D-doggy, . . . want doggy . . .' and he had to go down. Adam followed him.

Down below there were fewer people. This was where records, stationery, hammers and nails, espadrilles, etc., were on sale. It was very hot. The man, the woman and the bitch were standing at the electrical goods counter, inspecting lamps and lengths of flex. The bitch had sat down under a lamp-shade with her tongue hanging out. When she saw

74

Adam and the dog she got up; her leash was trailing on the ground. Her owners were apparently too busy shopping to notice anything at all. Adam sensed that something funny was going to happen; so he stayed where he was, at the record counter. He pretended to be looking at the shiny cardboard sleeves; but he turned his head slightly to the left and watched the animals.

And all of a sudden it happened. There was a kind of flurry in the crowd, with the sound of a guitar and the click of stiletto heels. The little blue light in the photomaton machine went on and off, a livid hand drew the curtains and he saw himself reflected, snow-white, in the metal structure. At his feet now, right against his feet, the black dog's woolly body was covering the bitch's yellow coat; minutes went by, while men and women still walked past and round them, pounding the linoleum with metal-tipped shoes. The bitch was now the colour of old gold, and beneath her sprawling, outstretched paws the floor undulated gently, flecked with highlights, with hundreds of overlaid, spectral shadows; in this vault of the shop, sunk below ground-level, people were talking louder, laughing more boisterously, buying and selling hand over fist. There was a constant clicking of photographs, and every time the magnesium flashed it shattered something in the middle of a white circle where the dogs seemed to be wrestling, openmouthed, their eyes wide in a kind of avid terror. Adam's forehead was damp with sweat; full of hatred and jubilation he stood motionless, whirling his brain round at high speed; a siren was shrieking in the middle of his skull; no one else could hear it, but it cried: 'Warning, warning!' as though war would break out at any moment.

Then the pace slackened, the bitch began to moan, almost in pain. A child came into the trampled space, pointed at the animals and laughed. Everything had rushed past. As

75

though a film had been speeded up for a few minutes there were still a few spasms of frenzy; but Adam had already turned his eyes away from the pile of dogs and was breathing again, as he pressed his fingerprints on the record-sleeves. The sound of the guitars died away and the cool lips that had spoken not long ago came again to the rim of the microphone and announced:

'The last models from our summer collection are being offered at reduced prices on the lingerie counter . . . Fancy petticoats, cardigans, English blouses, swim-suits and light jerseys, ladies . . .'

Then Adam turned round and, with an almost straight back, began to climb the stairs to the ground-floor, preceded by the black, wool-clad hero; behind them, in the midst of the shaded labyrinth, close beside the electrical goods counter, in the bitch's orange-coloured belly, they left a nothing, an emptiness—it was funny—which in a few months' time would be filled with half-a-dozen little mongrel puppies.

They went on together up the high-street. It was getting late; the sun was already going down. That meant that yet another day was over, one more to be added to thousands of others. They walked at a leisurely pace on the sunny side of the road.

There were more cars than pedestrians, and at a pinch one could feel almost alone on the pavement.

They passed two or three cafés, because it was one of those southern towns with at least one café to every building. Not one single man suspected that the dog wasn't with Adam, that it was Adam who was with the dog. Adam sauntered along, glancing now and again at the people who went by. Most of the men and all the women wore dark glasses. They didn't know him, or the dog either. And it was quite a time since they'd last seen this tall, ungainly fellow slouching along the street, hands in the pockets of his dirty old linen trousers. He must have been living for quite a while all alone in the deserted house at the top of the hill. Adam looked at their dark glasses and reflected that instead of going to live all by himself in a corner he might have done something else; such as buying a parrot that he could have carried on his shoulder wherever he went; so that if anyone stopped him he could have left the parrot to speak for him:

'Morning, how are you?'

'Morning, how are you?'

and people would have realized he had nothing to say to them. Or he might have got himself up like a blind man, with a white walking-stick and thick, opaque spectacles; then other people would have been shy of coming near him, except occasionally, to help him across the street; and he would have let them do it, without saying thank you or anything, so that in the long run they'd have left him in peace. Another thing would have been to apply for a little kiosk where he could have sat all day selling tickets for the National Lottery. People would have bought as many tickets as they wanted, and he would have prevented anyone from talking to him by calling out at regular intervals, in a falsetto voice:

'Tonight's last winning tickets,

Try your luck!'

Anyhow, the dog served the purpose well enough, for the few people who went by in the opposite direction scarcely glanced at him through their smoked glasses and showed not the faintest wish to exchange greetings. That proved that he was no longer quite a full member of their detestable race and that like his friend Dog he could go about the streets and nose round the shops without being seen. Soon, perhaps, he too would be able to urinate placidly against the hubs of American cars or the 'No Parking' signs and make love in the open air, on the dusty footpath, between two plane-trees.

At the far end of the high-street there was a sort of fountain, a greenish bronze affair such as one used to see all over the place in the old days. Set firmly in the pavement, with a handle to pump up the water and an iron-barred drain through which it ran away. The dog was thirsty, and stopped in front of this post-cum-fountain; he waited for a moment, doubtfully, sniffed at the grooved flagstone and then began to lick the grating, where faint traces of moss were clinging and empty cigarette-packets lay about, crumpled into balls. Adam came up silently behind him, hesitated, and then turned the handle. After a few gurgles the water came gushing out, falling on the dog's head and splashing the toes of Adam's shoes. The water flowed on as though the movement of the handle were manufacturing it, and the dog lapped up several mouthfuls with his jaws wide open; when he had finished he moved away from the fountain, shook his head, and trotted off. Adam scarcely had time to swallow two or three gulps of the water that goes on falling even after one stops turning the handle. He wiped his mouth as he walked away, and took a cigarette from his pocket.

Some rough-and-ready signal must have gone off somewhere in the town—a flight of pigeons perhaps, or else the fact that the sun was vanishing behind the five-storey houses; for the dog was now walking straighter and faster. He had adopted a gait that, without being hurried, indicated frank indifference to all that was happening around him; his ears were pricking forward and his paws only touched the ground very briefly, as though he knew he was drawing a straight line that could not possibly be deflected.

He trotted along, right in the middle of the pavement, doing five miles an hour in the opposite direction from the hooting cars and the red and green streaks of the buses. All this, no doubt, in order to reach a house somewhere in the town, where a plump woman, whom he could see only as far up as below the breasts, would set before him, down on the kitchen floor, a plastic plate of finely chopped meat and vegetables. Perhaps a red-and-white bone, bleeding like a scratched elbow.

Behind the dog came Adam, almost at the double, as they crossed a succession of identical streets, past gardens, park gates that were just closing, quiet squares; a succession of big doorways, brown benches where tramps were already asleep with their heads leaning on the back of the seat; men and women were getting into cars; two or three old men were hobbling nonchalantly along, all in black; red workmen were putting oil lamps round the crater-like holes where they had been working all day under the open sky. A man of indeterminate age was going down the road too, on the opposite pavement, carrying on his back a wooden box full of panes of glass; every now and then he turned his head towards the house-fronts with a strange, melancholy cry that sounded like 'Olivier! . . . Olivier! . . .' but which must have been 'On the way! On the way!'

That was what the dog was trotting among; along the streets, past the houses, below the roofs that bristled with television aerials and brick chimneys; through the maze of drain-pipes and glinting windows, right out in the grey street down below, at a jog-trot, his body hard as a sword.

That was how he scampered by without looking at the stretches of house-wall or the shrubs in the little gardens, notwithstanding the thousands of caverns that could have been disclosed by tearing away what was concealing them, the thousands of caverns in the depths of which people were nestling, ready to live among oak tables heavy-laden with flowers and baskets of fruit, velvet curtains, double beds and reproductions of impressionist paintings.

What the dog was doing was walking quickly, going home; it was, crossing a final street in the village which would soon be asleep, trotting the length of a final wall covered with posters, pushing with his muzzle to open one side of a wrought-iron gate, and vanishing from sight close by, somewhere between the house-front and the orange-grove—all his, all theirs, not Adam's.

What the dog had done now was to desert Adam at the entrance to the house, leave him standing with his back against the concrete gate-post with its engraved name and number—Villa Belle, 9—where he could stare through the gate's twenty-six bars, gaze at a shaggy garden as pink and green as in a child's picture-book, and wonder if it had been hot there that day or if it would rain there during the night.

H. There was something new in the empty house on the hill. This was a rat, of a handsome size, not black like most sewer-rats, but on the white side—between grey and white —with pink nose, tail and paws and two piercing blue, lidless eyes which gave him a courageous expression. He must have been there a long time already, but Adam hadn't noticed him before. Adam had gone up to the living-room on the first floor, where he had once lain on the billiard table with Michèle. He had not been back there since, presumably because it hadn't occurred to him; unless it was because he couldn't be bothered to climb the little wooden staircase to the upper floor.

Then he had remembered the billiard table and reflected that he might while away a few hours by playing billiards. That was why he had come back there.

So he opened the window and pushed back one of the shutters, so as to see properly. He hunted everywhere for the billiard balls; he thought the owners had hidden them away in a drawer and he broke open all the furniture with a knife. But there was nothing in the chest of drawers or in the sideboard or in the cupboard or in the little lemon-wood table, except old newspapers and dust.

Adam stacked the newspapers on the floor, intending to read them later on, and went back to the billiard table; he now found, on the right-hand side of the table, a kind of drawer, which was locked, where it seemed the balls must drop after falling into the pockets round the table. With his knife, Adam dug a groove round the lock. It took him a good twenty minutes to force the drawer. Inside, sure enough, he found nine or ten ivory balls, some red and some white.

Adam took the balls and laid them on the table. He still needed a cue to play with. But these the owners must have hidden carefully, perhaps in another room; perhaps they'd even taken them away with them, God knows where.

Adam suddenly felt tired of searching. He looked round him, hoping to find a substitute for the cues. There was really nothing except the legs of a Louis XV armchair; it would have meant taking them off, and besides they were twisted and gilded and Adam didn't want to dirty his hands with gold.

He now remembered that in the little front garden of the house he had seen two or three rose-trees, tied to bamboo props. He went down to the flower-bed, pulled up one of the rose-trees, and wrenched the bamboo shaft out of the ground.

Before going upstairs again he took his knife and cut one of the roses off the tree; it was not very large but it was a nice, round shape, with sweet-scented pale yellow petals. He put it into an empty beer-bottle, on the floor in his room, beside the heap of blankets. Then, without even looking at it, he went back upstairs.

He played billiards by himself for a few minutes; he sent the balls one against another without paying much attention to their colour. Once he managed to send four into the pockets at one stroke. But except for that once, which seemed to be more or less of a fluke, he had to admit he was not much good. Either he missed the balls he was aiming at, or he failed to hit the right spot: the cue struck the ivory surface a little to one side instead of in the middle, and the ball went off in all directions, spinning madly on its own axis. In the end Adam gave up playing billiards; he took the balls, dropped them on the floor and tried to play bowls. He was no better at this, please note, but as the balls fell on the floor they made a certain noise and set up certain movements, so that one could take more interest in the thing, even get some satisfaction out of it.

Anyhow it was while he was amusing himself like this, that he saw the rat. It was fine, muscular rat, standing on its four pink paws at the far end of the room and staring at him insolently. When Adam caught sight of it he lost his temper at once; he tried to hit the rat with a billiard ball, meaning to kill it or at least to hurt it badly; but he missed it. He tried again several times. The rat didn't seem to be frightened. It looked Adam straight in the eye, its pallid head stretched forward, its brow furrowed. When Adam threw his ivory ball the rat sprang to one side, with a kind of plaintive squeak. When he had thrown all the balls, Adam squatted down on his heels, so as to be more or less level with the beast's eyes. He reflected that it must be living in the house, like himself, though perhaps it hadn't been there so long. It must come out at night from a hole in some piece of furniture, and trot upstairs and down-stairs, hunting for food.

Adam did not know exactly what rats ate; he couldn't remember whether they were carnivorous or not. If it was true what the dictionaries said: 'Rat: s. Species of small mammiferous rodent with a long annulated tail.'

He could only remember the two or three legends related to the subject of rats, in connection with sinking ships, sacks of corn and plague. To tell the truth he had not even realized until today that there were such things as white rats.

Adam stared at this one, listened hard; and discovered in the rat something akin to himself. He reflected that he too might have gone to ground in the daytime between two worm-eaten boards and roamed about at night, searching for crumbs between the floor-boards and being lucky enough now and again, in some recess in a cellar, to come across a litter of white cockroaches that would have made a fine treat for him.

The rat still stood motionless, its blue eyes fixed on him; there were rolls of fat, or of muscle, round its neck. In view of its size, which was slightly above average, and of the above-mentioned rolls of flabby muscle, it must be a rat of advanced age. Adam didn't know how long a rat lives, either, but he would easily have put this one at eighty years old. Perhaps it was already half dead, half blind, and past realizing that Adam wished it ill.

Slowly, quietly, imperceptibly, Adam forgot that he was Adam, that he had heaps of things of his own downstairs, in the sunny room; heaps of deck-chairs, newspaper, all sorts of scribbles, and blankets that smelt of him, and scraps of paper on which he had written 'My dear Michèle' as though beginning a letter. Beer-bottles with their necks broken, and a sort of tea-rose that was spreading the ramifications of its hot-flower perfume, minute by minute, between four walls. The yellow scent of a yellow rose in a yellow room.

Adam was turning into a white rat, but by a strange kind of metamorphosis; he still kept his own body, his hands and feet did not turn pink nor his front teeth lengthen into fangs; no, his fingers still smelt of tobacco and his armpits of sweat, and his back was still bent forward in a crouching position, close to the floor, regulated by the S-shaped bend in his spine.

But he was turning into a white rat because he was

84

thinking of himself as one; because all of a sudden he had formed an idea of the danger that the human race represented for this breed of small, myopic, delicate animals. He knew that he could squeak, run, gnaw, stare with his two little round, blue, brave, lidless eyes; but it would all be in vain. A man like himself would always be sufficient; he need only resolve to take a few steps forward and lift his foot a few inches, and the rat would be killed, crushed, its ribs broken, its oblong head lolling on the floor-boards in a tiny pool of mucus and lymph.

And suddenly he stood up; he had turned into fear itself, been transformed into danger-for-white rats; his head was full, now, of something that was no longer anger or disgust or any form of cruelty, but a kind of obligation to kill.

He decided to set about it rationally. First of all he shut the doors and windows so that the creature should not run away. Then he went and picked up the billiard balls; as he came closer the rat drew back a little, pricking its short ears. Adam laid the balls on the billiard table and began to talk to the rat in a low voice, making strange, hoarse, throaty sounds.

'You're afraid of me, eh, white rat?' he muttered. 'You're afraid. You're trying to behave as though you weren't afraid . . . With those round eyes of yours . . . Are you looking at me? I admit you're a brave chap, white rat. But you know what's ahead of you. They all know, all the members of your species. The other white rats. And the grey ones and the black ones. You've been waiting a long time for what I'm going to do to you. White rat, the world is no place for you. You're doubly disqualified for living: in the first place you're a rat in a man's world, among men's houses and traps and guns and rat-poison. And in the second place you're a white rat in a country where rats are generally black. So you're absurd, and that's an extra reason . . .'

He counted the balls; there was one missing. It must have rolled under the cupboard. Adam scraped about with the bamboo stick and brought out the sphere of ivory. It was a red one, and cold, and held in the palm of the hand it felt bigger than the others. And consequently more lethal.

When everything was ready, Adam took up his stance beside the billiard table, resolute; all at once he felt himself becoming a giant, a very tall fellow, ten feet or thereabouts, bursting with life and strength. At a little distance, against the back wall, close beside the square of pale light falling from the window, the animal stood, planted on its four pink paws, displaying great patience.

'Dirty rat!' said Adam.

'Dirty rat!'

And he threw the first ball, with all his strength behind it. It crashed against the top of the skirting-board, an inch or two to the left of the animal, with a noise like thunder. A split second later the white rat squealed and leapt aside.

'You see!' exclaimed Adam triumphantly, 'I'm going to kill you! You're too old, you don't react any more, you beastly white rat! I'm going to kill you!'

And then he let himself go. He threw five or six balls one after another; some of them broke against the wall, others bounced on the floor and rolled back to his feet. One of the balls, as it broke, fired a splinter at the rat's head, just behind the left ear, and drew blood. The rodent began to run along by the wall, with a kind of whistling draught emerging from its open mouth. It rushed towards the cupboard, to hide there, and in its haste it bumped its nose against the corner of the piece of furniture. With a yelp it vanished into the hiding-place.

Adam was beside himself at this.

86

'Come out of there, you filthy brute! Filthy rat! rat! filthy rat! Come out of there!'

He sent a few billiard balls under the cupboard, but the white rat didn't budge. So he shuffled across on his knees and poked his bamboo stick about in the darkness. It hit something soft, close to the wall. Finally the rat emerged and ran to the far end of the room. Adam crawled towards it, holding his kitchen knife. With his eyes he thrust the animal back against the wall; he noticed that the stiff fur was slightly bloodstained towards the top of the head. The thin body was quivering, the ribs rising and falling spasmodically, the pale blue eyes bulging with terror. In the two black rings set in their limpid centres Adam could read an inkling of doom, the anticipation of an outcome heavy with death and anguish, a moist, melancholy gleam; this fear was mingled with a secret nostalgia relating to many happy years, to pounds and pounds of grains of corn and slices of cheese devoured with quiet relish in the cool dusk of men's cellars.

And Adam knew he embodied this fear. He was a colossal danger, rippling with muscles—a kind of gigantic white rat, if you like, ravenously craving to devour its own species. Whereas the rat, the real one, was being transformed by its hatred and terror into a man. The little animal kept twitching nervously, as though about to burst into tears or fall on its knees and begin to pray. Adam, moving stiffly on all fours, advanced towards it, shrieking, growling, muttering insults. There were no such things as words any longer; they were neither uttered nor received; from the intermediate stage they reissued eternal, veritable, negative; they were perfectly geometrical, sketched against a background of the unimaginable, with a touch of the mythical, something like constellations. Everything was written round the central theme of Betelgeuse or Upsilon Aurigae.

Adam was lost amid the abstract; he was living, neither more nor less; occasionally he even *squeaked*.

He grabbed some of the balls and hurled them at the beast, hitting the target this time, breaking bones, making the flesh clap together under the hide, while he yelled disconnected words such as 'Rat!' 'Crime! Crime!' 'Foul white rat!' 'Yes, yeh, arrah!' 'Crush! . . .' 'I kill', 'Rat, rat, rat!'

He threw the knife, blade foremost, and drowned the white rat's words by shouting one of the greatest insults that can possibly be flung at that species of animal:

'Filthy, filthy cat!'

It was by no means over yet; the myopic little beast, maimed though it was, bounded out of Adam's reach. It had already ceased to exist.

At the conclusion of a life full of concentrated memories it was a kind of pale phantom in ghostly outline, like a dingy patch of snow; it was leaking away over the brown floor, evasive and persistent. It was a lobular cloud, or a fleck of soft foam, dissociated from blood and terror, sailing on the surface of dirty water. It was what remains from an instant of linen-washing, what floats, what turns blue, what traverses the thick of the air and bursts before ever it can be polluted, before ever it can be killed.

Adam saw it gliding first left, then right, in front of him; a kind of fatigue added to his determination, sobering him.

Then he stopped talking. He stood upright again and decided to finish the fight. He took a billiard ball in each hand—nearly all the others were broken by now. And he began to walk towards the rat. As he moved along beside the skirting-board he saw the famous spot—he would mark it later on with a charcoal cross—where the white rat had begun to lose its life. Nothing remained on the parquet floor to testify to the beginning of the massacre except a few tufts of light-coloured hair, some scraps of ivory like splinters of bone, and a pool. A pool of thick, purple blood, dulled already, which the dirty boards were swallowing drop by drop. In an hour or two, the time required to penetrate bodily into eternity, it would all over. The blood would look like a stain caused by no matter what liquid—wine, for instance. As it coagulated it would harden or become powdery and one could scratch it with a finger-nail, put flies there and they wouldn't be drowned or be able to feed on it.

With a veil of moisture in front of his eyes, Adam walked up to the rat. He saw it as though he were trying to look through a shower-curtain, a nylon hanging with little drops of water trickling down it and a naked, flesh-coloured woman concealed behind, amid the dripping of rain and the smell of soap-bubbles.

The white rat was lying on its stomach, as though asleep at the bottom of an aquarium. Everything had drifted out of its ken, leaving a naked, motionless space: now very close to bliss, the rat was awaiting the ultimate moment when a half-sigh would die away on its stiff whiskers, propelling it for ever and ever into a sort of double life, at the exact meeting-point of philosophy's accumulated chiaroscuri. Adam listened to its calm breathing; fear had left the animal's body. It was far away now, scarcely even in the death-agony; with its two pale eyes it was waiting for the last ivory balls to come thundering down on its bones and despatch it to the white rats' paradise.

It would go down there, partly swimming, partly flying through the air, full of mystical rapture. It would leave its naked body lying on the ground so that all its blood could drain out, drop by drop, marking for a long time the sacred spot on the floor that had been the scene of its martyrdom.

So that Adam, patient, should stoop down and pick up its dislocated body.

So that he should swing it to and fro for a moment and then, weeping, fling it in a wide curve from the first-floor window to the ground on the hill-top. A thorny bush would receive the body and leave it to ripen in the open air, in the blazing sunshine.

I. Question:
'My dear Michèle,

I do wish you'd come up to the house again one of these days, I haven't seen you since we had that race, you remember, down below, along the headland. It's ridiculous how much time I waste doing nothing in particular; perhaps because it's so hot that I wonder if summer will ever come to an end. I found a dead white rat in an arbutus bush just under the wall of the house. It must have been dead for a good time, it was quite yellow except for some spots of blood, which looked like dust. And it had little concentric wrinkles round its eyes; the closed lids made an X shape; and it had fallen into a lot of thorny bushes; the arbutus berries or bilberries were ripe, and made hundreds of scarlet dots round its head. The thorns had torn it to pieces, unless it was the sun that had reduced it to that condition; I suppose a dead body decays more rapidly in the sun.

As well as this, someone has cut with a penknife on a cactus leaf, You say Cécile J.'s a Shit.

Cécile J. says Shit on you.

I wonder who on earth can have written that. Some little girl who happened to go past, or perhaps one of the idiots I sometimes see in the grass on Sunday afternoons, with fellows who have moustaches. She must have been angry because her moustached fellow had gone out with some other girl; so she took her penknife, and instead of doing the usual thing, carving a heart with compartments and putting

Cécile   Eric

on either side, she put

Cécile J. says Shit on you.

And I say it back to her.

What's fun sometimes is to sit at home, in the house, with my feet in the sun; I remember this kind of thing too. It happened a long time ago, but I remember it to this day; there was some sort of big Girls' School not far from my home. Four times a day they went past where I lived—at 8 in the morning, at noon, at 2 o'clock in the afternoon and at half-past 5. I was always there when they went by. They usually came along in groups of ten or twelve; they were all stupid, and most of them were ugly. But I'd picked out four or five who were vaguely pretty, and it amused me to see them go by like that, four times a day. I felt as if it gave me some kind of steady dates; I could do whatever I wanted, go fishing, go away for a week, be ill in bed—I'd know they were coming past regularly, just the same; it was nice, because it gave me the impression of having something to fill in my time. Like going home and seeing the four walls still there, and the table and the chair and the ashtrays just as you'd left them.

It's fun to remember that, here in a house that isn't my own—where the deck-chairs are deck-chairs stolen from the beach, and the candles are candles stolen from the chapel on the port. The newspapers taken out of dustbins in the town. The scraps of meat and potatoes, the tins of pineapple, the odds and ends of string, the charred wood, the sticks of chalk and all these three-quarter objects that prove I'm alive and that I steal things. I'm glad I found this house; I can have peace at last, even if I don't know how to fill in the twenty-four hours. Twenty-four hours of peace and silence, I'm caught up in the strip-cartoon I chose for myself. . . .'

Reply:

'I can't answer you, Adam, I can't answer your question about the girl who wrote those words on the cactus leaf; but I've thought of a whole lot of stories; it's rather as if I were afraid to tell them to myself and had to start writing so as to bring all these queer things out of the confusion they're in as a rule. In any case it's not disagreeable, because when they're all strung together—all the little happenings one sees everywhere, the bits of paper with three words written on them, the leaves on which somebody has carved a phrase with a penknife, the insults one sometimes hears while crossing the street, etc.—they amuse me and I believe I'm fond of them.

Yesterday I went to the cinema; it was a curious film, but it's made me feel talkative; I think you're wasting your time on things of no importance; you're wasting yourself; it won't get you anywhere; you're afraid of everything that's sentimental; I'd like to tell you a story. No matter what. No matter what.'

Reply:

'All right. Let's tell stories. They've not much connection with bloody reality; but one enjoys them; let's tell the most delicate stories imaginable, like the story of a garden we'll suppose to be covered in snow and at the same time bathed in sunshine. There'd be cherry-trees all over the place. Except at the far end of the garden, where there'd be a high wall, very white. The snow would have settled on the branches of the cherry-trees and along the top of the wall. But because of the sun it would be slowly melting and

93

it would fall on the grass, making a sound like drops of water, plop-plop.

And one of the trees would grumble: "Quiet! quiet! I can't get to sleep!" it would groan, creaking its boughs.

But the drops would go on falling, making even more noise. The sun would say:

"Sleep! Who's talking about sleep? Nobody is to sleep when I'm here on the watch!"

And the pear-trees would have plump, ripe pears on them, with scars for mouths. The scars would have been made by birds, but they might look very like lips all the same. And the pears would roar with laughter.

Then one of the cherry-trees, the oldest, would begin to grumble again:

"Be quiet! I must get some sleep! I must get some sleep! Or I shall never be able to flower!"

The drops would take no notice. Just before falling, while still hanging by their tails from the branches, they would call out in shrill voices:

"*Silence, silence! La queue du chat balance!*"
Just to tease.

It would be like that all over the garden. The little flakes of snow would be falling on the grass, softly, placidly, and the effect would be funny, because it would sound like rain although the sun would be blazing away. And everybody would be grumbling. The grass, because it's green and would like to change colour. The dead twigs, because they're dead. The roots because they would so much like to see the sky; the lumps of soil because they've had an overdose of phosphates; the blades of grass because they can't breathe. And the strawberry leaves because they're covered with soft, whitish hairs and it's somehow ridiculous, for a leaf, to be covered with soft, whitish hairs. Then the garden would change, little by little; there would be hardly

94

any snow left on the cherry-trees and none at all along the top of the wall. And there would be hardly any sun left, either, to melt it. The noises would begin to be different. For instance the cherry-tree would creak its boughs, to get its own back. The pears would suddenly become too ripe and fall; some of them would go squash, making a mushy patch of over-ripeness on the grass. The others would manage to escape, and would crawl away, dribbling juice through their scars. But the wall would still stand straight and calm and silent. All white. It wouldn't move. And the result would be that seeing the wall so handsome, so noble, all the rest of the garden would feel ashamed of its noisy excitability.

And then we should see the garden gradually becoming gentle and icy again. There would only be a spiritless turbulence here and there, microscopic in every respect. Another few hours and it would be all white, green and pink, like a beautiful iced cake, all tranquil; and sleep would descend, with nightfall, just at the right moment—yes, really just at the right moment—on all those leaves, eh.'
Reply:
'My dear Michèle,
Again today I've been thinking that summer's bound to finish one of these days, and wondering what I should do when summer's over, when it'll be less hot, without the sun, and we shall see the water seeping in everywhere, rain-water, all the time, drop by drop.

There'll be autumn, and then winter. They say it will be cold when summer's over. I've been thinking that I shan't know where to go then. I've been thinking that the people who live in this house will come back one evening, by car. They'll bang the car doors and climb up the path that cuts across the hill, and invade the house again. Then it occurred to me that they'll throw me out—kick me out,

95

perhaps. Unless they send for the police. And I shall be dragged off somewhere; it's sure to be some place where I shan't want to stay. That's as far as I can look ahead. After that it's all vague again, I don't know what will happen to me.

They'll certainly be angry with me for a whole lot of things. For sleeping here, on the floor, for days and days; for messing up the house, drawing squids on the walls and playing billiards. They'll accuse me of opening beer-bottles by smashing the necks against the window-sill: there's practically no yellow paint left on the wooden edge. I imagine I shall have to appear before long in a law-court full of men; I'm leaving them this filth as my testament; I'm not proud, but I hope they'll sentence me to some kind of punishment, so that I can pay with my whole body for the crime of being alive; if they humiliate me, whip me, spit in my face, I shall at last have a destiny, I shall at last believe in God. Perhaps they'll tell me I live in some other century, the 26th, for example, and you'll see how far I shall last into the future.

But I prefer to think of what I shall be able to do if they leave me free to go away.

It's hard to say, because I have masses of plans in my mind already. And that's funny, because I've not really given it much thought; I've had ideas, naturally, like everyone has, when I was strolling round the town by myself, or with you, Michèle, or wool-gathering in my own room, lying in my deck-chair.

For instance, I might go into mourning, a grey suit with a black band. I'd walk about the streets and people would think I'd lost a near relation, one of my parents, my mother. I'd attend every burial service and when the ceremony was over some people would shake hands with me and others would kiss me, whispering expressions of regret. In that case my chief occupation would be reading the "Deaths" column in the newspapers. I'd go to all funerals, handsome or shabby. And little by little I should get used to the life. I should discover what one's supposed to say, and the proper way to walk very softly, with downcast eyes.

I should like going to cemeteries, and I should enjoy touching dead people on the brow, seeing their pale, bulging eyes and empty jaws, and the marble slabs on the tombs; and I'd read what was written in the middle of the wreaths, on the ribbon that's hooked to the plaster violets:

"Regrets"

If necessary I could drone out:

"Nigher still and still more nigh
Draws the day of prophecy
Doomed to melt the Earth and Sky.
O, what trembling there shall be
When the world its Judge shall see."

Or I might travel; I'd go to a lot of towns I don't know, and make a friend in each of them. Then, later, I'd go back to the same towns: but I'd deliberately choose a day when I was sure not to meet my friend. For instance I'd go to Rio during the Carnival. I'd ring the bell at my friend's house—let's call him Pablo—and of course he'd be out. So then I could take a piece of paper and write him a note:

"My dear Pablo,

I came to Rio today to see you. But you weren't at home. I suppose you were at the Carnival, like everyone else. I'm sorry not to have been able to see you. We could have had a drink and a chat. Perhaps I shall be back this way next year. 'Bye for now.

Adam Pollo."

97

Or I'd go to Paris on the Fourteenth of July, or to Moscow for the procession in the Red Square, to Rome for the Council or to Newport the day of the Jazz Festival.

The real difficulty would be to choose my friends properly; I should need to be certain they'd be away when I came back to see them.

Otherwise my little game would go wrong, and I might not have the heart to carry on with it. I should muddle up my dates, and when I rang the bell their doors would be flung open and they'd exclaim, with beaming smiles of welcome:

"Adam Pollo? You here? What a delightful surprise! If you'd come tomorrow you'd have missed me, it's the Bull Fight . . ."

Yes, it would be just as well to plan that sort of amusement methodically. I must think about it often; perhaps I'll buy a diary where I can jot down the dates of festivals and important events in towns all over the world. Of course there'll always be the risk that one of my friends has been taken ill or turned eccentric and not gone to the fiesta. But risks like that give a spice of adventure to the thing.

These ideas I've been telling you about are only two among any number of others; I've thought up a whole heap of different schemes for fitting into the world. I might suffer from elephantiasis; I've noticed that always disgusts most people and keeps them at a distance. Or I might have a prognathous jaw; that makes people sorry for you and they never want to see how your bottom teeth jut out when you open your mouth. To limp because of eczema in one leg, to be a scoundrel, or to pick one's teeth with a little red celluloid spoon, the kind that's given away in packets of soap-powder—those aren't bad methods either. Or one can spend whole days trying to pick out decayed

98

places in one's teeth with the point of a knife. Generally speaking, anything in the nature of disease, madness or physical infirmity will do the trick.

But there are convenient situations in social life where people tend to leave you in peace; jobs like water-divining, pimping or gardening are particularly advantageous.

I've often thought I'd like to be a cinema operator, up in the projection-room. For one thing, you're shut up in a small room, all alone with the projector. There are no openings except the door and the slits that let the beam of light through. All you have to do is to put the reel on the spindle, and while it's running off, with a pleasant humming sound, you can smoke cigarettes and drink beer straight out of the bottle, keeping an eye on the blueish electric light bulb and saying to yourself that this is like being on board a liner during a cruise, one of the few people who aren't fooled by what's going on.'

Reply:

'My dear Michèle,

Now that it seems it's going to rain soon

Now that it seems the sun will be getting weaker, from day to day, from ray to ray, until it dies through being changed into a snowball, and that I shall be obliged to follow the cooling process, huddled up in my deck-chair,

Now that I have the impression that the triumph of the infirm and the crippled is about to begin,

Now that I am abandoning the earth to the termites, I think you ought to come.

Don't you really want, as I do, to come and sleep in the last remains of the light?

Do you really not want to come and tell me a quiet story while we drink beer or tea and hear sounds go past the window? And then we'd be naked, and we'd look at our bodies, we'd count something on our

99

fingers, and we'd relive the same day a thousand times.

We'd read the newspaper.

When are the people of the house coming back? I'd so much like you to tell me sometime who carved those things on the cactus leaf and who killed that animal, the white rat that died by being impaled perhaps with two blue eyes glazed with its courage in the tangle of arbutus-bushes and didn't rot but became embalmed and by now must be pierced through and through with the heat.'

J. It was raining. So the dog would not be on the beach today. Where would he be? Nobody knew. At home, no doubt; unless he decided to roam the streets all the same, hunching his broad woolly back under the raindrops.

Adam went to the beach to have a look, though with no great hopes. The beach was ugly in the rain. The wet stones were not like stones any longer, the concrete like concrete or the sea like sea. They had all run on top of one another and mixed into mud. Nothing to be seen of the sun, naturally. In its place in the sky there was a funny little knot of seagulls, and at the spot it usually shone down on there was another little knot, of black seaweed.

In the town, Adam found it was almost cold. He was uncertain where to go; he didn't know whether he liked the rain or not. If he hadn't liked it at all he would not have hesitated to go into a café and drink beer, quietly bored. But he wasn't sufficiently sure of not liking it, to take on that expense. Letting himself drift, he arrived in a kind of department store. Because of the rain there were three times as many people as usual inside. Adam edged his way between the counters, telling himself he wouldn't stay there very long.

Then he found himself stuck behind a fat woman who was looking at socks. Adam looked too, and saw there were all sizes. Blue dominated except in the children's socks, where it was white. The fat woman was principally interested in that category. She handled most of them, at random, stretching them between her big red hands. Lifting the hem of her pinafore-dress with the toe of his shoe, Adam saw she had varicose veins; they ran in a series of purplish lumps just under the skin and that made him want to look higher up, to see what happened on her thighs. But Adam was drawn away by a movement in the crowd, and left the woman before he could find out any more. He stopped at the record counter, waited a moment for his turn, and then asked the assistant:

'Have you got MacKinsley Morganfield?"

Adam looked at the girl before she answered, reflecting that she was pretty; she had the soft cheeks of a little girl in quite good health, nut-brown hair, and her best feature was a pair of full lips, not made up but very red, which were now parting silently so that a pearly drop sparkled in the middle of the warm cavity of her mouth; her voice would certainly flow from deep down in her throat and, with four vibrations of the upper vocal cords, put an end to that faint quivering at the corners of her mouth, complete the most recent of human apotheoses, half desire, half habit.

'What did you say?' she asked.

'MacKinsley Morganfield,' said Adam. 'A fellow who sings.'

'What does he sing?' said the salesgirl; her eyes hovered blank and evasive, round the circum-ocular part of Adam's face.

'He's an American singer,' said Adam, 'a Negro who sings blues.' The girl went to the other end of the counter, opened a drawer and began searching through some lined-up records.

Adam watched her from behind, looking particularly

at the back of her neck; it was bent and the nape was rounded and white, with thousands of little curly hairs growing up from it. He still didn't understand how an imaginary name, such as 'MacKinsley Morganfield' or 'Gallaher's Blues' or 'Ricardo Impres' could have power to bend, at will, the round necks of the little girls who sold records in multiple stores.

After a time she turned to him and said no, she hadn't got that record.

Adam wanted to see the nape of her neck again, so he threw out another name, at random.

'And Jack Crivine?'

But the girl seemed to have understood. With a faint smile, she replied:

'No, I don't know that name.'

Disappointed, Adam thanked her and went away. And yet, as he fled he could feel her eye, a big green eye, staring at his back.

There were books there, hooked onto a kind of wire turnstile; Adam reflected that he might come to the shop every day at the same time, for example, and read one page from a selected book. If the book had 251 pages it would take him 251 days to read it. Probably a bit longer, allowing for the covers, foreword and list of contents, and for days when he couldn't come. Adam took a book from the turnstile, at random, opened it towards the middle, and read:

114   *A HIGH WIND IN JAMAICA*

back into the bows for a fresh run: but at each charge his run grew shorter and shorter. The pig was hemming him in. Suddenly the pig gave a frightful squeal, chiefly in surprise at his own temerity, and pounced. He had got the goat cornered against the windlass: and for a few flashing seconds bit and trampled. It was a very chastened goat which was presently led off to his own quarters: but the children were prepared to love him for ever, for the heroic bangs he had given the old tyrant.

But he was not entirely inhuman, that pig. That same afternoon, he was lying on the hatch eating a banana. The ship's monkey was swinging on a loose tail of rope; and spotting the prize, swung further and further till at last he was able to snatch it from between his very trotters. You would never have thought that the immobile mask of a pig could wear a look of such astonishment, such dismay, such piteous injury.

Adam closed the book; strictly speaking there was nothing so very touching about that page; and yet as he hooked the volume back onto the wire turnstile, Adam smiled tenderly. He felt he would discover little by little, within his enclosed world, heaps of unknown things, battles between wild animals, decks of ships overloaded with coal and sunshine. With buckets of water and coils of tarred rope. He resolved to come back tomorrow, or later on, to read another page.

He was happy to be living in a scale model of the universe, all his own, a gentle place with a thousand different ploys to occupy it.

K. Adam left the shop abruptly. He put a cigarette between his lips; by squinting he could see it getting spotted with raindrops. When the paper was thoroughly soaked he lit the cigarette and listened to the tobacco sizzling as it struggled against the damp.

He went down several streets and emerged on the promenade.

Until today there had been no rain for a long, long time. You could tell that just from the smell of the rain as it mingled with the dust on the pavements.

Adam set out along the sea-front; the fresh water was trickling in streams over his temples, through his hair and down inside his shirt-collar. It was making its way in little rills through the layer of salt that months of sunshine and sea-bathing had deposited on his skin. The promenade was a funny place, a widish, tarred road running below the public gardens; at first it bordered the harbour with its quays; then it went round a succession of small inlets, used as beaches for the tourists. There was only one footpath, on the side nearest the sea. So going past on a fine day, you could gaze in wonder at a crowd of pensive sadists, backs bent, elbows resting on the handrail as they gazed at another crowd consisting this time of masochists, slumbering, naked, on the beach below.

You made your choice; sometimes you'd stay up above with the sadists, your goggle-eyes rivetted on somebody's stomach which was usually dented by a navel.

Sometimes you went down below, staggering over the scorching pebbles, and then stripped and lay on your back, arms outstretched, under the avalanche of heat and staring eyes. The proof is that on a day like this no one was leaning on the railings because there was no one crazy enough to be lying naked on the beach in the rain. Unless it was the other way about.

Anyhow, there was nobody there. Adam strolled along with his hands in his pockets. The rain had put out his cigarette; he threw it over the parapet and watched it drop to the quay below. When he raised his eyes he noticed two cranes and a boat, a good distance away.

Their black ironwork was absolutely motionless. The cranes stood with arms extended, frozen in a kind of sinister cramp; the ship was framed between them, hardly smoking at all. It was a dark red colour all over, and the rain was driving against its portholes. Half of a name could be seen curving round the stern in capital letters, thus:

'DERMY'
and
'SEILLE'

The part one couldn't see must be 'Commander' or 'Admiral' or 'Captain' or perhaps 'City of'. It could have been 'Pachy' or 'Epi' or any old thing. As for the other word, below, one could easily have betted ten million that it was 'Marseille' if one had had the ten million, or if it had been worth while.

But that was not all; the rain was still falling, and the rustle of dead leaves could be heard on all sides; the dirty landscape was ringing with this monotonous sound, the only one. Adam felt a disastrous listlessness creeping over him; he bent down slightly and leant on the iron balustrade. He closed his fingers round it and allowed the water to flow down his arms like blood onto the wet railings. He was also thinking, no doubt, of his approaching death, his drained body lying full length on the concrete of a rain-washed, nocturnal quay, his acquiescent corpse, white as morning, which would still be shining with a thin trickle of blood, a hair's breadth of daily life, the last root thrusting down into the bowels of the earth. He listened to the noise that came zooming out of the sea like a waterfall; everything ahead of him, right to the far end of the docks, was quiet and calm, yet quivering with menace and hatred. He could feel his heart beating harder and harder, faster and faster; and he crumpled up, with his chest against the iron rail. The deserted wharves were cluttered with abandoned mer-chandise, some of it covered with tarpaulins, some not.

Standing at the water's edge or floating on its surface, two cranes and a boat had been left about. They were sharpened ruins, collections of broken razor-blades that made a grating sound as they clove the raindrops in two. Everything had been deserted, owing to a bit of a storm; some object or other, the pale shadow of something left over from a murder, the scattered materials. There was no more work, and that meant death.

Perhaps, one never knows, there was still a faint breath of life here and there, hidden behind the rubbish. Not in the shell-holes, anyhow; nor down there, you can be sure. A tuft of grass, drunk with rain, bent double with the weight of coal-dust and still thrusting up through the veneer of asphalt. Perhaps a pair of ants, perhaps a cat, perhaps some kind of seaman, smoking his pipe in a vacated shanty-town. But those didn't count; they were merely Phantoms and Co.

You must understand that what was happening to Adam

on this particular rainy day might equally well have happened to him on any other day. On a very windy day, for instance. Or on a day during the equinox, or on one of those much-vaunted sunny days. With great patches of light spreading over the ground, there would have been an enormous crowd on the promenade, lots of women and children. The cars would have kept up a continuous roar behind him; he would have met groups of boys and girls in sweaters, T-shirts and blue jeans, passing him on their way to the beach; they'd have set their transistors yelling as they went by. This way:

'But darling darling
Keep in touch
Keep-in-touch
Keep-in-touch-with-me.'

And down there, on the docks, the cranes would have been set turning and the boat's funnel smoking, the men shouting, the barrels of oil rolling and the big rounds of cork would have been stowed; the ground would have been made to smell of coal and diesel oil and the air to ring with hammerblows banging on the rusty hulls of the cargo-boats. That's it, everything would have been done that is done on a sunny day. But Adam would have guessed, all the same; he would have sat down, quite dumbfounded, on a bench on the promenade and seen space being peopled with ghosts. He would have felt death invading all his movements, only instead of being grey and unoccupied death would have been red and white and industrious.

But one particular noise would have come spurting out of everything, drowning all other sounds—a noise bordering on rain, very close to the tumult of waterfalls or the hissing of steam-engines. This was a kind of fate; Adam had gone beyond the evidence of his senses, and for him, henceforth, nothing seemed to move. He reconciled all measures of time and motion, from the butterfly to the rock. Time, having become universal, was destroying itself through its own complexity. In the world as he now understood it, everything was explicitly alive or dead.

After that it didn't matter so much that he should have stood up and walked on again beside the hand-rail, whistling a waltz tune through his teeth. That he should walk the length of a big puddle of yellow water that was boiling under the rain. That with the toe of his shoe he should crush an empty matchbox that had (I 25 A) written on its under-side. Nor did it matter that as he went along he should try to catch a glimpse of the little stucco temple an old bourgeois family had erected at the far end of their garden in more prosperous days. Or that he should happen to pass a group of seminarists, shivering in their long, black cassocks and whispering:

'At Castelnaudry, didn't you know?'

'And yet he told me it was better not to' and laughing.

No, it didn't matter much, because the breath of real life was no longer in them; they were no longer bright and vic-torious, they were nothing but lean spectres who brought forewarning of a great void that would open up some day. They predicted all possible causes of death—the burst of machine-gun fire from a passing car, the chopper of the guillotine, smotherings under pillows, stranglings, poison-ings, murders by axe, embolisms, or just simple runnings-over in the street by four vulcanised rubber tyres.

Adam expected some such violent end whenever he put a foot forward. It wasn't difficult to imagine. He might be struck by lightning; they would bring him down from the top of the hill on a stretcher, black and charred, amid the rumbling of the storm. He might be bitten by a mad dog. Poisoned by water. Or else, drenched as he was by the rain, he might very easily get pneumonia. Trailing his hand along the balustrade, he might scratch himself on a jagged piece of metal and develop lockjaw.

An aerolite might fall on his head. Or an aeroplane. The rain might cause a landslide so that the promenade would collapse, burying him under tons of earth. A volcano might erupt beneath his feet—there—at any moment. Or he might simply slip on the wet asphalt, or on a banana skin, why not, and fall backwards, fracturing his cervical vertebrae. A terrorist or a lunatic might choose him for a target and send a bullet into his liver. A leopard might escape from a menagerie and tear him to pieces at a street-corner. He might murder somebody and be sent to the guillotine. He might choke himself on a sugared almond. Or war, sudden war, might touch off some gigantic calamity, some kind of bomb, send up a mushroom of smoke surrounded by flashes of lightning, and annihilate him, vaporize him— Adam, poor, puny Adam—in a microscopic contraction of the atmosphere. His heart would stop beating and silence would spread through his body; in a chain reaction, the cold would creep slowly along his limbs until with tremendous stupefaction he would vaguely recognize that his furthest recesses of red flesh, which used to be warm, now had something corpse-like about them.

At every step he faced some new peril: that a beetle would fly into his open mouth and block his windpipe; that a wheel would come hurtling off a passing lorry and decapitate him, or that the sun would be extinguished; or that he himself would be gripped all at once by a suicidal impulse.

He suddenly felt tired; tired of living, perhaps, tired of constantly having to defend himself against all these dangers. It wasn't his actual end that mattered, so much as the moment when he would decide he was ready to die. He had a horror of that bizarre transformation, which would certainly take place one day or another and prevent him from thinking about anything any more.

Adam sat down on the back of a bench; he had got beyond the docks some time ago, to where the promenade ran round the rocky inlets. A man came past on a bicycle; he wore oilskins and seaman's boots. In his right hand he was carrying a dismantled fishing-rod, its sections held together by three sock-garters. The saddle-bags on his bicycle seemed to be full—of rags, or fish, or a wool jersey; as he pedalled along the road, his tyres making a sticky noise on the tarmac, he turned his head to look at Adam. Then he pointed over his shoulder and called out, sounding as though he had a cold:

'Hey! There's a drowned man back there!'

Adam followed him with his eyes. Thinking he had not understood, the man—a long way off already—looked round and shouted again:

'A drowned man!'

Adam said to himself that the man was right; as everyone knows, a drowned body is the choicest possible entertainment for anyone who is wandering aimlessly along the sea-front, soaked to the skin and sometimes sitting on the back of a bench. As he got to his feet he reflected that all over the place there must be one such case of drowning every day. To show others how to set about it, summoning them, likewise, to meet their end.

Adam walked on again, faster; the road was bending round a sort of cape, and one could see nothing. The drowning must have occurred on the other side; perhaps at the Roc-plage, or along by the German blockhouse, opposite the Seminary. He was ready to bet that in spite of the rain there would be a lot of people staring down at the sea, a lot of people, all enjoying themselves, despite the faint contraction of their nostrils and hearts, where shamelessness would pause for an instant, just long enough to become tinged with embarrassment, before hurtling ahead, mingled with the thick breath of meals and wines, towards *this*, towards the *object*. And indeed, as soon as Adam got round the corner, he saw a gathering of people, still some distance along the road. It was a group of men, mostly fishermen in oilskins. There was a firemen's van as well, with its back doors open. As he drew nearer, Adam noticed another car, but this was a private one, and foreign, Dutch or German or some such. A couple of tourists had emerged from it and were standing on tiptoe, trying to see.

The closer Adam came, the more activity he seemed to perceive. He leant over the parapet and saw down below, on the beach, a yellow plastic inflatable raft and two frogmen taking off their diving gear.

It couldn't have been long since they fished the body out, for on the short flight of steps leading up to the road there were still some puddles of sea-water, not yet washed away by the rain. One of them had shreds of seaweed in it. When Adam arrived they let him through to the front row without comment, perhaps because after being out in the rain so long he looked like a drowned man himself.

And Adam saw that in the middle of the ring of bystanders, laid flat on the gravel like a heap of rags, there was that insubstantial, ridiculous thing which had nothing terrestrial about it any more, and nothing aquatic either. This amphibious monster was a man of no particular age, just a man like any other. His only peculiarity—and it made you want to laugh, a deep, throaty laugh—was the quantity of water he represented, what with his flesh and his clothes, in the middle of this wet scene; it was the fact of being a drowned man out in the rain. The sea had already ravaged his body. A few hours more and he would have looked like a fish, one felt. His hands were blue and swollen and on his feet—one bare, the other shod—there were tufts of weed. From the depths of his clothes, which were twisted round him, soaked and saturated with brine, his head and neck hung out limply. His face, though dead, was curiously mobile, crawling with a kind of movement quite alien to life, because of the water that puffed out his cheeks, eyes and nostrils, and rippled beneath the skin with every drop that fell from the sky. Within a few hours this man of about forty, honest and hard-working, had become a liquid man. Everything had melted, in the sea. His bones must be jelly now, his hair seaweed, his teeth tiny stones, his mouth an anemone; and his eyes, which were wide open, staring straight up to where the rain came from, were veiled by a kind of glaze. Air mingled with vapour must be bubbling invisibly between his gill-shaped ribs. The bare foot, screwed into the trouser-leg like an artificial limb, had emerged from the depths of the sea with the skin greasy or grey and a suggestion of embryonic webbing between the toes. He was a giant tadpole, floated down accidentally from the mountains, where lonely pools of water lay in the hollows of the peaty ground and shivered beneath the wind.

When one of the firemen turned the man's head over, the mouth opened and vomited. 'Oh!' said one of the lookers-on.

The idlers had lost their excitement and now stood rooted to the spot like stone images, while the rain poured down on their heads. Only the firemen were still active, slapping the corpse with the flat of their hands, talking together in undertones, manipulating little bottles of spirits.

But the drowned man lay alone, huddled on the ground, muddy-eyed, ready for some imaginary reflex action, perhaps for a leap that would carry him back towards the element in which resurrection must find him. And the heavy rain was still falling on his blue flesh, splashing louder than ever, as though hitting the surface of a pond.

113

Then things began to happen very quickly; a white stretcher was brought; the firemen pushed back the ring of spectators; there was a brief glimpse of a strange, grey, confused body retreating towards the ambulance. The doors banged. There was a noise, the crowd took a step forward; and the ambulance drove off townwards with its dripping burden. In the middle of the road, where just for a few hours people would still avoid treading, a strong smell of seawater now hovered, despite the rain. The wheel-shaped pool was slowly absorbed by the gravel, and everyone's heart shrank at the strange passing—for now the dead man's body was quietly shedding its ludicrous memory. It was flowing down at the back of their minds, they were no longer even trying to hold it, to imagine it tossed from mortuary to pauper's grave. He had become a queer archangel, white or clad in armour. He was at last the victor, single and eternal. His blue-gloved hand pointed imperiously, showing us the sea where he had been born. And the sea's edge, the fringe of waves washed up with refuse, invited us to approach. Sirens disguised as empty hair-oil bottles, headless sardines, jerrycans and half-peeled leeks, chanted their hoarse-voiced summons; we were to go down the steps, still puddled with salt water, and without undressing, entrust our bodies to the waves. We should cross the edge, with its floating orange-peel, corks and patches of oil, and go straight to the bottom. In a little mud, stabbed with pangs of osmosis, tiny fish swimming into our mouths, we should be motionless and gentle.

Until a group of men dressed like monsters came to look for us, thrust hooks into the back of our necks, dragged us to the surface and drove us away in ambulances towards the mortuary and paradise.

L. When you've seen a drowned body, only just taken from the water, still lying on the road, you don't find much to say. Especially when you have understood why some people drown themselves, one day or another. The rest doesn't matter. Whether it's raining or fine, whether it's a child or a man, or a naked woman with a diamond necklace, etc., makes no difference. Those are the particular settings of an unchanging tragedy.

But when people haven't understood, well . . . When they allow their attention to be distracted by the details that seem to justify the event, give it a certain reality, but which in fact are merely stage effects; then there is a great deal to say. They pull up, get out of their cars, and join in the game. Instead of seeing, they compose. They lament. They take sides. They celebrate and write poems.

He asks whence comes this subterranean dust
to take its place on things. Reigning gently.
all amidst the cogwheels granite in crumbs.
it petrifies the level surfaces, he says.
he wishes for yet more tedium and taste: ashes.
he listens. then one must leave him thus
await his pleasure, the high priest.
he looks to every form to remind him
of a forgotten wish: one would think he waits for war.

true, he may be mistaken
War may Be no longer the Giver of Courage
but the Breaker of Stones
It may Be War that Grinds the Granite to crumbs
It may Be War that Fabricates the Hardest Dust
The millimetric Abrasions

He asks
He wishes He waits
He counts on his fingers
and gathers himself to leap

he—yes—LOVES
the hard dust
that is why he does not know
that there is the sand,
what is called sand
what is called ashes
and the yellow leaves and the bird-droppings
and the rainy soil
the lavas and other seeds
yes, all that.
which is called gentle dust.

And of course (since he who writes is shaping a destiny for
himself) they little by little become one with those who
drowned the chap.
   One of them, his name's Christberg, says:
'But what happened?'
'There was an accident' says his wife, Julia.
'You saw how swollen he was? He must have been a
hell of a time in the water. It seems it was two days . . .'
says a fisherman called Simonin.
   'Do they know who he is?' Christberg enquires.
   They all stayed where they were, though. In a circle

round the patch of sea-water with bits floating in it. As though the-man-just-now, the drowned man, had begun to shrink until he was only a tiny insect, almost invisible, still swimming in the middle of the pool.

'Was it a man or a woman?' asked Julia.

'I saw one like that last year. At much the same place. A bit further along, though. Beyond the restaurant over there. I was on the beach and there was a woman going up to people and asking, "You haven't seen Guillaume?" Asking everybody, like that. They all said no. She—she went on doing that for quite a time. Afterwards something was seen floating a little way out, not so very far from the shore. There was a fellow who was a good swimmer and he went in after him. It was Guillaume. It was the——— He was just a kid, about, about twelve, I remember. When the chap brought him to land he wasn't a pretty sight, I can tell you. They, they laid him down on the shingle and he was all purple. They wanted to prevent his mother seeing him, but they couldn't, it was too late, she got through all the same. She saw him and she began turning him over and over on the shingle, crying, and calling out, like this:

"Guillaume, oh, Guillaume!"

Well, she turned him over so often that you know, everything came out of his mouth. Bile, and milky stuff, the lot. And gallons of sea-water. But a funny thing, eh, he was dead all the same', said the narrator, whose name was Guéraud.

'But what exactly happened?' Christberg asked again.

'It seemed he was drowned,' his wife whispered.

'D'you suppose he's dead?' asked Bosio.

'After two days I don't see how he could still be alive,' said Joseph Jacquineau.

'They always vomit when they're turned over. They've swallowed such a lot of water, you understand, the least

jerk makes them throw it up. Not a pretty thing, death,'
said Hozniacks.

'Even with all the things, the injections they give them
in the heart, and everything? They say they can be saved
even when they've been dead for days,' said Bosio.

'Do you believe all that stuff?' asked Simone Frère.

'Dunno,' said Bosio.

'How can one tell,' said Hozniacks, 'I . . .'

'I saw a fellow once, but it wasn't the same thing. He was
a fellow who'd been knocked down by a car. Without
exaggeration, the two lots of wheels had run right over him,
one across his neck and the other across his legs. Funny
thing, that kind of car leaves the marks of the tyres on the
skin. Well, I tell you for sure, they could have given that
chap all the injections they wanted to. It wouldn't have
brought him round. There was blood everywhere, even in
the gutters. And both eyes had popped out of his head.
Like a squashed cat, exactly like a squashed cat,' explained a
man leaning on a walking-stick, who was known as M.
Antonin.

'It took them three hours to find him,' said Véran. 'They
looked everywhere along the coast. And here, they hunted
for three hours. Three whole hours, they hunted. I saw
them right from the start, because I was walking along the
seafront. I just happened to see them.'

'So they knew he was missing?' said Guéraud.

'Must have,' replied Véran.

'Perhaps he committed suicide. Left a letter at home and
they found it,' said Hozniacks.

Some people were going away already, walking beside
the parapet. They were getting into cars and slamming the
doors, and groups of idlers were calling to one another:

'Hey, Jeannot! You coming?'

'Yes, wait for me!'

'Hurry up!'

'Paul! Paul!'

'Hey, Jeannot! Well, then?'

'It's all over, there's no point in staying here, come along!'

The rain drove them away, one by one; a few new arrivals slowed down, in cars or on foot, but went on again at once, slightly bothered by not discovering what had happened; those who remained had broken up the circle. Now they had turned away from the last traces of the puddle of salt water and were looking out to sea. The horizon was veiled, uncertain, because of the grey mist. There were few gulls flying, and the earth looked as though it were round.

'Was he in a boat?' asked Hozniacks.

'Unless he was fishing from a rock and fell in,' said Olivain.

'No, no, it must have been a boat that capsized, he was too far from the shore,' said Véran.

'Perhaps he fainted? It does happen,' said the spectacled woman, Simone Frère.

'Yes, but two days ago the sea was very rough,' said Bosio.

'And in two—in two days, he may have drifted a long way. There are strong currents round here,' said Olivain.

'That's true—must be why they've been looking all over for him,' said Hozniacks.

'I saw one drowned man last summer. Young chap. He'd dived in, fully dressed, from one of those cycles on floats. Showing off, probably. And he'd gone down like a stone. They fished him out and tried everything, artificial respiration, massage, injections, the works. But he never came round,' said Jacquineau.

'Yes, I remember seeing about it in the papers,' said Véran.

'But this one wasn't a young man, was he?' said Hozniacks.

'A lot of people get drowned along this coast,' said Simone Frère.

The rain was trickling down their chins and plastering their hair to their heads; if they'd only known, or seen, how they were getting to look more and more drowned. There was only one group left now, with five people, viz.:

Hozniacks –	– fisherman
Bosio – –	– fisherman
Joseph Jacquineau –	pensioner
Simone Frère	– wife and mother
Véran – –	– no occupation

They couldn't tear themselves away. The last memory of the man who had lain dead before their eyes and who still haunted the spot a little, was keeping them together, exposed to the rain. It was their human memory that gave them a fellow-feeling even without love, and made them dread the long, lonely journey over the abyss even more then death or pain. This would go on until the day when— in a month, a week, or less—one of them would refer to the incident for the very last time.

Let's say it would be Hozniacks. In the café, on his way home, he'd tell the story just once more:

'The other evening I was walking along by the sea, coming in from fishing because it was raining. I saw a drowned man. He was all swollen with water, quite blue, and no one could bring him round. There was something in the paper about it next day.

Tired of Life

M. Jean-François Gourre, 54, travelling salesman for a toilet-soap firm, was found drowned yesterday. Accident seems to be ruled out, and a verdict of suicide was returned at the inquest. The unfortunate man is believed to have taken his life by throwing himself from a hired boat. When the body was found it had been in the water for three days. M. Gourre, who was much esteemed in the trade, seems to have given way to a fit of depression. We offer our sincerest sympathy to his family and friends.

'Yes, I felt sure it was suicide. I said so to the others. The chap looked like a suicide; I felt sure from the start that he hadn't been drowned naturally.'

Swathed in black, M. Gourre's widow and her daughter Andrée, aged fifteen and a half, will make their way along the corridors in the Mortuary, following a little bent, white-overalled man who jingles bunches of keys in his pocket as he leads them to the big cold-storage room. He will open the door, turn his bald or pallid skull towards the women and say to them softly:

'This way, please.'

They will follow him; they will watch him scanning the numbers on the drawers; he will pull aside a kind of very clean white sheet from drawer No. 2103 V, and whisper:

'This is the one.'

After identifying the fresh, pink corpse, the little corpse of M. Jean-Françoise Gourre, husband of one and father of the other, they will go away without a word. The subject will never be mentioned again, not at table, not in the living-room, among relatives and friends, nor even to the tradespeople when they do their shopping. At the very most somebody, now and then, may venture to say to one or other of them: 'My deepest sympathy . . .' without even shaking hands.

Between them and him, all will be over; he was not a good man; he often told lies, deceived his wife, used to peer at his daughter through the bathroom keyhole when she was getting into the bath, quite naked. He was a good man. He was a good father. He never went to cafés and was not believed to go often to a brothel. He went to church sometimes on Sundays; and above all he earned an honest, regular living.

He had even promised to buy a television set. He had never existed.

Her husband had been killed in the war, dying a hero's death during the attack on a Japanese stronghold. Andrée's father had been killed in a car or plane crash when she was only three. He was handsome, rich and affectionate. Too bad that fate should have carried him off so soon!

That was pretty much what must have happened, apart from Adam, among a few people, the day that chap was found drowned and then dragged to the roadside, when it was raining and everything was drenched.

So now, as a result, there is a kind of God dwelling in each of them by turns and calling them to Himself, at the hour of His choice, that they may live in what they had never seen before, dead men.

M. They would be forgotten. They would be left to lead their own lives, go home, do what they had to do, all those others, Hozniacks, Guéraud, Bosio, Simone Frère, Olivain, Véran, Joseph Jacquineau, Christberg and little Guillaume. Adam allowed them to pass him on the road. He had been one of the first to leave, but because he was tired, fearfully tired, he had dragged along the seafront. He had stopped for a minute under a plane-tree, to shelter from the rain. But the leaves were heavy with water and the shower easily came through. So he had trailed on again, soaking, his pockets full of rain. He wanted a cigarette, but the packet was wet and the cigarettes spoilt: the paper and tobacco had dissolved into a lumpy paste that lined his pocket.

The idlers were going home in little groups; one could still hear vague snatches of conversation, not all connected with the accident. There was talk of drowning, avalanches, fainting-fits, fly-fishing and politics.

Adam had a stitch in his side. He did not feel at all alone now. He had even stopped trying to understand. He was beginning to remember that he must very often have been mistaken.

When he got to the harbour he paused under the awning of a Bar-Tabac. He looked at the postcards on the revolving stand; there were coloured ones and black-and-white ones.

There was a batch of several showing a young woman with a rather plain face but a lovely figure, wearing a bikini. Adam went into the bar and bought this, together with a packet of cigarettes. Then he came outside again and stood under the awning, sheltering from the rain and looking at the photo. It was in five colours and showed the young woman kneeling on a kind of pebble beach and smiling very hard. With her right hand she was pulling down the bottom half of her biniki, disclosing a patch of plump brown hip. With the other hand she was hiding the tips of her breasts. To make it quite clear that they were bare, her bra was lying on the ground beside her. And to make it quite clear that it was a bra, it had been laid out flat on the pebbles, with the cups sticking up. The whole thing was pretty ridiculous; the card was good quality, shiny, rich in texture, creamy, translucent as sugar, gleaming all over. Running his eyes over it and scratching it with the nail of his middle finger, Adam reflected that it was about a thousand times more erotic than the half-naked woman in the photograph. When you came think of it, the communicative power of this commonplace object was completely separate from its pornographic intentions; the collective message was feeble and not likely to call forth more than laughter or melancholy; but its true essence lay far beyond, it rose to the heights of geometry or technique; sawdust and cellulose formed a halo that sanctified the girl, proclaiming her to all eternity virgin and martyr, blessed among women. She seemed to reign over the world like a madonna, remote from blasphemy, onanism and giggles; the glossy surface of the photo could preserve her for centuries, as safely as a glass case in a museum. A large drop of water, blown by the wind, fell off the edge of the awning, splash into the middle of the postcard. Here it spread out, suddenly, somewhere between the Venus's navel and her left breast.

Adam turned the card over; all it said on the back was:

'Photo Duc' 'A genuine photograph, all rights reserved.' '10, Rue des Polinaires, Toulouse.'

For Adam, who had been betting he would find 'Pretty girl on the beach', or else something vulgar, 'Come down and see me sometime'—that kind of thing—this was a disappointment.

Adam tramped the streets until nightfall. About eight o'clock he ate a piece of bread; he sat on a bench in the bus station. He watched people going past, sharing an umbrella or belted tight into raincoats.

On the other side of the square, behind two or three parked buses, there was a cinema. The front was lit up and a small queue had formed in the rain, waiting for the doors to open. The cinema was called the Rex; the name was written in red neon lighting, which blinked now and then. Under the name 'Rex' there was a big poster, showing some man in a raincoat kissing some woman in a raincoat on a kind of breakwater. They both had red faces and yellow hair, as though they had stayed too long on the beach. The background of the poster was a black blur, except for a big yellow globe just beside them, which looked like a street lamp. But the weird, sinister thing was that this man and woman had such crudely coloured faces, frozen into clumsy stiffness; their eyes were ugly, rolling skywards, their eye lashes were broken, and their gaping mouths looked like wounds bleeding side by side.

The film was called 'Pick-up on South Street', or something like that; Adam thought Samuel Fuller would have been glad to see the poster that had been designed for his film. For a moment he was tempted to go into the cinema. But he remembered he hadn't enough money left. He ate the rest of his bread, and lit a cigarette.

125

A little further along, under the arches, two or three girls were waiting for their bus. They were decked out in flowered dresses, shawls, flesh-coloured stockings, umbrellas, imitation leather handbags, and probably scent if one had gone close enough to smell it. Adam wondered whether it was Saturday. He tried to work it out, but in vain. In the end he decided it must be Saturday, Saturday the dance-hall night, etc. He thought of going to one of the places where he used to spend evenings in the old days, the Pergola, the Shooting Star or the Mammouth Club. To drink a glass of beer and have a girl for a few hours. What stopped him was that he had never enjoyed dancing. He not only danced badly, but everyone knew he danced badly. So, he said to himself, what would be the use? No one would learn anything new. Besides, he hadn't enough money left.

A bus arrived and carried off the girls; a few minutes later they were replaced by other girls, curiously similar in appearance. Near by, watching them and smoking, were two Algerian workmen. They said nothing, just smoked their cigars, and while they smoked they stared at the girls' legs.

There were three buses like this, one after another, and each one took away a little group of girls and workmen. It really must be Saturday. A short time before the fourth bus arrived, a ragged man came in under the arches, dragging a bundle of old cardboard boxes and discarded newspapers, which he must have found in a dustbin. He propped his burden against one of the pillars, right opposite Adam's bench, and sat down on it to wait for the bus. In this position he looked more like a tramp or a beggar than anything else. Adam noticed he wore spectacles.

Adam suddenly got up and walked over to the man, determined to speak to him. After some mutual hesitation they exchanged a few brief remarks, almost in whispers. The spectacled tramp did not look at Adam. His head was

126

bent slightly sideways, slightly forward, and he was staring at the toes of his shoes. Now and then he scratched himself, on the leg, under the arms, or on the head. He did not seem surprised or nervous, only a bit contemptuous, and bored. With his left hand he was steadying the bundle of cardboard and newspapers on which he sat, to keep it from toppling over. He was dirty, unshaven, and he stank. He made no gestures, except that once he pointed vaguely in the direction where the buses came from. He said he didn't smoke, but asked Adam for money all the same; Adam wouldn't give him any.

When the bus arrived the man rose unhurriedly, picked up his bundle of newspapers and cardboard, and got in without so much as a glance at Adam. Following him with his eyes, Adam watched him through the window of the bus as he rummaged in the pockets of his overcoat, which was too big for him, and found the money for his ticket. His bony head was tilted forward, and with his left hand he steadied his glasses because of the jolts, which sent them sliding down his nose a millimetre at a time.

Adam hadn't the courage to wait for the fifth bus. Men were eternal and God was death. Men were eternal and God was death. Men were eternal and God was death. Men were eternal and God was death.

Going into the 'Magellan', you found the cloakrooms and the telephone on your left, at the far end. When you had finished with the cloakroom and opened the door marked 'Gentlemen', while the water gurgled and splashed out of the tank, you looked on a shelf below the telephone to find the directory. To make a call, you had to give the number to the barman. He wrote it on a scrap of paper— 84.10.10—dialled it on the telephone that stood on the counter, and then put the call through to the other telephone, under its sound-proof hood at the far end of the bar. As he did so he waved to you, saying:

'Your number!'

Whereupon you pressed a little red button in the base of the telephone, and heard a nasal voice replying:

'Hello? Hello?'

'Hello? Michèle?'

'This isn't Michèle, it's her sister. Who . . .'

'Oh, I see. Tell me, Germaine, isn't Michèle there?'

'No.'

'Is she out?'

'This isn't Michèle, it's her sister. Who . . .'

'Listen, you don't happen to know where she is?'

'But who's that speaking?'

'A friend of Michèle's, Adam.'

'Adam—oh, Adam Pollo?'

'Yes, that's right.'

'Yes—you've got something important to say to her?'

'Well, yes, rather . . . That's to say—I just wanted to know what, what's become of Michèle. I've not seen her for quite a time, and you understand . . .'

'Yes.'

'You don't know where she's likely to be now?'

'Michèle?'

'Yes, Michèle.'

'Listen, I don't know—she went out about two o'clock, taking the car. She didn't say anything special as she left.'

'And . . . about what time do you think she'll be back?'

'It all depends, you know. It all depends where she's gone.'

'But in the ordinary way?'

'Oh, in the ordinary way she's always home by—by eleven or thereabouts . . .

'Do you mean you don't know whether she's coming back this evening?'

128

'This evening?'

'Yes, all night.'

'Oh, I shouldn't think—I shouldn't think she'd be out all night. It does happen sometimes, of course; she has a girl friend with whom she sometimes spends the night. But I shouldn't think so, all the same. When she's not coming home she usually lets us know, either by ringing up or as she's going off. So as she said nothing to me, I imagine she'll be back before long.'

'I see. And—you think after eleven o'clock?'

'Oh, before that, I think. I don't know.'

'Yes.'

'Listen, the best thing—if you have a message for her, would be to leave it with me, and I'll tell her as soon as she gets home.'

'The thing is, I've no message. I wanted, I wanted just to ask how she was getting on.'

'I know. But if you want to arrange to meet her, or something. Or if you'd like her to ring you back when she gets in. Have you a telephone number or something?'

'No, I haven't got a telephone. I'm in a bar.'

'Then the best thing would be for you to ring back in an hour or two. Before midnight, of course.'

'Before midnight?'

'Yes, about eleven.'

'Yes—the trouble is, I can't. You see I have a train to catch an hour from now. I have to get the boat for Senegal. I'd have liked to say goodbye to her before leaving.'

'Ah—you have to catch a boat for Senegal?'

'Yes, I——'

'Oh, I see . . .'

'Listen: do you think Michèle may be with that girl friend now?'

'I don't know at all.'

129

'You don't know at all. And—you couldn't give me her friend's name? What is it?'

'Sonia. Sonia Amadouny.'

'Has she got a telephone?'

'Yes, she's got one. Would you like me to go and find you the number?'

'If you would, yes.'

'Half a minute, I'll go and see.'

Adam was sweating beneath the sound-proof hood. All sorts of strange noises were going on close to his ear: footsteps, incomprehensible phrases, and then a kind of far-off explanation, between the living-room and the stairs to the first floor: 'Who was that, Germaine?' 'A friend of Michèle's, Mummy, he's going off to Senegal and he wants to say goodbye to her.' 'To Senegal?' 'Yes, and he wants Sonia's telephone number—what is it, exactly, 88.07.54 or 88.07.44?' 'Whose number?' 'Sonia's—you know, Sonia Amadouny.' 'Oh, Sonia Amadouny—88.07.54.' '88.07.54 —you're sure that's it?' 'Yes . . . Are you going to give it to him?' 'Yes.'

'Hello?'

'Yes?'

'88.07.54.'

'88.07.54?'

'Yes, 88.07.54. That's right. Sonia Amadouny, 88.07.54.'

'Thank you very much.'

'Not at all.'

'Good, then I'll give her a ring. Anyway, if Michèle did happen—did happen to come in before eleven . . .'

'Yes?'

'No, never mind, it doesn't matter. I'll try to get hold of her like that, otherwise it doesn't matter. Just tell her I rang up.'

'Right.'

'Right, thank you. Excuse me, and thank you.'
'Goodbye.'
'Goodbye, Mademoiselle.'

Once you begin playing about with the telephone there must be no hesitation; you must never stop to think, not even for a few seconds. What can I say to Amadouny? Isn't it too late to ring her up? Michèle probably won't be there; and so forth. You must go right ahead, call the bar-man, shout '88.07.54', add 'Please, it's very urgent!' rush over to the other telephone, press the red button, and let yourself slip into that spectral language where the words seem to rise up towards invisible clouds, like a mystic's cries of pain. You must cast aside all misgivings, all fear of being laughed at, confer humanity upon the swarthy instru-ment that skids about in your damp clutch, presses its filter-shaped mouth to your ear and, while waiting to establish some nasal communication, murmurs its mecha-nical chant. You must wait, with your head almost invisible between the bakelite shells, warmed by their electricity, until the hissing stops, the sparks begin to click, and from the depths of an abyss there rises a treacherous voice whose falsehood will enfold you, lead you on to a point at which, whether you believe in it or not, you will be obliged to say —hearing your own voice as it passes along the wires and mingles with those distant hellos:

'Hello—Monsieur Amadouny? Could I speak to Sonia, please?'

If she's not there you must stick to it, explain you're leaving for Senegal in half an hour and absolutely must get hold of Michèle. You then learn that Michèle and Sonia have gone out together in Michèle's car. That you missed them by two minutes. That they may have gone into town to dance; but that in any case they've certainly not gone to the cinema, because they talked about that at dinner and said there was nothing worth seeing. They went off together, apparently, not more than two or three minutes ago. They probably won't have gone to dance at the Pergola or the Hi-Fi or the Mammouth, because those are too crowded on Saturday evenings. That leaves the Staréo and the Whisky. Sonia wouldn't mind which, but if Michèle's a snob she'll no doubt have chosen the Staréo. Michèle is 67 per cent snob.

Sixty-seven chances out of a hundred that she'd have dragged Sonia Amadouny to that pretentious night-club, with its fake indirect lighting, its fake easy-chairs upholstered in fake red satin, and its fake gigolos dancing with the fake daughters of fake tycoons. Luckily no one was taken in by it.

There was nobody at the Staréo; the regulars avoided it on Saturday evenings, preferring to come on Mondays, when it was crowded. Adam made his way through the darkened room, looking for Michèle or for Sonia Amadouny; they were not there. He went up to the bar and asked loudly:

'Do you know Sonia Amadouny?'

The barman turned a bored face towards Adam. He had grey temples and a silk tie. He shook his head. Soft music was coming from a pick-up. Leaning on the bar beside Adam there were two smiling, fair-haired pansies.

Adam stared at them and at everything else; it was all really very quiet, very gentle, very nauseating. It was the first time for ages that one had breathed such pure air; one felt like staying here, in this species of oblivion, and waiting for anything or nothing; drinking a little whisky out of a big, cold glass, and standing next to these two handsome, effeminate boys; next to their soft-hued, short-lived suede jackets, next to their over-red lips, their over-white skin, their long, over-blond hair; with their bursts of laughter, their hands, their black, faintly dark-ringed eyes.

But before that, one must walk as far as the Whisky, about a hundred yards away; it was on the first floor, and was probably the most popular night-club in the town. Two adjoining rooms, one with a bar, the other surrounded by leather benches. Adam put his head in at the door. Here the air was tense, packed with noises; the lamps were blood-red, everyone was dancing and shouting. To a jazz record by Coleman, Chet Baker, Blakey. A woman standing behind the cash-desk bent forward and said something to him. Adam couldn't hear. She beckoned to him to come closer. Finally he caught a few words: he took a step towards her and shouted:

'What?'

'I said—come in!'

Adam stood motionless for ten seconds, without thought or speech; he felt he had burst in all directions, was spread out over at least ten square yards of noise and movement. The woman at the cash-desk yelled again:

'Come in—come in!'

Adam made a trumpet of his hands and shouted back:

'No. Do you know Sonia Amadouny?'

'Who?'

'Sonia Amadouny?'

'No.'

The woman added something, but Adam had already stepped back and didn't hear her; what with the darkness, the red lights, the convulsively jerking legs and hips, the two rooms were roaring like engines. It was like being suddenly flung into a steel shell, the cylinder of a motor-cycle, for instance, and imprisoned in four metal walls, with thickness, violence, explosions, petrol, and flames, smuts, coal, explosions, and the smell of gas, thick oil, as

133

viscous as melting butter, bits of black and red, flashes of light, explosions, a great heavy, powerful gust of air that tears you limb from limb, kneads you and crushes you against four cast-iron walls, splashings, metal filings, clicks, forward-reverse, forward-reverse, forward-reverse: *heat*.

Adam shouted again: 'No, I want . . .'

And then, louder: 'Sonia Amadouny!'

'. . . Sonia Amadouny!'

The woman said something in reply and then, as Adam still couldn't hear, shrugged her shoulders and grimaced 'No!'

The rain had almost stopped; just a few drops from time to time. The town was drenched. Adam walked the streets all night. From 9.30 in the evening till 5 in the morning. It was as though there had been a huge sun burning everything along its path, reducing it all to heaps of ashes.

While he walked, Adam was thinking:

(I took the wrong line. I was too off-hand about things. I went wrong. Idiot. What I wanted to do was to trail that girl Michèle. Like I did the dog. I wanted to play a game, like one, two, three, four five, six, seven, eight, nine, ten, eleven, twelve—are you ready?—thirteen, fourteen, fifteen, sixteen, seventeen, eighteen—are you ready?—nineteen, twenty, twenty-one, twenty-two, twenty-three, twenty-four —I'll count up to thirty—twenty-five, twenty-six, twenty-seven, twenty-eight, twenty-nine, twenty-nine-and-a-half, twenty-nine-and-three-quarters—and, and—thirty! and then hunt everywhere in the town. In the angles of walls, in doorways, in night-clubs, on beaches, in bars, in cinemas, in churches, in the parks. I wanted to look for you until at last I'd find you, dancing the tango with a medical student, or sitting in a deck-chair by the sea. You'd have left clues, of course, to help me find you; that would have been in the rules of the game. A name or two, Amadouny Sonia-Nadine, Germaine, a handkerchief on the ground with a streak of pinky orange lipstick on it, a hairpin in a deserted avenue. A conversation between two boys in a self-service restaurant. Some sly hint left under the blue plastic table-cloth at an all-night cake-shop. Or two initials—M.D.—stamped with the tip of a fingernail on a horsehair bench in a No. 9 trolleybus. And gradually I'd have begun to tell myself '*I'm getting warm!*'

And then, at twenty-five past six in the morning, when I was absolutely whacked, I'd have found you at last, belted into your man's raincoat, your lips firm, your hair wet with dew, your wool dress a bit creased; your eyes tired from staying open all night. Alone, nobody with you, cuddled up in a deck-chair on the promenade, looking towards the grey sunrise.

But nobody waits for anybody; there are more important things in the world, of course. The world is over-populated and starving, with tensions on all sides. One ought to search that real world, investigate its minutest details; the lives of individual men and women don't matter.

Much more serious was the universe as a whole. Two thousand million men and women getting together to build things, cities, to prepare bombs, to conquer space.

The newspapers announce: 'The space-ship Liberty II has made seven circuits of the earth.'

'The 100 megaton H Bomb has burst in Nevada.'

And really it was as though a big sun had been shining everywhere, all the time. A pear-shaped sun that could be measured by the Beaufort scale, a sun with down-geared dawns. They were weaving an impenetrable net all round the planet. They were ruling it systematically into squares by extending lines xx', yy', zz'. And inspecting every square.

135

Society was arranging itself in groups of specialists:
That's to say the army, the Civil Service, the doctors, the butchers, the grocers, the metal-workers, the electronic engineers, the Merchant Navy captains, the Post Office clerks.

People were putting up buildings twenty-two storeys high and then planting television aerials on the roofs. Underground they were putting drainpipes, electrical cables, metropolitan railways. They were making the earlier chaos bristle with posts and dykes. They were digging, sinking, burning or blasting. Dynamos were starting up with a soft purring sound and throwing their magnetic fields to every corner of the sky. Aircraft were taking off, with a noise like tearing paper. So were rockets, in saffron-yellow clouds, making straight for the unknown spot in the middle of outer space. And then dissolving into black plumes.

Everything was returning to a new dawn, to a daybreak consisting of millions of united determinations. Above all there was this host of men and women, thirsting for violence and conquest. They were assembled at the world's strategic points; they were drawing maps, naming countries, writing novels or compiling atlases: the names of the places they populated were lined up in columns:

Ecclefechan	Scotland	55.3. N.	3.14.W.
Eccles	England	53.28.N.	2.21.W.
Eccleshall	England	53.28.N.	2.21.W.
Echmiadzin	Armenia	40.20.N.	44.35.E.
Echternach	Luxembourg	49.48.N.	6.25.E.
Echuca	Victoria	36.7. S.	144.48.E.
Ecija	Spain	37.32.N.	5.9. W.
Ecuador, Rep.	South America	2.0. S.	78.0. W.
Edam	Netherlands	52.31.N.	5.3. E.
Eddrachillis	Scotland	59.12.N.	2.47.W.

and their own names filled the books that lay on the shelves in cafés:

Revd. William Pountney
Francis Parker
Robert Patrick
Robert Patton
John Payne
Revd. Percival
Robert de Charleville
Nathaniel Rayner
Abel Ram, Esq.

It was among them that he should have hunted. Then he'd have found everything, including Michèle seated at dawn in a deck-chair, cold and wet with dew, shivering amid these interwoven forces. They were all living the same life; their eternity was slowly fusing with the raw materials of which they were the masters. Fusion, the fusion brought about in blast furnaces, the fusion that boils amid smelting metal as though in a crater, was the weapon that raised them above themselves. In this town, as elsewhere, men and women were cooking in their infernal stew-pans. Protuberant against the hazy background of the earth, they were awaiting something, some supreme event, which would wrap them in eternity. They lived among their machines; naked, stubborn, invincible, they were making their earth resplendent. Their almost completed world would soon wrest them for ever away from all things temporal. It was as though an iron mask were already being laid over their faces; in another century or two they would be statues, sarcophagi: within their bronze and concrete moulds there would live on, concealed, frail but immortal, a kind of particle of electric fire. Then will come the reign of timeless matter; all will be within all. And it seems likely there will be only one man, only one woman, left in the world.

Adam was everywhere at once in the town streets. Outside a park drowned in the darkness, outside a dogs' cemetery, under a hewn-stone porch; sometimes along the tree-lined avenue, or seated on the cathedral steps.

Alone on this plain of stone and metal he kept an eye on everything; he was seen to smoke a cigarette beside the Fontaine Fusse and another under the railway bridge. He was quite incidentally under the arches of the Grand-Place, in the middle of the garden in the Square, or leaning on the railings of the promenade. Or on the beach, confronting a motionless sea. Being ubiquitous, he sometimes passed himself in the street, coming round the corner of a house. At this time, a quarter to four in the morning, there may have been 4,000 or 5,000 adams, the genuine article, going about the town. Some were on foot, others on bicycles or in cars; they were quartering the whole town, filling up even the smallest recesses in the concrete. An adam-woman, in a tight-fitting mauve dress, ran after the adam-man, her stiletto heels tapping loudly, and said:

'Coming with me, baby?'
and the adam-man followed her, as though reluctantly.

Further east in the town, other adam-men were going off to work, whistling. An aged adam-man lay asleep, curled up on a vegetable-barrow. Quite possibly another one of him was dying, with faint cries, in his old yellow, sweat-soaked bed. Or yet another was hanging himself with his belt, because he had no money left, or no woman.

In the Square, in the middle of the lawn, Adam halted at last; he leant back against the pedestal of a statue of himself; then, at about five o'clock, he stopped again, outside a laundry window. Drunk with fatigue and joy, he felt a kind of tears running down his cheeks; he suddenly began

138

to weep, without looking at the hundreds and thousands of windows that were opening behind him. The adams ran past along the echoing pavement; with an effort, as though praying, he repeated two lines of a poem to himself. Exactly fifteen hours ahead of time, a strip of neon lighting reddened at the back of the window, performing a passage from a sunset.

With an effort, as though praying, no longer conscious of darkness or daylight, Adam repeated two lines from a poem:

'"Tis ye, 'tis your estrangèd faces,
That miss the many-splendoured thing.'

N. Sunshine, a man and woman lying on a double bed in a room with half-closed shutters, a terracotta ashtray between them on the sheet, which is grey in some places and scorched in others. The room is square, beige, squat, really set in the middle of the block of flats. All the rest of the town consists of concrete, hard corners, windows, doors and hinges.

On the night-table beside them a wireless set is turned on, pouring out a flood of words only interrupted every eight minutes by an islet of music.

'So we can safely say that the coming year will be, will prove more favourable to the tourist industry and we cannot fail to be gratified by this in view of the considerable importance the emphasis that has always been placed on the tourist industry and particularly on the influx of foreign tourists from which our beautiful country draws its chief source of income (. . .) for this purpose we have already made considerable improvements in our hotel system all along the coast, developing those hotels which were inadequate, improving those which offered no more than a modicum of comfort and thus establishing with more modern hotels the whole tourist organization which is becoming more and more necessary owing to competition from abroad and particularly from the Southern countries such as Italy, Spain and Yugoslavia (. . .) well Monsieur

Duter we are most grateful for the information you have so kindly given us and we shall soon be on the air again for another interview dealing with local tourist resources (. . .) it is exactly nine minutes thirty seconds past two o'clock, Radio-Montecarlo has chosen Lip to give you the correct time (. . .) Two o'clock in the afternoon is the time to relax, but not to relax just anyhow the only relaxation that does you good relax with a cup of coffee (. . .) appreciate the flavour of good coffee, hot or iced as you prefer and relax relax rela . . .'

There is no alarm-clock or clock of any kind on the night-table. The man is still wearing his wrist-watch, which makes a little leather coat right round his skin: apart from this he is naked. The woman is naked too; she has a wedding-ring on the fourth finger of her right hand. Between the first and middle fingers of that hand she is squeezing a cigarette; its crushed, sweat-damped paper shows the outlines of the strands of tobacco. And she is smoking.

Their clothes are rolled up carelessly on a chair, pushed right into the angle between the back and the seat. On the front of the wireless set there is a photo, slipped into the frame round the list of wavelengths; it shows the same man and woman, clothed this time, in a street in Rome; he is smiling, she is not. On the back of the photo they have written their names:

Mme and M. Louise and Jean Mallempart

They wrote their names like that two years ago, for a joke, because they were getting married next month; so they supposed. But that must be old stuff by now. Two hot summers, during which the heat from the valves of the wireless may have twisted the photograph right out of shape. There is nothing terribly tragic, or absurd, in the bedroom where, at this hour, at the third pip exactly ten minutes past two, with sun, closed shutters, sweat, cinema-organ music, nothing definite is moving, except the woman's hand as she smokes, and the round eye of the man, Jean Mallempart, shining below his forehead.

In the grocer's shop on the ground floor of this newish modern block of flats, in the grocer's shop called 'Alimentation Rogalle', the calendar says it is late August, getting near the end of August, something like the 26th or the 24th. This is marked on the square of white paper of the calendar which is sold as 'comic' because it has a joke every day, today's joke is 'What goes "ninety-nine *bump*"? A centipede with a wooden leg.' Above this is a square of cardboard with a picture of a blonde in a spotted dress. She is holding up a glass, and we are told, in red capital letters, that what she is drinking is 'B Y R R H' 'Apéritif'. The place is hot, almost boiling, with that sickly smell of geraniums and that sound of tyres gliding along the streets. We're in summer, and nearing the end of August. On the beaches the deck-chairs creak under the weight of broad, sunburnt, oily backs; dark glasses groan when folded up. In one or two dining-rooms, simultaneously, a red ant is eating straight off the greenish leaf of plastic that imitates a yellow rose or a pink carnation.

Men and women are entering the water; they bathe placidly, waiting a moment with their arms in the air for the slight ripple set up by a motorboat some way from the shore to reach them and wet another few inches of their stomachs; then they throw themselves forward, heads up, out of their depth, and advance through the water which gradually strips them of their names, making them absurd, breathless, jerky.

The water is quite round, and painted a gaudy blue; a mere eighteen inches from the shore a little boy in a bathing-suit is sitting in the sea, counting on his fingers the refuse washed up by the tide. He finds:

one banana-skin
one half-orange
one leek
one piece of wood
one strip of seaweed
one lizard, headless
one empty Artane tube, all twisted
two brown masses, of unknown origin
one piece of what looks like horse-dung
one scrap of cloth (Bedford cord)
one cigarette end (Philip Morris)

On the promenade, still in the sun, where it crosses the Boulevard de la Gare, an old lady is dying of sunstroke. She dies very easily, so easily she almost does it several times. Falling flat on her face on the pavement, without a word, she knocks her hand against the front mudguard of a parked car, and her old, dried-up hand begins to bleed imperceptibly, while she dies. While people go past, while they look for the police, the priest or the doctor, and a woman looking on stiffens and murmurs below her breath

'Hail Mary
Full of Grace
The Lord is with Thee
etc.'

An Italian, sitting on a bench, takes a packet of Italian cigarettes out of his pocket. The packet is three-quarters empty, so that the word 'Esportazione' loses its luxurious implications and meanders over the paper like a drooping pennon. He takes out a cigarette, and the expected happens: he begins to smoke. He looks at the breasts of a girl who walks by. One of those tight-fitting sailor-type jerseys they sell at the Prisunic. Two breasts.

What with all these buildings, these huge grey rectangles, concrete upon concrete, and all these angular places, one soon gets from one point to another. One's home is everywhere, one lives everywhere. The sun is exerting itself on the rough-cast walls. What with this series of old and new towns, one is landed full in the hurly-burly of life; it's like living in thousands of books piled one on top of another. Every word is an event, every sentence a series of events of the same kind, every short story an hour, or more, or less, a minute, ten or twelve seconds.

With flies buzzing round his head and that child yelling down in the yard like a scalded cat, Mathias is trying to write his detective story. He is writing it by hand, on exercise-book paper.

'Joséphime stopped the car:
"You want to get out here?"
"Okay, sonny," said Doug.
The moment he was out of the car he regretted it.
"You shouldn't have played the bloody fool."
The beautiful Joséphime had pulled out a little revolver inlaid with silver, a jewel of Belgian craftsmanship, and was now pointing it straight at Doug's stomach.
"It's really too bad," Doug reflected, "Now the women are beginning to want to put slugs into me too. Where's my well-known sex appeal?"
"So what's going to happen now?" sneered Doug. "You know, my life's insured."
"For your widow's sake I hope it's for a fat sum," said Joséphime.
And she pressed the trigger.'
and Douglas Dog died, or didn't die.

But there are still quite a lot of green, blue-sulphated vines to be seen from many windows. The children pick up snails along the narrow paths, in the sunshine: the snails have curled up in their shells, blindly trusting their lives to the thin layers of rubbery secretion that hold them to the branches of the oleanders. The café terraces are packed. At the Café Lyonnais, people are sitting under the red awnings, talking:

On the beach perhaps?
Waiter, a beer. A beer.
A beer.
Tickets for the National Lottery! Who'll have the prize?
Not me, thank you.
Waiter, a glass of vin rosé.
A vin rosé, yes Sir.
There you are, Sir.
How much?
One franc twenty, Sir.
Including service?
Yes, Sir.
Thank you.
Jean, where shall we sit?
I saw Monsieur Maurin yesterday, and d'you know what he said to me?
Oh yes, he's a funny fellow.
Never. It's impossible, absolutely impossible.
After that I shall go, at any rate; I've got my shopping to do you know, quite a lot of things to get butter meat ribbon for the dressing-gown . . .
Shall we go? Waiter?
But what the hell does it matter, I ask you, what the hell does it matter, so then he said to me all the same . . . But what the hell does it matter to him, eh, what the?

It's a stylish café, where dark red predominates, on the tables as well as on the walls; the tables, all round ones, are arranged geometrically on the pavement, so precisely that on a sunny day when the awning is up, anyone looking out of a second-storey window might think they were seeing the pieces of a one-coloured set of draughts arranged for a game. The glasses on the tables are plain ones, and sometimes show on their edges a semicircle of whipped cream and lipstick, mixed together.

The waiters have white uniforms; with each order they put on the table, at the same time as the glasses, saucers whose colour varies according to the price of what was ordered; the men and women sit eating, drinking and talking quietly; and the waiters move silently, gliding past with empty or laden trays in their hands and napkins under their left arms, undulating along like skin-divers. Most of the noise comes from the street; it is manifold, though in its diversity it combines into a rich sound, more or less monophonic, such as is made by the sea, for instance, or the steady swish of rain; one audible note with millions of variants, tones, modes of expression accompanying it—women's heels, horns tooting, the engines of cars, scooters and buses. A tuning 'A' played simultaneously by all the instruments in an orchestra.

The movement of matter is all of one kind—the grey mass of cars, nose-to-tail in the background. There are no clouds in the sky, and the trees stand perfectly motionless, like dummies.

Whereas animal movement is at its height: strollers and pedestrians are walking along the pavement; arms are swinging and waving; legs are tensed to take the weight of a body, about twelve or thirteen stone; they bend slightly for a second and then become levers on which the rest of the body describes a tiny parabola. Mouths breathe, eyes turn rapidly in their moist orbits. Colours take on movement and their purely pictorial quality is attenuated; the white

146

man becomes more animal in movement. The black man, more Negro.

It is all this that gives him his gentleness, his slightly sinuous, slightly sour disdain, as though he had invented the moon or written the Bible.

He walks along the streets and sees nothing. He goes through whole squares, down entire boulevards—deserted, bordered with plane-trees or chestnuts—he goes past real police-stations, town-halls, cinemas, cafés, hotels, beaches and bus-stops. He waits for friends, for girls, or for nobody; often they don't come and he gets tired of waiting. He doesn't try to find reasons, that kind of thing doesn't interest him, and perhaps after all it's none of his business. So then he walks on again all alone, the sun scatters itself through the leaves, it's cool in the shade, hot in the sunshine. He wastes time, gets excited, walks, breathes, waits for darkness. We can bet he has seen *Libby* on the beach and talked to her, sprawling on the dusty shingle. She talked to him about clothes, boys' and girls' interests, classical music, etc. The bad film she saw.—It's in attending to such matters that one forgets the others; it does you good in the end, and you feel you're gradually recovering your invulnerability, a hero again, projecting all your concentrated brains on a heap of dirty shingle and the noise of retreating waves. Afterwards, an hour later, you go back to the street, quite proud of yourself and reeling like a punch-drunk boxer. Tragedy is a thing of the past? Who cares—we've still got petty details, general ideas, ice-cream cornets, pizza at five o'clock, Film Clubs and Organic Chemistry:

SUBSTITUTIONAL REACTIONS

H atoms may be successively replaced by certain atoms of identical value, such as Cl. Must be exposed to light.

(and bromide) (Br)

$$CH_4 + Cl_1 = CH_3Cl + ClH$$
$$CH_3Cl + Cl_2 = CHaCL_2 + ClH$$
$$CH_2Cl_2 + Cl_2 = CHCl_3 + Cl_4$$
$$CHCl_3 + Cl_2 = CCl_4 + Cl_4$$

(Carbon tetrachloride)

To begin with we've got no psychological reflexes any longer, we've lost them. A girl is a girl, a chap going down the street is a chap going down the street; he's sometimes a copper, a pal or a father, but he's first and foremost a chap going down the street. Ask, and what answer will you get? 'It's a chap going down the street.' Not that we're scatter-brained—not at all; in fact we're more like bureaucrats: under some kind of pressure: off-peak bureaucrats.

Like that woman, Andrea de Commynes. The only one with a face that was rather sallow, rather pale, among all the brown, shining ones; the only one who conceals green eyes behind dark glasses and who is reading, one hand hooked into the curve of her bronze necklace, the other holding her leather-bound book. The pages are worm-eaten and the title runs across the spine of the book, stamped in crooked letters from which the colour has faded:

INGOLDSBY LEGENDS

Not forgetting that plane that's silently crossing the naked sky; not forgetting that statue on which the sun shines in torrents from six a.m. onwards, and which also represents a naked man, in the centre of a basin. And the pigeons, and the smell of earth underneath the paving-stones, and the three old women sitting on the bench, nodding over their everlasting knitting.

Or the beggar—known as the Whistler. The kind of fellow you don't often come across. They call him that because when he isn't begging he walks along all the streets whistling an old tango tune :'Arabella'. Then he stops, settles down in some corner of an old wall, preferably all yellow from dogs and children peeing there; he pushes up his trouser-leg on the side that has the stump, and he calls to the tourists as they go by. When one of them stops, he explains:

'I live as best I can. I manage.

I sell waste paper. I suppose you wouldn't have anything for me?

A small coin for an old cripple?'

The other man says:

'Afraid not, I'm completely broke today,' and adds:

'Do you like—er—that kind of life?'

He replies:

'Well, I've no complaints,' and adds: 'So you really mean it? Not even one little cigarette for me? Sir? For a poor cripple?'

His stump develops scabs in the open air. It often looks like that sort of vegetable that's sold in the market in summer. Thousands of cars are making their way in Indian file to the 'Grand Prix Automobile'. One or two drivers may be killed, perhaps. They'll scatter sawdust on the ground and wait for Monday's paper. There it'll be: 'Tragedy Mars Big Car Race', handled no worse than anywhere else.

Hornatozi is having his wife followed. Hornatozi, the Son in Hornatozi & Son, Corn Merchants. He goes to work in his light-panelled office, and now and then he takes his wife's photograph out of his pocket. Hélène is tall, young and auburn-haired. Like Joséphime and Mme Richers, she often wears a black dress. Hornatozi knows that the day before yesterday, between 3 and 3.30 in the afternoon, she went to No. 99 Avenue des Fleurs. On the

149

negative, which is smeared with finger-prints, Hélène Hornatozi is smiling into space, her head tilted a little to the left. She bears this drifting smile, and from her curved lips there flutters out the mysterious holy spirit that establishes relationships among men; it is as though she lay there dead, laid out on the marble surface of the film, offering beneath her glazed effigy the last vestiges of her woman's body, a parcel of white bones on a black background, a mask from which the flesh has been scooped out and where the colours are reversed; hovering between the air and this translucent screen, Hélène's memory contracts in her negative rigor mortis and her eyes, white pupils on black sclerotic, bore two holes through the rampart that surrounds the living, causing them to believe once and for all in ghosts. It is from this memory fixed by the developing fluid that the woman derives all her power; an insubstantial trace of maleficence draws all eyes to her voluptuous body, formed for love; in Hornatozi's fingers the white figure outlined in black burns with a thousand jealous fires. His thumbs, pressing on the edge, are sweating slightly and will yet again leave the greasy ridges of their prints behind them. He bends forward now, his hypnotized gaze plunging straight into the big hollow orbits where night seems to be falling; for he longs to make the journey, if only as a slave, and come at the end of his sufferings to the delicious intimacy of earlier days, the warmth of being hidden in being, the innocence, the assuaged yearnings, an almost alcoholic inhumation. But she, the woman of whom he is no longer sure whether she is dead or whether she has been unfaithful, shuts him out from her strange domain merely by indicating its celluloid walls; and it is vain for him to bend over the shiny card, vain for his breath to quicken, his mouth throwing rings of steam onto her picture, vain for his temples to swell and his shoulders to sag. Already, he perceives, the wickedness has faded to an abstraction, the powers of evil have destroyed themselves; nothing sharp remains in the photograph except a glint of light reflected from the window onto the rippled surface of the paper, running from side to side, captive, irrational and therefore human, like a bubble on a plate of broth.

Down below lies the long, flat, dusty expanse of the quays, still in the full glare of the sun; boats and derricks; the Customs House; the docks, with eleven dockers working there. Every three minutes the pulley lowers a bale of cotton or a cord of wood. In the globe of stale smells, the rattle of chains, the whiteness, the quivering air, the loads collapse onto the dock.

In a dark hotel room a Negro student is reading a Série Noire detective story. Old women are searching the depths of attic rooms through field-glasses.

Louise Mallempart, a pale dimness amid the silky folds of the sheets, is thinking of a table covered with a damask cloth and bearing enthroned in its centre one large glass of cold water.

All this comes of the heat that is branching out, crawling low down, just above the ground. A tiny, trembling breath of air makes wrinkles round the objects it meets. Earth, water and air consist of masses of black and white particles, mingling in a blur like a million ants. There is nothing really incoherent any more, nothing wild. One would think the world had been drawn by a child of twelve.

Little Adam will soon be twelve; one evening at the farm, one wet evening, while he can hear the cows being brought in along the lanes, while he listens to the Angelus and feels the earth withering, he picks up a big piece of blue cardboard and draws the world.

At the top of the blue cardboard, on the left, he draws a red and yellow ball with his coloured pencils; it's like the sun, except that there are no rays coming out of it. To balance it he draws another ball on the other side, high up on the right—a blue one, with rays. That must be the sun, since there are rays coming out of it. Then he draws a straight line right across the cardboard below the sun-moon and the moon-sun. With his green pencil he makes a lot of little vertical strokes going down into the horizon. These represent corn and grass. Some of them are barbed—those are fir-trees. Black in the white chalk sky, a horse with spider's legs is about to trample on a man put together from cylindrical tins and hairs. And wherever there is space left on the cardboard he draws big stars, brown or mauve stars ringed with yellow. In the middle of each star is a kind of black dot that transforms it into a live animal, watching us with its bacteria-nucleus, its strange, solitary maggot's eye.

A weird universe he is drawing, all the same, the little boy Adam. An arid, almost mathematical universe, where everything is easily understood in terms of a cryptographic code whose key is immanent; in the brown line round the cardboard a large population can be established without fatigue—shopkeepers, mothers, little girls, devils and horses. They are set there, line for line, in an indissoluble, independent, subdivided matter. Almost as though there were a kind of god in a box, giving orders for everything, with eye and finger, and saying to each thing, 'be.' It's also as though everything were contained in everything, to all infinity. That is to say, in this clumsy drawing by the little boy Adam as well as in the calendar from the wholesale grocer's or a square yard of checked cloth.

To give another example of a type of madness with which Adam had grown familiar, one might mention the well-known Simultaneity. Simultaneity is one of the necessary elements of that Unity of which Adam had one day had an inkling, either during the business at the Zoo, or because of the Drowned Man, or in connection with many other incidents we are deliberately omitting. Simultaneity is the total annihilation of time and not of movement; an annihilation to be conceived not necessarily as mystical experience, but by a constant exercise of the will to the absolute in abstract reasoning. The idea is, that when engaged in any particular action, smoking a cigarette for instance, one shall be indefinably aware, all along, of the millions of other cigarettes which are presumably being smoked by millions of other people all over the world. That one shall have the sensation of millions of flimsy paper cylinders, part one's lips and let a few grammes of air mingled with tobacco smoke filter through them; and then the gesture of smoking becomes single and unique. It is transformed into a Stereotype; the habitual mechanism of cosmogony and myth-making can come into play. In a way this procedure is the reverse of the ordinary philosophical method, which begins with an action or sensation and leads up to a concept that contributes to knowledge.

This process, which holds good for myths in general, such as birth, war, love, the seasons, death, can be applied to anything: any object whatsoever, a match-stick on a polished mahogany table, a strawberry, the striking of a clock, the shape of the letter Z, can be recaptured without limit in space and time. And by thus existing millions and milliards of times, as well as their *own* time, they become eternal. But their eternity is automatic: they need never have been deliberately created, and are to be met with in every century and every place. All the components of the telephone are present in the rhinoceros. Emery paper and magic lanterns have always existed; and moon is really sun and sun moon, the earth is Mars, Jupiter, a whisky and soda and that queer instrument that will soon be invented to create objects or destroy them, its structure being known by heart already.

To understand this properly one would have to follow Adam and try the path of certitudes, which is that of materialistic ecstasy. Then time shrinks and shrinks; its echoes become briefer and briefer; like a pendulum allowed to run down, what used to be years soon become months, the months dwindle to hours, to seconds, to quarter-seconds, to thousandths of seconds; and then all at once, abruptly, to nothing. One has reached the only fixed point in the universe and become virtually eternal. In other words, a god, since one needs neither to exist nor to have been created. It is not a question of psychological immobilization nor, strictly speaking, of mysticism or asceticism. For it is not prompted by the search for a means of communication with God, or by the desire for eternity. It would be only one more weakness in Adam were he to attempt to overcome matter, his own matter, by employing the same impulsions as matter itself.

It is not purely and simply a question of desire; just as, a while back, it was not purely and simply a question of the cigarettes people may be smoking *all over the world*. No, what drives Adam is reflection, lucid meditation. Starting from his own human flesh, from the sum of his present sensations, he annihilates himself by a dual system of multiplication and identification. Thanks to these two methods he can reason in the future as well as in the present and the past. Provided one takes these words at their proper value, that is to say as words. Whether close at hand or far off. He gradually obliterates himself by self-creation. He practises a kind of sympoetry and ends not in Beauty, Ugliness, Ideal, Happiness, but in oblivion and absence. Soon he no longer exists. He is himself no longer.

He is lost, a weak particle that still moves, still describes itself. He is no more than a vague ghost, solitary, eternal, measureless, the terror of lonely old women, who creates himself, dies, lives and lives again and sinks into darkness, hundreds, millions and milliards of an infinite time, neither one nor the other.

O. This is how, later on, Adam described what happened next; he told the story carefully, writing with a ball-point pen in a yellow exercise-book which he had headed 'My dear Michèle', as though beginning a letter. The whole thing was found later, half-burnt. Some pages were missing altogether, either because they'd been torn out to wrap something up in—basketball shoes, household refuse—or even as a substitute for toilet paper, or because they had been too badly burnt. So they will not be given here, and their absence will be indicated by blanks of about the same length.

'A few days before the owners would normally be coming back and throwing me out of the house, I got into trouble in the town. I'd gone down there as usual, about two or three o'clock in the afternoon, to try to see Michèle, or the dog, or somebody else, but more especially to buy cigarettes, beer and something to eat. I particularly wanted to see Michèle, because I needed to borrow another 1,000 or 5,000 francs from her; I had made a short list on the back of an empty cigarette-packet,

fags
beer

chocolate
stuff to eat
paper
newspapers if
possible take
a look round

and made up my mind to follow it in that order.

The cigarettes I found at a tobacconist's on the way into the town. A little bar, quiet and fairly cool, called "Chez Gontrand". There were picture postcards on the walls. The counter at the tobacconist's end was a wooden one, painted brown. The woman behind it was between sixty and sixty-five years old. She wore a striped dress. An Alsation dog lay asleep at the far end of the bar; the rolls of fur round his neck hid the aluminium plate rivetted to his collar and the name—Dick—that was engraved on it.

I bought the beer at a self service grocery which was spacious, clean and airy. As I went in they gave me a red plastic basket with perforated sides, to hold whatever I bought. Into it I dropped just one bottle of light ale, making a noise of glass hitting plastic. I paid and went out.

The chocolate, in the same shop. But I stole that. I pushed the tablet inside my shirt, one end wedged behind the belt of my trousers. It made a bulge, so as I went past the pay-desk I had to pull my stomach in hard, to hide the lump. I could scarcely breathe. The girl at the desk didn't notice, nor did the big lout who's supposed to watch what goes on along the shelves. It seems to me they don't give a damn, in that joint.

This left the stuff to eat, the newspapers and the paper.

The stuff to eat:

I bought a tin of stew at the Prisunic.

The newspapers:

I found these in my usual way, you know, by hunting in the refuse-bins that are hung on the lamp-posts. I found a magazine in good condition, the local dental magazine. Good-quality paper with lots of blank spaces; I said to myself this makes a change, I shall have fun mixing it all up, sockets and dentures, molars and killing the nerve by method B.

The paper:

At the Prilux, a school exercise-book. (This one is almost finished already; when I've filled three more like it I can begin to think about finding a publisher. I've already got a striking title—The Complete Bastards.)

The most important thing was: if possible take a look round.

~~That is to say, while I was walking round the town, keep a look out for things that might be useful later on, perhaps try to find an empty house, even a tumble down one, where I could live when the one up on the hill becomes impossible, and try to see the dog, lots of animals, play games of my own, have a bath at the Public Baths, and borrow 5,000 francs from Michèle. In the first place don't forget that I~~ If I could find some kind of work, something that didn't need much attention, some physical job, washer-up in a restaurant, layer-out at the Mortuary or crowd work at the film studios, I'd be satisfied with that. I should earn just enough to buy a packet of cigarettes when I want, once a day, for ex., & paper to write on, and a bottle of beer too, once a day. Anything more is luxury. I wish I could go to the ~~USA, they say one can live like that over there, and have sun in the South, and nothing to do except write, drink and sleep. Another idea would be to take holy orders, why not?~~

I once knew a fellow who was a potter. He married a woman called Blanche and he lives in a house up in the hills. I went to see him one day, at three in the afternoon; it was very hot, and there were beans climbing over a pergola. The sun was hardening everything into scabs. He was working under the pergola, half naked. He was scratching Aztec patterns on some kind of earthenware pots; and the sun was drying the clay, making little specks of powder all round the vase; afterwards he laid on the colours and they were fired in the oven, heat on heat. It was all in harmony. There was a salamander with a forked tail asleep on the sun-baked ground. I don't think I had ever in my life seen so much heat upon heat. The outside temperature was 39° Centigrade and the oven temperature was 500°. That evening his wife Blanche cooked the beans. He was a good chap; he was always nearly dead by the end of the day. Quite white, a patch of dancing air, an equilateral cube gradually baking.

I said to myself that I too might have a house in the country. On the side of a kind of flinty mountain; under the scorching stones there'd be snakes, scorpions and red ants.

This is how I should spend my day: I'd have a patch of ground, all covered with stones, exposed to the sun from morning till night. In the middle of it I would make bon-fires. I'd burn planks, glass, cast-iron, rubber, anything I could find. I'd produce kinds of statues, like that, straight out of the fire. Black objects, scorched in the wind and dust. I should throw on tree-trunks and burn them; I should twist everything, blacken everything, coat everything with a crackling powder, send the flames soaring, thicken the smoke into heavy coils. The orange-coloured tongues would make the earth bristle, shake the sky right up to the clouds. The livid sun would fight against them for hours on end. Insects would come by thousands to fling themselves on my bonfire and burrow head-first into the colourless layer at the foot of the blaze. Then, blown upwards by the heat,

159

they would climb the flames like an invisible column and fall back in a soft shower of ashes, delicate and fragile, transformed into charred specks on my head and my bare shoulders; and the blast of the flames would blow on them and make them shudder against my skin; it would give them new legs and new wing-sheaths, a new life that would carry them into the air and deposit them in swarms, soft as crumbs of smoke, in the holes between the stones, right down to the foot of the mountain.

About five o'clock in the afternoon—let's say—the sun would win. The sun would burn up the flames, leaving only a round black patch in the middle of the bonfire area, with all the rest as white as snow. The black patch would look like the sun's shadow, or a bottomless hole in the ground. And nothing would remain except charred tree-trunks, lumps of metal looking as though struck by lightning and melted, twisted glass, drops of steel like water among the ashes. Everything would have grown like dark plants, with grotesque stems, driblets of cellulose, crevices full of glowing coals. Then I'd collect all these convulsed shapes together and pile them up in a room in the house. I should enjoy living between a mountain of white stones and a burnt-up jungle. It's all connected with heat. It would decompose everything so as to reconstitute a world blighted by drought; heat, pure and simple. Thanks to that everything would be white and hard and set. Like a block of ice at the North Pole it would represent material harmony, so that time would cease to flow on. Yes, it would be really beautiful. By day it would be heat plus heat, and by night, blackness plus coal.

[

And one day I'd take an old car, run it into the middle]
of the bonfire site, and pour petrol over it. Then I'd pour
petrol over myself, get into the car and set fire to it.

And I should keep on my dark glasses, so that when they
found my charred body, my round skull, there would be a
funny, black caricature of an insect there, its plastic body
would have sunk boiling into the sockets of my eyes. Two
wire rods, like spindly legs, would be sticking up on either
side, making antennae for me.

I hope no one would recognize any trace of me in that
blistered mummy. Because I would very much like to live
all naked and all black, once and for all burning, ~~once and
for all created.~~

Michèle.

I made a very thorough search for you.

First of all there was that fellow Gérard, or François, I
forget his name. I knew him in the days when I used to
play pinball. Or when I was a student of some kind. He
didn't recognize me, because since then I've grown a
beard and I wear dark glasses. He told me he'd seen you
going down towards the Vieux Port.

I went down there and sat on a bench in the shade. I
waited a bit, with the idea of having a rest. I was just
opposite the jetty and there were two Englishmen there,
dressed up like yachtsmen, talking. They were pretending

161

to be deathly bored with the Mediterranean, and one of them said:

"I am looking forward to the Shetlands."

Quite a lot of people were going past, pointing out the white boats to their children.

An hour later I went up again to the Grand-Place, the one with the fountain. In the Café I ran into a girl you must know, called Martine Préaux. I told her that Gérard, or François—anyhow, that dark chap in the pink shirt—had seen you going down towards the Vieux Port. She said something like this:

"He's crazy, I've just seen Michèle in the other Café, further down. She was with an American."

"An American? An American sailor?"

"No, not a sailor, just an American. A tourist."

I asked her if she thought you'd still be there. She said:

"I really don't know. Perhaps; it's not so very long ago," and added: "You'd better go and look."

You weren't in the other Café any longer, always supposing you ever had been. The waiter didn't know. He didn't want to know. It would have meant tipping him, and I couldn't afford it; so I sat down all the same and had a glass of grenadine-and-water.

As I wasn't sure what to do, and as I mostly can't think without doodling on a piece of paper, I tore out the first page from my exercise-book and drew a plan of the town, cross-hatching the places where you might be. It took me nearly an hour. In order of importance, the places were:

> at home
> the cafés in the Place
> the shops in the Avenue
> the seafront
> the church

the bus-station
the Rue Smolett
the Rue Neuve
the Descente Crotti

After that I got up, paid for the grenadine, and went straight off to look for you. I had about 50 francs left. Luckily I'd still got the [

what you said to me. He had a rather flabby face, a crew-cut, and long, fat legs. As it was dark, I went to the far end of the bar and asked for a glass of red wine.

At first I hadn't meant to drink so much. If I'd wanted to get tight I'd have started with something else; beer, for instance; I can't carry red wine. When I begin drinking that I always throw it up in the end, and I don't care for throwing up. It's the same with excrements, I don't like to think I'm leaving part of myself somewhere. I want to remain complete.

Why I drank too much this time was that I had the 5,000 francs in my pocket, I'd nothing else to do, and I didn't like the look of the American. I began by ordering:

"A glass of red wine"

when I might just as easily have said: "A Misty Isley" or "An espresso and two croissants".

The point is that after that I was too tired to call a different order to the waiter. I'd say:

"The same again."

"Red?" he'd ask.

And I'd nod.

A funny thing happened then. The Bar was crowded, the waiters were hurrying to and fro, and you were sitting near the door with that American fellow. I looked at all of you, one after another, and you were all doing the same thing, that's to say drinking, talking, crossing your legs, smiling, smoking and puffing out the smoke through your nostrils, etc. You all had faces, arms and legs, backs to your heads, sexual organs, hips and mouths. You all had the same lump of reddened skin on your elbows, the same tear-glands, their edges showing, the same double cleft in the small of the back, the same type of ears, curled like a shell, no doubt cast in the same mould, hideously identical. Not one of you had two mouths, for example. Or a foot in place of the left eye. You were all talking at the same time and telling one another the same things. You were all, all, all alike. You were living in twos, in threes, fours, fives, sixes, tens, twenty-nines, one hundred and eighty-threes, etc.

I amused myself by reconstructing your talk:

Suzanne's in a nursing-home.

    Of course not, never, why on earth? There's no reason!

It's because of Georges, I saw him the other evening at the Mexico, he

    It's true in a way. But Ionesco isn't

    stinker if anyone asks you that say it's

    Hi! Jean-Claude, want a cigarette? You know

165

half a pint of draught you wouldn't have twenty
  francs
It's Henri, a pal of Jackie's. I've a job
Then what's the matter?
D'you want to know the truth? You know the truth?

necessarily modern, he's in the tradition of the
me, afterwards. I've had enough of this, shall we go?
on Thursday, when it rained, well, the thing worked
at the City Stores I unload packing-cases twice
to put a record on it's not worth mentioning
so then I had a good shower. He said to me it's
He tells you stories, okay, they're good ones, but you get
  tired of them, there isn't
realists, you know, of Monnier, Henri Monnier, for instance.
It's not ten o'clock yet, let's wait another
All the same I went to Monaco
it's all washed up now   here?
a week, it's quite well paid and it gives me a bit of exercise
no use counting on me for the next match
Hi, Claude!   No news
a word of truth in it all any more
five minutes anyhow. I'm sure he'll come, he kept saying
  he would.

But there was no sense in all these words, all these intermingled phrases. You were all men and women, and never
until then had I felt so strongly that you constituted a race.
I suddenly wished I could take refuge with the ants and
learn as much about them as I knew about you.
I drank four or five more glasses of wine; I'd had nothing
to eat, and drink on an empty stomach always makes me ill.
I drank more than a bottle of red wine, down there at the
far end of the bar.

I had a kind of sick taste on my tongue. It was very hot, and everything felt clammy. I remember tearing a page out of the exercise-book and writing in the middle of it:

Interrogation concerning a disaster
among the ants.

Then I wrote some stuff on the back of the sheet; but I've lost it since then and I can't remember what it said. I think it mentioned powder, mountains of white powder.

When I left the bar I was pretty well plastered. Going past you I saw you were showing some photographs to the American. I felt ill, so I went for a long walk in the Old Town. I staggered along, leaning against the wall. Twice I vomitted into the gutter. I had no idea what time it was, or what I was doing. I sat down on the rim of the Fontaine Saint-François; I put the parcels of food and the exercise-book down beside me. I smoked two cigarettes one after another. A cold breeze was flapping the awnings outside the shops.

My matchbox was empty; I made it into a boat, sticking a burnt match upright in the lid. I threaded a scrap of paper onto the match, to make a sail, and put the whole thing into the fountain. It began to drift across the black surface. Puffs of wind hit the sail and sent it zigzagging towards the middle of the basin. I watched it for over a minute, and then suddenly lost sight of it. The fountain swallowed it up in a shower of drops and hid it behind a curtain of mist. The water began to bubble round it, and a few seconds later it vanished downwards like a shadow and evaporated in the tumult of greyness and black whirlpools.

That was the moment when I'd have liked to hear somebody say, somebody say to me, Bastard!

[

In the end I went away after all, because a police car
had seen me and slowed down. I went round through the
Old Town and up again to the gardens behind the Bus
Station. I thought I could lie down on a bench and get
some sleep.

In the gardens I found you and the American fellow.
When I recognized you I thought I'd have a ball, because
it was dark and you looked as though you were enjoying
yourselves. I sat down beside you and began telling you
stories. I forget what they were, riddles, ghost stories or dis-
jointed phrases. I have an idea I told you about my great-
grandfather, who was Governor of Ceylon. But I forget.
The American lit a cigarette and waited for me to go. But I
didn't feel like going. I asked you for another 1,000 francs.
Michèle said she'd given me enough for the time being; I
replied that she had never returned the raincoat I'd lent
her, and that it was certainly worth more than 5,000.

Michèle, you lost your temper and told me to clear out.
I laughed, and said give me 1,000 francs. The American
threw away his cigarette and said:

"Now, come on, get going."

I replied by swearing in American. Michèle got scared
and gave me the 1,000 francs. The American stood up and
said again: "Hey, get going". I repeated the same oath.
Michèle threatened to call the police. But the American
said not to worry, he'd manage by himself. I couldn't see

168

straight. He made me get up off the seat and pushed me backwards. I came back at him, still talking, saying whatever came into my head, I can't remember what. I think I was telling him about the raincoat, that it had cost 10,000 francs, that it had a cloth lining; and also about everything we'd done that day up in the hills. Michèle began to walk away, saying she was going for the police. The police station was just across the gardens.

The American hadn't understood a word I was saying, because I'd spoken very fast, in a muffled voice.

He came back at me to push me backwards again, but I grabbed him by the collar. Then he hit me, first to the left of the chin and then again, under the eye. I tried to land a kick in his groin, but I missed. Then he began thumping me in the face and the stomach, with his fists and knees. Until I fell on the gravel path. He didn't stop at that. He put his two fat knees on my chest and bashed my face as hard as he could. He nearly knocked me out, and he broke one of my front teeth; in doing that he must have hurt his fist, because he left off at once. He got up, panting, and went out of the gardens, calling Michèle.

After a minute I managed to turn over, and I crawled on all fours to the bench. I sat down and wiped my face with my handkerchief; I didn't feel any pain except from my broken tooth, but I was bleeding a lot. He must have driven his fist into my nose. In any case both my eyes were swollen up like oranges. As I wiped away the blood I was muttering under my breath; I was still a bit tight, and I could find nothing to say except:

"Because of that stinker I shall have to go to the dentist, because of that bastard I shall have to spend 2,000 francs on going to the dentist."

Not more than five minutes later I saw the American and Michèle coming back with a copper. I just had time to get away through the bushes and over the hedge. I went back to the Old Town and washed my face and hands under a fountain. I had a cigarette to relax myself. My tooth was beginning to jag; it was half broken and felt as though the nerve had grown out through the enamel like a blade of grass. I thought to myself, I must be getting home, to the deserted house at the top of the hill.

I went back there as quickly as I could. Passing the church by the harbour I saw it was five-and-twenty to five. There were cars going by with their lamps alight, and animals all over the place, in pairs, uttering weird cries. I was thinking all the time, "I've been sick twice and to-morrow I shall have to go and see the dentist, the dentist—dentist." I was thinking all the time about the leather chair and the steel levers whirling and the sickly smell of fillings, in the square of stale, cool air, very hygienic.'

[

]

At this point three pages of the exercise-book have been torn out. The fourth has a drawing on it, an aerial view of some sort of town. The streets are drawn in with a ball-point pen. A red spot, like a Square, has been made by pressing on the paper a thumb covered with blood from a scratched pimple. A cigarette-end has been crushed out at the bottom left of the page. All this with considerable application, it would seem, and great self-satisfaction—as evidenced by an eyelash that must have fallen off during the exaggerated time for which Adam's head was bent over the paper. One may reckon that about three or four days elapsed between the page before the missing ones and the page that follows the gap. This is the last page in the famous yellow exercise-book. There are only a few lines on it, also written with a ball-point pen. The bottom of the page has been torn off, and there is a lot of scratching-out; in some places the words underneath are still legible, in other places they are completely obliterated. There are gaps in a few of the words, where the pen skidded on the greasy paper.

'Sunday morning, my dear Michèle,
Michèle and the American must have gone to the police and given away my hiding-place. Very early this morning I was woken by a noise; alarmed, I got up and looked out of the window. I saw two or three men climbing the hill, not talking. They were walking fast, and looking up at the house every now and then. ~~I thought at once they must be coppers,~~ anyhow I had just time to grab two or three things and jump out of the window. They didn't see me because there's a line of ~~rose-bushes beans~~ rose-bushes in front of the window. I went uphill a bit, above the house, then I sloped off to the left and doubled back along the dry bed of a stream. ~~I passed not~~ very far from them, and at one moment I caught sight of them clambering up through the patches █████████ of briars. I took care not to make a noise by kicking any loose stones. The ███████ of them.
I came out on the road; at first I walked along the bank at the side, then I got down on the road. It wasn't long after sunrise; there was a glimpse of the sea to the left, between the pines. The scent of pines and grass was overpowering. After that I strolled along as though I were out for a walk. Five hundred yards further on I came to a narrow lane running down to the seashore, so I took that. I thought it was better not to keep on the main road, because the coppers would be bound to recognize me if they came past by car. I'd left my watch behind in the house, but by the sun it was eight o'clock, not more. I was hungry and thirsty.
Down below, near the beach, there was a café just opening. I had a cup of chocolate and an apple fritter. My broken tooth was hurting again. And I had about 1,200 fr.

left. I began to wonder whether I oughn't to go into exile.
To Sweden, Germany or Poland. The Italian frontier
wasn't far off. But it wouldn be   y with no passport
or money. ~~Or I thought I might perhaps go and see my
mother.~~ I no longer needed to write it on the back of an
empty cigarette packet: what I was going to do was to take
a look round. In a town there are two kinds of houses one
can live in—ordinary houses, and homes. There are two
kinds of homes—mental homes and homes for the night.
Among homes for the night, some are for rich people and
some for poor people. Among those for poor people there
are some with separate rooms and some with dormitories.
Among those with dormitories there are some that are
cheap and some that are free. Among those that are free
there's the Salvation Army. And the Salvation Army won't
always take you in.

That's why, by and large, it was nice to live all alone in a
deserted house at the top of a hill.

Of course it was short on what people call comfort.
You have to sleep on the floor unless the owners have left a
bed, which they hadn't in this case. The water is nearly
always cut off (except the stand-pipe in the garden, you
remember, Michèle?). You have no protection against
burglars or animals: it means taking care of yourself; and
when one's alone one rea   doesn't de   oneself efficiently against bugs, mosquitoes, spiders, or even scorpions
and snakes. And then the owners are always liable to turn
up suddenly. S   mes they get angry when they find
there's somebody in their house. One hasn't much of an
excuse, especially in hot weather and when one's a young
chap, as tough as the next, in other words quite able to
work—and particularly when one had a room of one's own
in the town, with everything one needed. They may go so
far as to call the police, and one's soon picked up, a tramp

172

declared to be "of no   wn   ress", a thief, a deserter—
breaking and entering, confidence trick, blackmail or
mendicancy.

I'm not blind or crippled. I shall go off to the cold
countries; I shall travel in a goods-train and bed in the
street in Rotterdam. I shall sit on a bollard beside a fishing-
net and go down to the beach to bathe. The dog will perhaps
come past here today, Sunday, 29th August, nearly nine
o'clock in the morning. It's hot and sultry; it seems there'll
be fires on the hill-sides round about. Here I'm hidden
away.

Unf [

]
On the back of the exercise-book Adam has signed his
name, in full: 'Adam Pollo, martyr.' Although one can't
say for certain, it is extremely probable that the above
passage was concluded in the place where it accidentally
turned up later on, in the 'Gents' at the Torpedo Snack-Bar.

P. Towards the end of the morning, about noon or nearing one o'clock, he had become just a man in the middle of the beach. His long, skinny body was stretched out on the scorching pebbles. To let the air through a little and reduce the roasting effect of the sun, he had propped himself backwards on his elbows, leaving a narrow gap between his spine and the ground. He had settled close to the water's edge, so that whenever a motorboat rushed past out at sea, towing somebody on water-skis, it wetted the soles of his feet with the ripples in its wake.

At a distance, and from behind, he looked much the same as ever. He was still wearing the dark blue shorts with oil-stains on them, and the sun-glasses with gilt wire frames. His clothes were folded in a heap beside him, topped by a two-month-old magazine; this had originally been open in the middle, at a page dealing with a railway accident; but the wind, blowing from one side, had closed it again; now it was the back cover that lay upwards, showing a little boy eating spaghetti and cheese. Further along the beach another little boy was playing all by himself, paddling barefooted in the water. Adam was not looking at him; Adam was about thirty years old now.

Adam Pollo had a longish head, with a slightly pointed top. His hair and beard, roughly hacked with scissors, were full of tangles and matted locks. His whole face had some lingering trace of good looks, rather large eyes, or perhaps a soft, immature nose, cheeks that were boyish, *beardless* under their covering of yellow beard. He had a narrow torso filled with dozens of ribs; it was stretched by his drawn-back arms and did not look very sturdy. His shoulders were bulgy in front, with muscles no doubt; his arms were bony. His hands were shortish, broad and plump, with an undeniable air of hands that couldn't undo the fastening on even the easiest bra. The rest was in proportion. But seen at close quarters, with the sun making patches on it, and the splashes of sea-water, Adam's body looked as though it were being gradually spotted with all kinds of colours, from bright yellow to blue.

Thus camouflaged, he was caught in a multitude of other spots—brown, green, black, black-and-grey, white, ochre, dirty red; from far off he looked like a small child, from nearer, like a young man, and from close to, like a kind of funny old man, centenarian and innocent. He was breathing rapidly. Each time he breathed in, the hairs round his navel straightened up to denote the fleeting presence of about 2 litres of air, which penetrated his bronchial tubes, dilated them down to the smallest, stretched his ribs and pushed away the top of the stomach and the smaller intestine with a thrust of the diaphragm. The air went right down inside, echoing with his heart-beats, the furthest recesses of his flesh turned blood-red and his veins were shaken at regular intervals by a great blue tide that swept up through his body. The air filtered in everywhere, warm, laden with smells and microscopic scraps. It invaded the mass of meat and skin and sent tiny electric shocks through and through it. Everything functioned along its course: the valves closed, the capillaries of the windpipe drove out the dust, and in the lowest depths of the great damp cavity, stained purple and white, the carbon dioxide accumulated, waiting to be driven upwards, ready to be exhaled and to mingle with the atmosphere; it would go to hover here and there on the beach, in the holes between the stones, on the sweating foreheads, adding to the density of the steel-grey skies. Deep down inside Adam was an agglomeration of cells, nuclei, plasma, atoms combined in any number of ways; nothing was airtight any longer. Adam's atoms could have mingled with the atoms in the stones, and he might have been drawn down quietly through the ground, the sand, water and slime; everything would have crumbled together, as though into an abyss, and have vanished into the blackness. In Adam's left femoral artery an amoeba had formed its cyst. And the atoms were revolving like infinitesimal planets in his immense, cosmic body.

Yet in confrontation with others, as he lay in the foreground of the beach with both feet trailing in the sea, he was an individual; the sun's yellow-white rays fell vertically on his sugar-loaf skull, and with his projecting jaw, his scrubby beard and his general air of being a specimen, he looked more and more like a character in the first part of a Greek play. Just now he was smoking a cigarette; sun-blinks flew past his eyes like artificial flies and then burst like bubbles. Salt whitened on the hairs of his body. And the same little boy paddled about in the sea, singing in a drone:

'. . .Criaient la gloire
de Dieu,
Chantaient l'amour
de Dieu . . .'

He stopped for a glance at his mother, who was lying further up the shingle, abandoned to sleep; and then began again, on the wrong note,

'. . . *Criaient la gloire*
de Dieu, etc.'

Planes flew overhead without a sound, between two layers of atmosphere. People were going off to lunch. A wasp with one wing half torn off was running over the stones; twice it nearly wheeled inland, but losing its sense of direction in this chaotic desert it made a mistake and crawled to meet its death—towards the sea, where a single drop of salt water drowned it in the sunshine. Now the little boy was singing:

'Oh Sarimarès
belle amie d'autrefois,
en moi tu demeures vi-ive.'

in steadier voice. Then he climbed up the beach, knocking Adam's magazine to the ground as he went past. After which he went on more cautiously, staring at Adam's back with his two small, heavy-lidded eyes; until he reached the bath-towel where his mother lay asleep, pulled it towards him, sat down and forgot.

Not long after this, Adam got up and went away. He walked quickly to the Post Office nearest to the harbour and went to the Poste Restante window. The clerk gave him a bulging envelope, a fat letter. On the envelope was written:

Adam Pollo,
Poste Restante No. 15
and the address.

Because it was cool there, and perhaps because he didn't quite know where else to go, Adam opened the letter in the Post Office. He sat down on a bench not far from the table with the telephone directories. Beside him was a girl making out a money-order. She had to have several shots at it, with pauses for mental arithmetic; she was sweating, and tightly clutching a ball-point pen with an advertisement printed on it and a rubber band twisted round it.

Adam unfolded the letter; there were three pages of large writing, much more like drawings or hieroglyphs than the Roman alphabet; it must have been traced by a heavy hand, a not very feminine hand, accustomed to bearing down weightily on flat surfaces, and more especially on sheets of paper. A touch of fantasy in the arrangement of the letters and the slope of the final 's's suggested affection, liveliness, or perhaps simply the faint irritation of having to write on the off-chance, with no guarantee that the letter would be read. The pages lay there, undeniably, offering a message which one must be able to read between the lines, kind of ingenuously cunning riddle. Changeless, at all events, as though engraved on some stone in a wall, a message from a mortal hand which could never be effaced by time, which offered itself, clear as a date, abstruse as the chart of a maze.

The letter had been waiting in its pigeon-hole at the Poste Restante for over a week.

19th August

My dear Adam,

When your father and I found your note in the letter-box we were very much surprised, as you can imagine. We were not expecting anything of the kind—neither what you have done, nor your way of telling us about it. We hope you aren't keeping anything from us—that there's nothing serious behind all this. Though neither your father nor I liked your showing so little confidence in us. We still feel hurt, I assure you.

Your father was terribly against the idea of writing to you Poste Restante, as you asked us to do in your note. We

178

had a long argument about it and, as you see, I've gone against his wishes and taken it upon myself to indulge your whim.

But I feel somehow that I'm wrong, because I don't know what to say. I wish I could have a quiet talk with you, get you to explain why you acted as you did, and try to guess what it is you need. I don't feel that a letter will do much good in that way—particularly a surreptitious one like this. But since you wanted it, I'm writing it all the same. I'll try to make it a friendly one, to get you to understand the foolishness of your behaviour and the dreadful anxiety it is giving your father and me. As soon as you receive this letter, answer it by return, no matter what your plans are and what you may be doing. Tell me why you went off like that without a word, where you are now, and if there's anything you need. You must realize that's the first essential, so as to relieve our anxiety and soothe our feelings. Do that to please me, Adam, it's all I ask.

I'm enclosing the note you left us when you went away. If you read it you will understand that it was nothing like enough to set our minds at rest. We weren't expecting anything of the kind. You'd said nothing to us about a journey, or about holidays. We thought your national service had tired you and that you'd stay with us for a rest—we were thinking we might all go to stay in the country with your aunt for a time. We didn't say much about it, of course, but you had seemed tired lately, and I knew you didn't like making plans. Needless to say, this has put an end to our holidays.

Philippe had written to us the week before. He'd agreed to join us at Aunt Louise's as soon as he could get away from his work, and to have a family August. Your father had managed to get leave for the whole month, and I took it for granted you would like the idea. I was looking forward to being all together again, like old times; you and Philippe are grown up now, but you know we only have to get together, the four of us, and you're both my boys again and I forget your age and my own. Your father was very angry when he knew what you'd done. Why didn't you say anything about it beforehand, Adam? Why not have told us? Or at least told me, your mother? Yes, why didn't you try to explain things to me? If you had to go away for some reason or other, if it was absolutely necessary for you to be away for a time, you can be sure we should have understood. We'd have made no objection——

Remember the time before, fifteen or sixteen years ago, when you wanted to leave home—— You weren't twenty-nine then, only fourteen; but you remember I made no objection to the idea. I felt you needed to get away from us for a while. The quarrel with your father was a silly business, of course, but I could feel it went deeper than a row about breaking the blue bowl. Your father's a quick-tempered man, as you know—— He didn't really mind about the blue bowl either; but he thought you were being cheeky, defying his authority, and that was why he boxed your ears. He was wrong, and he apologized—but remember what I did. I caught you up on the stairs and asked you to think it over—I explained that you were too young to go away all by yourself, into the world—I said you'd do better to wait a bit and get over your anger. I said you might wait a week or two and then, if you still wanted to leave, you could look for a job somewhere, apprentice yourself, for instance. You could have made an honest living on your own, if that was what you wanted. You thought it over carefully, and you understood. You cried a little, because your pride was wounded and you felt you'd lost a battle. But I was glad for you, because I knew it was the only thing to do.

So, Adam dear, what I can't understand is, why didn't you do the same this time as over the blue bowl? Why didn't you come and talk to me? I'd have advised you like I did then, and have tried to help you. You can't imagine how your note hurt me, it was so short and cold, and it put me in a position where I had no chance of helping you—— Your father was angry, but with me it's different. All these years of trust and affection can't just be washed out, my darling boy. I'm sorry you didn't think of all this before going away—for I'm certain you didn't. But I hope it's all nearly over now. As soon as you get this letter, do come home; we won't criticize you or ask you to explain —it will soon be forgotten. You're grown up, you came of age long ago, and you are free to go wherever you choose. We'll talk about that, if you like. If you don't want to come home right away, send us a long letter, addressed to both of us. But Adam, I do beg you not to leave us with the bad impression of a hasty note, scribbled at a café table. Don't leave us feeling worried and disappointed. Send us an affectionate letter, Adam, to show that we're still your parents, and not a couple of strangers you dislike. Tell us what you mean to do, where you want to work, how you're getting along, where you intend to go—— I see in the papers that teachers are wanted in central Africa and Algeria; it's not particularly well paid, but it might do as a beginning and lead to something else.

Then there are appointments as assistant professor of French in Scandinavia—and there must be lots of others like that. With your qualifications you could easily find a job in one of those countries, unless you'd rather stay here. In that case you could take a room in town, in whatever district you like. We would lend you the money, you could pay us back later on. You'd come to see us now and then during the week, or you'd write to us. In any case we should know what you were doing, if you were well, whether you were having difficulties about money or anything.

You see, Adam, you must realize things can't go on like this for ever. You can't spend the rest of your life with a wall between yourself and us; you can't arrange your life on a mere whim. You mustn't. Sooner or later you'll have to be on friendly terms with one or other of us—or else you'll have to get along with strangers. You must form a circle of friends, where you can find affection; otherwise you'll be unhappy and you will probably be the first to suffer for it. So as in any case you will have to give up this abrupt, suspicious attitude, why not do so right away, and with us? Everything your father and I have done for you we have done in the attempt to overcome your unsociability and shyness—we persist in our affection because we don't want other people to criticize you, because you're our own child. The Pollo clan, as you used to call it, must hold together. It mustn't split up, even over such a difficult member as you are. Please, Adam, do realize that we form a scrap of something indestructible. We brought Philippe up to look at it that way, and that's how we should have liked to bring you up.

So Adam dear, nothing is lost. With good will all round, everything can go back to what it was. In spite of the way things may seem to you, we are still the Pollo clan. You're called after one of our ancestors—your great-grandfather's name was Antoine-Adam Pollo. You have to be an important member of the clan, even if you behave differently from the others—even if you stand out in other ways. There are a thousand ways of sticking together, Adam, remember that. You can choose the one that suits you; and you can rely upon it that it will always suit me.

I shall look forward to a letter from you tomorrow, a long, friendly one. Be sure and tell me what you need. I'll put aside a little money for you and give it to you when you come to see us—enough to keep you going till you begin to earn your own living. And I'll get some clean clothes ready for you as well, if you like, some shirts and a suit and some underclothes.

There, that's all I wanted to tell you—forgive me for reminding you of the humiliating business about the blue bowl. But I feel so certain you haven't changed since the day I caught you up on the stairs and persuaded you, gently, that you ought not to go away like that. We'll keep all this a secret between the two of us, shall we? and we shall understand each other much better when you come to see us——
So I shall expect you very soon, Adam dear, I love you very much and I have great hopes of you.

Your affectionate mother,
Denise Pollo.

Adam folded up the letter; there was a scrap of paper in in the envelope as well. It was all crumpled and dirty. A few hurried lines were pencilled on it, in a different handwriting. They said:

'Don't worry about me. I'm going away
for a time. Write to me at Poste Restante
15, down by the harbour. Don't be anxious
about me, everything's all right.
Adam.'

When he finished reading, Adam put the letter and the note back into the envelope, slipped it inside his magazine, picked up his belongings and left the Post Office. A kind of sweat was plastering his hair down on his forehead and his shirt to his back.

Everything was all right, indeed. The weather was still

lovely, for the end of summer, and the Promenade by the sea was swarming with people. Outside the cafés, boys in T-shirts were strumming guitars and handing round the hat. Everything was so white in the light that it might have been black. The whole scene had a sunburnt skin. A huge ink-pot, why not, had emptied its contents onto the earth; it was like looking at the world through a photographic negative.

Adam was no longer following anybody; in fact he was perhaps the one who was being followed now. He no longer strolled along casually. Each lingering step on the lozenges of gravel was calculated; he went straight ahead along the sea road, in the spirit in which one fills up an application-form.

Surname................................ First names...................
Date and place of birth...
Address ....
Occupation ....
Are you (*) a Civil Servant
            Employee of the Gas or Electricity Board
            Local Government employee
            Unemployed
            Student
            Old-age Pensioner
            Voluntary Welfare Worker
(*) Strike out which does not apply.

On the other side of the street there was a wireless shop with an ice-cream stall next door to it. Adam bought an ice cornet and looked at the TV show: two kids, a boy and a girl, dressed in black tights and dancing to the tune of 'Paper Moon'; further back in the shop three other TV sets were tuned in to the same programme. They all looked terribly human, with their identical white rectangles traversed by thousands of greyish motes; superimposed on the picture, Adam's tall figure was reflected in the shop window, with his two eyes, one nose, one mouth, ears, a trunk, four limbs, shoulders and hips.

Adam smiled at all this, with a kind of smile that meant he was just getting over not understanding; he licked the ice-cream slowly, and for the first time for some days, he talked to himself aloud. He spoke in a melodious, rather deep voice, articulating each syllable distinctly. His voice rang out, fine and strong, against the plate-glass, drowning the bursts of music and the street noises. It was all that could be heard, as it emerged from Adam's lips in the form of a pyramid and spread over the surface of the window like a cloud of steam. From the very first second it appeared to be self-sufficient, to require no addition or response, rather like the words in balloons coming out of the mouths of the characters in children's comics.

'What I wanted to say. Here it is. We're all alike, all brothers, eh. We have the same bodies and the same minds. That's what makes us brothers. Of course it seems rather ridiculous, don't you agree, to make such a confession—here—in broad daylight. But I'm telling you because we are all brothers, all alike. Do you know something, do you want to know something? My brothers. We possess the earth, all of us, just as we are, it belongs to us. Don't you see how it resembles us? Don't you see how everything that grows on it and everything that lives on it has our faces and our style? And our bodies? And is indistinguishable from us? For instance, just look round you, to left and right. Is there one single thing, one single element—within sight, which isn't ours, which isn't yours and mine? Take that street-lamp I see reflected in the shop window. Eh? That street-lamp belongs to us, it's made of cast-iron and glass, it's upright as we are, and topped by a head like ours.

The stone jetty down there by the sea belongs to us as well. It is built to the scale of our feet and hands. If we'd wanted, it could have been a thousand times smaller, eh? Or a thousand times bigger. That's true. The houses are ours, houses like caves, with holes pierced in them for our faces, full of chairs for our buttocks, beds for our backs, floors that imitate the ground and consequently imitate us. We are all the same, comrades. We have invented monsters—yes, monsters. Such as these television sets or these machines for making Italian ices; but we have remained within the confines of our own nature. In that we show our genius— we have made nothing that merely cumbers the earth, like God himself, my brothers, like God himself. And I tell you, eh, I give you my word, there is no difference between the sea, the tree and television. We make use of everything, because we are the masters, the only intelligent beings in the world. There you are. The TV is us, men. It is our strength we have poured into a mass of metal and plastic, so that it may answer us back one day. And that day has arrived, the mass of metal and plastic answers us now, captivates us, enters our eyes and ears. An umbilical cord links this object with our own bellies. It is the useless, many-splendoured thing in which we are adrift, in which we lose ourselves, in a little pleasure, yes, in our general happiness. Brothers, I am the Telly and you are the Telly and the Telly is within us! It has our particular anatomy, and we are all square, all black, all electric, all sonorous with purrings and music when, drawn to the Telly by sight and hearing, we recognize in its voice a human voice and on its screen a figure identical with ourselves. Judge for yourselves, brothers. We share this image like love, and our vague, obscure unity begins to appear; behind that glazed surface it is as though thick, warm blood were flowing, it is like a set of chromosomes, with one extra

186

pair, which is at last going to make us into a race again. Who knows if we shall not draw the cruellest revenge from this, for having been so long separated. Having misunderstood one another. Having believed falsely. Who knows if we may not at last again discover some tyrannosaur, some ceratosaur, some deinotherium, some huge pterodactyl bathed in blood, against which we can fight side by side. Some opportunity for sacrifice and slaughter, which may prompt us to clasp our hands again at last and pray in a whisper to pitiless gods. And then there will be no more TV, brothers, no more trees or animals or earth or dancers in tights; there will be only *us*, brothers, for ever, us alone!'

Adam was now on the opposite pavement. He had laid his parcel of belongings and his magazine on the ground beside him. He stood with his back to the sea, and the wind flapped his yellow trousers. There was something slightly pedantic in the stance he had adopted: behind him the rail with its cross-pieces of painted iron; through the gaps one could see the stretch of quays and docks, with the dockers at work. All this bustle was supposed to form a contrast to Adam's impassive, vaguely oblong face. One felt that had there been a bench just there, Adam would have been standing on it. And yet his attitude was not that of a public speaker; he managed to convey a general impression of nonchalance by his whole bearing. His voice was now less vibrant in the lower register, at times it struck a shriller, rather flat note. In any case he was not trying to make a harmonious effect: nothing, in fact, was more discordant than the presence of this man, standing upright and motionless amid the shifting chiaroscuro of his surroundings; and nothing more disagreeable than the idea of this man talking aloud, all by himself, in front of a crowd of idlers, under the sun at approximately 1.30 p.m.

Adam was now speaking more distinctly; he had assumed a tone half-way between fanatical ranting and wedding-breakfast oratory. He was saying:

'Stop, ladies and gentlemen, and listen to me for a little. You don't pay enough attention to the speeches that are made to you. Although you hear them all day and every day, hour by hour. On the wireless, on the television, at church, at the theatre, at the cinema, at banquets and at fairs. Yet words come easily, and nothing is nicer than a tale told like that, at point-blank. Off the cuff. You're used to it. You are not human beings, because you are not conscious of living in a human world. Learn to speak. Try it for yourselves. Even if you have nothing to say. Because, I tell you, the floor is yours. Why not try, just as you are, to act as substitutes for your own machines: go ahead, talk, right and left. Spread the good word. You'll see, before long you won't need the radio or the telly any more. You'll just meet yourselves at the corner of a street, as I did today, and you'll tell yourselves stories. No matter what. And you'll see, your wives and children will come flocking up and listen to you with all their ears. You can go on telling them the loveliest things, indefinitely.'

By this time an audience had gathered, consisting more or less of:

(1) a dozen women, men and children, the hard core;

(2) about twenty others who moved on after a minute or two.

Altogether, an average of about thirty listeners, gathered in a knot on the pavement.

'I'll tell you something. Listen. I—a little time ago now, I was sitting on some steps, up in the hills, smoking a cigarette. There was a fine view from there, and I was enjoying it a lot. Across from where I sat there was a lower hill, and then the town, stretching away to the sea, and the

188

long curve of the shore. Everything was very quiet. The sky took up three-quarters of the view. And below, the earth was so peaceful that one would have said—that it was a continuation of the sky. You see the kind of thing. Two hills, a town, a small river, a bay, a little sea, and a column of smoke curling up to the clouds. All over the place. I'm describing these features so you'll understand what comes next. You understand?'

Nobody answered, but a few people nodded, laughing.

Adam singled out one bystander, at random, looked at him and asked:

'You understand?'

'Yes, yes, I understand,' said the man.

'And—haven't you anything to tell us yourself?'

'Me?'

'Yes, you, why not? Do you live in the country?'

The man made as if to draw back, and the crowd seemed to do likewise.

'No, I——'

'Are you selling something?' asked a woman.

'Yes, the word,' said Adam.

The first bystander seemed to understand this:

'So you're a Jehovah's witness? Eh?'

'No,' said Adam.

'Yes, you—you're a prophet?'

But Adam did not hear him; he turned back to the mysterious enigmas of his embryonic language, to his desperate isolation, the blockade protecting him from being overrun by the populace, and he went on with what he had begun:

'Suddenly, on the earth, everything was different. Yes, at one stroke I understood everything. I understood that the earth belonged to me, and not to any other living species. Not to the dogs, not to the rats, not to the vermin, not to

189

anything. Not to the snails or the cockroaches or the grasses or the fish. It belonged to the human beings. And so to me, since I was a human being. And do you know how I came to understand that! Something extraordinary had happened. An old woman had appeared. Yes, an old woman. An old woman. You'll see what I mean. The road I was sitting beside was one of those steep, mountain roads. From where I sat, on these steps, I could see it sloping down and vanishing round a bend. Ahead of me there was just a bit of road, not more than a hundred yards; it was tarred, and shining under the clouded sun. Suddenly I heard muffled sounds, coming in my direction, I looked down the road, and there, coming into sight slowly, terribly slowly, was an old woman, a fat, ugly old woman, in a flower-printed coat that billowed round her like a flag. First I saw her head, then her shoulders, then her hips, her legs, and finally the whole of her. She was toiling up the tarred road, on her fat, blotchy legs, puffing like a cow, her mind a blank. I watched her emerging from the hill, like getting out of a bath, and coming up towards me. She cut a paltry figure, a black silhouette against the cloudy sky. She was, that's it—she was the only moving thing in the whole region. Nature all round her was unvaried, motionless—except that—how should I put it?—it was making a halo round her head, as though she had the earth and sky for her hair. The town was still stretching away towards the sea, so was the river, the hills were still rounded and the trails of smoke still vertical. *But they extended from her head.* It was as though it had all tipped up. It had altered. It was she, you understand, she who'd made it all. The smoke, yes, that was a human thing all right. So were the town and the river. So was the bay. The hills—the hills had been cleared of trees and covered with telegraph poles, they were crisscrossed with lanes and gulleys. The

190

road and the steps, the walls, the houses, the bridges, the dams, the airplanes—it wasn't the ants, all that! It was she. A quite commonplace old woman. Fat and ugly. Not even fit to live. Organically incapable. Bulging with fat. Unable to walk straight. With bandaged legs, varicose veins, and cancer somewhere about her, in her rectum or somewhere. It was she. The earth was round and tiny. And human beings had worked it all over. There isn't a single place on this earth, d'you hear me, not a single place on this earth that hasn't got a road, a house, an aeroplane, a telegraph pole. Isn't it enough to drive you mad, to think we belong to that race? It was she. It was she, this bundle of rags, full of entrails and stuff, of dirty, bleeding things, this dotty, muddy-eyed animal with a skin like a dried-up crocodile, its dewlap, its shrivelled uterus, its collection of drained-out glands, its lungs, its goitre, its yellow tongue all ready to stutter, . . . its gasps, like a stunned cow, its . . . its heavy cry . . . Huh-huh . . . huh-huh . . . swollen belly . . . broken veins . . . and its skull . . . bald, its hairy armpits scabbed with seventy-five years of sweat. It was she. She . . . You—you see?'

Adam was speaking faster and faster; he was getting to the point where one no longer forms sentences, tries to make oneself understood. He was pressing right back against the painted iron railing; all that could be seen of him now was his head, which rose above the crowd and faced them, with something prophetic, something friendly about it; he was the man people point at, the one that sends them hurrying for the police, the one for whom they go to fetch their cameras, the one who's either jeered at or insulted, according to choice.

'Want to tell you. Wait. Can tell you a story. You know. Like over the wireless. Dear listeners. I can argue. I can argue with you. Who wants to? Who'd like to talk to me?

Eh? Can we argue about something? We can talk about the war. There's going to be a war—— No . . . Or about the cost of living. What's the price of potatoes? Eh? It seems potatoes are enormous this year. And turnips quite tiny. Or about abstract painting. If no one has anything to say. Haven't you anything to say? I can tell a story. That's it. I can make up fables for you. On the spot. Here—I'll give you some titles. Listen. The legend of the dwarf palm that wanted to travel in Eastern Europe. Or the ibis turned into a girl by a commercial traveller. Or Asdrubal the two-mouthed. And the Love-story of a carnival king and a fly. Or How Zoe, the Queen of Peloponnesus, found the treasure of the rock-tomb without really trying. Or The courage of trypanosomes. Or How to kill rattlesnakes. That's easy. You need to know three things. Rattlesnakes. Are very vain. Don't like jazz. And as soon as they see an edelweiss they fall into a cataleptic trance. So. This is what you have to do. You take a clarinet. When you see the snake you pull an ugly face at him. Being vain, they get in a rage and rush at you. At that moment you play them Blue Moon or Just a Gigolo. On the clarinet. They don't like jazz. So they stop short. They hesitate. At that precise instant you take out. You take out of your pocket a real edelweiss, picked in the snow. And they fall into a cataleptic trance. So then. All you have to do is grab them and slip a p onto them somewhere. When they recover from the trance. They see they've become merely. That they've become merely prattlesnakes. And as they're so terribly vain, this kills them. They prefer to commit suicide. They hold their breath. For hours. In the end it kills them. They turn quite black. Do you hear? etc.'

Adam talked from 2.10 p.m. to 2.48 p.m. The crowd of listeners had grown appreciably. They were beginning to

192

look really wary, and their interruptions drowned Adam's voice at times. He was talking faster and faster and more and more incoherently. He was hoarse with fatigue, and a kind of irritation had stolen over his face.

There were two deep furrows across his forehead now, and his ears were red. His shirt was clinging to his back and shoulders. He had talked so much, shouted so much, that he scarcely overtopped the crowd any more; he was fused with it, and his pointed head, with the thick hair and beard, seemed to hover among the listeners like somebody else's head; instead of degrading it, despair had carved it into an effigy. It was as though a dull hatred had severed it from the trunk, on the threshold of some peculiar revolution, and as in days of yore, the populace, aroused by the hero, was carrying in its sticky centre, like a sea, a noble countenance that was still alive. At once innocent and shameful, the eyes shone madly in their deep sockets, caught in the mass hysteria like marbles in a string bag. Among them all they had built up an agglomeration of human flesh and sweat, indivisible in aspect, where nothing that was comprehended in it could continue to exist. Sudden cries, laughter, jests, the roar of engines, motor-horns, the sea and the boats, were all stripped of logic. Everything was coming and going confusedly, in jerks, with the sound and colours of a riot.

The truth is hard to register; all of a sudden the pace quickened alarmingly. In a second, it was over. There was an eddy in the crowd, with cries, of anger perhaps. After that everything followed its natural course. Except for this strange, unexpected detail, nothing was left to chance. What I mean is that it was so simple and so automatic that when the crowd took action it was at least two hours ahead of its own schedule.

BEN BELLA SCORES TRIUMPH AT ORAN:
"One-party System Essential."

BETWEEN MAN-DELIEU AND LE TRAYAS FIRES CUT THE RAILWAY LINE IN SEVERAL PLACES

Many trains held up. Several houses threatened. A camping site hastily evacuated.

At Tizi-Ouzou, 100,000 Kabyles

cheer the G.P.R.A.

GENERAL STRIKE OF SAILORS AT MARSEILLES UNTIL TOMORROW AFTERNOON

Sailings for Corsica and Africa are cancelled until further notice.

VAR RESIDENT ON HOLIDAY MEETS DEATH BY DROWNING AT PALAVAS-LES-FLOTS

Montpellier. On holiday at Palavas-les-Flots (Hérault), M. Seyne-sur-Mer (Var) was accidentally drowned yesterday morning.

Overcome while in the water, M. Mages was brought to land by fellow-bathers and taken to hospital at Montpellier, where he died soon after admission, despite all attempts to revive him.

MYSTERY DEATHS IN CORSICA

The bodies of 2 German tourists were found in the sea, two miles away from each other, near Anghione beach.

The man's death appears to be due to a fractured skull. The woman showed no signs of violence.

(See page 7)

● Missing from his home near Toulon since June 30, a farmer is found dead in a ravine. Accident, suicide, or foul play?

● *Ariane district: A boy of twelve drowned in the Paillon.*

MANIAC ARRESTED AT CARROS

Young maniac barricaded in a school at Carros.
Police make arrest.
Short chase terminates escape of mental patient at Carros.

Strange behaviour

On Sunday afternoon the crowd strolling along the Promenade was alarmed by the strange behaviour of a young man, Adam P., who, clearly not in his right mind, was haranguing the crowd in an incoherent manner. Things

would have gone no further, but that, for some unknown reason, the young man became so distracted that before the eyes of the spectators he began

(See page 7)

Verdict in the Locussol case:

STEFANI, 20 YEARS WITH HARD LABOUR ARTAUD, 5 YEARS

(Achard found guilty in absentia for the 2nd time)

MANIAC ARRESTED AT CARROS

(Continued from page 1)

what can only be described as a display of indecency.

Eventful chase

The police, sent for at once, set off in pursuit of the deranged youth, who had made his escape. They searched the upper part of the town; but it was not until the late evening, towards 10.30, that their quarry was reported to have been seen in a nursery school in the Carros district, which he had entered after climbing the wall of the playground. The young man then barricaded himself into one of the empty classrooms. When called upon to emerge, he threatened suicide. The police were obliged to drive him out with tear-gas bombs, whereupon he surrendered. He was armed with a kitchen knife.

Removed to mental hospital

Pending his appearance before the magistrate on several charges, the young man, the son of a good local family, is to be examined by a psychiatrist. It seems clear that he acted under the influence of sudden mental derangement. If Dr. Pauvert, who is a psychiatrist from the Institut Pasteur, finds him to be of unsound mind, he will remain at the mental home for treatment and the legal proceedings will be dropped. Otherwise he will be brought to trial on two charges—breaking and entering, and committing a nuisance. We understand that Maître Gonardi will appear on his behalf. The police ask all those who have or believe themselves to have suffered any loss or damage through the behaviour of the accused, to report the circumstances to the police station immediately.

As we go to press, we learn that the young man is alleged to have admitted, without apparent cause, to being responsible for fires in the district. He is said to have declared repeatedly 'I am an incendiary, an incendiary'. The information so far available seems to point to amnesia. Early this morning, however, two further complaints were lodged with the police—one by M. L., who declares that the accused broke into his house and caused damage, and one by Mlle. M., alleging indecent assault. The young man will be removed to the mental hospital at noon today, for examination by the psychiatrist.

MYSTERY IN CORSICA *(Continued from page 1)*

The bodies of a man and a woman were found yesterday morning on the beach at Anghione, a bathing resort on the east coast of Corsica, not far from Bastia.

The gruesome discovery is surrounded by considerable mystery.

It was about 7 a.m. and the camping-ground at Anghione, where many holiday-makers are enjoying a quiet seaside holiday, was beginning to wake up, when two amateur fishermen rushed to the manager's office to report that a woman's body was floating about 300 yards from the shore. A few minutes later the Moriani police arrived on the spot. Scarcely had the

body been recovered from the sea, when the police sergeant was informed by telephone that another body had been found by a bather on the beach at Pinarello, two miles further north.

FIRST OBSERVATIONS

It was at once discovered that the bodies were those of a German couple who had been camping at Anghione since June 28 and were intending to leave Corsica yesterday. The man was about 50 years old, the woman 42, and both were employed by a Hamburg firm. The bodies were clothed, and neither of them showed bullet-wounds. The man's forehead

bore very extensive bruises, but the woman's body showed no traces of struggle or injury.

Nevertheless, when brought out of the water, both of them bled freely from the ears. Dr. Marchesi, called to the spot, made a rapid examination and declared that the man, at least, had a fracture of the skull.

PUZZLING FEATURES

Questioned, the management declared that the couple were just like many others in the Camp and had attracted no special attention. It was said, however, that the man always carried a brief-case and never let it out of his hands.

A waitress had noticed that

MYSTERY IN CORSICA (Continued)

Bastia removed the bodies to the mortuary, where Dr. Colonna will carry out an autopsy.

the couple were not on good terms and frequently quarrelled.

Asked whether they had quarrelled on Wednesday evening, a few hours before their death, she replied: 'No, they didn't come to the canteen that evening.'

Another curious point is that only two days after they arrived the woman asked to be moved to another hut, saying that her husband snored and kept her awake.

A strange couple indeed: did she discover for the first time, on this holiday, that the man in her life snored so loud as to keep her awake?

The obvious conclusion was that they were not married. Had they run away together? According to Dr. Marchesi, death had occurred at about 9 o'clock the previous evening.

THE INVENTORY

As required by law, the head of the municipality, M. Leonello, Mayor of Castellare di Casinca, was present when an inventory was made of the contents of the man's hut. Apart from the usual toilet articles and clothes, the police found the mysterious brief-case; but this proved to contain only some dirty handkerchiefs and other trifles. There was also a fairly considerable sum of money in French and German notes.

Theft could not, therefore, have been the motive of the crime. In the course of a thorough search of the hut, the police found some letters, which yielded no clues, a number of cuttings from literary newspapers dealing with philosophical or theological subjects, studies of man, the future, extinction, etc.

It was discovered later that neither of the couple was fond of bathing. They used to spend the day in the shade and never went on the beach.

Pliers in handbag

The first discovery which seemed to offer a promising clue was that the woman's handbag contained . . . a brand-new pair of pliers, bought in Germany. A curious possession for a woman! Did she intend to use it as a weapon of defence or attack? Several kinds of tranquillisers were also found, together with prescriptions showing that the dead man and woman had both been treated in Germany for nervous depression.

At 3 p.m. the representatives of the Public Prosecutor arrived —MM. Ricci, the Assistant Prosecutor, Leonello, examining magistrate, and Colonna, official pathologist. After they had inspected the scene of the discovery, the ambulance from

VIEWS ON THE CASE

It is difficult to draw any conclusions at this early stage. Certain hypotheses may be ventured upon, however. It is said that cries were heard about midnight; but this is not the hour indicated by the medical evidence. Moreover, the launching of a new yacht was being celebrated somewhat noisily that night in a neighbouring restaurant. The cries heard were no doubt those of the festive guests.

As for the boats which are reported to have passed soon after nightfall, they were probably fishing-boats, of which several put out every evening.

Was this a double crime, perpetrated by a killer who had come to pay off some score?

The police considered this possibility. But the following theory seems more convincing.

Did the woman discover that the man she loved was about to leave her? That the end of the holiday would mean the end of her love? The man was not physically strong (he also had a slight limp); did she knock him on the head, throw him into the water, and then drown herself?

All this, of course, is pure hypothesis; and unless the postmortem yields some fresh clues the police will have a difficult task.

R. At last he was in the shade, sitting in a cool, clean little room which faced north and was thus hermetically sealed against the sun. Not a sound to be heard except the faint plash of water flowing into a tank somewhere in the distance, and the cries of children playing a long way away, at 5 o'clock in the afternoon, in some park with sand-pits and benches. The walls seemed to match these faint sounds, for they did not look strong; they were of hollow bricks, plastered over and then painted; the paint was cream-coloured and grainy-surfaced. These walls must be pleasantly damp with condensation, summer and winter alike. There was an open window in the exact centre of the outer wall. It was barred, and the sun, thus intercepted, threw vertical and horizontal shadows across the blankets on the bed and Adam's striped pyjamas. The bars—three vertical and two horizontal—divided up a sky that was just like the walls. It was an arbitrary yet harmonious division into squares, and their number, twelve, brought a quaint reminder of the Celestial Houses as described by Manilius.

Adam was thinking of it at this very moment, as he sat in his striped pyjamas on the edge of the iron bed. They had given him permission to smoke, and he was making use of it and of a plastic ashtray. His cigarette, smouldering tip downwards at the bottom of the ashtray, was helping him to pursue an unlimited train of thought which could not be interrupted as long as the tobacco lasted. They had cut his hair and shaved him, and his face looked very young again. It was turned towards the monochrome rectangle of the window; Adam had already got as far as choosing one of the compartments formed by the intersection of the bars; owing to his bad taste, or perhaps accidentally, he had chosen the eighth, starting from the left. In any case, whether his choice had been deliberate or no, Adam was well aware that, according to Manilius, the Eighth Celestial House is that of Death. Knowing this made it virtually impossible for him to be sincere; there was no importance in anything he might imagine or believe on the basis of this single fact (irrespective of the data relating to angles, quadrille, sextile, etc., whether or no they could be confirmed by the ecliptic, the North–South line, the meridian or the First Vertical, or assimilated to the famous points on the equator, 30° and 60°—Whether or no one agreed with Manilius that the Eighth Celestial House was potentially the Third); he had chosen to play that game as he might have played Battleships, Consequences, hopscotch or Animal, Vegetable or Mineral—prepared from the start to keep to the basic rules.

That having been said, it was not too exactly himself, any longer. And what is more, it was not too exactly the window-bars either; it was six crosses intermingled, in the style of:

Elohim   ADONAI ZEBAOTH   Eloher

which made frames for other symbols, such as Aglaon and Tetragrammaton, with 2 Maltese crosses, one inverted swastika, and one Star of David, or else Ego Alpha et Omega, or perhaps an alternation of Stars of David and suns.

If one had suddenly been transformed into that window, or if one had been facing Adam, one would have seen that he was sitting bolt upright on the raised edge of the mattress, with his head bent slightly forward and his hands resting on his knees, like someone just looking at the time. Seen thus, he looked as though he were thinking or as though he felt cold. He kept on staring at the same point, to the left.

The floor beneath his parallel feet was covered with dark red tiles, which had once been glazed; they were hexagonal in shape, and so strictly geometrical as to resemble a scale model of the room itself. The light coming through the window must undergo prolonged reverberation, as though the walls were covered with bevelled mirrors. It was the shiny paint and the innumerable facets of its grainy surface that reflected the light and threw it back continuously from point to point. He, Adam, knew the room well, having inspected it carefully at the very beginning: he granted it, despite its small size, a familiar, even family appearance, in fact soothing. It was deep and hard and austere. Everything, particularly the walls, stood out in cold, unmistakable relief. Yet it was this very coldness that he appreciated, without seeing it; he did not dislike the matter of the place, because of the implication that a game was in progress, a game that required him, Adam, to adjust himself, to give way, and not the things around him. He knew he was succeeding, by stages; he remained hard, insensitized, motionless, and his temperature was going down. From 36.7°C. to 36.4°. Sitting to the right of his cigarette, he was bathed in the cream-coloured half-light, grainy, moist, with no thought of passing time. There were lots of such moments in the day. He had been collecting them since early childhood: for instance when you're lying in the bath and you feel the water changing gradually from hot to warm, warm to cool and cool to cold; and you lie stretched out, up to your chin in an alien element, looking up at the ceiling between two layers of steam and wondering how long the water will take to get icy cold again; you pretend you're in a boiling pot and that by sheer force of will (or of Zen) you're enduring the heat, getting the better of something like 100°C. You are destined to emerge shamefaced, deserted, naked or shivering.

And the bed: he often thought that later on, when he had money, he would get his bed put on wheels, and have himself pushed out of doors. He'd be warm, knowing it was cold outside, and he would keep himself to himself under the blankets, while remaining completely in touch with the outer world. The room was so cramped, so stifling, that he felt sure of this. That was perhaps what he wanted more than anything else. In any case it seldom happened to him, in fact hardly ever. He felt certain that if he fell asleep there he would have no need to turn over noiselessly in bed in the middle of the night and look all round, trying to understand what he was seeing, translating mentally, here an empty coat-stand, there a chair and a towel, further on the shadow of a bar enlarged by the moonlight, etc. No more need, before getting into bed, to learn by heart where things stood; no more need to lie with his head towards the door, so as to keep watch. Here there was a bolt on the door and bars across the window. He was enclosed, alone, the sole one of his kind, right at the centre.

Adam was listening slowly, without moving his eyes half an inch; there was nothing he needed. All sounds (the gurgle of water in the pipes, the dull thuds, the bursting of seed-pods, the cries from far away that came into the room,

201

cut off one by one, the whispering of a fall of dust nearby, somewhere beneath a piece of furniture, the slight vibrations of the phagocytes, the tremulous awakening of a pair of moths because of a heavier knock on the other side of the wall) seemed to come from inside him. Beyond the walls there were more rooms, all of them rectangular, architecturally designed.

The same design was repeated in every section of the building, room, corridor, room, room, room, room, room, room, room, room, room, W.C., room, corridor, etc. Adam was glad to detach himself like that, with 4 walls, 1 bolt and 1 bed. In the cold and in a clear light. It was comfortable, if not durable. One ended sooner or later by suspecting as much and calling for it.

Outside, outside the sun was perhaps still shining; there were clouds, perhaps, in little wisps or perhaps only half the sky was covered. That was all the rest of the town; one felt that people were living all around, in concentric circles, thanks to the walls; one had, wasn't that so, a great many streets, going in all directions; they divided the blocks of houses into triangles or quadrilaterals; these streets were full or cars and bicycles. By and large, everything was repetition. One was practically sure to find the same planes a hundred yards further on, with exactly the same basis angle of $35°$ and the stores, the garages, the tobacconists, the leather goods shops. Adam was working out the plan in his head and adding a lot of things to it. If you took an angle of $48.3°$, for instance, well, you could be sure of finding it somewhere in the Plan. It would be a funny thing if there were no place for that angle at Chicago; and then, after finding it again, one need only look at the drawing to realize at once what had to be done. At that rate Adam could never get lost. It was the curves that were the hardest; he didn't understand how to react there. The best thing was to draw a graph; the circle was less complicated: one only had to square it (so far as possible, of course) and decompose it into a polygon: then there were angles, and one was saved. For instance he would extend the side *GH* of the polygon and get a straight line. Or he could even extend two sides, *GH* and *KL*, which would give him the equilateral triangle *GLz*, and then he would know what to do.

The world, like Adam's pyjamas, was striped with straight lines, tangents, vectors, polygons, rectangles, trapezoids of all kinds, and the network was perfect; no parcel of land or sea but was divided with great precision and could be reduced to a projection or a diagram.

In fact one need only start out with a polygon of about 100 sides, drawn on a piece of paper, and one would be sure of finding one's way about, anywhere in the world. By walking on along the streets, following one's own vectorial inspiration, one might perhaps even—who can say?—get as far as America or Australia. At Chu-Cheng, on the Chang, a little hollow house with walls of papyrus is waiting patiently in sunshine and shade, amid the soft rustle of leaves, for the messiah-surveyor who, compass in hand, will one day come to reveal the obtuse angle that is splitting it asunder. And many others as well, in Nyasaland, in Uruguay or in the heart of Vercors, all over the world, on stretches of arid, eroding land, among the bushes of broom, covered with millions of angles swarming like vermin, with millions of squares as fatal as signs of death, of straight lines splitting the sky on the far horizon with lightning gestures. One ought to have gone everywhere. One ought to have had a good plan, plus faith; a complete confidence in Plane Geometry and a Hatred of all that is curved, all that undulates, sins on the side of pride, the circle or the terminal.

In the room at that moment, with the daylight coming in

through the window, leaping forward and back in all directions and enfolding him as though in a sheet of sparks; with the cool, monotonous sound of waters; Adam was growing more tense; he was watching and listening intently, he felt himself growing, becoming a giant; he saw the walls extending to infinity, squares being added to squares, larger and larger, always a little larger; and little by little the whole earth was covered with this scribble, lines and planes intersecting with sharp cracks like rifle-shots, marked at their intersections by big sparks that fell away like round balls and he, Adam Pollo, Adam P . . . , Adam, not severed from the Pollo clan, was in the centre, right at the heart, with the drawing all made out, all ready for him to take to the road, and walk, go from angle to angle, from segment to vector, and name the lines by scratching their letters in the ground with his forefinger: xx', yy', zz', aa', etc., etc.

Quite naturally Adam took his eyes off the eighth intersection of the bars and let himself fall backwards on the bed. He reflected that he still had two or three hours before supper-time. After that he would smoke his last cigarette of the day, and go to sleep. He had asked for paper and a black ball-point pen as well; but those were evidently not allowed, for the nurse had not mentioned the subject that morning, nor at lunch time. In any case he realized he had nothing much left to write. He had lost the wish to do anything tiring. He wanted to eat, drink, urinate, sleep, etc., taking his own time, in the cool, in the silence, in a kind of comfort. He had a vague impression that there were trees over there, all round. Perhaps one day they'd let him go out in the garden, in his pyjamas. Then he could carve his name surreptitiously on the tree-trunks, like that girl Cécile J. had done on the cactus leaf. He would steal a fork to do it with, and dig it in hard, in capital letters. Then the name would harden slowly into a scar, under the action of sun and rain, for a long time—for twelve years or twenty, for as long as a tree lives:

ADAM POLLO   ADAM POLLO

He threw the bolster off the bed and laid his head flat on the mattress; then he stretched his legs as far as possible, so that his feet stuck out beyond the end of the bed. The night-table was on his right, close beside his head; it had two movable aluminium shelves without doors. On the bottom shelf there was an empty chamber pot. On the top shelf were: a pair of sun-glasses with gilt wire frames; one bottle of tranquillizer pills with passiflora and quinine as their chief ingredients; one cigarette, but no matches— when he wanted a light he had to ring for the nurse; one handkerchief; *La Sarre et son Destin*, by Jacques Dircks-Dilly, out of the hospital library; one glass of water, half full; one white comb; one photo of Zsa-Zsa Gabor, cut out of a magazine. All the furniture and cubic space in the room was supposed to form a setting for Adam alone, as he lay flat on the bed with his arms at an oblique angle and his feet together, as though crucified in sloth and repose.

And, a little before 6 in the afternoon, long after he had finished his cigarette and his thoughts—if they could be so called—the nurse pushed back the outside bolt and came into the room. She found Adam asleep. She had to put a hand on his shoulder in order to wake him. She was a young woman, and attractive, but so completely annihilated by her nurse's uniform that it was impossible to make out her age or whether she was really pretty or really commonplace. Her hair was tinted a red-gold shade and her palish complexion stood out against the beige walls of the room.

Without saying a word, she picked up the plastic ashtray

205

from the floor where Adam had deposited it, and emptied it into the slop-pail. Time did not in any case pass quickly in this place; and the position she thus suddenly took up, for some obscure reason deriving, perhaps, from the thousands of hours she had given to waiting on the mentally sick, seemed to place her in contradiction to herself, render her more ridiculous, reduce her by repercussion to four colour-slides projected on walls which had become a screen; her body bent sharply at hip-level and stayed like that, stuck, for an indefinite period of time. Awakening echoes of toil and distress in the world, memories of days without food, of degradation and old age. Abolishing all colour-contrasts by a succession of possible movements on different planes where a watery grey was dominant. Driving to madness whoever had the misfortune to catch sight of her and to shut his eyes immediately afterwards. For now the colours were reversed—her white face and apron were ink-black, the once-yellow walls powdered with a sort of cloak of bitter slate-grey and every cool, soothing colour suddenly transformed to a hellish atrocity. Nightmare drew close, pressing against the temples, making every object shrink or expand at its will. The woman seen just now was a medium putting the final touch to delirium in its most horrible form—the fear of going really mad. She clung to the eyeballs like a twining root, multiplying her faces to infinity. Her eyes were immense, wide open like caverns. She emerged from a dark pyrosphere, shattered the ramparts of the background like glass, and stood there, half-revealed, bending over a world simulated in her own image, awaiting some infinitesimal changes. Slowly she shrivelled, until her bones could be seen; until she resembled a drawing traced heavily with the pen, a pattern stamped on some object made of snake-skin; some figure, or rather some strange letter, a capital Gamma, piercing the brain through and through. Within a few seconds she had been devoured by incandescent fire, she had overthrown boundaries; in the ebb and flow that was now slowing down she stood motionless, became mechanical, was transformed into a dead bough that the flames have left behind. She offered every possibility of lingering in her torment, a thousand ways of perpetuating her gesture; Adam's choice was to sit up up the edge of the bed. Then, drained of all volition, he waited for the nurse to begin moving again; her movement led up to words, pleasant ones, for she asked:

'Well? Had a nice nap?'

And he replied:

'Yes, thank you, very nice,' adding, 'Have you come to do the room?'

She moved the slop-pail a few inches before saying:

'That I have not. You should do a little work yourself today, don't you think? We can't afford to pay for chambermaids for you here, you know. So make your bed, nice and tidily, and then sweep the floor a bit. I've brought you a broom and a dust-pan. All right?'

'All right . . .' said Adam. 'But . . .' he added, looking with curiosity at the young woman, 'But—shall I have to do this every day?'

'I should think so,' she retorted, 'Every morning. Today it was rather different, because you're new here. But from now on you'll have to get down to work every morning at ten o'clock. And if you're a good boy you'll soon be allowed out, like the others. You'll be able to go out in the garden and read, or dig flowerbeds, or talk to the rest of them. You'd like to go out in the garden, wouldn't you? You'll see. You'll enjoy being here. They'll give you little jobs to do, making little wicker baskets, or decorations. There's even a carpenter's shop with all the gadgets, planes, electric saws and so forth. You'll see, you'll enjoy it. Provided you do just as you're told, you understand? To be going on with, make your bed now, and sweep the floor. Like that, everything will be tidy for visiting time.'

Adam nodded, got up, and set to work at once. He did it well, while the young woman in her white uniform watched him. When he had finished, he turned to her and asked:

'Will that do?'

'Is the pot empty?'

'Yes,' said Adam.

'Good. Then that'll do. We shall get along splendidly.'

She picked up the slop-pail and added:

'Right. Visiting time is an hour from now.'

'Is someone coming to see me?' queried Adam.

'I'll come and call you then.'

'Is someone coming to see me?' he asked again.

'I should just think so.'

'Who? My mother? Tell me.'

'Half a dozen gentlemen will be round to see you an hour from now, with the head doctor.'

'From the police?' Adam asked.

'Oh no,' she laughed, 'Not from the police.'

'Then who?'

'Some gentlemen who're interested in you, you inquisitive boy! Some very solid citizens, who can't wait to meet you! You'll behave nicely, won't you?'

'Who are they?'

'They're what I've told you. Half a dozen of them. Very much interested in you.'

'Journalists?'

'Yes, that's it. Journalists, in a way.'

'They're going to write some stuff about me?'

'Well, that's to say—they're not exactly journalists. They won't talk about you in the papers, certainly . . .'

'Then they're the people I saw when I came in here?'

The nurse picked up everything she had to carry away, and took hold of the door-handle with her left hand.

'Oh no, not them. Young men like yourself. They'll come to the infirmary with the head doctor and ask you questions. You must get on the right side of them. They may be able to help you.'

'You mean coppers, don't you?' Adam persisted.

'Students,' said the nurse as she left the room, carrying the slop-pail. 'Students, if you must know.'

Adam went to sleep again till they arrived, at about ten past seven.

The nurse woke him as she had done the first time, shaking him by the shoulder, told him to make water, to straighten his pyjamas and comb his hair, and then led him to the door of a room just across the corridor. She left him to go in alone.

The room was even smaller than his own cell, and full of people sitting on chairs. There was a medicine cupboard in one corner and a weighing-machine in another, to show that this was the infirmary. Adam made his way between the seated people, found an empty chair at the far end of the room, and sat down on it. He sat there for a little time in silence. The other people seemed to take no notice of him. Except when Adam asked a girl who was sitting next to him whether she happened to have a cigarette; she said yes, opened her black leather handbag and held out the packet to him. They were rather expensive Virginia cigarettes, Blacks or Du Mauriers. Adam asked if he might take three or four. The girl told him to keep the whole packet. Adam took it, thanked her, and began to smoke. After a few minutes he raised his head and looked at them; there were seven in all, young ones, some male, some female, aged between nineteen and twenty-four, and a doctor, a man of about forty-eight. None of them was looking at him. They were talking in undertones. Three of the young ones were making notes. A fourth was reading something in an exercise-book; this was the girl who'd given him her packet of cigarettes. She was twenty-one and a bit, her name was Julienne R., and as it happened she was slim and astonishingly pretty; she had fair hair twisted into a chignon and a beauty-spot above her right ankle; she was wearing a dark blue cotton dress that had a leather belt lined with gold plastic. Her mother was Swiss. Her father had died of an ulcer ten years ago.

She was the first who really looked at Adam. She gazed at him with grave eyes, faintly dark-circled, full of gracious understanding. Then she folded her arms, locking her little finger into the bend at each elbow, scarcely moving the tips of the first fingers, and craned her neck slightly forward, more than usual. Her forehead had a faint suggestion of something childish, yet material; it was broad but not vulgarly so, it made way naturally for the roots of her hair, which began by parting to right and left and was then brought up at the back of the head and coiled down again at the end of a twisted parting.

She was unquestionably the one who had listened most to the others, whether to the doctor or to her fellow students. One could sense this in her remarkably well-proportioned features; they had a symmetry which, instead of hardening the lower part of the face, particularly the lips, gave an added tenderness, an extra touch of enquiry. She opened her mouth slightly in breathing, and gazed unblinkingly. Her gaze, by infinitesimal degrees, bore down Adam's, took on a thousand presumed emotions, a thousand delicate touches, an intimacy as powerful as sin, as perfect as incestuous love. She was a citadel of consciousness and knowledge, not vindictive, not violent, but almost senile in its sweet confidence.

She was the first to speak; at the nodded permission of

the doctor, she leant slightly forward towards Adam, as though to take him by the hands. But her arms were still folded. She said, in her deep voice:

'Have you been here long?'

'No . . .' said Adam.

'How long?'

Adam hesitated.

'A day? Two days? Three days? Or more?'

Adam smiled.

'Yes, that's it—three or four days, I think . . .'

'You think?——'

'Three or four days?' asked a boy in dark glasses.

Adam hesitated again.

'Do you like being here?' asked Julienne.

'Yes,' said Adam.

'Where are you?' asked another girl, whose surname was Martin.

'Do you know where you are, here? What the place is called?'

'Er——the lunatic asylum,' said Adam.

'And why you're there?' asked the Martin girl.

'Why you're here?' Julienne repeated after her.

Adam pondered this.

'The coppers brought me here,' he said. The girl made a note—of his reply, no doubt—in her exercise-book. A lorry was grinding up a steep bit of road, somewhere outside the window. The dull roar of its engine came into the infirmary like the drone of a bluebottle, weaving a web of sound-waves between the white-tiled walls; it was a garbage-lorry, no doubt, climbing the mimosa-bordered hill that leads to the incinerating plant. Lead pipes, rolls of cardboard and heaps of springs would fall pellmell over the sides of the artificial mountain, waiting to be thrust into the annihilating flames.

'How long will they keep you here?' asked Julienne R.
'I don't know—they haven't told me.'
Another young man, a tallish boy on the other side of the room, raised his voice now:
'And how long have you been here?'
Adam looked pensively at him.
'I've told you already. Three or four days.'
The girl glanced round and made a sign of disapproval at the young man. Then she went on again, in a slightly softer voice:
'What's your name?'
'Adam Pollo,' said Adam.
'And your parents?'
'The same.'
'No—I mean, your parents? They're still alive?'
'Yes.'
'Do you live with them?'
'Yes.'
'You always have done?'
'Yes, I think so.'
'You have lived somewhere else?'
'Yes—once . . .'
'When was that?'
'Not long ago.'
'And where was it?'
'It was on a hill. There was an empty house.'
'And you lived in that?'
'Yes.'
'Were you comfortable?'
'Yes.'
'You were alone there?'
'Yes.'
'Didn't you see anybody? Didn't anyone come to see you?'

'No.'
'Why not?'
'Because they didn't know where I was.'
'Did you like that?'
'Yes.'
'But you don't sug . . .'
'It was nice. A fine house. And the hill was nice, too. One could see the road at the bottom. I used to sunbathe with nothing on.'
'You like that?'
'Yes.'
'You don't like wearing clothes?'
'Not when it's hot.'
'Why not?'
'Because one has to button them. I don't like buttons.'
'What about your parents?'
'I'd left them.'
'And gone away?'
Adam took a flake of tobacco out of his mouth.
'Yes.'
'Why did you go away?'
'Where from?'
The girl jotted down something in her exercise-book; now it was she who hesitated, hanging her head. Adam saw that the parting turned round the top of her head in an S shape. Then she looked up and her big, heavy, sleepy eyes rested on Adam again. They were huge eyes, blue, intelligent, inflexibly and resolutely hypnotic. Her voice seemed to flow along her gaze and slide to the depths of Adam's guts. Before it reached maturity, three other questions, fired at him by two girls and a boy, were left unanswered:
'Are you ill?'
'How old are you?'

'You say you don't like clothes. But—do you specially like being naked?'

At last Julienne R's words burst out from the midst of a kind of fog, like a spark running through damp gunpowder. Like a match used for picking one's ear, on which the wax-coated phosphorus is consumed without a flame and gives off an acid smell of singed flesh. Like a burning torch thrusting through the opposing layers of water.

'Why did you leave your parents' house?'

Adam had not heard this; she repeated, without annoyance, as though speaking into a microphone:

'Why did you leave your parents' house?'

'I had to go,' said Adam.

'But why?'

'I don't quite remember,' he began. They all made notes of this. Only Julienne R. did not lower her head.

'I mean to say——'

'Were you in trouble?'

'Had you quarrelled with your parents?'

Adam waved his hand. The ash from his cigarette fell on Julienne's shoe; 'Excuse me,' he murmured, and then went on:

'No, not in trouble, exactly. Put it this way, I ought to have gone a long time before. I thought——'

'Yes? You thought?' asked the girl. She seemed to be really listening.

'I thought it would be better,' said Adam. 'I wasn't having trouble with my parents, no but—— Perhaps I was just giving way to a childish need to be alone . . .'

'Children are usually pretty sociable,' said the boy with dark glasses.

'Yes, if you like—— Yes, that's true, they are pretty sociable. But at the same time they try to establish a kind of—how can I put it?—a kind of faculty of communication

214

with nature. I think they want—they easily give way to purely egocentric—anthropomorphic—needs. They try to find a way of getting inside things, because they're afraid of their own personality. It's as though their parents had made them want to minimize themselves. Parents make their children into *things*—they treat them like objects of poss— like objects that can be possessed. They give this object psychosis to their children. So some children are afraid of company, of the company of grown-ups, because of a vague inkling that they're on an equal footing there. It's equality they're afraid of. They have to play their part. Something's expected of them. So they choose to withdraw. They try to find some way of having their own universe, a rather—well—mythical universe, a make-believe universe where they're on a level with dead matter. Or rather, where they feel they've got the upper hand. Yes, they'd rather feel superior to plants and animals and what have you, and inferior to grown-ups, than on an equality with anything at all. If necessary they'll even reverse the situation, making the plants play their role, the children's role, while they play at being grown-ups. You see, for a kid, a Colorado beetle is always more like a man than another kid. I—yes . . .'

By this time the girl was bolt upright on her chair. Her eyes were shining like spectacles; she was frowning, as though in thought. The weighty appearance of her brow and nose had altered a little, deviating into a kind of snobbish pleasure at the incongruous encounter between elements reputed to be incompatible; it was like writing whimsical associations of words right in the middle of a blank page. This kind of thing:
'proton—already'
    'Jesus—bather'
        'grandmother—cracker'
            'island—belly'

One would have said she was now showing the reverse side of her mask; she seemed like, heaven knows what, a young Methodist girl who'd discovered a spelling mistake in a paragraph of the Bible—she looked half amused and half disgusted.

The boy in dark glasses leant forward and said:

'But you—you're not a child any longer!' The others giggled; the doctor cut them short by saying:

'Please, please. We are not here to amuse ourselves. I suggest you go on with your interview. Though I warn you that so far it's not very satisfactory. How can you expect to form any interesting ideas unless you manage the questions and answers better? You put your questions anyhow, at random, you pay no attention to the patient's behaviour, and then you're surprised that you can't diagnose the trouble. You let the clues escape you.'

He got up, took the spectacled student's notebook from him, glanced at it briefly and handed it back.

'You don't know how to set about the thing,' he said, and sat down again. 'You jot down a whole lot of useless details in your notebooks. You put "doesn't remember how long he's been in hospital—three or four days", and further on, "doesn't remember why he left home," and then, "doesn't like wearing clothes. Reason: dislikes buttons." That's all quite pointless. Whereas what might have been interesting, you don't mention—instead of writing all that, you need only have put: lapses of memory—sexual obsession accompanied by rejection of responsibility through fabulization —and there you would have had the beginnings of a diagnosis. But never mind, go ahead.'

Turning to Julienne R., he added:

'Come along, Mademoiselle. You'd made a good beginning.'

Julienne R. thought for a moment. During this time,

216

there was silence except for the creaking of chairs, the rustle of one or two exercise-book pages, the swallowing of saliva, and a curious smell of sweat and urine given off by the walls of the infirmary, or perhaps by Adam himself. He had managed to prop his elbows on his knees without hunching his shoulders too much, and in this position, with his right arm quite vertical, his hand was level with his chin and the butt-end of his cigarette just opposite his mouth. It was a pose carefully calculated to involve the minimum of effort. Allowing for the uncomfortable effect, in this company, of striped pyjamas and hair cut too short, almost shaved, and for the general chilly atmosphere of the infirmary, Adam was getting along fairly well. With his long, lanky body, thin arms and closed mouth, he gave an impression of exceptional, eccentric intelligence together with a slight tendency to pose. Moreover, his bare feet in their felt slippers were exactly parallel. One could see he had ceased to expect anything much—a breath of air, perhaps, a little fresh-turned soil, the sound of a wash-basin emptying; he had been a long time in the world, there was nothing about him that could be restored to life or firmly resist the heavy gaze of the fair-haired girl with the pair of blue eyes, deep as bottles, strained, avid to encircle the whole world, himself included, in the power of knowledge. He could read her, and the rest of the group, like a postcard. But he stopped at that. And he was outstripped, carried away on a black stream, amid whirlpools of pulverized granite, between the shifting layers of immense zinc plates where he was reflected an infinite number of times, a solitary, weedy man.

Julienne R. did not look at the others again. It was difficult to tell whether she was ashamed, afraid, or what. She said:

'Why are you here? Why are you here?'

217

It might pass for just another question; but it was almost a compassionate appeal, almost a diffuse love-formula. She repeated:

'Can you tell us—— Will you tell me why? Why you're here? Do try to tell me . . .'

Adam refused. He took another cigarette out of the packet and lit it from the stub of the first; then he dropped the stub on the floor and crushed it out, lingeringly, with the toe of his slipper. The girl watched him, her fingers clenched on her exercise-book.

'You won't—tell me why you're here?'

The other girl, Martin, put in:

'You don't remember.'

One of the young men nibbled the end of his pencil.

'Just now you were saying something interesting. You were talking about children, about minimization, etc. Don't you think—don't you think that may be an obsession with you? I mean, mightn't it be that you assimilate yourself to these children? That is—I mean——'

'How old are you?' asked the boy with the dark glasses.

'Twenty-nine,' said Adam; then, turning to the first speaker:

'I see what you mean. But I don't feel one can answer that kind of question. I think—— Unless that belongs to the general attitude of a lunatic, a nut. In which case it wouldn't matter much if I answered yes or no.'

'Well then, why did you mention it to us?' asked the young man.

'To explain,' said Adam. 'I'd mentioned the solitary spirit of children. I wanted to explain it. Perhaps it wasn't worth while.'

'But it was you we were talking about.'

'Yes, of course—anyhow, it answered your question.'

'Because you're a case of micromania.'

218

'Or perhaps because one may still have something childish about one even at twenty-nine.'

The girl opened her mouth to say something, but she was forestalled:

'Have you done your national service?'

'Yes.'

'And your job?'

'What work were you doing?'

'Before?'

'Yes, before——?'

'I did all kinds of things,' said Adam.

'You had no settled job?'

'No——'

'What things have you done?'

'I don't know, really . . .'

'What work did you have that you enjoyed doing?'

'Odd jobs, I enjoyed them.'

'What odd jobs?'

'Well, washing cars, for instance.'

'But you——'

'I enjoyed being a bathing attendant, too. But I've never been able to do what I'd have liked. I'd have liked to be a chimney-sweep or a grave-digger or a lorry driver. But one needs references.'

'You wanted to do that all your life?'

'Why not? You do find old grave-diggers, you know . . .'

'But you've had a good education, haven't you?'

'Yes.'

'Have you any qualifications?'

'Yes, a few.'

'Wh——'

'I have a diploma in Regional Geography, for one thing . . .'

'Why didn't you make use of it?'

'I wanted to be an archaeologist—or an excavation over-seer, I don't quite remember which . . .'

'And——?'

'It didn't last . . .'

The fair-haired girl looked up and said:

'Honestly, I can't think what you're doing here——'

Adam smiled. 'You mean you don't think I'm a nut? is that it?'

She nodded. Her eyes were unfocused, inscrutable. She turned towards the head doctor and asked:

'Who said he was insane?'

The doctor stared hard at her and then slowly drew his legs in under his chair.

'Listen, Mademoiselle. This should be a lesson to you. You always jump to conclusions before you have collected all the facts. At least wait till you have finished this conversation. You know what he did?'

She nodded, her brow slightly furrowed. The doctor's expression was amused.

'You know. Not all cases are equally simple. Not all cases are as simple as the last one. You remember, the sailor? This may surprise you, but the fact is that there are no extremes in madness. There is no real boundary between a madman who commits murder and one who seems perfectly harmless. You came here expecting to see extra-ordinary people, taking themselves for Napoleon or unable to utter two coherent words, and you're disappointed to find nothing of the kind. Sometimes, like today, you even come across a patient who is extremely intelligent.'

He paused, cautiously.

'Well, as this is an exceptionally difficult case, I will help you. According to you, the patient is quite sane. But let me tell you that the first psycho-pathological tests for which I gave instructions when he was admitted showed him to be not merely abnormal, but definitely insane. I'll read you the results . . .'

He picked up a sheet of paper and read:

'Systematized paranoid delirium.

Tendency to hypochondria.

Megalomania (sometimes reversing to micromania).

Persecution mania.

Theory of justified irresponsibility.

Sexual deviations.

Mental confusion.

In short, the patient is in a permanent manic-depressive state which may evolve towards confusion or even to acute psychotic delirium. In such cases as his the delirium takes on what I might call an orderly appearance, owing to memories of culture and to the patient's potential intelligence. But his condition is dominated by frequent changes of mood, relapses and depressive states, and most of all by mythomania, confusion, and the different phases of sexual obsession.'

The doctor passed his hand over the back of his neck, which was rather greasy although he rubbed it with lavender-water several times a day. He seemed to relish more and more the embarrassment he had brought upon his audience. In the case of Julienne R. he was particularly pleased. He leant slightly forward in her direction.

'So you see, Mademoiselle, we have come to very different conclusions. Try to check mine by continuing your conversation with M. Pollo. I am sure you will persuade him to say some very interesting things—— No, seriously, depressive patients respond tremendously to a sympathetic attitude. What do you say to that, M. Pollo?'

Adam had only heard the last words, all the rest having been uttered in a confidential tone intended only for the students. Adam glanced for a moment at the doctor and then at the tip of his cigarette, projecting, white and slender, from his fingers; and said:

'I'm sorry, I didn't hear the beginning of your question.' Then he lapsed into a kind of torpor. He could already feel himself slipping away from his real surroundings. Julienne R. cleared her throat and said:

'Very well—let's go on . . . What do you think? I mean, what do you think is going to happen to you?'

Adam looked up:

'What did you say?'

Julienne repeated: 'What do you think is going to happen to you now?'

Adam looked into the girl's eyes, two cavities that were almost familiar by this time; she had prominent brow ridges, so that the light falling from above cast two grey-blue shadows on her white cheeks, like the eye-holes of a plaster skull. Adam sighed faintly.

'I've just remembered a queer thing,' he said. 'I don't know what reminded me of it—it's funny . . .'

Looking at the edges of Julienne's eyelids, he went on:

'It was—let's say when I was twelve. I knew a funny chap, his name was Tweedsmuir, but they called him Sim, because his first name was Simon. Simon Tweedsmuir. He'd been brought up by the Jesuits, so there was a kind of style about him. He was friendly enough, in his own way, but he didn't talk much to the rest of us. He liked to keep himself to himself. I think it was because he knew that all we other fellows knew his father used to beat him with a stick. He would never talk about it to anyone. He was certainly the cleverest chap I've ever known, and yet he was always at the bottom of the form. But you could feel he could have been top if he'd wanted to. Once he had a bet with another boy that he would come out top in Latin composition and algebra. And he did. And the funny thing is that nobody was surprised. Not even the boy who'd had the bet. I think Sim regretted it afterwards, because the masters began trying to take an interest in him. He got himself expelled from school on purpose and no one ever heard of him again. The only time he ever really spoke to me was at the end of the Christmas term, just before he left the school. He'd turned up that morning black and blue with bruises, and in the cloakroom at break he told me about his way of praying. He said he thought the only way to get nearer to God was to do over again, in spirit, what God had done in the material sense. One must gradually rise up through all the stages of creation. He had already spent two years as an animal; when I knew him he'd just got up to the next level, the Fallen Angels. He was going to have to worship Satan out and out, until he managed to establish perfect communication with him. You understand. Not merely what one might call a physical relationship with the Devil, like most saints or mystics. Like St. Anthony or the Curé d'Ars. Complete communication, that's to say a state where he would understand the Works of the Evil One, their aim, their relation to God, to the beasts and to mankind. Put it this way, God can be understood as well through his opposite, his Devil, as through Himself, in his own essence. Every evening for two and a half hours, Sim was giving himself up entirely to Satan. He had written prayers and hymns of praise to him; he made him offerings —sacrificing small animals, and sins. He'd tried magic too, rejecting what he felt to be too childish or too daring, in view of his age and of the twentieth century. It was a stage in the manner of the Khlystys, you know, or Baron Samedi. But the difference was that for Sim this was only one step in the religious life. Taken entirely for love of God. From a wish to re-enact the Creation in the spiritual sense. He'd determined——'

Adam paused, then decided to go on. The fair-haired girl was sitting very stiffly on the edge of her chair, and trembling. Her fingers had made damp sweat-marks on the cover of the exercise-book. Every now and then a shadow travelled along the line of her eyebrows, thrown by a flight of birds passing the window; after so many long-drawn-out words and memories there was no difference any more between her and the fabulous characters in dreams. The words were alive, or she was, or the unicorn and the Yink, or anything.

'Yes—he'd determined to get through his worship of Satan by the time he was about sixteen—sixteen or seventeen. So he would have four years left before coming of age, four years to devote to the stage of human beings. Then nine years for the Angels. And then, by the time he was thirty, if he worked without ever letting up, if he didn't indulge his personal ambitions or pleasures, he could have ceased to exist except in God, in Him, through Him and for Him. In the ineffable—bang in the ineffable. No longer Sim Tweedsmuir, but God in person. You see. You see.'

One would have said his words had rung strangely in the infirmary, that cramped little room with its white-tiled walls like the walls of a bathroom or a public lavatory; one would have said there was an immense rectangular emptiness somewhere on earth and that this altered the depths of the sentences and dimmed the meaning of the words.

'Tweedsmuir. Tweedsmuir' Sim Tweedsmuir. He never talked to me again after that, after that day. I believe I heard that he'd died some time ago. He must have caught syphilis somewhere, during his satanic period. While honouring the Devil with a tart. You see the kind of thing. In a way, yes, he was an intelligent fellow, and all that. If he'd managed to see it through, he'd have ended by getting into the newspapers.'

Adam gave a short laugh. 'You know the funny thing about it? It's that if he'd been only the slightest bit more sociable lots of the chaps at school would have followed him, and his religion. I would have, for instance. But he didn't want any of that. He distrusted people. He wouldn't even listen if one mentioned Ruysbroek or Occam. In fact he had a petty side to him, and that was his downfall . . .'

'You're sure you didn't follow him a little way all the same—I mean his religion, his doctrine?' Julienne asked.

'How old did you say he was?' added the boy with the dark glasses.

'Who, Sim?'

'Yes.'

'He must have been a little older than me, about fourteen or fifteen . . .'

'Yes, that makes it easier to understand. It must have been the kind of mysticism kids do invent for themselves at that age—no?'

'You mean it was unsophisticated?'

'Yes, and I——'

'That's true. But it was rather fine, all the same. I think—I think if one remembers he was at the age for being confirmed, and all that, it seems rather fine, don't you think?'

'And you yourself thought it so fine——'

Julienne R. frowned, as though her head had suddenly begun to ache.

'——so fine that you followed him, didn't you?'

The head doctor agreed with this. 'Yes, that was it,' he said. 'And I would even go further and ask whether you are sure the whole story isn't about you. This Sim what-d'you-call-him—did he really exist?'

'Sim *Tweedsmuir*,' said Adam.

He shrugged his shoulders; the cigarette was burning the

nail of his first finger and once again he had to crush it out on the floor with the toe of his slipper.

'After all, I . . . I couldn't tell you. I mean it doesn't really matter whether it was I or he, you understand? In fact it doesn't really matter whether it was you or me or him.'

He thought for a moment, then swung round to face the fair girl and asked abruptly:

'What have you put me down as? A schizophrenic?'

'No, a paranoiac,' replied Julienne.

'Really?' said Adam, 'I thought—I thought you'd have put me down as a schizophrenic.'

'Why?'

'I don't know. I don't know. I thought so. I don't know.'

Adam asked if he couldn't have a cup of coffee. He pretended he was thirsty, or cold, but what he really wanted was to make a slight change in the appearance of the room. He was tired of being in an infirmary, with infirmary chairs, an infirmary discussion, an infirmary smell and a great infirmary emptiness. Anyhow the doctor rang for the nurse and asked her to bring a cup of coffee.

His cup of coffee came very quickly; he put it down on his left knee and began stirring it slowly, to melt the sugar. He drank in sips, seldom raising his head. There was something in his mind, a kind of swelling; he couldn't make out what it was. It might be like the memory of a dead person, the absurd idea of someone being dead and gone. Or, at a pinch, like being on a boat at night and remembering thousands of things, the waves for instance, and the gleams that are hidden by the darkness.

'So you don't know—do you know what you're going to do now?' Julienne began again; then she broke off and asked 'Can you let me have a cigarette?'

Adam held out the packet. She lit her cigarette with a little mother-of-pearl lighter she took out of her handbag. She had clearly forgotten the others, and that might mean, at a pinch, that she would soon forget Adam too.

'You don't know what will happen to you . . .'

Adam made a gesture that brought his hand down on his trouser-leg, a fraction of an inch away from the kneecap.

'No—but I have a pretty good idea, and that's enough for me.'

She made a last effort to talk to him.

'So there's nothing you want?'

'Yes there is—why?'

'Well, what do you want? To die?'

'Oh, not at all!' smiled Adam. 'I don't in the least want to die.'

'You want——'

'You know what I want? I want to be left in peace. No, not exactly that, perhaps . . . But I want lots of things. To do what isn't me. To do what I'm told. The nurse told me when I first came that I must be good. There! That's what I'm going to do. I'm going to be good. No, I don't really want to die. Because—because it can't be so very restful to be dead. It's like before birth. One must be bursting with eagerness to be born again. I think I should find that tiring.'

'You've had enough of being by yourself . . .'

'Yes, that's it. I want to be with people now.'

He breathed in the smoke as it came out of Julienne's nostrils.

'I'm like that bloke in the Bible, you know, Gehazi, the servant of Elisha. Naaman had been told to bathe seven times in the Jordan, or something like that. To cure his leprosy. When he was cured he sent Elisha a present, but Gehazi kept it all for himself. So then, to punish him, God

227

gave him Naaman's leprosy. You understand? I'm Gehazi. I've caught Naaman's leprosy.'

'You know what?' said Julienne—'Do you know what are the most beautiful lines of poetry ever written? It seems pretentious, of course, but I'd like to say them to you. May I?'

Adam nodded. She began:

'It goes: *"Voire, ou que je——"* '

But her voice faltered. She cleared her throat and began again:

'Voire, ou que je vive sans vie
Comme les images, par coeur.
Mort!'

She looked to the left of Adam, a couple of inches to the left. 'That's by Villon. Did you know it?'

Adam drank some coffee and made a negative gesture with his hand. He looked at the others, who had been listening, a little embarrassed, a little ironical. And he wondered why he was left in pyjamas the whole blessed day. So he shouldn't escape, perhaps? And perhaps, in spite of the vertical stripes, the things were not pyjamas. This might be the uniform worn in an asylum, or by sick people. Adam picked up the coffee cup from his knee and drank the rest. A little damp sugar was left at the bottom. He scraped it out with the spoon and licked it. He would have liked another cup of coffee, dozens of cups of coffee. He would have liked to talk about it, too. To the fair-haired girl, perhaps. He'd have liked to say to her, stay with me, in this house, stay with me and we'll make coffee at any time of the day or night, and then drink it together; there would be a big garden all round, and we could walk about in it until morning, in the dark, with the planes flying overhead. The young man with dark glasses took off his glasses and looked at Adam.

'If I've got it right,' he said, 'the idea of your friend's religion was a kind of pantheism—or mysticism. A sort of link with God by means of knowledge? The path of certitude, what?'

Julienne R. added:

'But what does it all matter to you? This stuff about mysticism? What does it all mean? Does it really interest you so much?'

Adam flung himself back in his chair, almost violently.

'You haven't understood. Not in the very least. It's not God that interests me, you see. It wasn't God for Sim either. Not God as such, as the creator, or what have you. Responding to a sort of craving for the final or the absolute, there, like a key unlocking a door. Good heavens, you'll never understand in that way! That doesn't interest me. I don't need to have been created. It's like this discussion. It doesn't interest me for what it is, for what it appears to be. Only because it fills a vacuum. A terrible, unbearable vacuum. Between two levels of life . . . Between two stages, two periods, you see what I mean?'

'But then what good does it do, all this mystical stuff?' asked the spectacled student.

'None at all. Absolutely none. It's as though you were talking to me in a language I don't understand. What good do you expect it to do? I can't tell you. It would be like trying to explain why I'm not you—— Take Ruysbroek, for instance; what good did it do him to draw distinctions between the material elements, earth, air, fire and water? It might have been poetry, of course. But it wasn't. Mysticism served to raise him to the level—not the psychological level, eh? not that—the level of the ineffable. It doesn't matter where that level lay. No matter what level. The important thing is that at a certain moment in his life he believed he had understood everything. Since he had

229

made the connection with what he had always called God, and that God being by definition eternal, omniscient, omnipotent and omnipresent, Ruysbroek too was all those things. At least during his attacks of mysticism. And towards the end he may even have been permanently at his level, his state of full effusion. That's it. It isn't knowing that matters, it's knowing one knows. It's a state in which culture, knowledge, speech and writing become worthless. By and large, if you like, it might be a sort of comfort. But never an end in itself, you see, never an end in itself. And at that level, of course, there haven't been so very many real mystics. You understand—speaking in the dialectical manner—but the relationship is different, of course—or perhaps one is oneself. It's simply a state. But when you get down to it, it's the only possible outcome of knowledge. In any other way, knowledge leads to a dead end. And then it ceases to be knowledge. It takes a form in the past tense. Whereas there it's suddenly exaggerated, it becomes so enormous, so overwhelming, that nothing else matters. One is that one is—— Yes, that's it. To be is being . . .'

Mlle R. gave a faint shake of the head; her lower lip quivered, as though she were torn between contradictory ideas.

'Very clever, all that,' said the spectacled fellow, 'But that's all one can say for it . . .'

'It's meaningless, a lot of metaphysical bombast,' another student interrupted. The spectacled fellow went on:

'I don't know—I don't know if it has occurred to you that it's a kind of argument that has no end to it. Like the reflections in a triple mirror. Because, for instance, I can reply that one is that one is that one is that one is. And so forth. It seems to me to be more like rhetoric. The type of rhetoric that amuses a boy of twelve. Syllogisms. This kind

230

of thing: a boat takes six days to cross the Atlantic, therefore six boats will take one day.'

'I don't——'

'Because, because the concept of existence implies a unity. A unity which is the consciousness of being. And because this consciousness of being is not the same as its definition in words, which can be multiplied *ad infinitum*. Like anything imaginary. There's no reason why it should ever stop. Eh?'

'That's not true,' said Adam. 'That's not true. Because you're making a confusion. You're confusing existence as real experience with existence as *cogito*, as the point from which thought starts and to which it returns. You think I'm talking about psychological concepts. That's what I dislike about you. You're always trying to drag in your blasted analytical systems, your psychological stunts. You've adopted a particular system of psychological values, once and for all. Useful for analysis. But you don't see, you don't see that I'm trying to make you think—of a much wider system. Something that goes further than psychology. I'm trying to get you to think of a huge system. Of a kind of universal thought. Of a purely spiritual state. Something representing the culmination of reasoning, the culmination of metaphysics, of psychology, philosophy, mathematics, the lot. Yes, it's exactly that: what's the culmination of everything? It's to be to be.'

He switched to Julienne R.

'It's because just now I said something about a state of ecstasy. So you assumed it was a psychological condition. Something that will yield to treatment. Something like paranoid pathological delirium and so forth. I don't give a damn for that. I'll try to tell you what it is, and have done with it. After that, don't ask me what I think about Parmenides, because I shan't be able to tell you any longer . . .'

Adam pushed his chair back and wedged his shoulders against the wall. It was a cold, solid, white-tiled wall that one could easily take into partnership, either for a struggle or for a doze. Besides, it would certainly re-echo the vibrations of Adam's vocal chords, transmitted through his back, and carry them all over the room, thus sparing him the fatigue of speaking loudly. Adam explained, his words hardly articulated:

'I could tell you about something that happened a year or two ago, and which has nothing to do with stuff about God or self-analysis or anything of that kind—— Of course you're at liberty to analyze it by the usual psychological criteria if you want. But I don't think that would be any use. In fact that's the very reason why I'm choosing something that seems to have no connection with God, metaphysics and all that stuff.'

He stopped and looked at Julienne. He saw her face move almost imperceptibly, at the base of the nostrils and round the eyes, as though stirred by some complicated rage. And suddenly, without anyone else having noticed the change, he felt terribly ridiculous. He bent forward, away from the supporting wall, exposing himself to the biting gaze of his enemies. And he said calmly, aware throughout his being that only this fair-haired girl could understand him:

'Yes . . .'

At intervals of 7 seconds he said again:

'Yes—— Yes.'

She said: 'Go on.'

Adam reddened. He drew his legs in under his chair, as though about to get up. It was as though thanks to those few seconds, to a dark-ringed glance from an unknown girl and to the words 'Go on', brought out in a muffled tone after an infinitesimal mental hesitation, a pact of friendship

232

had been signed between them. In her turn she crushed out her cigarette end with the toe of her black court shoe. In form and substance, the situation curiously resembled that of a man and woman, strangers to each other, suddenly aware of having been photographed side by side by some street photographer.

'It's not worth it,' Adam grunted, 'you don't like the anecdotal style.'

She said nothing, simply bent her head; not quite as low as the first time, however, so that only the front half of the S came into view. On the other hand the movement was sufficient to loosen the front of her dress, and Adam saw two silver threads, the two sides of a chain, that met in the cleft of her breasts. The chain certainly ended lower down, between the cups of her brassière, with a little mother-of-pearl cross, or a medal of the Virgin set in aquamarines. The idea of concealing something rather sacred, the picture of a divinity, against the most eminently biological part of a woman's body was slightly fantastic. It was childish, touching, or else pretentious. Adam looked round at the others. Except for the spectacled student, who was writing in his notebook, and the Martin girl, who was talking to the head doctor, they all showed signs of weariness. Embarrassment had given way to boredom and was taking strange, nightmarish forms, prompting, it seemed, a perpetual repetition of the same gestures, sounds and smells.

Adam sensed that this might last for another fifteen minutes, certainly not more, and decided to make the most of what time remained to him.

'No, I'll tell you, it's not worth while. For one thing you don't like the anecdotal style, and for another thing, in a way, from the point of view of truth, from a realistic standpoint, that's not it, either . . .'

'Why not?' said Julienne.

233

'Because it's literature. Just that. I know we're all more or less literary, but it won't do any longer. I'm really tired of—— It's bound to happen, because one reads too much. One feels obliged to put everything forward in a perfect form. One always feels called upon to illustrate the abstract idea by an example of the latest craze, rather fashionable, indecent if possible, and above all—and above all, quite unconnected with the question. Good Lord, how phoney it all is! It stinks of fake lyricism, memories, childhood, psychoanalysis, the springtime of life and the history of the Christian religion. One writes cheap novelettes full of masturbation, sodomy, Waldensians and sexual behaviour in Melanesia, when it isn't the poems of Ossian, Saint-Amant or the canzonettas placed in the tabulary by Francesco da Milano. Or 'Portrait of a Young Lady' by Domenico Veneziano. Shakespeare. Wilfred Owen. Joâo de Deus. Léoville Lhomme. Integralism. Fazil Ali Clinassi, etc. etc. And the mysticism of Novalis. And the song of Yupanqui Pachacutec:

Like a lily of the fields I was born
Like a lily I grew tall
Then time went by
Old age came
I withered
And so died.

And Quipucamayoc. Viracocha. Capacocha-Guagua. Hatunrincriyoc. Intip-Aclla. The promises of Menephtah. Jethro. David's kinah. Seneca the Tragedian. Anime, parandum est. Liberi quondam mei, vos pro paternis sceleribus poenas date. And all that: Markovitch cigarettes, the Coupe Vétiver, Wajda, Cinzano ashtrays, ball-point pens, *my* ball-point pen, BIC No. 576—reproduction

234

"APPROVED 26/8/58, Pat. Off." All that. Eh? Is it correct? Does it mean anything? Is it correct?'

Adam ran his hand through his close-cropped hair. He felt that the gesture gave him an American air.

'You know what?' he said, 'You know what? We spend our time turning out rubbishy cinema. Yes, cinema. Theatre as well, and psychological novels. There's hardly any simplicity left in us, we're croakers, half-portions. Weary Willies. You'd think we'd been invented by some writer of the 'thirties, who'd wanted us to be affected, handsome, refined, full of culture, full of filthy culture. It sticks to my back like a wet coat. It sticks to me all over.'

'Eh—what *is* simple, at that rate?' The rather ill-timed interruption came from the spectacled student.

'How d'you mean, what's simple? Don't you know? Haven't you even the faintest idea, then?' Adam's hand went to his pocket in search of the packet of cigarettes, but stopped, tense, before getting there.

'Do you really not see it, life, life the whore, all round you? You don't see that people are alive, alive, that they're eating, etc.? That they're happy? You don't see that the man who wrote "the earth is blue like an orange" is a lunatic or a fool?—— Of course not, you say to yourself there's a genius, he's dislocated reality in a couple of words. You run them off, "blue, earth, orange". It's beautiful. Whatever you like. But I personally need a system, or I go mad. Either the earth is orange or the orange is blue. But in the system that consists of employing words, the earth is blue and oranges are orange. I've reached a point where I can't stand freak talk any longer. You understand, it's too difficult for me to find my way to reality. Maybe I've no sense of humour? Because according to you it takes a sense of humour to understand that stuff? You know what I say? I'm so far from lacking a sense of humour that I've gone much further than you. And there it is. I've come back ruined. My kind of humour lay beyond words. It was hidden and I couldn't give it expression. And as I couldn't put it into words, it was much vaster than yours. Eh? In fact it was boundless. You know. Myself, I do everything that way. The earth is as blue as an orange, but the sky is as bare as a clock, the water as red as a hailstone. Or better still—the coleopterous sky floods the bracts. To want to sleep. Cigarette cigar besmirches the souls. 11th. 887. A, B, C, D, E, F, G, H, I, J, K, L, M, N, O, P, Q,R, S, T, U, V, W, X, Y, Z & Co.'

'Wait, wait a minute, I——' the girl broke in. Adam continued:

'I'd like to stop this silly game. If you knew how I'd like to. I'm crushed, soon nearly crushed . . .' he said, his voice not weaker but more impersonal.

'You know what's happening?' he asked. 'I'll tell you, just you. What's happening is that people are living, here, there and everywhere; what's happening is that some of them are dying of heart-failure, quietly, at home, in the evening. What's happening is that there are still people who are unhappy, because their wife's left them, because their dog is dead, because their little boy chokes when he swallows. You know—— And we, we, why do we have to put our oar in?'

'Is that why you did all THAT?' the girl demanded.

'All WHAT?' shouted Adam.

'Well, those things—all those things that they——'

'Wait!' said Adam. He was hurrying, as though ashamed of explaining himself:

'I've had enough of it! That's enough psychopathology for today—I mean—there's nothing left to understand. It's all over. You're you and I'm me. Stop trying to put yourself in my place all the time. The rest is balls. I've had enough of it, I—do please stop trying to understand. You know, I—I'm ashamed—I don't know how to put it. Don't talk about it all any more . . .'

He suddenly lowered his voice and bent towards Julienne R., so that only she could hear him.

'This is what we'll do: I'll talk to you very softly, just to you. And you must answer in the same way. I'll say to you hello, how are you? and you'll say to me, I'm very well, thank you. You see how I want it to be: and then, what's your name, you're pretty, I like the colour of your dress, or of your eyes. What's your sign? Scorpio, Libra? You'll answer yes, or no. You'll talk to me about your mother, what you had for your meal, or the film you've seen at the cinema. The countries you've been to—Ireland, the Scilly Isles. You'll tell me something that happened during your holidays, or your childhood. The first time you ever used lipstick. The time you got lost on a mountain. You'll tell me whether you like going for walks in the evening, when it's getting dark and one can hear hidden things moving. Or about when you went to look at the exam results, standing out in the rain, and what you were thinking as your eye ran down the list of names. You'll talk to me very softly, telling me such tiny things that I shan't even need to listen. Stories of storms or equinoctial gales, autumn in Brittany with heather growing above your head. When you were scared, when you couldn't get to sleep and you used to go and look out into the darkness through the slats of the shutters. And for the others, for the others, I'll go on with my own story. You know, that complicated story that explains everything. The mystical business. Shall we?'

The others were leaning foward, watching; some of them —the fair-haired boy, for instance—were grinning sarcastically. They didn't take the thing seriously; they were all eager for this other-world rigmarole to come to an end, so that they could get home, have dinner and go out for the evening. There was something on at the cinema and at the Opera it might be Gluck.

Adam could read consent all over the girl—on her neck, all round her neck, in the corners of her mouth, on her shoulders and breasts, down her spine and right down to her feet, which were rigid in their gold-buckled court shoes set at an infinitesimal angle. He pushed back his shoulders until they touched the wall; he stretched out his legs till they brushed against her bare knees. He could feel the red and black pyjama-stripes on his skin; they extended from him to a kind of solid, impenetrable surface that was now forming between himself and the group of students. He groped in the jacket pocket and found the packet of cigarettes. The student with the sun-glasses held out a box of matches to him at arm's length. There were five matches in the little cardboard drawer, three of them used and two fresh. Adam lit the cigarette flawlessly; as the only temporal detail in his successful bearing, a drop of sweat ran down from his armpit and fell like a cold pin-prick, level with his second rib. But it happened so rapidly, and was after all so well tolerated, that nobody could have guessed. Julienne R., hunched up on her chair, showed the greater fatigue; she was obviously waiting for something. Not anything novel or strange, something socially inevitable; something calm and icy, like crossing out a word in a sentence, for example.

'A year or two ago,' Adam began, '—to go on with the story I was telling just now——'

Julienne R. picked up her exercise-book and prepared to jot down essentials.

'I was on the beach with a girl. I'd been bathing, but she'd not gone in; she was lying on the shingle, reading a science-fiction magazine. There was a story in it called "Bételgeuse", I think. When I came out of the water she was still there. I could see she was hot, and I don't know why—probably to annoy her—I put my wet foot on her back. She was wearing a bikini. At that she jumped up and said something to me. I don't remember what it was. But that's the important thing. Two minutes later she came back to me and said, "Because you made me all wet just now, I'm going to take one of your cigarettes." And she felt in the pocket of my trousers, which were lying beside me on the beach, to find the cigarette. I said nothing, but I began to think. Two hours later, I remember, I was still thinking about it. I went home and looked in the dictionary. I swear this is true. I looked up every word, so as to understand. And even then I couldn't understand. I spent the whole night thinking about it. By about 4 in the morning I was crazy. I'd got what the girl had said on my brain. The words were flying in all directions. I could see them written up everywhere. On the walls of my room, on the ceiling, in the squares of the windows, along the edge of the sheet. It was bothering me to death. Then I began to get things straight again. But it wasn't the same now. It was as though everything had become either false or correct, from one day to the next. I said to myself, no matter how I twist The Sentence, or the facts that are parallel to it, it MUST be pure logic. I mean I began to understand everything, clearly. And I thought I must go, push my motor-bike into the sea, and all that. I said to myself that the——'

But Adam had already become invisible to them all, as he had been obliged to do with his mother, with Michèle and with many other people; sitting alone at the lightest end of the infirmary, he seemed to be hovering slightly, with his thin limbs, his egg-shaped head and his left hand, from which the cigarette stuck out horizontally. His body, stiffly upright on the metal chair, seemed to be smoking amidst involuntary chaos; some mere trifle, his prognathous jaw, his sweat-beaded forehead and perhaps his triangular eyes, was turning him into a prehistoric creature. It was as though he were perpetually climbing out of some muddy yellow water in the form of a lacustrine bird, its feathers flat against its skin and every tiny muscle in movement to raise it skywards. His voice rolled down over the terrestrial population, no longer particularly comprehensible, and carried him along on its waves like a kite. Above him, close to the ceiling, two blue globes were bumping together, the shock of their clashing curves reverberating in magnetic storms. It was like the idea of a God of destiny, a knot of mysteries and canonizations, born one day from the spark between two cog-wheels in a locomotive. Adam was turning into a sea. Unless he had fallen asleep, without the pose, owing to the magnetic influence of Julienne R.'s gaze or the hypnotic persuasion of a mere striped pyjama suit. In any case he was drifting backwards, soft, transparent, undulating, and the words were rattling together in his mouth like pebbles, with strange rumbling noises. A bubbling network had lined the cramped room, and the others were in danger of following it. When Adam stopped talking and began to emit feeble grunts, the doctor decided to intervene; but it was too late. He called out two or three times 'Hello! M. Pollo! M. Pollo! Hey!', shaking Adam by the shoulder. Then he noticed a kind of grin across Adam's bony face, sharpening his parchment-coloured features. It began high up, just below the cheekbones, and split the face in two without parting the lips or revealing even the tip of an incisor. At this he gave up all hope and sent for the nurse. Slowly, one by one, they left the cold room, while Adam was led away, tottering, down the corridor.

From the depths of his slumber, Adam felt them going; his lips moved and he almost whispered 'goodbye'. But not even a grunt came out of his throat. Somewhere or other a blue ball-point pen was squeaking slightly as it crossed the page of an exercise-book and wrote the one word: 'Aphasia.'

While Adam went round one corner of the passage and then another, leaning on the nurse's warm arm, he was entering a region of fable. He was thinking, perhaps, very softly, very tenuously, far ahead of his frozen vocal cords, that he was really in his proper place. That at last he had found the beautiful house of his dreams, cool and white, built amid the silence of a wonderful garden. He was telling himself that he was happy, all alone in his beige-painted room, with its single window through which the sounds of peace flowed in unbroken. He had no objection; it was to be his at last, that perennial repose, that boreal night with its midnight sun, with people to look after him; out-door walks and subterranean slumbers; even, now and then, a pretty nurse whom one could lead into a thicket at dusk. Letters. A visitor from time to time, and big parcels of chocolate and cigarettes. There would be the annual celebration on Founder's Day, April 25 or October 11. Christmas and Easter. Perhaps tomorrow the blonde girl would come to see him. Alone this time. He would take her by the hand and talk to her for a long time. He would write her a poem. After a couple of weeks, all being well, he would be allowed to write letters. Then, towards the late autumn, they'd be able to stroll in the garden together. He would say to her, I can stay here for another year, perhaps not so long; after that, when I leave, we'll go and live in the South, at Padua or Gibraltar. I'll work a bit, and in the evening we'll go to night-clubs or to a café. Now and then, when we feel like it, we'll come back here for a month or two. They'll be glad to see us and they'll give us the best room, the one that looks over the garden. Outside the dead leaves are crackling in the sun and the living leaves are rustling in the rain. One can hear a train. The corridors smell of vegetable broth, everything seems to be hollow, warm and yet cool. That's the moment to dig oneself a hole in the ground, pushing aside the twigs and crumbs of earth, and get into it, feet first, well hidden, to spend an invalid's winter. After that there'll be the cup of *tilleul* and then darkness, closing over the clouds of the Last Cigarette as though over Sinbad's magic smoke. At a pinch, a bell may ring. A mosquito is prowling round the lamp, making a noise like a marble-polishing machine. That's the moment to surrender the earth to the termites. The moment to escape backwards and pass through the stages of past time. One is caught in the torpor of the evenings of childhood, as though in bird-lime; one is smothering in the fog, after some meal or other, in front of a curiously empty holly-patterned plate with smears of soup left on it. Then comes the cradle period and one dies, suffocated in swaddling-clothes, choking with rage at being so small. But that's harmless. Because one has to go back even further, through blood and pus, to one's mother's womb and there, arms and legs curled into an egg-shape, with one's head against the rubber membrane, fall into a dark sleep, peopled by strange terrestrial nightmares.

Adam is all alone; he lies on his bed beneath strata of draughts, expecting nothing any more. He is enormously alive, staring up at the ceiling, at the spot where No. 17's haemorrhage came through three years ago. He knows that everyone has gone away now, right away. He is going vaguely to sleep in the world allotted to him; opposite the high window, as though to counterbalance the six swastikas formed by the bars, a single cross hangs on the wall, mother-of-pearl and pink. He is inside the oyster, and the oyster is at the bottom of the sea. He still has a few bothers, of course; he will have to keep his room tidy, give samples of urine for analysis, answer test questions. And one is always at the mercy of being unexpectedly released. But with any luck he'll be here for a long time, attached to this bed, these walls, that garden, this harmony of bright metal and fresh paint.

While awaiting the worst, the story is over. But wait. You'll see. I (please note I haven't used that word too often) think we can count on them. It would be really strange if one of these days there were not something more to say about Adam or some other among him.

J.M.G. LE CLEZIO, WHO IS HALF ENGLISH AND HALF FRENCH, WAS BORN IN NICE IN 1940. THIS NOVEL, HIS FIRST, WON THE PRIX RENAUDOT, TIED FOR THE PRIX GONCOURT, AND CAUSED MORE COMMENT THAN ANY OTHER FIRST BOOK IN MANY YEARS.